GENDER, POWER, AND COMMUNICATION IN HUMAN RELATIONSHIPS

LEA's COMMUNICATION SERIES
Jennings Bryant/Dolf Zillmann, General Editors

Selected titles in Interpersonal/Intercultural Communication (W. Barnett Pearce, Advisory Editor) include:

Cupach/Spitzburg • The Dark Side of Interpersonal Communication

Daly/Wiemann • Strategic Interpersonal Communication

Hewes • The Cognitive Bases of Interpersonal Communication

Kalbfleisch • Interpersonal Communication: Evolving Interpersonal Relationships

Leeds-Hurwitz • Semiotics and Communication: Signs, Codes, Cultures

For a complete list of other titles in LEA's Communication Series, please contact Lawrence Erlbaum Associates, Publishers.

GENDER, POWER, AND COMMUNICATION IN HUMAN RELATIONSHIPS

Edited by

Pamela J. Kalbfleisch
University of Wyoming

Michael J. Cody
University of Southern California

LAWRENCE ERLBAUM ASSOCIATES, PUBLISHERS
1995   Hillsdale, New Jersey   Hove, UK

Lawrence Erlbaum Associates, Inc., Publishers
365 Broadway
Hillsdale, New Jersey 07642

Cover design by Kate Dusza

Library of Congress Cataloging-in-Publication Data

Gender, power, and communication in human relationships / edited by
    Pamela J. Kalbfleisch and Michael J. Cody.
            p.   cm.
        Includes bibliographical references and indexes.
        ISBN 0-8058-1403-5 (alk. paper).—ISBN 0-8058-1404-3 (pbk.
    : alk. paper)
        1.   Interpersonal   relations.   2.   Man–woman   relationships.
    Communication—Sex differences.   4. Sex differences (Psychology).
    5. Interpersonal communication.   I. Kalbfleisch, Pamela J.   II. Cody,
    Michael J.
    HM132.G44   1995
    305.3dc20   94-36468
                                                                    CIP

Books published by Lawrence Erlbaum Associates are printed on
acid-free paper, and their bindings are chosen for strength and durability.

Printed in the United States of America
10   9   8   7   6   5   4   3   2   1

In memory of Paul Kalbfleisch
(July 10, 1918–August 17, 1993)
Father, mentor, friend
He taught me to laugh and to smile,
to love the West and its mountains,
to have faith, and
to never lose sight of my dreams
—PK

In celebration of Julia Cody
(April 23, 1982)
Daughter, inspiration, and hope
for the future, may she live
in a world of equality and peace
—MC

Contents

PART III   WOMEN AND MEN TOGETHER

PART IV   WOMEN AND MEN IN SOCIETY

Contributors

James J. Bradac, Department of Communication, University of California, Santa Barbara, Santa Barbara, CA 93106.

Camille Buckner, Department of Psychology, University of Texas-Austin, Austin, TX 78712.

Diane M. Burns, Department of Speech Communication, University of Alabama, Tuscaloosa, AL 35487

Judee K. Burgoon, Department of Communication, University of Arizona, Tucson, AZ 85721.

Daniel J. Canary, Department of Speech Communication, Pennsylvania State University, University Park, PA 16802.

Ankila S. Chandran, Annenberg School for Communication, University of Southern California, Los Angeles, CA 90089-0281.

Michael J. Cody, Department of Communication Arts and Sciences, University of Southern California, Los Angeles, CA 90089-1694.

Leda Cooks, Department of Communication, University of Massachusetts, Amherst, MA 01003

William R. Cupach, Department of Communication, Illinois State University, Normal, IL 61761.

Leesa Dillman, Department of Communication, University of Nevada at Las Vegas, Las Vegas, NV 89154

Mary Anne Fitzpatrick, Department of Communication Arts, University of Wisconsin-Madison, Madison, WI 53706.

Nancy M. Henley, Department of Psychology, 405 Hilgard Avenue, University of California, Los Angeles, Los Angeles, CA 90024-1563.

Thomas M. Hirata, Annenberg School for Communication, University of Southern California, Los Angeles, CA 90089-0281.

Pamela J. Kalbfleisch, Department of Communication and Mass Media, University of Wyoming, P.O. Box 3904, Laramie, WY 82071-3904

Joann Keyton, Department of Communication Studies, 143 Theatre and Communication Building, University of Memphis, Memphis, TN 38152

Lynn Carol Miller, Department of Communication Arts and Sciences, University of Southern California, Los Angeles, CA 90089-1694; Department of Psychology, University of Southern California, Los Angeles, CA 90089.

Yvette Montagne-Miller, Department of Speech Communication, San Diego State University, San Diego, CA 92182.

Charlene L. Muehlenhard, Department of Psychology, University of Kansas, Lawrence, KS 66045

Anthony Mulac, Department of Communication, University of California, Santa Barbara, Santa Barbara, CA 93106.

Davis Patterson, Department of Sociology, DK-40, University of Washington, Seattle, WA 98195.

Judy C. Pearson, School of Interpersonal Communication, Ohio University, Athens, OH 45701.

Joi L. Phelps, Department of Psychology, University of Kansas, Lawrence, KS 66045

Rhonda K. Reinholtz, Department of Psychology, University of Kansas, Lawrence, KS 66045

Jeffery D. Robinson, Department of Sociology, University of California-Los Angeles, Los Angeles, CA 90024-9122.

Everett M. Rogers, Department of Communication, University of New Mexico, Albuquerque, NM 87131-1171

Sadina Rothspan, Department of Psychology, University of Southern California, Los Angeles, CA 90089

Arthur T. Satterfield, Department of Psychology, University of Kansas, Lawrence, KS 66045.

Pepper Schwartz, Department of Sociology, DK-40, University of Washington, Seattle, WA 98195.

John Seiter, Department of Speech Communication, Utah State University, Logan, UT 84322

Janet T. Spence, Department of Psychology, University of Texas-Austin, Austin, TX 78712.

Sara Steen, Department of Sociology, DK-40, University of Washington, Seattle, WA 98195.

Preface

There is power in a word or a gesture. There is power when women and men live together, work together, talk together, or are simply in each other's company. There is power in a smile, a caress, and there is power in sex.

There is power in money, there is power in education, and there is power in access. In some situations, who you know can matter more than what you know. Who you can know may affect what you can become.

There is power in a fist, a gun, and anger. There is power in how we choose to resolve our conflicts, and how we negotiate the most intimate aspects of our lives.

There is power in how we are portrayed in our music and our media; power in what we read, what we see, and what we hear. There is power in how we treat each other both as intimates and as strangers.

As much as we are bound in our society by the ways things are, we are equally drawn to the way things ought to be. This text provides an opportunity to look into the past and to draw conclusions about the future.

This edited book establishes a state of the art perspective on theory and research on gender, power, and communication in human relationships. In one volume are both theoretical essays and review chapters that address issues relevant to female and male differences in power, dominance, communication, equality, and expectations/beliefs. All contributors to this volume share two commonalities. First, each contributor provides a 1990s assessment of power and equality in female and male relationships. Second, each contributor reviews respective programs of research and focuses attention on the relevance of this research on understanding the relationships of women and men.

This volume is unique because it incorporates a multidisciplinary approach to the study of gender and the communication of power in human relationships. This book provides both scholastic breadth and centralized treatment of issues that form the very foundation of social and personal relationships. This edited work will appeal to scholars working in the disciplines of communication and psychology, as well as other areas of social science research. This book includes the original work of intellectuals with national and international reputations in the social sciences. Each of these chapters presents a state of the art review or a theoretical essay augmented by an empirical investigation of a central concept.

Pamela J. Kalbfleisch
Michael J. Cody

Part I

Introduction and Overview

Chapter 1

Power and Communication in the Relationships of Women and Men

Pamela J. Kalbfleisch
University of Wyoming

Michael J. Cody
University of Southern California

> *Men who run the world today are ". . . a bunch of shallow, bald, middle aged men with character disorders. They don't have the emotional capacity it takes to qualify as human beings. One good thing about these white, male, almost extinct mammals is that they are growing old. We get to watch them die."*
> —a 36-year-old female trucking-company executive (Gates, 1993, p. 49)

> *I want everything to be just like it was before.*
> —D-Fens quoted from the movie, *Falling Down*

WHY THIS BOOK NOW?

We write the introduction to this volume in January 1994 exactly 1 year after the inauguration of Bill (and Hillary) Clinton. The Clintons promised change, changes in leadership, welfare program, health care program, domestic programs and, of course, changes in women's roles. Make him president, Bill said, "and you get two for the price of one." "You do not have to tear a woman down to build a man up," Clinton admonished during his campaign. Now, 1 year into their term in office, we have witnessed some (limited) changes in public power held by women. Of course, critics are plentiful—changes too slow, changes too fast, or as D-Fens mourns, change should be reversed.

We advocate change in roles for men and women, and our goal in this volume is to chronicle changes, both the changes that are occurring and changes that need to occur. Indeed, all the contributors to this volume are familiar with change: All have devoted considerable attention to women and men in this society and changes that have or that should have occurred. Of course, we are not interested in change just for the sake of change. We are guided by two goals: equality for women and men (in power, income rights and privileges), and improved quality in female/male relationships and human relationships in general. It is clear, considering that what some people have to say (such as those quoted in the introduction), that some women loath men for not changing, and that some men are anxious, defensive, or angry about the changes that have already occurred. Obviously, there is much work to do in order to facilitate change and to improve relationships.

Further, it is clear that all matters concerning relationships between women and men are of paramount interest to scholars and are clearly in the center stage of the public's focus. Of course, there are (highly visible) stories: reactions to the movie *Thelma and Louise*, to the Hill–Thomas hearings, to the Tailhook Incident, to the spousal abuse trials of the Bobbitt couple, and so forth. However, general issues are proven to be important *every day*. Consider a few of the highlights from the *Los Angeles Times* for 1 week during fall 1993:

> *Los Angeles Times*, September 30, 1993, "Early Obesity Tied to Social, Economic Woes for Women." by John Schwartz, *The Washington Post*. This article reports on a publication in the *New England Journal of Medicine* detailing how overweight women complete less education, are 20% less likely to get married, hold poverty rates at 10% higher than non-obese women, and earn $6,710 less per year than non-obese women. Only one of these findings was replicated for men: Obese men were 11% less likely to be married than thinner men.

> *Los Angeles Times*, October 2, 1993, "Women a Comedy Force? No Joke," by Chuck Crisafulli, in a "Special to the Times." The article deals with the fact that women have to work hard to break into the comedy circuit, or find ways to nurture a career outside the "boys' club" mainstream clubs.

> *Los Angeles Times*, October 2, 1993, "Wilson Signs Bills to Expand Rape Laws," by Daniel M. Weintraub and Mark Gladstone, *Times* staff writers. Incredulous as it seems, only in 1993 did the Governor of California (a state accounting for more than 11% of the nation's population) sign a bill changing the rape laws so that "spousal rape" is now considered a felony, the same as the rape of a stranger. Spousal rape (because of the "assumed consent" for sexual relationships between a husband and a wife) used to warrant a misdemeanor. Governor Pete Wilson also signed a "gender-neutral rape bill" that will now allow women who commit sex crimes with minors to be punished as rigorously as men.

> *Los Angeles Times*, October 4, 1993, "Is Violence a Male Hormone Problem?": "Dear Dr. Brothers . . . It seems that almost all this tendency to violence is somehow related to testosterone. Has anyone considered a medicine that would lessen the amount of this male hormone and act as an antidote to violence?"

Los Angeles Times' Youth Opinion, October 4, 1993, "Does Rap Music Disrespect Women, Girls?" As one 17-year-old woman observed:

> Rap gives women a bad image when it calls them things like bitch, slut, and whore. Videos make them seem like sex objects. They focus on their bodies, not their intelligence or their minds. All you ever see is girls in bikinis. Guys listen to that music, and it influences how they talk to girls. If guys look up to rappers, that's a bad role model for them to be following.

> Women also give themselves bad images. In Dr. Dre's song, "Nothing But a G-Thing," women do things for the video they didn't have to do if they didn't want to. Women shouldn't put themselves in the position of putting themselves down. If they took a stand, it would help the [women's] cause. ("Does Rap," 1993, p. E5)

Los Angeles Times, October 5, 1993, "Women's Groups Re-emerge in Workplace," from Associated Press. The article details a few successes in the workings of a "Women's Advisory Committee" that promotes the advancement of women in top positions of management. Indeed, J.C. Penney is credited with creating such an advisory committee 3½ years ago in order to help place more women in senior positions. The history of such advisory committees, however, is not overly positive. When such "networking" groups were formed in the 1970s, many were discouraged by management because they were perceived as "adversarial." Still, some died out in the early 1980s when women did make some advances on managerial positions. Frustration with employment during the last recession has prompted networking groups (or "mentoring" partnerships) to organize again. However, the article points out some trouble spots:

> Still, high-level women executives often don't participate in the corporate groups, said Dana Friedman, co-president of the New York-based Families and Work Institute. "They have the attitude, 'If I did it, why can't others?'" Friedman said. "Women at the top rarely advocate for women's issues." ("Women's Groups," p. D15)

Los Angeles Times, October 8, 1993, "Caught in a Vicious, Bitter Trap," by Dianne Klein, Times Staff Writer, documents the problem of men who marry noncitizen brides from the Philippines and elsewhere, and the women ultimately are abused. If the women complain, the husbands withdraw sponsorship and the INS deports the woman. Unless laws are changed, an unknown number of women will live in jeopardy, fear, and pain.

If such issues and problems surface in only 1 week, it is clear that society (the media, governments, etc.) are decidedly and keenly focused on reflecting on men and women, their relationships, and their problems.

Further, it is clear that despite several decades of advocacy, persistent problems plague women, their concerns, and their progress. Programs of research that have focused on improving equality of women and men date back to the middle of this century. However, in some ways, little seems to have changed. Today, women's salaries still lag behind men's, and fiscal inequality directly relates to dyadic power inequality among couples. Women's occupational status is strongly and adversely affected by dated stereotypes. Women have hit glass ceilings and they do not appear to benefit from the same mentoring relationships that benefit men on the job. They, until recently, watched spouses who raped them be charged with only mild misdemeanors, they are devalued in music videos and lyrics, they are judged harshly on the basis of physical appearance, and they watch as backlash occurs whenever solid progress has been made in political, domestic, and employment areas (Faludi, 1991).

What happened? Are things as bleak as they appear to be from reading newspapers and watching talk shows concerning interpersonal relationships?

In sum, we edited this book in order to document research on women and men living, working, and being together. Our concern is to have scholars in special areas chronicle their line of research (theory and empirical evidence) and report on the progress (or lack of) in equality and relational quality. An assessment is long overdue and timely—both given the focus on gender studies today and given the particular time in history in which leaders advocate deliberate, planned changes for gender roles. As we approach the year 2000, just how much have women and men progressed as participants in interpersonal relationships and in society as a whole?

OVERVIEW OF THE VOLUME

This edited book establishes a state-of-the-art perspective on theory and research in many (but admittedly not all) aspects of power in female/male relationships. The goal of the volume is to provide in one text both theoretical essays and review chapters that address issues relevant to female and male approaches to power, dominance, communication, equality, beliefs, and expectations. All contributors to this volume share two commonalities. First, each contributor provides a 1990s assessment of power and equality in female/male relationships. Second, each contributor reviews perspective programs of research and focuses attention on the relevance of his/her research on understanding the relationships between men and women.

The chapters are organized into three parts (Parts II–IV). First we focus attention on *gender-based expectations and beliefs*. Chapters in this part deal with issues concerning our expectations about how men and women are, or have been stereotyped, their roles, their characteristics, and their behaviors as "appropriate" for females and for males. Although expectations and beliefs based on gender are important in the lines of research discussed later in the book, the contributors in this section capitalize in the formation and maintenance of long-term, enduring, gender-based beliefs concerning verbal and nonverbal behaviors and the roles of women and men. Part III focuses attention on men and women interacting with one another—dating, negotiating safe sex, giving and receiving advice, influencing, coping with anger and conflict, and facilitating intimacy in their relationships. It is the longest of the three parts for the obvious reason that *communicating* and *dyadic power* is of central concern to most scholars, students, and members of society. Part IV adopts a macrolevel view of gender research. Contributors to this section focus directly on proposed *major* changes in television portrayals, in social influence and perceptions of women and men, and in how gender and power are studied by the research establishment. These chapters also propose some fundamental changes in how research should be conducted in the areas of persuasion, relational communication, and gender studies.

In Henley's chapter, she reexamines, extends, clarifies, and defends her 1970s work on "Body Politics" (Henley, 1977). Henley provides a set of testable hypotheses, emphasizing the association of specific nonverbal behaviors to social power. She continues her goal of revealing how certain nonverbal behaviors are seemingly irrelevant to power (behaviors reflecting two functions: intimacy and dominance) and reflect a fundamental gender bias at the societal level, allowing males greater license and freedom to behave and dominating asymmetric unequal patterns of behaviors.

In a companion piece on nonverbal communication and power, Burgoon and Dillman review literature concerning the "classic" view of "gender displays" in nonverbal behaviors. Although previous research clearly suggests that males typically communicate with more gestures, dominance, and behaviors, Burgoon and Dillman's study indicates that men and women tend to use many of the same behaviors to express dominance, and that women can and do communicate dominance behaviors with some frequency. However, the authors note that gender differences persist in that males and females differ in their ability to intensify or modify messages being sent. Males more effectively communicate dominance, whereas female behaviors reflect more solidarity and intimacy.

Mulac and Bradac, in chapter 4, overview research on linguistic variables in analysis of gender differences in powerfulness or powerlessness. Considerable evidence has been provided concerning "female speech," the "female register," "men's language," and "women's language." These authors indicate that some of the earlier research from the 1970s is too often accepted at face value or is rarely challenged, despite the fact that many of these early investigations were limited in a number of ways. Most problematic is the fact that most scholars (until recently) critically questioned which of the linguistic variables validly reflected the concept of "power," and few projects sampled male and female discourse from *ongoing interactions*. As Mulac and Bradac note, communicators often adapt or accommodate to their interactants' communication style or pattern; thus, expected differences between females and males, or power and powerlessness styles of communicating, may disappear as individuals communicate. Mulac and Bradac's results indicate that the *expectations* and *beliefs* that we tend to hold regarding "gender-based" language are probably too simplistic and invalid.

In the final chapter on expectations and beliefs, Spence and Buckner seek to clarify the models that have been proposed regarding the meaning of masculinity and femininity. Spence and Buckner characterize the concepts of "femininity" and "masculinity" as some of the muddiest in social psychology. Models reviewed include (a) the unidimensional model of femininity and masculinity, (b) the dual model of two separate, uncorrelated factors of masculinity and femininity, and (c) a "multifactorial model" that is centered around the notion of "gender identity" but that allows males and females to hold differing beliefs and experiences part of the psychological sense of being "male" and of being "female."

Part III of the volume focuses on men and women living, working, and being together. Research colleagues Rineholtz, Muehlenhard, Phelps, and Satterfield pointedly illustrate how popular media (films, rap music, pop music) contain insidious if not pervasive messages concerning sexual beliefs regarding male power and dominance and female response and submissiveness. These researchers suggest that the common messages and themes influence how people "naturally" accept messages about sexuality and sexual coercion. These messages can have alarming if not dangerous consequences for those who are about to date and for those who are dating.

Professors Miller, Burns, and Rothspan (chapter 7) present, in our opinion, one of the most alarming reports in our volume. In their chapter, Miller and her colleagues outline how major discrepancies in sexual practices among African Americans produces a situation in which African-American women have significantly reduced levels of power and are treated with little equality in their intimate relationships. This disparity can place these women at a distinct disadvantage in using safe sex when their partners are unwilling. The implications of this power discrepancy for the spread of AIDS among the African-American community are particularly disquieting.

This report is followed by Kalbfleisch and Keyton's description (chapter 8) of the power inequality that exists between women and men working together, as men make use of mentoring relationships to advance their careers, women falter in developing these helping relationships. These researchers suggest that women may make use of a differing model for mentoring, and that understanding this model may assist in facilitating the development of these supportive relationships.

In chapter 9, Fizpatrick and Mulac examine the influence of interpersonal or noninterpersonal relationships on the use of "feminine gender preferential" language and "masculine gender preferential" language by both female and male interactants. They find that for men the relationship is a factor in language usage, with men employing more "masculine gender preferential" language with strangers, and more "feminine gender preferential" language with their spouses.

The differing abilities and styles of conflict management and coping with anger is examined by Cupach and Canary in chapter 10. These researchers indicate that the popularly accepted stereotype that men are more aggressive than women may not be supported in the cumulative research findings. In their chapter, this proposition is explicated and tested with a sample study and references to past research that has failed to support this stereotype of the female and male approaches to conflict and anger.

In the final chapter of this section (chapter 11), Schwartz, Patterson, and Stein argue that financial inequalities play havoc with the nature of female/male equalities and power. Specifically, it is the financially less stable female who is in jeopardy of never really achieving equality, and who is also suffering from a reduced status position, reduced levels of self-esteem, and other problems. Further, Schwartz and colleagues outline a number of problems in the self-concepts of both females and males. For example, women are affected by taboos as to who is to initiate sex and who should or should not control the frequency of sexual contact. On the other hand, men are affected by reduced levels of esteem when they suffer loss of income because so many of them subscribe to the role of "male as provider."

Part IV of this volume deals with females and males in a global, societal level. First, Rogers and his colleagues (Hirata, Chandran, and Robinson) overview the various attempts made around the globe to increase the status of women—especially in the United States of America and in India. They report on a representative study in the United States and on another one in India. The U.S. study deals with how males and females are portrayed on television, demonstrating a clear attempt (in the shows of the 1990s) to show women in various working roles and to show men in more nurturing roles (among other things). The India study taped receivers' reactions to television shows designed to prompt receivers to rethink the "traditional" roles of women in Indian society. Still, it may require considerably more time to actually change gender-based expectations concerning roles and behaviors relying on a media-only based approach.

In chapter 13, Cody, Seiter, and Montagne-Miller review 30 years of persuasion research in an attempt to show that women (or some subset of women) are more easily susceptible to influence than men. Actually, if one assesses an individual's goals, resources, and beliefs concerning purchases, male/females abilities, and so on, men are substantially more easily influenced than women (they spent more money in less time, agreed with more tactics, and spent more time shopping when assisted by a female, compared to when the salesclerk was a male). Still, women were also influenced by a number of tactics when shopping; but generally it is women who are competent shoppers (for clothing); they resist influence, take more time shopping, buy fewer items that are returned, and shop more economically.

In the final "macrolevel" chapter, Pearson and Cooks present a historical and critical view of gender research and provide a number of valuable insights and critiques of how scholars have progressed or not progressed over the decades in studying gender. Of particular interest are their suggestions on how we are to best proceed in order to provide more valuable research conclusions regarding gender and power.

TOWARD INTEGRATION, EQUALITY, AND IMPLICATIONS FOR HUMAN RELATIONSHIPS

The authors of the chapters in this volume review substantial bodies of research, offer intriguing research investigations, present provocative perspectives, and offer unique solutions or implications for the study of women and men, power, and human relationships. Most of these authors are experts and pioneers in their respective areas of study. Their advice, perspectives, and research endeavors bring us to an understanding of the state of the art in the 1990s.

In an attempt to integrate and unify this volume for the reader we offer Table 1.1 as a précis of these contributions, and as a method for placing these chapters into an overarching perspective. However, the synopses contained in this table are no more than an overview designed to assist the reader in digesting what is sometimes an enigmatic volume. The reader should keep in mind that the summary paragraphs are the work of the editors, and that to reach a full and complete understanding of each author's outlook, the individual chapters should be examined and considered at length. It is our hope that this volume will move both scholar and student toward an understanding of the relationships of women and men as we reach the end of this century and stand poised at the precipice of the future.

REFERENCES

Crisafulli, C. (1993, October 2). Women a comedy force? No joke. *Los Angeles Times*, pp. F1, F12.

Does rap music disrespect women, girls? p. E5. (1993, October 4). *Los Angeles Times*.

Faludi, S. (1991). *Backlash: The undeclared war against American women*. New York: Doubleday.

Gates, D. (1993, March 29). White male paranoia, *Newsweek*, pp. 48–53.

Henley, N. (1977). *Body politics: Power, sex, and nonverbal communication*. New York: Prentice-Hall.

Is violence a male hormone problem? p. E6. (1993, October 4). *Los Angeles Times*.

Klein, D. (1993, October 8). Caught in a vicious, bitter trap. *Los Angeles Times*, pp. A1, A23.

Schwartz, J. (1993, September 30). Early obesity tied to social, economic woes for women. *Los Angeles Times*, p. A23.

Weintraub, D.M., & Gladstone, M. (1993, October 2). Wilson signs bills to expand rape laws. *Los Angeles Times*, p. A21.

Women's groups re-emerge in workplace. pp. D11, D15. (1993, October 5). *Los Angeles Times*.

TABLE 1.1
Gender, Power, and Communication

Outlook	Henley (Chapter 2)
History of research	Professor Henley revises and explicates her 1977 book, *Body Politics*, reviewing 25 years of research on nonverbal behaviors and nonverbal communication in interpersonal transactions, including experimental research, observational analyses, surveys, and mass media portrayals. One of the central propositions is that nonverbal behaviors that might otherwise appear "meaningless" and unrelated to power are in fact behaviors strongly associated with status and power, and are related to "sex privilege." Special attention is given to behaviors associated with *space, touch, gaze/visual, facial expression, posture, gesture, body movement,* and *compliance.*
Equality: "he good and the bad	In the view of the editors, Henley's work can be credited with significantly increasing the *awareness* of how subtle power displays are in all human interaction, especially when focusing attention on asymmetric expressions of dominance and intimacy. However, despite the fact that many men and women are more *aware* of the meanings of behaviors, and some may alter their behaviors (such as avoiding touch that denotes dominance, or refusing to accept and legitimize a potentially dominating action), gender equality is extremely elusive. For example, Henley notes that increased smiling by women and minorities are clearly present in media portrayals, but women and minorities do not "in real life" smile more than men and "Whites;" thus, stereotypes persist. Further, Henley provides a set of guidelines concerning how research needs to be improved in order to more competently and directly study *gender equality* and the *subordination hypothesis.*
Female and male relationships	A case can easily be made that the relationships between men and women have been, and continue to be, improved given greater awareness of the meanings communicators assign to nonverbal behaviors. However, Henley argues that some of the most important research has yet to be undertaken. Parallel work with ethnic groups and subordinate groups is important not only for its own sake, but also as additional support for the general subordination hypothesis. In regard to male/female relationships and social change, some commendable recent research includes work on identifying which types of men are likely to be aggressive, and how women's "little voices" (or gut instincts) enable them to sense that they are interacting with an aggressor, a potential rapist.

11

TABLE 1.1 *(Continued)*

Outlook	Burgoon and Dillman (Chapter 3)
History of research	Reviewed are decades of research on "gender displays" on nonverbal communication, research that certainly escalated in the 1980s. This chapter focuses on *dominance cues*, and the authors conclude that women's nonverbal behavior is just as capable of communicating dominance and power as is men's—especially effective are non-normative distance, touch, and eye contact.
Equality: The good and the bad	The general consensus is that gender differences have been overexaggerated in some recent research. However, the present results indicate that males and females are equally effective in displaying identifiable dominance behaviors. The authors conclude that there are more similarities than differences between men and women. However, women were rated as more *composed* and as more *affectionate* than males, still suggesting that women are perceived as more calm, likeable, and trustworthy (see results in chapter).
Female and male relationships	Gender differences, when significant, did not account for much of the variance, suggesting fairly equal reactions on the part of observers. However, the study contains little information concerning the frequency of occurrence of the displays in "real life," and is limited primarily due to the fact that results are not embedded in any contextual framework involving situations, environments, or goals (i.e., if people expect males to display dominance cues in certain situations, will these expectations "cause" observers to see more [male-related] dominance cues?).

TABLE 1.1 *(Continued)*

Outlook	Mulac and Bradac (Chapter 4)
History of research	Starting with Lakoff's work in the 1970s, traditional research in the area of linguistics posits that women use particular forms of linguistic markers denoting tentativeness, uncertainty, powerlessness; indeed, the term the *female register* was coined to characterize the "coherent code of powerlessness" in females' use of language. However, over the last two decades, more and more scholars have challenged this "traditional" view, arguing instead that (a) female use of certain linguistic devices has little to do with "power" and more to do with being socialized into different cultures, and (b) there is little evidence in support of a "coherent code" of markers that signify "power." The "cross-situational" consistency of such codes communicated by females is questionable.
Equality: The good and the bad	The authors concluded that they failed to find more than "weak support" for the power-discrepancy hypothesis. Secondly, the authors found that although woman's language was in fact rated lower in *dynamism* than men's language, women's language was actually rated higher in *sociointellectual status* and *aesthetic quality*. Generally, it was concluded that there is no strong evidence in favor of female's use of low-power speech. Among other things, the authors argued that future research needs to focus on the age of the interactants, because (a) males and females may express different levels of power at different times in the life cycle, or (b) different generations may be socialized into using more (or less) power in their language when maturing in the 1950s, 1960s, 1970s, and so on. In sum, there appears to be more equality in fe/male language than what one would expect based on observations made in the 1970s.
Female and male relationships	Today, there is no strong or convincing reason to expect females to demur or to use less powerful language than men (except that there is consistent evidence that females appear to be less *dynamic*). Additional research needs to confirm and replicate the present results, but it appears that male and female language is more similar than one would expect. Future research also needs to assess whether or not similarities in male/female language will translate into similarities, or equality, in outcomes related to language production—persuasiveness, credibility, impression management, and other perceptions.

TABLE 1.1 *(Continued)*

Outlook	Spence and Buckner (Chapter 5)
History of research	Despite decades of research employing the terms *masculinity* and *femininity*, the terms remain some of the "muddiest" constructs in both theory building and research in the social sciences. Adding new terms (sex-role orientation, sex typing, and gender schema) hardly aids in the understanding of the terms femininity and masculinity. Spence and Buckner review both theoretical and empirical uses of the terms, explicate current models of femininity and masculinity, and present an alternative model that provides a better fit to existing empirical data.
Equality: The good and the bad	The authors argue that rejection of the unifactorial model (i.e., masculinity and femininity are bipolar extremes of a single dimension) is long overdue. Further, the two-factor model (positing one dimension of femininity and one dimension of masculinity) is also problematic. A superior approach is one in which scholars adopt a gender identity theory that allows for gender-related phenomena to fall into multiple categories of traits, behaviors and attitudes. In regard to equality, the proposed theory rejects relatively simplistic notions of females or males as being fairly homogeneous types of people who differ from one another on one or two clusters of traits. Women and men are allowed (as evidence indicates) to be quite similar to one another on some categories, while differing on others.
Female and male relationships	Both men and women possess, though in different levels or amounts, and at different intensities, a variety of both masculine and feminine characteristics; characteristics involving more than a composite of basic traits. Although Spence and Buckner do not explicitly address the issue of the quality of male and female relationships, their claim concerning how we study gender equality allows for considerable freedom for the individual to seek out and identify with a range of potential gender related roles, traits, rules and behaviors. Thus, not only are individuals equal on some criteria and different on others, the multifactorial model holds that we should avoid "typecasting" individuals into limited categories of "masculinity" and "femininity." An initial starting point for improved relationships between females and males is to avoid stereotypes. Perhaps social scientists should start by abolishing the words "masculinity" and "femininity" from social science research (and ultimately from "pop psychology").

TABLE 1.1 *(Continued)*

Outlook	Reinholtz, Muehlenhard, Phelps, and Satterfield (Chapter 6)
History of research	Previous research looked at "mistakes" in flirting and characteristics of date rapists and situations involving rape. The present chapter assesses the messages and themes in popular media that establish or create how we think about sexual coercion. Messages and themes that are pervasive and insidious in society.
Equality: The good and the bad	The situation looks bleak for equality, as it does for improving male and female relationships. Pervasive sexual messages include: Males cannot control sexual behaviors, females are responsible, romance = nonrational behavior, sex is a force of nature, men are untrustworthy, women ask for it, and so on. Virtually all forms of media reinforce attitudes and beliefs that perpetuate a climate of sexual coercion.
Female and male relationships	With few exceptions, movies, novels, and music continue to transmit messages concerning women as submissive, responsible, yet powerless—and they do so with great consistency. Obviously, the first concern in changing the current situation deals with an awareness of how both males and females are influenced, even manipulated, by these messages. More importantly, a critical need exists in adhering to a more enlightened, mature, (egalitarian) set of messages concerning "romance."

TABLE 1.1 *(Continued)*

Outlook	Miller, Burns, and Rothspan (Chapter 7)
History of research	For a multitude of reasons (war, disease, poverty, etc.), there has often been a disproportionate sex ratio in societies over time, with women often outnumbering males. At such times, women's positions and roles in society may either be elevated, or devalued. Specifically, confronted with a shortage of "available" men, women are likely to be devalued when they have a sense of powerlessness, an inability to select a mate, and when they possess a lack of both "dyadic" and "structural" power. Such devaluation (along with an individual's skills at communicating and negotiating safe sex practices) affects a woman's ability to propose safe sex practices and to overcome resistance to unsafe sex practices.
Equality: The good and the bad	Among many minority members in American society, women possess substantially less power than do men; this is especially true in the African-American culture. Men indicated greater promiscuity than women, both in and out of committed relationships. Confronted with a shortage of available men, women often (but not always) work harder on forming and maintaining interpersonal relationships, being instrumental in using condoms, being persistent in their use, and working to overcome resistance to the use of condoms. However, as economic power decreased, women were more likely to simply focus on the sexual experience and were more likely to be at risk, reflecting extremely low levels of power and equality among the lower SES individuals. Both the current and future potential for creating and maintaining equality between males and females is disturbing.
Female and male relationships	Improved interpersonal relationships are hampered by interpersonal dynamics stemming from a disproportionate sex ratio, by poverty, which reduces structural/economic power, and (often) by a lack in dyadic power. Women continue to work diligently toward two goals: to work on committed relationships, and simply to reduce risk from serious and deadly diseases. It appears the situation is bleakest among the poorest; extremely poor females might use sexual experiences as part of an arsenal to solve short-term economic and financial goals, giving less immediate thought to serious, and possibly long-term health risks. The need for research and intervention, is critical.

TABLE 1.1 (Continued)

Outlook	Kalbfleisch and Keyton (Chapter 8)
History of research	The existence of mentors and proteges has been chronicled throughout history. Examples of the presence of these relationships abounds in literature, biography, film, popular press, and social scientific research. Modern research efforts have demonstrated what has been anecdotally described in the literature and popular media. Specifically, mentors significantly facilitate the career success of their proteges.
Equality: The good and the bad	Women have not been as successful as men in developing mentoring relationships. Males appear to be reluctant to enter into mentorships with females. On the other hand, females are more likely to mentor other females than they are males. However, there are relatively few women in positions where they can successfully mentor other women, and those that are in positions of power may hesitate to develop these mentoring relationships. There is evidence that part of the problem women may be facing is that the traditional framework for male–male relationships may not fit female–female relationships, nor female–male relationships. Finding alternate frameworks that successful mentoring relationships use may help empower nontraditional mentors and proteges by giving them a reference for developing mentorships.
Female and male relationships	Women and men are the least common mentoring partners that are found in academe and in business. Mentors and proteges more often seek members of their own sex for these partnerships. Ultimately this leads to a waste of resources and limitation of the sources for professional and social support. One of the problems faced by women and men working closely together may be gossip and innuendo on the part of co-workers and scrutiny by superiors, as well as jealousy expressed by spouses and loved ones. Sexual tension is another problem women and men may face in close working relationships. This sexual undercurrent can lead to mistakes in interpreting friendly behavior as flirting or seductive behavior, issues of sexual harassment, and perhaps the development of romantic relationships that could complicate the working relationship. One suggested possibility is for women and men to learn to transform sexual energy and attraction into mutual creativity and a robust, exciting working relationship. Another suggestion is to look for other models of relationships from which to draw useful frameworks for the development of mentoring relationships between women and men.

17

TABLE 1.1 (Continued)

Outlook	Fitzpatrick and Mulac (Chapter 9)
History of research	Considerable evidence on the Gender-Linked Language Effect supports the general notion that males and females vary significantly in the use of language (specifically, specific linguistic and prosodic features of speech). For example, males tend to use language involving more elements of *dynamism*, whereas the language of females often reflects higher levels of *aesthetic quality*, and sometimes higher levels of *sociointellectual status*. The research supports a general notion, or stereotype, that males and females represent two different sociolinguistic groups. However, much of the existing research has examined language examples taken in isolation of context and in isolation of the effects of the partner (male, female, spouse, etc.)
Equality: The good and the bad	Research reported in the chapter generally supports the claim that women and men vary in use of language, summing over all settings and interactional partners, and reflected only as a weighted combination of variables. More importantly, evidence indicates that communicators did not consistently use certain types of linguistic variables. Husbands used masculine gender preferential language with women strangers, but converged toward their wives' feminine preferential style when interacting with them. Wives, however, did not converge toward husbands and maintained the same feminine style in interactions with others. The conclusions/implications: In home settings, or when interacting with intimates, there is substantially more "equality" or similarity between men and women than what one would expect from extrapolating from the context-free language samples of college students.
Female and male relationships	The results of the reported study, if explicated, represent good news for male and female relationships. Some previous research in speech accommodation indicated that females were more likely to converge toward males (than vice versa), for reasons pertaining to increased social skills, or motivation to show similarity, or linking, or to be liked by the partner. The present results indicate that males are more likely to switch speaking patterns to accommodate to an extremely important area of social participation: intimate settings. Males and females appear to communicate with similar levels of aesthetic quality, sociointellectual status, and dynamism when speaking together.

TABLE 1.1 *(Continued)*

Outlook	Cupach and Canary (Chapter 10)
History of research	The assumption that men are more aggressive and less cooperative than women in conflict is not supported by the years of research on the topic. The literature reveals that men and women are equally capable of cooperating, competing, or avoiding the partner during conflict interactions.
Equality: The good and the bad	The news regarding equality is quite good. Because men and women largely engage in similar behaviors, neither sex is privileged in this type of interaction. Men, however, should not interpret women's tears as a sign of weakness or acquiescence. In addition, educators should stop perpetuating stereotypes and oversimplified men's and women's conflict behaviors.
Female and male relationships	Conflict probably affects relationships more powerfully than do most other types of interactions. It appears that the dissatisfied person seeks to engage the partner who may want to withdraw. In other instances men and women in conflict tend to mirror each other's behaviors. If the couple engage in the sequences of competitive actions or in demand withdrawal patters, then the relationship may suffer. If the parties to conflict can break out of competitive sequences, then the relationship will likely be served.

TABLE 1.1 (Continued)

Outlook	Schwartz, Patterson, and Steen (Chapter 11)
History of research	Two variables powerfully related to status inequality among married individuals are *money* and *sex*. Schwartz and colleagues document qualitative and quantitative research on power and dominance among married or cohabitating heterosexual couples, and among gay and lesbian couples. The "traditional" model involving income discrepancies is that if both the wife and husband believe in the "male-breadwinner ideology," the husband tends to have more power in major decisions, even if his wife has a higher income than he does. The "traditional" model of sexual activities assigns power to the male in terms of both the initiation of sexual activity and the frequency of sexual activity. However, the dynamics of sex and money as resources affecting power and domination often operate differently in homosexual couples.
Equality: The good and the bad	The "male breadwinner/male initiator" orientation is deeply entrenched in society and is hard to change. Even among couples who adopt an equalitarian philosophy, or among couples in which wives earn more money than husbands, people are susceptible to the biases of the male as the decision-maker/initiator. The traditional, dominant practice strongly affects the self-concept of both males and females; males' self-esteem is intimately linked to being a "good provider": Females often find it difficult to be the initiator of sex. Conclusion: Equality remains elusive, and probably will only follow after significant economic opportunities for women improve (and remain available consistently through recessions, etc.), and both men and women become aware of the way in which the traditional orientation affects their behavior and how they view themselves.
Female and male relationships	There always have been, and there always will be, problems in relationships that are attributable to disputes over money and sex. Being aware of the impact such variables have on power and domination, however, is no guarantee that conflicts can be avoided. Working women may, in fact, find that their income is likely to go entirely toward household expenses, freeing the husband's income to be spent as he sees fits. Lesbian couples know that money exerts a strong effect on power and domination, but they often confront a different kind of problem: They are so in tune with the corrupting effects money has on equalitarian relationships that they become sensitive to even small imbalances in money. However, the view looks especially bleak for working-class wives.

TABLE 1.1 (Continued)

Outlook	Rogers, Hirata, Chandran, and Robinson (Chapter 12)
History of research	After showing women engaged in domestic activities for years, television programs of the 1980s and 1990s incorporate social science theories in a concerted effort to promote the role of women—in several different countries. Although improved roles are portrayed on some programs (which clearly raise awareness of roles), they have yet to produce major changes in beliefs and attitudes.
Equality: The good and the bad	The "good" news is that more and more television shows plan to promote positive roles and egalitarian actions for and by women. Consciousness is raised, topics are debated, and female viewers identify with the plights of women shown on television; perhaps modeling their behaviors. The "bad" deals with the fact that messages are often not as consistently portrayed as we'd prefer, and sometimes female receivers actually identify with a character they were not intended to identify with (e.g., the self-sacrificing grandmother in "Hom Log").
Female and male relationships	Some males "don't get it," some receivers refuse to believe stories presented, and some have begun to backlash against the prowomen messages (e.g., in one story line an Indian girl [a child bride] died. Rather than accept the intended message that children are too young for marriages and giving birth, many males attributed other causes for the death, even blaming the victim of poor health practices. An actual improvement in female/male relationships may rest on combining changes in both interpersonal settings (schools, families, etc.), along with the media (movies, music, as well as television)(like other successful social planning campaigns).

TABLE 1.1 (Continued)

Outlook	Cody, Seiter, and Montagne-Miller (Chapter 13)
History of research	Decades of research in persuasion struggled to show women (or some group of women) as more easily influenced than men. Actually, men were often more easily influenced than women, depending on motives, beliefs, laws, and how resources are allocated.
Equality: The good and the bad	Soon (the authors hope) the myth of female influenceability will cease to persist. But research on "gender differences" probably will persist as scholars in marketing and advertising continue to examine how to appeal to women in "traditionally male" domains (as some recent titles have had it). Nonetheless, the simplistic notions of influenceability based only on gender is a thing of the past.
Female and male relationships	Men are not competent shoppers, which is obviously unfortunate, because shopping should be considered a fundamental or essential aspect of living. Yet, the double inequality for women today exists in that women do engage in shopping more often than do men, but society (or men, at least) de-values the importance of shopping. Such a situation may take time to change, starting (on one hand) with both parents becoming involved with both daughter and son; and with the acceptance of shopping as an important task any adult should be able to complete competently, and on a budget.

TABLE 1.1 *(Continued)*

Outlook	Pearson and Cooks (Chapter 14)
History of research	As a concluding chapter to the volume, the authors share a dialogue and discuss a chronological series of events leading up to today's orientations on research (and the basic questions of what, and how) "gender" issues are to be addressed and research.
Equality: The good and the bad	Awareness of biases in all fields of study is fundamental, followed by understanding and explaining behaviors from the *experience* of women; relying on *experiential knowledge*—cumulative life experiences, values, language, and so on. "Bad:" Most social science research is descriptive or relies on hypothesis-testing: methods that hardly allow a scholar to capture the essence of actual experiences. The authors propose some guidelines for conducting research. A challenge is for scholars not to dogmatically reject the "new," and to be open to productive lines of inquiry.
Female and male relationships	A fundamental problem since the 1960s in calling for "equality" is that equality was "good," so long as the basic rules of society are not changed—"equality""enlightened" men may accept. However, impacting on male and female relationships today is the fact that "equality" also means that the rules themselves change. Hence, some may feel that too many changes occur too quickly, prompting alienation, backlash, and adversarial reactions. The challenge will be to co-exist and integrate experiential worlds that are quite different, not to degenerate into separatist environments in which two spheres of knowledge and ideology remain isolated.

Part II

Gender-Based Expectations and Beliefs

Chapter 2

Body Politics Revisited: What Do We Know Today?

Nancy M. Henley
University of California, Los Angeles

In 1977 my book *Body Politics* (Henley, 1977) reviewed the literature on "power, sex, and nonverbal communication" and put forward from this review a set of theses, which I summarize below for the sake of those who are not familiar with them (and as a reminder for those who are). The theses are here categorized into three broad topic areas (all appear in Henley, 1977, pp. 179–200; the original numbers given them in the book are given below to aid identification).

The first topic area covers *nonverbal behavior/communication* (NVB/NVC) and the previously neglected *domain of power* within NVC studies. Like many others, I stated that nonverbal behavior is a major medium of communication in everyday life. But unlike others, I further stated that power/status/dominance is a major topic of nonverbal communication; that nonverbal behavior is a major avenue for social control and interpersonal dominance; that nonverbal power gestures provide the micropolitical structure, the thousands of daily acts through which nonverbal influence takes place, which underlies and supports the macropolitical structure; and that because of general cultural ignorance of nonverbal communication, its interpretation is highly susceptible to social influences (e.g., explanations utilizing sex stereotypes) that further maintain the status quo (theses 1, 2, 3, and 4).

Later theses were about the *definition and exercise of (social) power*: Borrowing from typical social science formulations, I defined *power* as the capability of influencing or compelling others, based on the control of desired resources (power, status, and dominance are different, though related and often confounded, concepts[1]). The ultimate underpinning of power, I maintained, is force, although force is the last-ditch, not the front-line defense. Power is exercised along a continuum, from least to greatest application of force; generally speaking, the mildest form of force that is effective will be used. Nonverbal behavior occupies a crucial point in the force continuum, between covert and overt control and between covert and overt resistance (theses 10, 11, 12, 13, 14).

The final topic area interrelates *nonverbal communication, power, and gender*: I claimed that the overwhelming bulk of sex-differentiated behavior is learned and is developed to display otherwise unobtrusive differences, and that many nonverbal behaviors that seem meaningless and non-power-related in fact are aspects of sex privilege or reflect societal biases ultimately founded in power differences (theses 8 and 9). I stated that sexual attraction cannot sufficiently explain men's greater usage of gestures that indicate both intimacy and dominance. Further, usurpation of the nonverbal symbols of power by subordinates may be ignored, denied, or punished by others, rather than accepted (theses 15 and 16). And much of women's behavior that is interpreted as self-limiting may in reality be the end of a sequence in which assertion was attempted, and suppressed, on the nonverbal level (thesis 18).

In this area I made a number of testable hypotheses, supporting them whenever possible with empirical data collected by others and, sometimes, myself. These are listed individually below so that we may examine their validity in the light of subsequent research; they are preceded by their thesis number from *Body Politics.*[2]

5. Nonverbal control is of particular importance to women, who are more sensitive to its cues and probably more the targets of such control.
6. Many nonverbal behaviors have the dual function of expressing either dominance or intimacy, according to whether they are asymmetrically or symmetrically used by the partners in a relationship.
7. The behaviors expressing dominance and subordination between nonequals parallel those used by males and females in the unequal relation of the sexes.

Table 2.1, taken from *Body Politics*, illustrates some of the parallels in behaviors of which I wrote.

---

[1]I understand *dominance* in a more personal and interactional way; it may be used to designate individual personality tendencies or dyadic relationships. *Status* concerns a person's social ranking relative to others, one's position in a hierarchy. Because they are highly interrelated concepts, and all three are used at different times in the nonverbal investigations reviewed herein, I will use the terms more or less interchangeably, although attempting to stick with the term or concept used in a particular study I am referring to. Edinger and Patterson (1983, p. 32) also used *status*, power and *dominance* interchangeably, citing other researchers' similar usage as well.

[2]Some readers may wish to question the particular theses I select to treat as testable hypotheses, considering that others of the list should be treated in the same way; however, my own position is that most of the theses are summing up the theoretical framework offered in the book. I believe the ones I have selected are the ones that other researchers have tried to test.

TABLE 2.1**

Gestures of Power and Privilege, Examples of Some Nonverbal Behaviors with Usage Differing for Status Equals and Nonequals, and for Women and Men.

Behavior	Between Status Equals		Between Status Nonequals		Between Men and Women	
	Intimate	Nonintimate	Used by Superior	Used by Subordinate	Used by Men	Used by Women
1 Address	Familiar	Polite	Familiar	Polite	Familiar?*	Polite?*
2 Demeanor	Informal	Circumspect	Informal	Circumspect	Informal	Circumspect
3 Posture	Relaxed	Tense (less relaxed)	Relaxed	Tense	Relaxed	Tense
4 Personal space	Closeness	Distance	Closeness (option)	Distance	Closeness	Distance
5 Time	Long	Short	Long (option)	Short	Long?*	Short?*
6 Touching	Touch	Don't touch	Touch (option)	Don't touch	Touch	Don't touch
7 Eye contact	Establish	Avoid	Stare, Ignore	Avert eyes, watch	Stare, Ignore	Avert eyes, watch
8 Facial expression	Smile?*	Don't smile?*	Don't smile	Smile	Don't smile	Smile
9 Emotional expression	Show	Hide	Hide	Show	Hide	Show
10 Self-Disclosure	Disclose	Don't disclose	Don't disclose	Disclose	Don't disclose	Disclose

*Behavior not known. **From Henley (1977). Reprinted by permission.

17. Denial of nonverbal power gestures made by women often takes the form of attributing the gesture to sexual advance rather than dominance.

MUTUALITY, RECIPROCITY, AND STATUS

One fact important to me and sometimes lost on others is that I did not claim that nonverbal behavior between males and females was based on dominance and submission *rather than* on affection, attraction, and other nonhierarchical motives. Although I felt the need to emphasize the neglected point that there is a power basis to nonverbal behavior, which was manifest in cross-sex interactions as well as under other circumstances, I fully acknowledged the existence of both vertical and horizontal social dimensions (e.g., Henley, 1977, pp. 5, 106–108, 180–181). This duality was in fact at the heart of *Body Politics*.

Thesis 6, based on work by Brown (1965) and Goffman (1967) is a cornerstone of the book's argument, explaining one reason that it is hard to understand, or verbalize, the power that underlies some gestures. What turns gestures of intimacy such as "gazing into another's eyes," "caressing," and "moving closer" into gestures of dominance such as "staring," "pawing," and "invading space" is the absence of mutuality. The same behavior could be used for different purposes, and might be seen in different ways, by the different participants in a social situation.

A corollary of this thesis that certain nonverbal behaviors express closeness or distance when used symmetrically but dominance or subordination when used asymmetrically is the idea that the mutuality or nonmutuality of the gesture is a clue to its function. In particular, one can speculate that reciprocating a power gesture can be a way of reasserting one's dominance, and not reciprocating it can be a way of showing acceptance of another's dominance. Although this thesis was not stated explicitly in *Body Politics*, I had earlier hypothesized (Henley 1973, p. 91) regarding touch, and will list here in a generalized form as thesis X, that:

X. The failure to reciprocate a dominance gesture by another indicates an acceptance of the legitimacy of the other's dominance, and reciprocation indicates a reassertion of one's own status (as not subordinate).

These theses primarily provided a theoretical framework, borrowing largely from previous theoretical work and integrating across subfields of study for interpreting nonverbal behavior in the context of unequal social status. This framework was presented with particular (but not exclusive) attention to communication within and between genders, and to gender-comparative studies. My intent was to break away from stereotype- and role-influenced interpretations of behavior and to incorporate the realities of social and political context: Much communication takes place between social unequals, and communicates—indeed, helps to create and perpetuate—this inequality. In my writing I have tried continually to place gender in the context of social inequality, and note that gender is a status dimension and a domain of power. The arguments made about gender power are meant to apply to other domains of power (e.g., socioeconomic status, racial/ethnic hierarchy).

LaFrance and I (Henley & LaFrance, 1984) later elaborated and generalized these original theses, hypothesizing that subordinate persons in any group difference context would show more nonverbal readability (encoding skill), sensitivity (decoding skill), accommodation (adjustment of one's nonverbal behavior to others), and submissiveness.

A question that arises is, how well have these various theses stood the test of time? Have they been supported or refuted by subsequent studies? In these pages I attempt to summarize pertinent work since the publication of *Body Politics*; my own assessment, perhaps naturally enough, is that the basic ideas put forward in *Body Politics* have been supported, and interestingly expanded, by subsequent research.

NONVERBAL COMMUNICATION AND POWER/DOMINANCE

First, the importance of power and dominance as topics of nonverbal communication has, I believe, been well supported, directly by the research findings and indirectly by the plethora of work on the topic in the past 15 years (e.g., Edinger & Patterson, 1983; Ellyson & Dovidio, 1985). The review by Edinger and Patterson of the role of the social control function in determining patterns of nonverbal involvement summarizes: "In contrast to the common assumption that nonverbal behavior usually reflects a spontaneous and consistent affective reaction, this research strongly suggests that in many instances nonverbal behavior may be managed to influence the behavior of others" (p. 30).

NONVERBAL COMMUNICATION AND GENDER

The thesis that nonverbal control is of particular importance to women (5), who are more sensitive to its cues and probably more the targets of such control, contains several points. The first clause was not meant to be a hypothesis about how important women consider nonverbal communication to be, but rather a statement that was part of the theoretical framework. Nevertheless, we may note that the importance of gender as a topic of nonverbal communication study has also been well supported. One type of evidence for this assertion is the consistent finding of significant sex differences in variables of interest to research psychologists. Frances (1979), for example, found that subject sex had a significant effect on many nonverbal behaviors displayed during conversations. Hall (1984), reviewing previous quantitative summaries of sex differences in various attributes, abilities, and behaviors, wrote: "How strong are sex differences for these [other than nonverbal] behaviors compared to sex differences for nonverbal skills and behaviors? The answer is clear: sex differences are larger for the nonverbal variables" (p. 145; see also Hall, 1985). Similarly, Hyde (1990) concluded from the evidence of meta-analyses of gender differences in various social behaviors that differences in nonverbal behaviors were generally larger than those in other areas (It should be noted that Hyde's conclusions are apparently based entirely on the work of Hall.).

The second point, that women are more sensitive to nonverbal communication (than men) has been a major topic of nonverbal communication research on gender. The studies of Rosenthal, Hall and their colleagues (Hall, 1978, 1984; Hall & Halberstadt, 1981; Rosenthal, 1979; Rosenthal, Hall, DiMatteo, Rogers, & Archer, 1979) proliferated with evidence of gender differences in nonverbal sensitivity, and Hall (1984) concluded on the basis of meta-analysis "that females are better decoders of nonverbal expressions than are males, and that this result is very consistent and of moderate size" (p. 27). This question is considered in more detail later in this chapter.

NONVERBAL BEHAVIOR, POWER, AND GENDER: TESTING HYPOTHESES

Much of the subsequent work relating to this framework has focused on thesis 7, the parallel I posited between male–female and dominant–subordinate nonverbal behaviors. Thesis 6, regarding the dual function of nonverbal behaviors, has been tested to a certain extent, in that various studies have attempted to examine the dominance and intimacy dimensions of various gestures, and often to determine whether one shows greater strength than the other. Radecki & Jennings (1980) in a self-report study of dominance and sexual behaviors between the sexes in work settings, found that "… intimacy and sexual behaviors were expressible on the same continuum as traditional dominance behaviors" (p. 78).

There is less work on the related theses stating that women's power gestures are often interpreted as sexual (17) and that subordinates will not, and superordinates will, reciprocate a dominance gesture by another (X).

In the rest of this chapter I will attempt to review the studies testing these hypotheses, citing only work printed after the publication of *Body Politics*, but with the *caveat* that any such review must be incomplete, because of the plethora of studies carried out in the past 15 years on the topic.[3] (I apologize to those whose studies I do not mention here and hope that my presentation is evenhanded.) The channels of nonverbal behavior that I will review include proxemics (use of space), touch, gaze/visual behavior, facial expression (mainly smiling), and kinesics (pos-

---

[3]Marianne LaFrance and I have previously attempted to summarize parts of this research elsewhere (Henley & LaFrance, 1984; LaFrance & Henley, in press).

ture, gesture, and body movement), all subjects of chapters in *Body Politics*;[4] in addition, other pertinent questions of communication accuracy, interpretation of nonverbal communication, reciprocity, and explanatory theories will be discussed.

THE PRESENT REVIEW IS ORGANIZED ACCORDING TO THE THREE TYPES OF QUESTIONS THAT EMPIRICAL STUDIES IN THIS AREA HAVE ADDRESSED.

1. *Behavior*. This type of study asks: How do people actually behave nonverbally? Here, additionally, we ask: How do people behave nonverbally as a function of gender and/or power/status/dominance? In particular, are certain behaviors consistently associated with dominance or subordination, and do the gestures of power parallel the gestures of (male) gender? In addition, Are dominance gestures used asymmetrically between social unequals, and symmetrically between social equals? Do equals and superiors respond to power gestures by others with reciprocating power gestures, and do subordinates not do so?

2. *Perceptions/attributions*. This type of study asks: How do people interpret nonverbal behavior that they observe? Here we ask: How do observers' interpretations of nonverbal behavior differ according to the gender and/or power relationships of the actors? In particular, are behaviors ordinarily associated with power reinterpreted to lessen or deny power when the actors are subordinates, and are women's power gestures more likely than men's to be interpreted as sexual? Are certain gestures perceived as dominant when used asymmetrically, and non-dominating when used symmetrically?

3. *Skill/accuracy in encoding/decoding*. This type of study asks: How well do the attributions made by observers match the communicative/expressive intentions of actors? Here we ask: How do gender and/or power/status/dominance affect decoding skill (sometimes called sensitivity)and/or encoding skill (sometimes called expressivity)? In particular, do subordinate persons show greater decoding skill than superordinates, and do females show greater decoding skill than males? [Henley & LaFrance (1984) predicted subordinate persons should show both greater expressivity ("readability") and sensitivity.]

After reviewing the recent empirical evidence in these three types of study, we will turn to questions of theory: why these particular findings, what systematic logical structure best explains their pattern?

---

[4]Three domains that were the subjects of chapters in *Body Politics* but that will not be examined here are those that have proved less popular for the study of gender issues—time, environment, and demeanor. The issues of gender and power in language, subject of another chapter in *Body Politics*, have spurred a burgeoning of the literature too large to be covered here (for recent reviews, I particularly recommend Graddol & Swann, 1989, and Penelope, 1990).

BEHAVIOR: HOW DO PEOPLE ACTUALLY BEHAVE NONVERBALLY AS A FUNCTION OF GENDER AND/OR POWER/STATUS/DOMINANCE?

Addressing this question involves observation (either naturalistic or experimental) of the relationship, if any, between nonverbal behaviors and operationalized power, dominance, or status. Experimental researchers may set up conditions of social inequality and observe nonverbal behaviors associated with higher or lower status (e.g., Dovidio and Ellyson, 1985; Leffler, Gillespie, & Conaty, 1982). Or they may manipulate nonverbal behaviors and observe whether these behaviors create conditions of power or influence, as observed by others' behaviors, such as compliance (e.g., Patterson, Powell, & Lenihan, 1986; Ridgeway, 1987). Naturalistic researchers may identify people with certain characteristics, say, of gender, job status, wealth, race/ethnicity, and so forth, and observe the nonverbal behaviors that go with those characteristics (e.g., Major, Schmidlin, & Williams, 1990; Street & Buller, 1987); or observe nonverbal behaviors and characteristics simultaneously (e.g., Borden & Homleid, 1978; Willson & Lloyd, 1990); or observe nonverbal behaviors and then determine characteristics (e.g., Hall & Veccia, 1992; Willis & Briggs, 1992).

In the realm of behavior, a considerable amount of evidence has accrued to support the hypothesis that certain behaviors are consistently associated with dominance or subordination, and that males are more likely to exhibit these behaviors. These include the following factors.

Space

In *Body Politics* I gave evidence (Henley, 1977) for five ways in which use of space (also known as proxemic behavior) reflects dominance in animals and in humans:

1. Dominants control greater territory.
2. Dominants are freer to move in others', or common, territory.
3. Dominants are accorded greater personal (bodily) space.
4. Subordinates yield space to dominants when approached, or in passing.
5. Dominants occupy positions associated with, and/or controlling, desired resources.

Gillespie and Leffler (1983), in a later review of the proxemics literature, also concluded that "correlational, causal, and gender research all support the theory that status is a powerful organizer of proxemic behavior" (p. 141).

Access to close proximity is associated with male gender as well as dominance/control. Leffler, Gillespie, and Conaty (1982) conducted an experiment that examined the effects of both specific status (experimental role) and diffuse status (gender) on proxemic and other nonverbal behaviors. Female and male subjects, randomly assigned, served once as teacher and once as learner for experimentally assigned teaching situations. Both teachers, holding higher specific status, and males, holding higher diffuse status, took up significantly more space with their bodies and their possessions than did learners and females, respectively.

An imaginative application of proxemic research on gender is the armrest study of Hai, Khairullah, and Coulmas (1982), in which 852 subjects were observed for their use of the armrest in the coach section of airplanes. Men had a much greater tendency to use the common armrest, with or without control for size. And those subjects who were accustomed to using the armrest but could not felt angrier when they had been denied it.

That women's personal space is smaller than men's, that is, that both men and women are observed in greater proximity to women than they are to men, is commonly observed in studies of interpersonal spacing (see also Hall, 1984). A frequent explanation for this has been women's greater affiliativeness and friendliness, and/or an expectation of aggressive response among men. However, Hall observed that "while previous analyses found a tendency for females to place themselves closer to others than males do …the much stronger and more consistent tendency is for females to be approached more closely by others than males are" (p. 94; see also the review by Gillespie and Leffler, 1983). Henley and LaFrance (1984) also pointed out that in studies in which *women are in control of their own spacing* (when they choose their own seating or may control another's approach distance), males are not allowed as close to them as are other females. Hence the closer proximity of others to females may be, in the case of approaching males, an exercise of male prerogative, not of females' preference for more intimate spacing.

Moore & Porter (1988) showed ethnic dimensions of spatial use that were also consistent with cultural status relationships: among Hispanic and Anglo children observed in same-sex group tasks, Hispanic females used less vertical and horizontal space than Anglo females, and were less likely to physically intrude on group members. (These differences did not apply, however, for Hispanic males, who were more likely than Anglo males to use vertical or upward movements and physical intrusions.)

Touch

Between-gender touching has been studied, sometimes in imaginative ways, in the years since the publication of *Body Politics*. Following are some of them.

In a role-playing experiment, Alber (1974, cited in Major, 1981) cast subjects into dominant or submissive roles of a play, a portion of which they were asked to rehearse, and observed significantly more touching by those playing dominant roles than by those playing submissive ones.

Borden and Homleid's (1978) observational study investigated the relationship between hand-holding, lateral positioning, and handedness in heterosexual couples, asking "Are men still strong-arming women?" Male–female couples were observed (on centrally located walkways, not street-side), either holding hands or not, and their lateral positioning was noted (who was on left or right). The persons were then asked about their handedness. When both were either right-handed or left-handed, and especially when the partners were touching, females were significantly more often on the side of the male's dominant hand than would be expected by chance.

Leffler et al. (1982) also found in their experiment (described under "Space" above) that higher diffuse status (male) and specific status (teacher) subjects touched their partner's *possessions* more than lower status subjects (females and learners) did.

Support for the operation of tactile dominance within the family is found in the research of Grusky, Bonacich, and Peyrot (1984), who conducted interviews with 48 families and examined their posed portraits for touching patterns. They found significant touch asymmetries for parent gender (fathers were significantly more likely to touch mothers than vice versa, and mothers were significantly more likely to be touched than fathers); generational status (parents were significantly more likely to touch children than vice versa, and children were significantly more likely than parents to be touched); and, to some extent, age status among children (younger children were significantly more likely to be touched than older children; however, the hypothesis that older children would touch younger ones more than vice versa could not be tested, because there was insufficient inter-child touching in their sample). They did not find any significant effect of child gender on family touch patterns. Grusky et al. (1984) concluded that there was "moderately strong, consistent support" for the hypothesis that higher status members within the family would initiate more and receive less physical contact than those of lower status.

Along another status dimension (or dimensions—both legitimate authority and social status are involved), Street and Buller (1987) observed physician–patient interactions. The doctors showed more dominance/control-type behaviors, including social touch, than the patients.

Major's studies have been the largest and most careful on touch and gender (Major, 1981; Major, Schmidlin, & Williams, 1990). In a review that included a report of new data as well, Major (1981) concluded both that females are touched more than males and that males are more likely to touch females than vice versa. Regarding touch initiation in general, she found more precisely that males were more likely than females to initiate touch in cross-sex encounters, but not in same-sex encounters.

Hall (1984; see also Stier & Hall, 1984, which covers essentially the same data), however, in an extensive review of studies of gender differences in touching, concluded that they showed "a clear trend … favoring females in touch initiation" (p. 108), but no clear sex differences in receipt of touch (p. 110). However, Hall's reviews combined studies without regard to gender combinations in testing both touch initiation and touch receipt overall, and when they did look at cross-sex touching separately, combined studies without regard to intentionality of touch (for elaboration, see Hall, 1984, p. 113). Therefore they do not constitute a true test of the theses of *Body Politics* (see also Henley & LaFrance, 1993; Major, Schmidlin, & Williams, 1990).

Major et al. (1990) noted several points of contrast between Major's 1981 findings and those of Stier and Hall (1984), and pointed out that both those reviews had observed that inconsistencies in the literature could be due to the fact that researchers had not systematically considered four factors: "the intentionality of touch, the age of the participants, the nature of the relationship between the participants, and the setting or context in which touch was observed" (p. 635). Major et al. (1990) designed their research to replicate Henley's (1973) original study, observing only intentional touch and taking into account the other previously neglected factors. They report a total of 799 observations of touch, from both a small midwestern city and a large industrialized eastern city (some of the data had been reported in Major, 1981). Although their findings are too extensive to report in full here (and interested readers are referred to their study for in-depth analyses), a few excerpts summarize their major conclusions:

> As predicted, when only intentional touch between adults was examined, men were more likely to touch women than women were to touch men, and cross-sex touch was more than twice as frequent as same-sex touch. In contrast, when children were involved, no evidence of gender asymmetry was observed, and same-sex touch was twice as likely to occur as cross-sex touch.

> In public nonintimate settings similar to those observed by Henley (1973), all of the predictions for adults were confirmed; in fact, the patterns were even more pronounced.

> Henley's (1977) main-effect hypotheses—that men, by virtue of their higher status, are more likely to initiate touch than are women, and that women, by virtue of their lower status, are more likely to be the recipients of touch than are men—also were examined. Although in the aggregate these hypotheses appeared confirmed, the significant interactions observed between sex of initiator and sex of recipient indicated that such a conclusion is misleading. Whether a man or a woman is more likely to initiate or receive touch is highly dependent on the sex of the partner. (Moore et al., 1990, p. 640)

Hall and Veccia (1990, 1992) also reported new observational studies of touch, in public places and at a professional convention (though with smaller numbers than Major et al. had), with careful attempts to note various characteristics of toucher and touched. Their findings are also too many and complex to repeat in full here, and LaFrance and I have examined them in detail elsewhere (Henley & LaFrance, 1993). Hall and Veccia (1992) summarized their findings as showing little support for touch asymmetry favoring males, although they do admit that a consistent finding "seems to be emerging in this field of study: males do seem to touch females with the hand more than vice versa" (pp. 94–95).

Self-Report.   There have been a number of self-report studies of touching. Radecki and Jennings (1980) had participants respond to a survey of dominant and sexual behaviors in work settings with regard to employees of the other sex. They found a complex pattern of responses with regard to gender differences and dominance behaviors, concluding that both sex of subject and occupational status produced significant differences in the predicted direction in two of their four scale comparisons. However, the authors also found some results in the opposite direction from that predicted, and themselves questioned whether social desirability might have affected responses, especially those of males.

In another self-report study, Willis and Rinck (1983) asked subjects to keep a personal log of touches received. They found that women were more likely to initiate personal (as opposed to impersonal) touch, but that there was no gender difference in receiving personal touch. However, they looked only at *overall* reports of receiving or giving touch and not at the interaction of subject and toucher gender; thus the touches received from women lump male (n =17) and female (n =59) recipients together and could reflect higher same-sex touching among women than men, rather than greater women's touching of men than vice versa.

A study by Jones (1986) seems to raise more difficult questions. Jones used the method of personal logs kept by trained subjects, who noted touch events in which they were involved during 3 days, and noted relevant information regarding toucher/recipient gender, setting, and subject's interpretation of the meaning of the touch. Jones summarized his findings as follows: "Henley's hypothesis that males use touch as a means of establishing dominance or reminding females of their lower status was not supported in the present study. The results suggest that females initiate more touches to males than vice versa, and that they use touch more often as a direct means of control in opposite-sex relationships." (p. 238).

How can such results be reconciled with Henley's theory and previous findings? A partial answer could have to do with the subjects and their task. The subjects were students, and only "school days"—not "home days"—and nonintimate occasions were used in the analysis. Jones noted that the students "reported touches with status equals almost exclusively" and that this may have influenced the findings. "In business organizations or other situations where formal status and sex are more often confounded," he wrote, "Henley's hypothesis might receive more support" (p. 238).

Whereas it is true that we would expect no significant differences for true status equals (and the frequent use of status-equal situations to test hypotheses of status inequality has often hampered nonverbal research; see LaFrance & Henley, in press), my hypotheses encompass gender inequality as a status variable; therefore this situation does not seem to be enough to explain the sex differences—or lack of them—found in this study. One obvious difference between this study and most other studies of touching behavior is its method: self-report diaries. Event logs are an important tool of research for various reasons (see Jones, 1986, p. 229), but they also have their limitations. Differently from externally observed behavior, they have no control for inter-rater reliability, and they conjoin observer, experiencer, recorder, and interpreter all in one. Sufficient training and adequate log sheets seemingly should eliminate the problems associated with this conjoining, but nevertheless the method seems almost like an invitation to write one's own story, especially when one may not realize one is working with a pre-written script (i.e., from gender socialization and expectations).

Gaze/Visual Behavior

As had been found previously, Frances (1979) found that females in conversational interaction (in a laboratory setting) spent more time gazing at their partners, and she found this for both gazing while listening and gazing while speaking.

Lamb (1981) studied initial eye gaze as a means of nonverbal control in same-sex dyads and triads; he found a tendency for females to avert initial gaze and males to maintain initial gaze as they spoke first. "The first few seconds seem to be a 'dominance battle' for males but not for females," (p. 52) he wrote. Lamb's conclusion that females use the various behaviors seen as control measures in similar fashion to men seems warranted and interesting. However, the association of initial eye gaze with dominance has not been clearly established, and the mixed findings regarding correlations of initial gaze with other presumed indicators of dominance (initial speaking and talking time) did little to strengthen its basis, so it is hard to determine how these findings should be interpreted.

Hall and Halberstadt (1986; see also Hall, 1984) reported from their review of the gazing literature that females, both adults and children, gazed significantly more than males, with the effect size being greater for adults than children. However, attempting to test a dominance-status hypothesis, they claim little support for it, except for age status; using weighted effect size regressions, however, did lead them to conclude that there was some support for a dominance-status hypothesis (For a more detailed presentation and critique, see Henley & LaFrance, 1993).

By far the most thorough and systematic series of studies of visual behavior with regard to power has been that of Dovidio, Ellyson, and their colleagues. These follow the paradigm of earlier studies (discussed in *Body Politics*) by Exline, Ellyson, and Long (1975), in which *visual dominance behavior* (VDB) is defined as the ratio of looking while speaking ("look–speak," or LS) to looking while listening ("look–listen," or LL); that is, VDB = LS:LL.

These investigators found that those with greater social power (Dovidio & Ellyson, 1985), expert power, or reward power (Dovidio, Brown, Heltman, Ellyson, & Keating, 1988; Dovidio, Ellyson, Keating, Heltman, & Brown, 1988), either male or female, in same-sex and mixed-sex groups, showed greater visual dominance behavior. Dominant behavior associated with expert power was further found to be mediated by "gender-based familiarity" with the topics of expertise: each sex exhibited more power in discussing topics related to its gender (Dovidio, Brown, et al., 1988).

However, when there was no discrepancy in power, males tended to show greater visual dominance than females, a finding the authors describe as "robust" (Dovidio, Ellyson, et al., 1988); and in the gender-linked expertise study (Dovidio, Brown, et al., 1988), on the non-gender-linked task men displayed greater power in various channels, including visual, than did women. These findings offer strong and consistent support for the hypothesis that men's nonverbal behavior tends to parallel the behavior associated with dominance and power, whereas women's tends to parallel the behavior of the subordinate and powerless.

Kimble and Musgrove (1988) did not find higher display of visual dominance behavior by males than by females, but this result may be due in part to the fact that they had selected subjects on the basis of an assertiveness measure to have equal numbers of females and males above and below the median assertiveness for the sample (men's mean assertiveness was nevertheless higher than women's). The selection process may have produced abnormally equalized proportions of assertive and unassertive females and males; and if this scale-measured assertiveness had an effect on VDB, it might tend to equalize overall measured VDB of the two genders. One would expect, then, a significant effect of assertiveness itself on VDB, but this was not found either. Closer examination of visual dominance patterns, however, led the authors to conclude that "assertiveness in women was related to their visual dominance behavior and, especially, to the visual dominance behavior of their dyad partners" (p. 12), findings they considered specific to mixed-sex interaction, because previous studies had found personal dominance traits to be correlated with VDB in same-sex groups.

Kennedy and Camden (1983) made an especially intriguing discovery regarding whether one looks or does not look while speaking: Using videotaped discussion sequences of mixed-sex groups, they examined matched interruption and non-interruption sequences. They found women were more likely to be interrupted when they did not look at the person who became the next speaker; and "the women in this study were much more likely to lose their speaking turn via an interruption than were the men when the women were not looking at the turn-taker" (p. 102). These findings and others supported the authors' suggestion that aspects of non-verbal behavior are involved in cross-sex interruption patterns, in which males typically dominate. Low visual dominance behavior, as measured by Dovidio, Ellyson, and their colleagues, may be one of the cues that would-be speakers utilize (presumably unconsciously) to determine the potential success of an interruption.

Facial Expression

There are two topics of research that generally come under scrutiny in the area of facial expression: One is general or emotional expressivity, which is most concentrated in the face, and the other is facial positivity, or smiling. In this review, expressivity will be considered in the section on nonverbal skill and accuracy; at this time we will examine the literature on smiling.

The evidence for greater smiling by females than males has accumulated in the years since *Body Politics* was published, to the extent that it is a quite well established and, I think, noncontroversial finding (e.g., Deutsch, 1990; Frances, 1979; Halberstadt, Hayes, & Pike, 1988; Halberstadt & Saitta 1987; Hall, 1984; Hall & Halberstadt, 1986; Kennedy & Camden, 1983; Ragan, 1982). Halberstadt and Saitta reported an interesting comparison of media portrayals of smiling with actual smiling recorded in naturalistic observation of public behavior. In media portrayals, females smiled relatively more often than males, and African Americans smiled relatively more often than Whites; but in real life, these effects of gender and race were not reliably found. Thus the media images increased the association of subordinate groups with smiling.

In addition, there is new evidence of an association of smiling with power. One piece of evidence is the finding by Kennedy and Camden (1983) that women were more likely to be interrupted when smiling (as when not looking at the interrupter, reported earlier): "Overall, women tended to display more positive expression (laughing and/or smiling) than did men. ...There is a greater chance that a woman will be interrupted if she is displaying positive affect than if a man is. Positive expression seems to serve as an invitation for men to interrupt women but inhibits women from interrupting men." (p. 101).

Another indication of the association of smiling and power is from Deutsch's (1990) experimental study, in which female and male subjects were randomly assigned to high or low interactive status roles, in same-sex or mixed-sex pairs. Deutsch found significant effects for both status and gender, but the results are a little more complicated than that: She found that higher status males smiled less than lower status ones, although females' smiling did not significantly differ in the two status conditions. Furthermore, higher status females smiled more than higher status males *to* lower status males, but the smiling to lower status females did not differ, nor did the smiling of lower status males and females. Thus both gender status and interactive status contributed to the smiling observed, and a parallelism is seen between the two.

Hall and Halberstadt (1986) claimed to find little support for a dominance-status hypothesis in their review of studies of smiling. However, as LaFrance and I noted in greater detail elsewhere (Henley & LaFrance, 1993), that meta-analytic review does not and cannot make a valid test of the hypothesis, because the studies contain few true and unconfounded status comparisons and do not separate findings by sex combination.

Posture, Gesture, and Body Movement (Kinesics)

There has been less research on dominance through posture and movement than through touch or gaze, and what there has been has often utilized photographs and examined Goffman's (1979) thesis that head and body canting are signs of deference. There have been mixed findings regarding the association of canting with gender. Ragan (1982), in a study of about 1,300 photographs from high school and university yearbooks and media files, reported finding that females canted their heads significantly more than males. However, Willson and Lloyd (1990) found in their photographs of undergraduates more head canting in males than females (at the same time, they saw more headcanting in both female and male students in the stereotypically feminine arts than in those in the stereotypically masculine sciences).

Halberstadt and Saitta (1987), in their extensive study of nonverbal behavior in media portrayals and in actual public settings, examined head and body cant. In media portrayals, although they found no significant sex differences in head canting, they did find that African Americans canted their heads significantly more than Whites in advertisements but were not seen to do so in news photos. Females canted their bodies significantly more than males, again in advertisements but not in news photos, while African Americans canted their bodies significantly more than Whites in news photos but not in advertisements. Young adults canted their bodies significantly more than older adults or children. (For a more detailed analysis of this research, see Henley & LaFrance, 1993.)

In a finding similar to that with smiling (see "Facial expression" earlier), when comparing media portrayals and observed behavior in natural settings, Halberstadt and Saitta found that African Americans were shown with head and body cant more than Whites in advertisements and photographs, but that Whites did both types of canting more than African Americans in natural settings. These finding of media portrayals creating or exaggerating deferent behaviors to reflect social status seem strong evidence of Goffman's (1979) notion that media portrayals, especially advertisements, show hyperritualized social relationships (see also Henley, 1980).

Compliance

Another indication of the use of behavior to convey power is its success in conveying it, as seen in the touched person's tendency to submit or comply. Various studies have indeed found that touch increases subjects' compliance to a request in field experiments (e.g., Kleinke, 1977; Willis & Hamm, 1980). Patterson, Powell, and Lenihan (1986) found that an experimenter's initiation of touch during a request increased compliance by subjects (in time spent and amount of task completed), and also that an alternative explanation that the effect of touch on compliance was mediated by attraction was not supported. There is also support for a dominance effect of gaze in compliance studies. Various field experiments have found that gaze increased subjects' compliance to a request (e.g., Bull & Gibson-Robinson, 1981; Kleinke, 1977; Kleinke & Singer, 1979).

PERCEPTIONS/ATTRIBUTIONS: HOW DO OBSERVERS' INTERPRETATIONS OF NON-VERBAL BEHAVIOR DIFFER ACCORDING TO THE GENDER AND/OR RELATIONSHIPS OF THE ACTORS?

Researchers typically ask observers (readers of descriptions, viewers of pictures) their interpretation of particular nonverbal behaviors. This often involves posed or selected visual portrayals, the experimenter manipulating nonverbal behavior and behaviorer's gender, and asking subjects to rate the individual actors on scales of dominance/submission, liking, and so on. (e.g., Goldberg & Katz, 1990; Summerhayes & Suchner, 1978). More rarely, it may involve live actors who exhibit particular nonverbal behaviors and then are rated by subjects who interacted with them (e.g., Storrs & Kleinke, 1990), or descriptions of nonverbal behavior rather than visual or physical portrayal (e.g., Pisano, Wall, & Foster, 1986).

Space

Schwartz, Tesser, and Powell (1982) posed people in dyads to vary by gender and four spatial dimensions: higher/lower, ahead/behind, right/left, standing/sitting (really a postural variable). All five factors were found to be significantly related to subjects' judgments of which person was more dominant: the person who was more elevated, in front, on the right, in front, or male was more likely to be judged dominant than the one who was not.

[See also Henley and Harmon,1985, described later under "General," for a similar experiment, not exclusively spatial, but that included two spatial variables in a posed study—space invasion and towering over (standing versus sitting)—and also found that spatial positioning affected judgments of dominance.]

Touch

A number of studies examining dominance perceptions of touch as affected by gender have been published since *Body Politics*. Forden (1981), for example, reported a study in which videotaped female–male interactions, identical except that one of the parties did or did not touch the other, were judged by observers. She found that "The female was seen as most 'dominant'... when she touched, the male as most 'passive' ... when he was touched" (p. 889), consistent with the hypothesis of touch as a power symbol. Interestingly, the "no touch" and "male touch" conditions did not differ significantly, lending support to the notion "that the norm is for males to touch females...It is not noticed when a man touches a woman, but when a woman touches a man, personality perceptions change" (pp. 893–894).

Again, in perceptions of touch—as in touch behavior—relating to gender and power, Major has been in the forefront in research and interpretation. In her 1981 review of "Gender patterns in touching behavior," she examined the evidence for touch interpreted as a cue to power and status, both that presented by Henley (1977) and that from later studies. She wrote of the touch perception literature:

> In summary, research on the meaning of touch provides strong support for Henley's (1973, 1977) theory that touching implies power. Across experiments the initiator of touch is seen as more powerful, dominant, and of higher status than the recipient.
>
> A striking and consistent finding of these experiments was that the act of touch overwhelmed the impact of any other power indicators, namely, gender, age, and initial status. That is, regardless of the toucher's gender, age, or status, the toucher gained in perceived power relative to a person not touching. And regardless of the recipient's gender, age, or status, his/her power diminished relative to a person not touching. (Major, 1981, p. 26)

Major and Heslin (1982) further confirmed these conclusions in a study of perceptions of same- and cross-sex nonreciprocal touch. Touchers were rated significantly higher than both recipients of touch and no-touch controls on status/dominance and instrumentality/assertiveness, and on warmth/expressiveness as well. (Henley & Harmon, 1985, also found support for touch as a power signal, in the research reported under "General," later.)

Note that Major and Heslin's finding of greater attributed warmth is not a contradiction of the thesis of a dominance factor in touch, but rather a confirmation of the dual meanings of touch. The same reasoning applies in part to the findings of Pisano, Wall, and Foster (1986). These researchers asked college students to attribute meaning to 31 types of nonreciprocal touch in cross-sex romantic relationships that were presented in a questionnaire. Subject gender and subject- versus partner-touch had only "minor effects" on attributed meaning; Pisano et al. summarized that "subjects generally interpreted the touches in this study as expressing positive meanings (most typically warmth/love) and rarely as expressing dominance or control" (p. 38).

However, as the authors noted, there are various explanations for this finding other than that touching does not express dominance in romantic relationships. The result hardly seems surprising considering that the touches that were rated were predominantly those common to romantic relationships and were presented as occurring between the subject and a partner, described as "their most-preferred opposite-sex romantic partner" (p. 31). (The fact that this was a paper-and-pencil measure that did not use any visual stimuli, as most other studies of this type have, could also account for some of the difference in the findings.) Pisano et al.'s findings, therefore, are not seen as challenging the thesis that touch conveys power.

Kinesics

There has not been extensive study of perceptions of body posture and movement. Halberstadt and Saitta's (1987) third study utilized advertising photos in which models exhibited head or body canting and asked college students to rate them for dominance and other qualities. They found that head cant had no effect on ratings, and, contrary to Goffman's (1979) theory, that body cant was perceived as more dominant than was its absence. Henley and Harmon's (1985) experiment with posed slides, described in the next section, investigated the dominance effects of the postures of pointing and standing over (standing while the other interactant sits).

General

Supportive evidence for attributions of power made for four types of nonverbal power signal—touching, invading space, standing over, and pointing—represented visually were reported by Henley and Harmon (1985; the data are not examined separately by type of signal). Henley and Harmon had two females and two males pose, in pairs, in all gender combinations, in 64 poses involving one person making zero to three dominance gestures, while the other made none. Both males and females were rated higher in dominance when making dominance gestures than when not making them (all results reported had a probability of $p \leq .01$). In addition, Henley and Harmon found an additive effect of gestures: The more of these gestures made in a pose (from 0 to 3), the higher the dominance ratings given.[5] This effect, however, interacted with gesturer sex: Males were given higher dominance ratings than females for making the same dominance gestures; and when females made dominance gestures, subjects' dominance ratings remained the same when either two or three gestures were simultaneously portrayed, that is, ratings did not continue to rise as they did for male gesturers.

Rachkowski and O'Grady (1988) showed videotaped interviews, in which a female or male client displayed either feminine or masculine sex-typed nonverbal behavior, to college students who rated the clients' characteristics, problems, and prognosis. Although there were no main effects of gender or sex-typed nonverbal behavior, they found a client gender by sex-typed nonverbal behavior interaction, primarily due to the subjects' "pervasive tendency to stigmatize the female clients displaying masculine sex-typed behaviors, in comparison to male clients displaying these same behaviors" (p. 771).

In the realm of perception/attribution, Burgoon's research seems to be an exception in not finding status or gender as significant factors influencing interpretations. Burgoon and Walther (1990) found that the attractiveness of stimuli influenced expectancies and evaluations, whereas gender and status had limited effects. Burgoon (1991) found "gender initiator attractiveness," that is, the gender of the initiator of a gesture, the gender combination of the interaction, and initiator attractiveness to be more influential than status in moderating interpretations.

Richards, Rollerson, and Phillips (1991) carried out a study of the relation between nonverbal behaviors, males' perceptions of females' submissiveness, and women's victimization. In this study, males viewed videotaped females and rated the females' dominance/submissiveness. Other evaluators analyzed the women's nonverbal behaviors. The authors concluded that dominant and submissive women display visually different behaviors, that men form differentiated perceptions of dominant and submissive women, relying largely on nonverbal cues, and that men tend to select submissive women for exploitation.

---

[5]Archer and Akert (1980) proposed the concept of Additive Theory in interpreting social interaction, but theirs is a different notion from the additive one used by Henley and Harmon (1985). Archer and Akert's Additive Theory "suggests that accuracy accumulates as a more or less linear function of available information" (p. 398). [They did not find much support for it, finding more evidence for Diffusion Theory, which states that "virtually all interaction pieces will contain meaningful information" (p. 407).] The additive notion used by Henley and Harmon was one of *perception/attribution* rather than of *accuracy*, of attributing less tangible meaning to interactions rather than determining relationships or unseen events from visible behaviors, as was the case in the Archer and Akert scenes (although I would not belabor this point; there is some point at which the notions intersect). Whereas Archer and Akert tested Additive Theory by breaking up interaction scenes into parts, Henley and Harmon added additional indicators of dominance to see how these affected the degree of dominance perceived.

Acceptability of Behavior

Another indication of perceived power is the reaction to a dominance behavior: If a behavior conveys dominance, it should be considered more acceptable when coming from someone with perceived legitimate power or status than when from someone of lower rank. Several studies of perceived acceptability of being touched by another have been carried out. Major (1981), reviewing the literature to that time on responses to touch, found support for both the power connotations and gender implications of touch. In fact, bringing in the power interpretation clarified a theretofore muddy literature, as Major and Heslin (1982) succinctly summarized regarding Major's (1981) review:

> In those studies finding positive responses in both genders, the toucher was of higher status than the recipient, thus the touch was role-appropriate and did not alter the relative status of the two participants. In contrast, in those studies that found men reacting negatively and women reacting positively to being touched, the toucher was of equal or ambiguous status relative to the recipient. (Major & Heslin, p. 150)

This conclusion seems to be confirmed by a recent experiment by Storrs and Kleinke (1990) of the influence of gender and status factors on perceptions of touch. In this interview study with status, touching, and gender varied, male subjects turned out to be less favorable toward interviewers of equal status or female gender (lower gender status) who touched them than they were toward the higher status interviewers; and female interviewers who touched were evaluated more favorably when they also had high status. Female subjects' reactions, however, were not influenced by the status and sex of the touching interviewer as males' were.

In another acceptability study carried out since Major's (1981) review, Baglan and Nelson (1982) gave descriptions of nine different asymmetric behaviors (e.g., giving another a pat on the back, stepping to one side to allow another to pass), in which status or gender were (separately) varied, and had students rate their appropriateness. They found significant differences in appropriateness attributed to most behaviors when status was varied, dominant behaviors being deemed more appropriate to higher-status persons, but little corroboration for the gender-specified dyads. In fact, in two of the three behaviors on which gender combination had a significant effect, failure to laugh at another's joke and moving out of another's way, the rated appropriateness was the opposite of what has sometimes been observed (Henley, 1977). However, this could be because the behaviors are ones that are highly culturally standardized—that is, women not laughing at jokes (either because they are "dirty" jokes or because women are considered not to have a sense of humor) and men chivalrously standing aside to let a woman pass. The overall failure to find similar results for status and gender effects could be due to the nature of the task—overtly asking for judgments of appropriateness of what were often norm violations may have called on subjects' concern not to treat females and males differently. That the task was entirely a paper-and-pencil one also differentiates it from perceptual tasks in which visual portrayals are given.

Do Dominance Gestures Affect Perceptions of Behavior or Recipient of Behavior, or Both?

Most studies examining this question have focused on touch as the nonverbal channel. Although perceptions of touch as conveying power are a well-established finding by now, there have been discrepant findings as to whether more power is attributed to the toucher or less to the touched. When Summerhayes and Suchner (1978) showed photographs of mixed-sex dyads, of equal or unequal status, touching or not touching, and asked undergraduates to rate them on four power/dominance-related scales, they found that touching reduced the perceived dominance of the person *touched* (except when the toucher was a higher status woman), but did not affect the perceived dominance of the person *touching*.

But in a similar study using dynamic rather than static presentation, Goldberg and Katz (1990) obtained completely converse results. These authors, using videotapes of dyadic interactions involving various levels of touch reciprocity, found that college students raters (using semantic differential scales) characterized the *initiator* of touch as being more powerful and dominant than the receiver, but found no difference in the ratings given the *recipient* of touch.

Major and Heslin (1982) found the third possibility to be the case. Using slides of cross-sex and same-sex nonreciprocal touch and non-touching interactions, they found both that touchers were rated higher, and that recipients of touch were rated lower, on status/dominance (and other dimensions) than nontouching control interactors. Henley and Harmon (1985) also found that their power signals, which included touch, both enhanced ratings of the gesturer's dominance and lowered ratings of the target's dominance.

All in all, the preponderance of evidence seems to indicate still (as Major also concluded in 1981) that there are significant effects on the perceived power of *both* the giver of touch and its recipient.

Reciprocity

There has been hardly any new research on thesis X, that the failure to reciprocate a dominance gesture by another indicates an acceptance of the legitimacy of the other's dominance. In behavior, this thesis may be tested by the question: Is there less reciprocation of power gestures by subordinate than by dominant individuals? In perception, thesis X may be tested by the question: does reciprocation of a dominance gesture undermine or erase the greater dominance established by the gesture? Whereas almost all the perception studies have used dyadic stimuli with nonreciprocal dominance gestures, at least one tried to look specifically at the act of reciprocation as an influence in adjusting the perception of power. Goldberg and Katz (1990) videotaped silhouettes of males interacting, exhibiting non-reciprocated touch, reciprocated touch, or no touching, and showed them to female and male subjects. Although there was no significant difference in the power/dominance ratings made of actors who were not touching, Goldberg and Katz found, as have those researchers limiting their studies to nonreciprocal touch, that in nonreciprocated touch the toucher received significantly higher scores than did the recipient of touch. What is more, they found the same for reciprocated touch; that is, reciprocation of touch had no significant effect in neutralizing the perceived asymmetry. Goldberg and Katz concluded that it was *initiation* of touch, not touch per se, that communicated power/dominance. (It would be interesting to see whether this is true for other gender combinations than the male–male one these researchers used.) Although the results of Goldberg and Katz raise a serious question about the reciprocity hypothesis, the limited focus of their research (only male interactants) does not allow a full disconfirmation. Although the supporting evidence for the reciprocity hypothesis seems weak, the information on it is not quite sufficient to make a final judgment at this time.

Attributing Sexuality to Women's Power Gestures

There is very little research testing the thesis that power gestures made by women will tend to be interpreted as sexual rather than dominant (to a greater extent than is so for men). Major and Heslin (1982) attempted to test this notion in their study of perceptions of nonreciprocated touch in dyads, hypothesizing "that pairs where a female was touching a male would be perceived as conveying more sexual desire than pairs where a male was touching a female" (p. 158). However, they did not find this, and in fact did not find touching cross-sex pairs to convey more sexual desire than nontouching pairs. However, as Major and Heslin themselves noted, "this may have been due to the modality of touch observed—a hand to the shoulder. In addition, sexual desire was not rated separately for the two actors in each slide, thus we could not compare directly ratings of a female toucher with those of a male toucher" (p. 160).

Henley and Harmon's (1985) perceptual study, while also using a hand to the shoulder for touch, and other rather nonintimate power gestures (see "General," earlier), did have dominance and sexuality ratings made for individual gesturers, both female and male. They found that females' dominance gestures received significantly higher *sexuality* ratings than did those of males. Furthermore, there was an interaction of number of gestures made and gesturer's sex, in which females' sexuality ratings increased as they made more dominance gestures, but males' sexuality ratings did not increase with added dominance gestures. (These results are for both male and female raters; sex of rater had no significant main or interactive effects in this study.) I consider the research design a reasonable test, and the findings good support, for the thesis, but I may be biased; obviously, additional research on this question would be most helpful.

SKILL/ACCURACY: HOW DO GENDER AND/OR POWER/STATUS/DOMINANCE AFFECT DECODING SKILL AND/OR ENCODING SKILL?

Since Rosenthal et al. (1979) reported a sex difference in decoding ability by viewers of their Profile of Nonverbal Sensitivity (PONS) video, various studies have looked at decoding skill, and sometimes encoding skill, as affected by gender or status, or both. Some studies have used Rosenthal et al.'s PONS test to see how this nonverbal decoding skill is affected by varying characteristics of the decoders, such as gender and relative power (e.g., Hall & Halberstadt, 1981). However, the video PONS has only a female encoder, limiting our ability to interpret whether gender differences in decoding accuracy may be due to decoder skill or a gender-of-encoder by gender-of-decoder interaction. Others, with other tests, have separated encoding/decoding skills in subjects and un-confounded the gender issue by having both females and males do both encoding and decoding (see, for example, Buck, 1984, chapters 5 and 7; Costanzo & Archer, 1989). Still others have crossed gender with another source of status, such as teacher/learner, and had subjects decode in both roles to determine whether this accuracy is attributable to a person's gender or to another source, such as role status (e.g., Snodgrass, 1985, 1992).

Judith Hall and her colleagues (Halberstadt, 1985; Hall, 1978, 1979, 1984, 1985, 1987; Hall & Halberstadt, 1981) conducted numerous review and research studies examining gender and/or power as factors in decoding accuracy. As cited in the section "Nonverbal communication and gender" earlier, Hall concluded from her reviews that there is a very consistent, moderately strong finding of female superiority in decoding ability.

Hall (1985) reviewed both encoding and decoding skills for gender differences. Regarding *encoding* ability (expressivity), she summarized results from 22 studies she had reviewed in 1979, along with 20 additional ones, and wrote: "In both [earlier and later groups of studies], females were better expressors. Both groups, however, showed pronounced interchannel differences. ... female visual cues were considerably easier to judge than male visual cues, but for vocal cues there was no difference." (p. 205).

Regarding *decoding* ability, Hall (1985) summarized results from 75 earlier studies and 45 found since 1979; she wrote: "All in all, the two groups told the same story: females were better at decoding nonverbal cues than males" (p. 201). This basic theme is repeated in Hall (1987).

The support for female superiority in both encoding and decoding abilities thus seems quite strong, and LaFrance and I have accepted its evidence in our previous writings (Henley & LaFrance, 1984; LaFrance & Henley, in press). However, it should still be noted that there are repeated findings, especially with researchers using measures other than the PONS, that do *not* find female superiority in decoding (e.g., Archer & Akert, 1977; Hodgins & Koestner, 1993; Snodgrass, 1985, 1992). In fact, Hall's own reviews (1978, 1984) do not find a predominance of significant findings of female advantage in the studies reviewed: Only 31% of the earlier-reviewed 75 studies, and 20% of the later-added 50 studies, showed significant female superiority (however, 91% of the first set, and 52% of the second set, found female advantage, significant or not).

Buck (1984, p. 267), made a similar point, citing other studies, and also called attention to the finding by Fujita, Harper, and Wiens (1980) that females were better than males in decoding posed expressions, but not spontaneous ones. These results, Buck noted, make sense when considered with Rosenthal and DePaulo's (1979a,

1979b) findings that women lose their decoding superiority for "leaked," that is, less controlled, nonverbal cues. Women's decoding advantage may be limited to posed (less leaky) rather than spontaneous interaction.

Explaining Differences in Nonverbal Accuracy/Skill

There has been considerable controversy over explanation of the group differences in nonverbal skills. My explanation regarding sensitivity in *Body Politics* (in which I dealt very little with the topic) was based on power: "Greater social sensitivity itself may well be the special gift—or burden—of subordinates, for example, women in a male-dominated society, or blacks in a white-dominated one. ... Certainly it makes sense that when an oppressive social situation makes life a struggle, one becomes finely tuned to the nuances of that struggle." (p. 14).

In 1984, with LaFrance, I expanded this explanation to include encoding skill, theorizing that:

> [Readability] The higher status person will be less readable (in the sense of less expressive) than the lower status person. The lower power person in a relationship is more likely to be the more expressive one and the one of higher power will be seen as less emotional and less expressive.[6]

> [Sensitivity] The less dominant group will be more sensitive to cues coming from others, and particularly to those cues coming from the more dominant group, than will be the case for the dominants. (Henley & LaFrance, 1984, pp. 362–363).

Hall has over the years (e.g., 1978, 1984, 1985, 1987; Hall & Halberstadt, 1981) repeatedly addressed the question of explaining the source of the sex difference in nonverbal sensitivity, suggesting, at different times, several from among the following: gender "role" socialization, women's oppressed status, genetic predisposition, greater female empathy, attention and practice, politeness norms, and cerebral laterality. She has repeatedly rejected what she has named the "oppression hypothesis," referring to my ideas.

Similarly, Halberstadt (1985) conducted a review of studies of the effects of race and/or socioeconomic status on nonverbal decoding ability and concluded that, contrary to my subordination hypothesis, "young white and middle-class individuals are better decoders than young black and lower class individuals," although this white middle-class advantage is "attenuated and possibly even reversed by adulthood" (p. 235).

Clearly, Hall's and Halberstadt's interpretation of their reviews and research conflicts with the interpretation made by LaFrance and myself of this literature. LaFrance and I have given our critiques in other places (Henley & LaFrance, 1984; LaFrance, 1986, 1987, LaFrance & Henley, in press), and to explain sufficiently

---

[6]I have not discussed in this chapter the relationships between encoding, emotion, and expressivity; some sources that look at these relationships with regard to gender include Buck (1984); Hall (1984); Henley and LaFrance (1984); and LaFrance and Henley (in press).

our response to these authors' assertions would take at least another chapter in itself, so I will not repeat them here. Suffice it to say that we believe that the research of Hall and her colleagues on nonverbal sensitivity has asked peripheral questions, used questionable measures, made inappropriate comparisons, drawn unwarranted conclusions, and reported results in a biased manner (LaFrance & Henley, in press).

With regard to method, for example, the studies examined often have confounded variables, such as race and socioeconomic status, do not provide the actual contrasts claimed to be tested, and mix ages to obtain the lack of significant finding. Just as in behavioral studies, many of the decoding studies find little difference among children, but significant difference among adults, findings easily explained by social learning. For further detail, and a close reading of the Hall studies, I refer readers to our recent critiques (Henley & LaFrance, 1993; LaFrance & Henley, in press).

DEVELOPMENTAL TRENDS

There is a striking similarity in the findings by both Major et al. (1990) and Grusky et al. (1984) of no gender asymmetries in touch when children were involved. As Major et al. pointed out, this was the finding in Henley's original (1973) study of gender patterns in touching, and helps to explain the failure of Hall's (1984; Stier & Hall, 1984) meta-analyses to find greater male touching and female receipt of touch: Half the studies they examined involved touching of children.

In fact, there is growing evidence for developmental trends in many of the behaviors investigated here (e.g., Hall & Halberstadt, 1986; Halberstadt, 1985), but the researchers do not always recognize them. Halberstadt, for example, concluded that there is a White middle-class advantage in decoding rather than the Black, lower-class one predicted by subordination theory, and that it is attenuated or reversed by adulthood (see "Explaining differences in nonverbal accuracy/skill" earlier). But, as LaFrance and Henley (in press) pointed out, the finding is fully in accord with subordination theory when one admits the possibility of maturation of skill.

In another example, Halberstadt and Saitta (1987) found that young adults canted their bodies significantly more than older adults or children, and interpreted it thus: "Finally, the age effect of greater body canting during young adulthood might support the hypothesis of less frequent body canting associated with greater power; however, one would expect the childhood group to have conformed as well." (p. 262).

This comment ignores the plausible explanation that social learning might account for the reason children show less body cant than young adults, or that, as other studies of gender difference, for example in performance, have found, females' expressions of deference and subordination tend to come to the fore in adolescence.

As different reviewers have noted with regard to Hall's (1984) nonverbal sensitivity meta-analyses (LaFrance & Henley, in press; Major et al., 1990), these findings of asymmetry patterns in adults but not in children are consistent with a social learning explanation, but not easily with one invoking biological predisposition for gender differences in nonverbal sensitivity. One might even speculate that the reluctance to consider the developmental implications of many of their findings may stem from Halberstadt's and Hall's reluctance to accept any support for a subordination hypothesis.

THEORETICAL EXPLANATIONS

"Sex" versus "Status"

Some studies have tried to determine whether sex/gender or status is the key variable in determining nonverbal behavior or response to it. We must keep in mind when such a comparison is suggested, however, that gender incorporates, or *is*, a form of status, so that the comparison is a problematic one at best. If you contend, as I do, that power/status is the underlying factor in the gender effect so often found in nonverbal studies, it comes as no surprise that the most consistent finding when researchers attempt to assign a causal locus is that both of these variables are implicated. To understand how this question has been studied and what has been found, I will review some of the more relevant research, again in the order followed above, by the three main types of study.

Behavior.   In the realm of behavior, Lamb (1981) carried out research on visual and vocal dominance in same-sex, status-undifferentiated dyads and triads, to see whether both sexes used the same dominance behaviors when in single-sex groups. He summarized the findings of his research as indicating "that females are as consistent as males in using these forms of control with members of the same sex, which suggests that power rather than sex is the important factor in these nonverbal and paraverbal modes of communication" (p. 49).

Leffler, Gillespie, and Conaty (1982), acknowledging the status nature of gender, incorporated both specific status (teacher–learner) and diffuse status (gender) as variables in a study of nonverbal behaviors associated with status. These authors found significant effects of both types of status, but stronger effects for the specific than the diffuse (gender) status.

Dovidio, Ellyson, and their colleagues, in their exemplary series of studies of visual dominance behavior (e.g., Dovidio & Ellyson, 1985; Dovidio, Brown, Heltman, Ellyson, & Keating, 1988; Dovidio, Ellyson, Keating, Heltman, & Brown, 1988), have typically found both social power/status (based on social hierarchy, expertise, or reward power) and gender to affect visual dominance behavior. Dovidio, Brown, et al. (1988) reported rather comparable estimates of the proportion of variance accounted for by greater expertise alone (.18) and higher gender status alone (.13). Brown, Dovidio and Ellyson (1990) illuminated some of the relationships between gender and status, in this case through expert power. They set up mixed-sex dyads to discuss gender-linked and non-gender-linked tasks. Without any prior training in the tasks, subjects exhibited differences in visual dominance behavior due to gender; with training, these differences in VDB were eliminated.

Deutsch (1990) found both status and gender effects on smiling in interviews, and an interaction as well such that these effects were concentrated in the situations in which males were interviewers (i.e., of higher status).

Thus in all the studies cited, both gender and other forms of status are found to affect similar power-related behaviors; to me these findings indicate that the common denominator is status, whether that due to gender or that due to another factor.

Perception.   As reported earlier, Schwartz et al. (1982) found significant effects of both gender and spatial dominance: Being male and being in a position of spatial dominance led to perceptions of dominance by subjects. Henley and Harmon (1985) too found significant main effects for both dominance gestures made (the more gestures, the higher the rating), and gender of gesturer (males being given higher ratings), as well as for an interaction between the two (males' ratings increased with dominance gestures more than females' did).

Thus in perceptions of nonverbal behavior as in the behaviors themselves, both gender and other types of status are seen to influence observers.

Accuracy.   Although Hall and Halberstadt (e.g., Halberstadt, 1985; Hall, 1978, 1984, 1985, 1987; Hall & Halberstadt, 1981) claimed a reliable gender difference in nonverbal encoding skill, they have claimed to find little support, either in their own studies or in meta-analyses of others', for dominance or status-based difference. In answering their analyses, LaFrance and I (Henley & LaFrance, 1984; LaFrance & Henley, in press) have argued that their data at times do support a subordination hypothesis, and at others have been inadequate tests of the subordination hypothesis.

Snodgrass (1985, 1992), on the other hand, has found strong main effects for experimentally assigned status (teacher/learner) on ability to interpret another's feelings, and no significant main effect for subject gender. Her dependent variable was not a standard measure of decoding skill using posed displays, but rather the agreement between one interacting subject's impression of the other and that other's self-report. In addition, Snodgrass utilized random assignment to experimental conditions (1985) and replicated her findings using reversal of conditions, so that each subject occupied both status positions (1992). Thus her research presents a strong argument for the effects of status on decoding ability.

Thus the debate of "sex" versus "status" in nonverbal skill still rages hotly; my own belief remains that status will be found to be the variable underlying gender differences.

OTHER QUESTIONS OF THEORY

Many other theoretical questions remain, of course. People may mean different things by sex or gender (just as they may by power or dominance or status), and

Hall (1978; 1984, Chapter 3) has been helpful in differentiating, for gender differences in decoding accuracy, possible nonhierarchical explanations attributable to gender, such as: sex-stereotypical masculinity and femininity (adherence to sex role self-concept); greater female empathy; greater female attention and practice focused on nonverbal decoding; greater female accommodation to politeness norms. Most of these, however, may be classified as expected products of, and therefore variations on the theme of, gender role socialization. The explanations by Hall that are exceptions to this rule are biological: female genetic predisposition to nonverbal sensitivity through adaptive evolution, and greater male cerebral hemispheric specialization which may inhibit processing of nonverbal information.

Gillespie and Leffler (1983) reviewed four implicit models used in understanding nonverbal behavior (in particular, proxemic behavior): the *ethological* paradigm, which "asserts that nonverbal behavior is at least partly innate or genetically determined, with certain general patterns inflexible within species"; the *enculturation* paradigm, which "claims that nonverbal behavior reflects contingent, somewhat arbitrary, but individually stable norms inculcated in all members of a society through socialization"; the *internal states* paradigm, which "contends that nonverbal behavior, whether innate or learned, *fluctuates* as a function of ego's individual attributes or internal psychological states"; and the *situational resource* paradigm, which "asserts that nonverbal behavior is learned but varies within cultures and across internal states, depending on the statuses of all those concerned and on the constraints of the situation" (all quotations from p. 121). The situational resource, or power, model is the closest to that which I have put forward; as Gillespie and Leffler noted, "differential access to social resources produces asymmetric patterns of nonverbal activity whereas relatively equal access produces symmetric behavior. And individuals are predicted to change behavioral patterns when their relative rankings change" (p. 122; see also Note 1, p. 142). As cited earlier, Gillespie and Leffler concluded that status is a powerful organizer of proxemic behavior. They went on to state:

> Too, it has been contended throughout [this chapter] that research based on other paradigms also supports this theory. To review this argument: ethological findings suggesting a status component to proxemic behavior are most parsimoniously explained in terms of structural relations rather than in terms of genetic etiology: the latter explanation, besides resting on invalid assumptions about proxemic invariance, is also untestable. Similarly for enculturation/socialization research: Besides a questionable definition of culture and a tendency to produce conflicting results, this research confounds culture and subculture with stratum and fails to support its crucial claim of individual proxemic invariance. In consequence, it offers as much support for the situational resource postulates of status effects and individual change as for its own culturally deterministic tenets. Finally, although the internal states model lacks empirical substantiation, this very outcome may reflect a status discrepancy between staff and subjects across treatment groups. (p. 141)

In the broader task of explaining gender differences in interaction (not just nonverbal ones), Ridgeway and Diekema (1992) rejected a "simple status" approach to explaining nonverbal gender differences for a more elaborated expectation states theory (Berger, Conner, & Fisek, 1974) explanation, which makes a better accounting of status and gender effects than, for example, Eagly's (1987) social role approach. Ridgeway and Diekema concluded that "despite recent criticisms, a status approach to gender differences in interaction continues to provide more theoretical insight into gender inequality and more predictive power over behavior than other available approaches. This is true, in any case, if we employ the sophisticated status explanation offered by expectation states theory and focus on goal-oriented interaction." (p. 175).

Although I recognize the advance offered by expectation states theory, I am still not satisfied with it for explaining nonverbal behavior; however, I do not have a more comprehensive theory to offer at this time.

CONCLUSION

In this review of research attempting to test the hypotheses I put forward in *Body Politics* and elsewhere, I have tried to show both the support for my ideas and the challenges to them, and to show why I disagree with many of the research interpretations that are offered as refuting my hypotheses. At the same time, I have included references to the sources in which readers may see these challenges more thoroughly spelled out, or may read in more detail my own rebuttal to those arguments.

My own conclusion is, of course, that my ideas have been supported and further developed by the burgeoning research of the years since that book's publication. Support, often considerable support, has been found for most of the theses examined here, through studies of behavior, perceptions, and skill, across nonverbal channels such as use of space, touch, visual behavior, facial expression, and body movement. The duality of function of nonverbal behaviors for dominance or intimacy, and their parallel use in situations involving gender and other power dimensions, have been well established. The action of symmetry/asymmetry (including the act of reciprocation) in determining whether a behavior is used for or interpreted as solidarity or status has not, however, been much supported, or much examined; often it has been somewhat taken for granted in the design of an experiment (i.e., nonreciprocal behavior has been used when power is investigated). This question bears further examination in future research. What other directions ought research to move in? The research is already such a locomotive that it barrels along, many wheels churning, to its own destinations. One can have as much hope of influencing its direction as of (to switch metaphors) controlling a tornado, however, I will say a few things.

On the one hand, I am rather appalled at the paucity in both quantity and quality of research adequately addressing issues of race/ethnicity and social class (socioeconomic status). These seem particularly ripe areas for future research, but potential researchers should first learn about these variables in order to research them correctly, and take as much care with the research designs as they would for other variables. (At the same time, the quality of research on the variables of gender and dominance has not always been great, either.)

LaFrance and Henley (in press) suggested the following guidelines for tests of the subordination hypothesis with respect to decoding ability; although they seem obvious enough, it is amazing how rarely they have been followed:

1. An adequate measure of decoding skill should be used.
2. An appropriate operationalization of power/dominance/status should be made.
3. The design should incorporate appropriate contrasts; the test of the subordination hypothesis is whether the subordinate group is better at reading the superordinate group than vice versa, hence cross-group pairings and comparisons should be used (within-group pairings may be used for corollary hypotheses or controls).
4. Competing alternative explanations should be built into the design for explicit testing, rather than trundled in post hoc.
5. Ideally, experimental design with random assignment and repeated measures, subjects serving as their own controls, should be used when possible.

Similar guidelines apply, of course, for research on behavior or perceptions rather than sensitivity. When solid experimental procedure with appropriate tests has been followed, as, for example, in the research of Leffler et al. (1982), or Snodgrass (1985, 1992), results have supported and expanded the subordination analysis.

On the other hand, I am especially excited by the broader implications offered by some of the research, getting beyond testing simple hypotheses—for example, Kennedy and Camden's (1983) findings in which gender differences in nonverbal behavior are related to the probability that women will be interrupted; or the conclusion of Richards, Rollerson, and Phillips (1991) that men form differentiated perceptions of dominant and submissive women based on their nonverbal behavior and appearance, and tend to select submissive females for exploitation.

In this spirit, I offer my own suggestion for interesting and practical research, based on Warshaw's (1988) finding that women frequently report that they had heard, but had not acted on, a little warning voice about a man who subsequently raped them, Malamuth's (1989a, 1989b) identification of some men as more prone to rape than others, and Ambady and Rosenthal's (1992) demonstration that people can make fairly accurate judgments of others based on quite brief observations of behavior. Does the small warning voice that women hear emanate from their nonverbal impressions of potentially violent men, or is it the classic chance occurrence, sharpened in retrospective memory because of the subsequent event?

A laboratory experiment could pair women and men for a typical social psychological experiment interaction, and afterwards, while testing the man for his attraction to sexual aggression (ASA), ask the woman to evaluate him on, among other things, his potential for such aggression or whether they heard that warning voice. A better design might select subjects in advance, males for high and low

ASA and females for high and low decoding ability (probably with another measure than the PONS, which measures one's ability to read a woman's rather than a man's nonverbal cues). If women turn out to be able to identify sexually aggressive men (as risky situations have been identified), research might turn to whether any specific nonverbal behaviors are associated with high ASA.[7] Although laboratory research cannot provide a definitive answer to the question, it could be a first step toward greater awareness of the factors involved in sexual assault.

Whatever direction research moves in, it is extremely gratifying that it does move. The debates by different investigators (especially Hall and myself) about the meaning of their studies may seem tediously like the proverbial argument over whether the glass is half full or half empty. But to have wide recognition of the status as well as the solidarity aspects of nonverbal behavior, and such ferment over explanations of gender differences, where before there was little of either (recognition or ferment), seems to me to be a marvelous advance in the 20 years since I began to study nonverbal communication and power.

ACKNOWLEDGMENT

I wish to thank Diana Brief for her assistance with literature search; the UCLA Academic Senate Research Committee and Center for the Study of Women for financial support; and Cheris Kramarae and Marianne LaFrance, whom I did not consult directly in writing this paper (and who thus may not be blamed for it), but whose generously shared resources and ideas I have called upon.

REFERENCES

Ambady, N., & Rosenthal, R. (1992). Thin slices of expressive behavior as predictors of interpersonal consequences: A meta-analysis. *Psychological Bulletin, 111*, 256–274.

Archer, D., & Akert, R. M. (1977). Words and everything else: Verbal and nonverbal cues in social interpretation. *Journal of Personality and Social Psychology, 6*, 443–449.

Baglan, T., & Nelson, D. J. (1982, Spring). A comparison of the effects of sex and status on the perceived appropriateness of nonverbal behaviors. *Women's Studies in Communication, 5*, 29–38.

Berger, J., Conner, T., & Fisek, M. H. (1974). *Expectation states theory: A theoretical research program.* Cambridge, MA: Winthrop.

Borden, R. J., & Homleid, G. M. (1978). Handedness and lateral positioning in heterosexual couples: Are men still strong-arming women? *Sex Roles, 4*, 67–73.

Brown, C. E., Dovidio, J. F., & Ellyson, S. L. (1990). Reducing sex differences in visual displays of dominance: Knowledge is power. *Personality and Social Psychology Bulletin, 16*, 358–368.

Brown, R. (1965). *Social psychology.* New York: Free Press.

Buck, R. (1984). *The communication of emotion.* New York: Guilford.

Bull, R., & Gibson-Robinson, E. (1981). The influences of eye-gaze, style of dress, and locality on the amount of money donated to a charity. *Human Relations, 34*, 895–905.

---

[7]This proposal does not mean to suggest that male sexual aggression is an individual personality problem rather than a social problem, but it does accept that there is individual variation in men's sexual aggressiveness.

Burgoon, J. K. (1991). Relational message interpretations of touch, conversational distance, and posture. *Journal of Nonverbal Behavior, 15*, 233–259.

Burgoon, J. K., & Walther, J. B. (1990). Nonverbal expectancies and the evaluative consequences of violations. *Human Communication Research, 17*, 232–265.

Costanzo, M., & Archer, D. (1989). Interpreting the expressive behavior of others: The interpersonal perception task. *Journal of Nonverbal Behavior, 13*, 225–245.

Deutsch, F. M. (1990). Status, sex, and smiling: The effect of role on smiling in men and women. *Personality and Social Psychology Bulletin, 16*, 531–540.

Dovidio, J. F., Brown, C. E., Heltman, K., Ellyson, S. L., & Keating, C. F. (1988). Power displays between women and men in discussion of gender–linked tasks: A multichannel study. *Journal of Personality and Social Psychology, 55*, 580–587.

Dovidio, J. F., & Ellyson, S. L. (1985). Patterns of visual dominance behavior in humans. In S. L. Ellyson & J. F. Dovidio (Eds.), *Power, dominance, and nonverbal behavior* (pp. 129–149). New York: Springer-Verlag.

Dovidio, J. F., Ellyson, S. L., Keating, C. F., Heltman, K., & Brown, C. E. (1988). The relationship of social power to visual displays of dominance between men and women. *Journal of Personality and Social Psychology, 54*, 233–242.

Eagly, A. H. (1987). *Sex differences in social behavior: A social-role interpretation.* Hillsdale, NJ: Lawrence Erlbaum Associates.

Edinger, J. A., & Patterson, M. L. (1983). Nonverbal involvement and social control. *Psychological Bulletin, 93*, 30–56.

Ellyson, S. L., & Dovidio, J. F. (Eds.). (1985). *Power, dominance, and nonverbal behavior.* New York: Springer-Verlag.

Exline, R. V., Ellyson, S. L., & Long, B. (1975). Visual behavior as an aspect of power role relationships. In P. Pliner, L. Krames, & T. Alloway (Eds.), *Nonverbal communication of aggression* (pp. 21–52). New York: Plenum.

Forden, C. (1981). The influence of sex-role expectations on the perception of touch. *Sex Roles, 7*, 889–894.

Frances, S. J. (1979). Sex differences in nonverbal behavior. *Sex Roles, 5*, 519–535.

Fujita, B. N., Harper, R. G., & Wiens, A. N. (1980). Encoding-decoding of nonverbal emotional messages: Sex differences in spontaneous and enacted expressions. *Journal of Nonverbal Behavior, 4*, 131–145.

Gillespie, D. L., & Leffler, A. (1983). Theories of nonverbal behavior: A critical review of proxemics research. In R. Collins (Ed.), *Sociological theory* (pp. 120–154). San Francisco: Jossey-Bass.

Goffman, E. (1967). *Interaction ritual.* Garden City, NY: Doubleday.

Goffman, E. (1979). *Gender advertisements.* New York: Harper & Row.

Goldberg, M. A., & Katz, B. (1990). The effect of nonreciprocated and reciprocated touch on power/dominance perception. *Journal of Social Behavior and Personality, 5*, 379–386.

Graddol, D., & Swann, J. (1989). *Gender voices.* Oxford: Basil Blackwell.

Grusky, O., Bonacich, P., & Peyrot, M. (1984). Physical contact in the family. *Journal of Marriage and the Family, 46*, 715–723.

Hai, D. M., Khairullah, Z. Y., & Coulmas, N. (1982). Sex and the single armrest: Use of personal space during air travel. *Psychological Reports, 51*, 743–749.

Halberstadt, A. G. (1985). Race, socioeconomic status, and nonverbal behavior. In A. Siegman and S. Feldstein (Eds.), *Nonverbal behavior in interpersonal relations* (pp. 227–266). Hillsdale, NJ: Lawrence Erlbaum Associates.

Halberstadt, A. G., Hayes, C. W., & Pike, K. M. (1988). Gender and gender role differences in smiling and communication consistency. *Sex Roles, 19*, 589–604.

Halberstadt, A. G., & Saitta, M. B. (1987). Gender, nonverbal behavior, and perceived dominance: A test of the theory. *Journal of Personality and Social Psychology, 53*, 257–272.

Hall, J. A. (1978). Gender effects in decoding nonverbal cues. *Psychological Bulletin, 85*, 845–857.

Hall, J.A. (1979). Gender, gender roles and nonverbal communication skills. In R. Rosenthal (Ed.), *Skill in nonverbal communication* (pp. 32–67). Cambridge, MA: Oelgeschlager, Gunn and Hain.

Hall, J. A. (1984). *Nonverbal sex differences: Communication accuracy and expressive style.* Baltimore, MD: Johns Hopkins University Press.

Hall, J. A. (1985). Male and female nonverbal behavior. In A. Siegman & S. Feldstein (Eds.), *Nonverbal behavior in interpersonal relations* (pp. 195–225). Hillsdale, NJ: Lawrence Erlbaum Associates.

Hall, J. A. (1987). On explaining gender differences: The case of nonverbal communication. In P. Shaver & C. Hendrick (Eds.), *Sex and gender* (pp. 177–200). Newbury Park, CA: Sage.

Hall, J. A., & Halberstadt, A. G. (1981). Sex roles and nonverbal communication skills. *Sex Roles, 7,* 273–287.

Hall, J. A., & Halberstadt, A. G. (1986). Smiling and gazing. In J. S. Hyde & M. C. Linn (Eds.), *The Psychology of gender: Advances through meta-analysis* (pp. 136–158). Baltimore, MD: Johns Hopkins University Press.

Hall, J. A., & Veccia, E. M. (1990). More "touching" observations: New insights on men, women, and interpersonal touch. *Journal of Personality and Social Psychology, 59,* 1155–1162.

Hall, J. A., & Veccia, E. M. (1992). Touch asymmetry between the sexes. In C. L. Ridgeway (Ed.), *Gender, interaction, and inequality* (pp. 81–96). New York: Springer-Verlag.

Henley, N. M. (1973). Status and sex: Some touching observations. *Bulletin of the Psychonomic Society, 2,* 91–93.

Henley, N. M. (1977). *Body politics: Power, sex and nonverbal communication.* New York: Prentice-Hall.

Henley, N. M. (1980). Gender hype [review of E. Goffman, *Gender advertisements*]. *Women's Studies International Quarterly, 3,* 305–312.

Henley, N. M., & Harmon, S. (1985). The nonverbal semantics of power and gender: A perceptual study. In S. L. Ellyson & J. F. Dovidio (Eds.), *Power, dominance, and nonverbal behavior* (pp. 151–164). New York: Springer-Verlag.

Henley, N. M., & LaFrance, M. (1984). Gender as culture: Difference and dominance in nonverbal behavior. In A. Wolfgang (Ed.), *Nonverbal behavior: Perspectives, applications, intercultural insights* (pp. 351–371). Lewiston, NY: C. J. Hogrefe.

Henley, N. M., & LaFrance, M. (1993). *Sex difference in nonverbal behavior: Putting power back into the analyses.* Unpublished manuscript.

Hodgins, H. S., & Koestner, R. (1993). The origins of nonverbal sensitivity. *Personality and Social Psychology Bulletin, 19,* 466–473.

Hyde, J. S. (1990). Meta-analysis and the psychology of gender differences. *Signs: Journal of Women in Culture and Society, 16,* 55–75.

Jones, S. E. (1986). Sex differences in touch communication. *Western Journal of Speech Communication, 50,* 227–241.

Kennedy, C. W., & Camden, C. (1983). Interruptions and nonverbal gender differences. *Journal of Nonverbal Behavior, 8,* 91–108.

Kimble, C. E., & Musgrove, J. I. (1988). Dominance in arguing mixed-sex dyads: Visual dominance patterns, talking time, and speech loudness. *Journal of Research in Personality, 22,* 1–16.

Kleinke, C. L. (1977). Compliance to requests made by gazing and touching experimenters in field settings. *Journal of Experimental Social Psychology, 13,* 218–223.

Kleinke, C. L., & Singer, D. A. (1979). Influence of gaze on compliance with demanding and conciliatory requests in a field setting. *Personality and Social Psychology Bulletin, 5,* 386–390.

LaFrance, M. (1986). Reading between the lines [Review of Hall, *Nonverbal sex differences*]. *Contemporary Psychology, 31,* 793–794.

LaFrance, M. (1987). On taking the oppression hypothesis seriously. *Contemporary Psychology, 32,* 760–761.

LaFrance, M., & Henley, N. M. (in press). On oppressing hypotheses: Or differences in nonverbal sensitivity revisited. In L. Radtke & H. Stam (Eds.), *Power and gender* (pp. 287–311). London: Sage.

Lamb, T. A. (1981). Nonverbal and paraverbal control in dyads and triads: Sex or power differences? *Social Psychology Quarterly, 44,* 49–53.

Leffler, A., Gillespie, D. L., & Conaty, J. C. (1982). The effects of status differentiation on nonverbal behavior. *Social Psychology Quarterly, 45,* 153–161.

Major, B. (1981). Gender patterns in touching behavior. In C. Mayo & N. M. Henley (Eds.), *Gender and nonverbal behavior* (pp. 15–37). New York: Springer-Verlag.

Major, B., & Heslin, R. (1982). Perceptions of cross-sex and same-sex nonreciprocal touch: It is better to give than to receive. *Journal of Nonverbal Behavior, 6,* 148–162.

Major, B., Schmidlin, A. M., & Williams, L. (1990). Gender patterns in social touch: The impact of setting and age. *Journal of Personality and Social Psychology, 58,* 634–643.

Malamuth, N. M. (1989a). The Attraction to Sexual Aggression Scale: I. *Journal of Sex Research, 26,* 26–49.

Malamuth, N. M. (1989b). The Attraction to Sexual Aggression Scale: II. *Journal of Sex Research, 26,* 324–354.

Moore, H. A., & Porter, N. K. (1988). Leadership and nonverbal behaviors of hispanic females across school equity environments. *Psychology of Women Quarterly, 12,* 147–163.

Patterson, M. L., Powell, J. L., & Lenihan, M. G. (1986). Touch, compliance, and interpersonal affect. *Journal of Nonverbal Behavior, 10,* 41–50.

Penelope, J. (1990). *Speaking freely: Unlearning the lies of the fathers' tongues.* Elmsford, NY: Pergamon.

Pisano, M. D., Wall, S. M., & Foster, A. (1986). Perceptions of nonreciprocal touch in romantic relationships. *Journal of Nonverbal Behavior, 10,* 29–40.

Rachkowski, R., & O'Grady, K. E. (1988). Client gender and sex-typed nonverbal behavior: Impact on impression formation. *Sex Roles, 19,* 771–783.

Radecki, C., & Jennings, J. (1980). Sex as a status variable in work settings: Female and male reports of dominance behavior. *Journal of Applied Social Psychology, 10,* 71–85.

Ragan, J. M. (1982). Gender displays in portrait photographs. *Sex Roles, 8,* 33–43.

Richards, L., Rollerson, B., & Phillips, J. (1991). Perceptions of submissiveness: Implications for victimization. *Journal of Psychology, 125,* 407–411.

Ridgeway, C. L. (1987). Nonverbal behavior, dominance, and the basis of status in task groups. *American Sociological Review, 52,* 683–694.

Ridgeway, C. L., & Diekema, D. (1992). Are gender differences status differences? In C. L. Ridgeway (Ed.), *Gender, interaction, and inequality* (pp. 157–180). New York: Springer-Verlag.

Rosenthal, R. (Ed.). (1979). *Skill in nonverbal communication: Individual differences.* Cambridge, MA: Oelgeschlager, Gunn & Hain.

Rosenthal, R., & DePaulo, B. (1979a). Sex differences in accommodation in nonverbal communication. In R. Rosenthal (Ed.), *Skill in nonverbal communication* (pp. 68–103). Cambridge, MA: Oelgeschlager, Gunn and Hain.

Rosenthal, R., & DePaulo, B. (1979b). Sex differences in eavesdropping on nonverbal cues. *Journal of Personality and Social Psychology, 37,* 273–285.

Rosenthal, R., Hall, J. A., DiMatteo, M. R., Rogers, P. L., & Archer, D. (1979). *Sensitivity to nonverbal communication: the PONS test.* Baltimore: The Johns Hopkins University Press.

Schwartz, B., Tesser, A., & Powell, E. (1982). Dominance cues in nonverbal behavior. *Social Psychology Quarterly, 45,* 114–120.

Snodgrass, S. E. (1985). Women's intuition: The effect of subordinate role on interpersonal sensitivity. *Journal of Personality and Social Psychology, 49,* 146–155.

Snodgrass, S. E. (1992). Further effects of role versus gender on interpersonal sensitivity. *Journal of Personality and Social Psychology, 62,* 154–158.

Stier, D. S., & Hall, J. A. (1984). Gender differences in touch: An empirical and theoretical review. *Journal of Personality and Social Psychology, 47,* 440–459.

Storrs, D., & Kleinke, C. L. (1990). Evaluation of high and equal status male and female touchers. *Journal of Nonverbal Behavior, 14,* 87–95.

Street, R. L., & Buller, D.B. (1987). Nonverbal response patterns in physician–patient interactions: A functional analysis. *Journal of Nonverbal Behavior, 11,* 234–253.

Summerhayes, D. L., & Suchner, R. W. (1978). Power implications of touch in male–female relationships. *Sex Roles, 4,* 103–110.

Warshaw, R. (1988). *I never called it rape.* New York: Harper & Row.

Willis, F. N., & Briggs, L. F. (1992). Relationship and touch in public settings. *Journal of Nonverbal Behavior, 16,* 55–63.

Willis, F. N., & Hamm, H. K. (1980). The use of interpersonal touch in securing compliance. *Journal of Nonverbal Behavior, 5,* 49–55.

Willis, F. N., & Rinck, C. M. (1983). A personal log method for investigating interpersonal touch. *Journal of Psychology, 113,* 119–122.

Wilson, A., & Lloyd, B. (1990). Gender vs. power: Self-posed behavior revisited. *Sex Roles, 23,* 91–98.

Chapter 3

Gender, Immediacy, and Nonverbal Communication

Judee K. Burgoon
University of Arizona

Leesa Dillman
University of Nevada at Las Vegas

Power, dominance, and equality are, at heart, relational issues: They define the nature of interpersonal relationships. Much of that definitional process is accomplished nonverbally. Nonverbal relational messages signal how participants regard each other, their relationship, and themselves in the relationship. Central to that definitional process is determining *who* wields power within a relationship and *how* that power is manifested through nonverbal messages. Often examined under the rubric of dominance and status displays, nonverbal research has begun to tackle the task of profiling what cues express or are construed as power, dominance, and status or powerlessness, submissiveness, and subservience. Our interest here is in assessing the extent to which women and men differ in their nonverbal expressions of power and dominance, particularly through the use of immediacy behaviors.

Immediacy cues are behaviors such as conversational distance, lean, body orientation, gaze, and touch that engage the senses, signal approach or avoidance, and create psychological distance or closeness between interactants (Mehrabian, 1981). Apart from deserving particular attention because they are ever-present signals in face-to-face interaction, immediacy cues warrant close scrutiny because they are simultaneously oft-cited gender-linked behaviors and leading candidates for conveying messages of dominance and power (see, e.g., Henley, chapter 2, this volume; Mazur, 1985; Ridgeway, 1987; Burgoon, Buller, & Woodall, 1989).

Although these cues have often been studied in isolation, in reality relational messages are sent via *packages* of cues and must be understood within the context of other co-present nonverbal and verbal behaviors. We are more certain that a particular message such as dominance or submission was sent when multiple cues conveying a similar or redundant message are present. Moreover, the fact that nonverbal cues occur as behavioral complexes means that concurrent behaviors may bolster, complement, or neutralize the dominance and power message of any given behavior. Thus it becomes important to examine the meanings associated with various *combinations* of immediacy cues as well as to determine what surplus meanings are conveyed by immediacy behaviors beyond possible dominance interpretations.

Equally important is assessing whether meanings are constant across senders or vary according to gender and other power-related sender characteristics such as status and attractiveness. Ample evidence documents that men and women differ on many of their nonverbal displays (see, e.g., Eagly, 1987; Gallaher, 1992; Hall, 1984; Hall & Halberstadt, 1986; Jones, 1986; Mayo & Henley, 1981; Mulac, Studley, Wiemann, & Bradac, 1987; Stewart, Cooper, & Friedley, 1986; Stier & Hall, 1984; Willis & Briggs, 1992). When sex-linked differences take behavioral form, they become labeled feminine and masculine displays.

The question is whether these basic feminine and masculine display patterns reflect differences in power. Almost two decades ago, Henley (1977) forwarded the theory that men's nonverbal behavior is characterized by dominance and women's behavior, by submissiveness. Among the behavioral differences offered in support of this theory have been that men display more visual dominance than women, whereas women maintain a high degree of attentive gaze toward others; women display more appeasement or submission gestures such as smiling and the head tilt; women claim less space, are touched more, and tolerate more spatial intrusions than men; women use more rising intonations and questioning vocal patterns rather than authoritative ones; women are silent (or silenced), talk less, and are interrupted more than men, giving them less access to the conversational floor (e.g., Dovidio & Ellyson, 1985; Ellyson & Dovidio, 1985; Henley, 1977; Jaworski, 1993; Keating, 1985).

However, recent studies and meta-analyses have not only challenged some of these findings but also questioned whether the observed male–female differences should be attributed to males expressing dominance, power, and oppression and females expressing deference, submissiveness, and powerlessness (see, e.g., Halberstadt & Saitta, 1987; Hall & Halberstadt, 1986; Marche & Peterson, 1993; Staley & Cohen, 1988; Stier & Hall, 1984). One alternative interpretation consistent with Bem's (1981) gender schema theory and Eagly's (1987) gender role theory, is that many gender differences are attributable to women and men conforming to culturally defined gender role expectations, which include women being more affiliative, communal, supportive, and nonaggressive. Thus, at this stage it may be more fruitful to ask whether women's *dominance displays* are different than men's and whether nonverbal behaviors exhibited by women have the same dominance meanings as when exhibited by men.

Given the focus of this book on gender and power issues, the current chapter offers some modest and partial answers to these significant questions by examining nonverbal immediacy cues used to communicate dominance. It presents an investigation identifying (a) which nonverbal cues convey dominance, (b) what other relational messages simultaneously communicated by these behaviors might alter the ultimate dominance message, (c) the extent to which meanings assigned to these nonverbal behaviors differ for men and women, and (d) the extent to which sender status, sender attractiveness, and gender composition of the dyad modify interpretations.

DEFINITIONS

Before proceeding, some definitions are in order to identify the relationship of dominance to power. While dominance and power both are means to an end and imply influence, dominance is typically characterized as relationally based or interactionally based, whereas power is characterized as an individual quality that is resource-based. *Dominance* has been variously defined as a universal feature of social organization that is reflected in one's rank or position in a social hierarchy (Sebeok, 1972), as one's preferential access to valued resources (Liska, 1988), or as "behavior directed toward the control of another through implied or actual threat" (Ridgeway, 1987, p. 685). Regardless of the definition chosen, dominance can only be declared in relation to the response of another. For example, Omark (1980) described a dominance relation as one in which an aggressive act is necessarily followed by a submissive behavior. At its most extreme, dominance may take the form of fight and submission, the form of flight. Within these extremes, dominance is typically thought of as eliciting deferent or compliant responses from others.

Whereas some regard dominance as an individual trait (e.g., Weisfeld & Linkey, 1985), others see it as a socially acquired skill (e.g., Mitchell & Maple, 1985). Liska (1988) distinguished between vested dominance—that which originates from birth order, kinship, physical power, or some institutionally legitimated social status—and social dominance—that which is earned through strategic behavior, social skills, empathic abilities, creation of friendship networks, and the like. Our interest here is in this latter kind of dominance and the kinds of nonverbal displays that enable such dominance.

Because *power* is broadly defined as the ability to exercise influence by possessing one or more power bases (see French & Raven, 1959), dominance is but one means of many for expressing power. Even though power is not necessarily exhibited as dominance, it is generally the case that persons who are dominant also possess power. Harper (1985) noted that power and dominance are often highly correlated. Therefore, for our purposes interpretations of dominance will be considered as contributing to (but not necessarily synonymous with) power.

Relational Meanings Associated with Nonverbal Immediacy
Behaviors

Nonverbal cues are used to signal a number of different relational themes (Burgoon & Hale, 1984, 1987). Among these, the themes of dominance and intimacy are probably the most central in defining the nature of an interpersonal relationship. But intimacy itself is comprised of a number of subthemes, including affection, immediacy, depth, trust, receptivity, and similarity. Additional relational message themes include composure, arousal, formality, and task or social orientation. Because of the multiplicity of meanings associated with any one nonverbal cue, the same behaviors that signal dominance may also be responsible for signalling some of these other messages. These simultaneous multiple messages may attenuate or alter interpretations of dominance. For this reason, we need to consider the other concomitant relational interpretations beyond dominance ones.

A program of research by Burgoon and colleagues (Burgoon, 1991; Burgoon, Buller, Hale, & deTurck, 1984; Burgoon, Coker, & Coker, 1986; Burgoon & Hale, 1988; Burgoon & Koper, 1984; Burgoon, Manusov, Mineo, & Hale, 1985; Burgoon & Newton, 1991; Burgoon, Newton, Walther, & Baesler, 1989; Burgoon, Pfau, Birk, & Manusov, 1987; Burgoon, Walther, & Baesler, 1992; Le Poire & Burgoon, 1991), coupled with work by other nonverbal scholars (e.g., Harper, 1985; Henley, 1977; Mehrabian, 1967, 1981; Steckler & Rosenthal, 1985) has begun to catalog those nonverbal behaviors that are consistently associated with certain relational meanings. A thorough review of this literature can be found in Burgoon, Buller, and Woodall (1989) and Le Poire and Burgoon (1991), but here we present a brief description of the messages associated with varying levels of the three immediacy behaviors studied in the present investigation: touch, eye contact, and proximity.

Messages Associated with Eye Contact. In general, more eye contact has been found not only to express more dominance, persuasiveness, aggressiveness, and credibility than little or no eye contact but also to communicate affiliation, attraction, caring, and immediacy (Burgoon et al., 1984; Burgoon et al., 1986; Exline, 1972; Le Poire & Burgoon, 1991). Exline, Ellyson, and Long (1975) found that dominant people tend to look equally while speaking and listening, but submissive people tend to look more while listening than while speaking—a pattern they dubbed the visual dominance ratio. Further, Exline et al. (1975) and Rosa and Mazur (1979) reported that more dominant individuals engage in longer, unwavering stares while submissive individuals are likely to avert gaze or to break eye contact first.

Due to stereotypes associated with sex one may be tempted to infer that women display submissive visual behavior and men display dominant visual behavior, but the research is unclear or mixed about this conclusion. Dovidio and Ellyson (1982, 1985) found that the visual dominance pattern held for both males and females on a number of outcome meanings such as expert power and high status, Burgoon et al. (1984) found negligible gender differences in dominance interpretations associated with the amount of gaze, and Ridgeway and Diekema (1989) found that men and women confederates were seen as equally dominant despite the males actually enacting more "dominance" behaviors. In contrast, Burgoon et al. (1986) found that gaze interpretations were significantly influenced by confederate gender: With positively regarded confederates, a pattern of 90% gaze connoted dominance if displayed by a male but submissiveness if displayed by a female. Yet for negatively regarded females, high gaze was a fairly dominant cue. And normal to low amounts of gaze were consistently viewed as submissive when displayed by women but not necessarily so when displayed by men. Thus, the same behavior was capable of being interpreted differently not only for men and women but also for women of differing regard.

Messages Associated with Proximity. Dominant individuals command and are afforded more personal space than submissive or low status individuals (Altman & Vinsel, 1977; Burgoon, 1978), and Burgoon et al. (1984) found that among five immediacy cues, proximity was the biggest predictor of dominance interpretations. Because dominant people are allowed to violate conversational distance norms, both close and far distances are associated with more dominance than are intermediate distances (Burgoon, 1991; Burgoon et al., 1984; Burgoon & Hale, 1988).

However, gender may alter interpretations. Burgoon et al. (1984) found that confederate gender interacted with distance, gaze, and body lean in producing dominance judgments and Burgoon (1991) found that photographed males were seen as more dominant at close than at norm or far distances; for females, there were no differences across distances. Thus we might expect some gender differences associated with proxemic relational messages.

Messages Associated with Touch. Early work on touch interpretations and evaluations showed that touch was routinely designated a dominance or status cue and receipt of touch, a submission cue (Henley, 1977; Major, 1981). Burgoon's (1991) experiment using photographed touchers confirmed that the presence of touch is more dominant than its absence but also that type of touch made a difference, with such forms as handholding and handshaking being interpreted far less dominant. By contrast, observers failed to attribute greater dominance to touchers seen in videotaped vignettes in the Burgoon et al. (1984) experiment, and participants who received touches failed to ascribe greater dominance to their partners in the Burgoon et al. (1992) experiment. This suggests that touch is not inevitably equated with dominance.

Moreover, although gender can influence interpretations, it has not proven to do so uniformly. Several experiments (Burgoon, 1991; Burgoon et al., 1984; Burgoon et al., 1992) failed to find any gender moderator effects for touch dominance interpretations, even though gender affected other interpretations and other outcomes measures. However, Henley and Harmon (1985), who included touch as one component of their composite dominance displays, did find that the presence of more touch, pointing, and spatial invasion connoted more dominance for males but not for females; instead, these same cues were seen as conveying greater sexuality by women. Here again, then, the same displays had different meanings when presented by men versus women. Henley and Harmon concluded, "The attribution of dominance more readily to males than to females making the same gesture supports the oft-stated belief that dominance gestures do not work for females in the same way that they work for males" (p. 162).

Gender as a Moderator of Relational Meanings

The brief synopsis of findings related to gaze, proximity, and touch parallels other research producing mixed or weak findings regarding gender differences in the communication of power and dominance. For example, despite the aforementioned studies finding that gaze and proximity, when studied separately, were differentially interpreted when enacted by males versus females, Coker and Burgoon (1987) found that in combination, more direct gaze and closer proximity signalled high involvement regardless of the actor's gender. Canary and Hause's (1993) review of 15 meta-analyses likewise yielded a lack of evidence for gender differences. Effects due to gender alone generally accounted for only about 1% of the variance in any analysis and gender largely interacted with other factors such as the observational setting (laboratory vs. naturalistic), sex of the researcher, recency of the research, and relationship of the interactants (friend vs. stranger). They concluded that gender differences seem to be over-exaggerated in the research—especially recently.

The Social Meaning Model of nonverbal behaviors (Burgoon et al., 1984; Burgoon et al., 1985; Burgoon & Newton, 1991) can explain many of the preceding results. This model suggests that certain nonverbal behaviors carry consistent socially recognizable meanings and they are used with regularity among members of a social community. In other words, gender of the actor should make little difference in interpretations of certain cues. The Social Meaning Model does not presume that behaviors carry a single, invariant meaning. As noted previously, a behavior may have multiple or simultaneous meanings, but meaning can be determined by examining the "package" of behaviors that occur in concert. This model does suggest that while gender and other factors may moderate interpretations somewhat, "main effects" for the behavior's meaning will still emerge. Thus, the following main effect hypotheses, which replicate previous relational message studies, were forwarded in this investigation:

H1: The immediacy behaviors of (a) close and far conversational distance, (b) gaze, and (c) touch connote more dominance than normal distance, gaze aversion, and the absence of touch.

H2: The immediacy behaviors of (a) close conversational distance, (b) gaze, and (c) touch also connote immediacy, receptivity, affection, depth, trust, informality, and composure than do normal and far distances, gaze aversion, and absence of touch.

An alternative to the Social Meaning Model, Expectancy Violations Theory, posits that communicator and context characteristics can play a large role in determining meanings assigned to particular behaviors (Burgoon, 1978, 1993). Beginning with the assumption that people have expectations about appropriate behaviors for particular situations, Burgoon and her colleagues have demonstrated that a strict code of adhering to the social norm does not necessarily lead to the most beneficial outcomes. The meaning assigned to behaviors depends on a person's *reward valence* (i.e., how rewarding it is to be with and interact with an individual) and the *direction and magnitude of behavioral change*. A number of studies (see Burgoon & Hale, 1988; Burgoon, 1993, for summaries) have supported the notion that individuals who are positively regarded due to such characteristics as their attractiveness, status, knowledge, or skill will fare better in the eyes of others if they violate in either a positive or negative direction the normative behavioral expectancies. According to the theory, this should hold true up to a point where interaction becomes highly uncomfortable or threatening. For example, a move to decrease the distance between two individuals may become so close that one feels physically intimidated; evaluations assigned to the violator then become negative. On the other hand, those who have a low or negative reward valence will be evaluated most positively if they adhere to normative behavioral expectancies than if they attempt to violate the norm in either direction.

This theory makes explicit the notion that certain characteristics of the communicators themselves (including their gender) will play a role in how those communicators are evaluated. The earlier cited Burgoon et al. (1986) and Henley and Harmon (1985) experiments support this view in showing that the same behavior performed by a male or female will receive differential interpretations. In particular, high immediacy (touch combined with close proximity and gaze) is seen as far more dominant when exhibited by a male than a female. Other findings have confirmed that factors such as externally ascribed status and attractiveness can alter interpretations directly or interact with gender (e.g., Burgoon, 1991; Burgoon et al., 1992). Thus, the following hypotheses and research question are offered:

H3: Touch coupled with close proximity and gaze is interpreted as more dominant when performed by a male than by a female.

H4: Gaze by an attractive female is perceived as less dominant than gaze by an attractive male.

RQ1: Do (a) status and (b) attractiveness moderate gender or immediacy behavior effects?

In pursuing the issue of gender differences, we wished to learn whether particular combinations of behaviors represented a risk for men or women to use. Consequently, we examined the meanings associated with various behavioral combinations.

METHOD

Participants

Most participants ($n = 312$) were adults recruited from the jury assembly room of the Pima County (Arizona) courthouse, where they were awaiting voir dire. Others were recruited in public places such as shopping malls, bus station waiting rooms, and parking lots.

Procedures and Independent Variables

Participants were approached by students from an upper division nonverbal communication class and asked if they would be willing to participate in a brief study on first impressions. After agreeing to participate, they were shown a photograph of two people ostensibly engaged in interaction. While viewing the photograph, participants completed a brief questionnaire assessing impressions of the stimulus person and were thanked for their participation. Participants saw either a male or female stimulus person (hereafter called the initiator) interacting with a male or female target. The initiator, whom they were asked to judge, was presented in three-quarter profile; the person to whom they were apparently speaking was seen from a rear, one-quarter view. The photographed stimulus and target individuals were similar in age, height, build, and physical attractiveness.

The five variables systematically varied in the photographs were (a) initiator gender, (b) gender combination of the dyad (same sex or opposite sex), (c) immediacy behavior combination (six gradations in immediacy resulting from combinations of conversational distance, eye contact, and touch), (d) initiator attractiveness (high versus low), and (e) status relationship between the two (initiator higher status, both equal status, initiator lower status). The six immediacy combinations depicted were: (a) far distance, eye contact present; (b) normal distance, no eye contact; (c) normal distance, eye contact present; (d) close distance, no eye contact; (e) close distance, eye contact present; and (f) close distance, eye contact present, touch present. The two stimulus people were made to appear attractive in half the photographs and unattractive in half. Status was manipulated through questionnaire wording. Approximately one-third described the pictured stimulus person as higher status than the target, another third described the pictured person as lower status, and the remainder described them as equals. (The attractiveness and status manipulations are described more fully in Burgoon, 1991).[1]

Dependent Measures. Participants completed a 31-item version of Burgoon and Hale's (1987) Relational Communication Scale (RCS), which assessed their interpretations of the relational messages being conveyed by the

---

[1]The studies reported there were collected at the same time.

initiator to the target. The RCS included items measuring dominance, equality, immediacy, affection, receptivity, depth, trust, similarity, formality, and composure. The items were subsequently subjected to confirmatory factor analysis to reduce these dimensions to fewer composites and to assess reliabilities (reported under results). Participants also completed demographic questions and questions measuring perceived attractiveness and status (see Burgoon, 1991, for these results).

RESULTS

Preliminary Analysis of RCS Dimensions

Based on both the conceptual arguments advanced by Burgoon and Hale (1984) and empirical results from several previous investigations (e.g., Burgoon & Hale, 1987; Burgoon & Le Poire, 1993; Burgoon et al., 1992), it was anticipated that many of the intimacy subthemes would be intercorrelated and would need to be combined into composite subthemes. At the same time, it was anticipated that dominance would remain a highly independent factor, as would composure and formality.

Confirmatory factor analysis using Hamilton and Hunter's (1988) version of PACKAGE produced the following six factors that had the strongest primary and lowest secondary loadings and provided the most interpretable solution: Dominance, Immediacy/Receptivity, Affection/Depth, Similarity/Equality/Trust, Formality, and Composure. The factor loadings and cross-factor correlations are shown in Table 3.1. Respective coefficient alpha reliabilities were .65, .82, .75, .77, .55, and .68.

Hypothesis Tests

The data were analyzed with multivariate analyses of variance testing for linear and quadratic effects. Initially, all five independent variables were examined for their effects on each of the outcome measures or composites. However, the omnibus tests using saturated models revealed only main effects for attractiveness and status and no effects for gender combination.[2] Thus, in answer to Research Question 1, externally ascribed status and attractiveness did not moderate gender or immediacy behavior effects. Consequently, reduced models including only immediacy behaviors and gender were employed in the hypothesis tests so as to increase the power of the tests. Effects of presence or absence of individual immediacy behaviors on dominance interpretations were further tested with 1 df contrasts. The omnibus tests

---

[2]Status produced main effects on dominance, $F(2,168) = 27.44$, $p < .0001$, $\eta^2 = .10$; immediacy/receptivity, $F(2,168) = 3.65$, $p = .028$, $\eta^2 = .02$; similarity/equality/trust, $F(2,168) = 27.44$, $p < .0001$, $\eta^2 = .10$; and formality, $F(2,168) = 6.19$, $p = .003$, $\eta^2 = .05$. Attractiveness produced main effects on affection/depth, $F(1,168) = 6.34$, $p = .013$, $\eta^2 = .03$, and composure, $F(1,168) = 6.65$, $p = .011$, $\eta^2 = .03$.

TABLE 3.1
Factors, Factor Loadings, Average Correlations within Factors, and Cross-Factor Correlations for Confirmatory Factor Analysis on the Relational Communication Scale

	RCS	Factor Loadings (decimals omitted)					
	Item	*(1)*	*(2)*	*(3)*	*(4)*	*(5)*	*(6)*
(1) Immediacy/Receptivity	01	*61*	03	36	01	20	16
	15	*67*	-10	-08	39	42	45
	17	*71*	05	22	14	30	28
	24	*62*	2	17	17	37	44
	27	*72*	9	3	44	60	50
	11	*60*	8	-6	29	38	33
	12	*71*	9	15	42	53	47
	19	*66*	8	-11	36	46	40
(2) Formality	03	12	*81*	3	10	17	5
	08	-4	*63*	13	-16	-25	-19
	20	6	*74*	14	10	24	5
(3) Dominance	04	26	6	*75*	-8	3	5
	10	20	5	*74*	-17	3	4
	18	-26	1	*65*	-28	-33	-25
	28	16	26	*66*	10	7	11
(4) Composure	05	13	-9	-14	*71*	19	26
	13	48	2	1	*74*	43	45
	16	35	3	-13	*78*	43	46
	23	24	10	-18	*62*	29	26
(5) Similarity/Equality/Trust	07	31	5	2	22	*69*	38
	21	48	1	-25	44	*71*	39
	25	55	24	-12	37	*72*	46
	09	44	-3	3	30	*70*	48
	22	44	-2	6	36	*77*	48
(6) Affection/Depth	02	28	0	-11	39	37	*58*
	06	32	-8	3	24	44	*67*
	26	55	-6	-2	33	47	*74*
	29	45	3	3	41	44	*78*
	31	43	-4	2	39	44	*76*
	Factors						
		(1)	*(2)*	*(3)*	*(4)*	*(5)*	*(6)*
Average correlation within factors		36	29	32	35	40	37
Correlation among factors							
(1)			6	13	42	62	57
(2)				13	2	7	-4
(3)					-15	-7	-2
(4)						47	50
(5)							61

Note. The primary loadings on each factor appear in italics.

results for each relational message theme are presented first before discussing support for the hypotheses and the impact of behavioral combinations on relational interpretations.

For *dominance*, initiator gender and immediacy behaviors produced a significant interaction and significant main effects for each factor: $F_{sex \times immed}(5,300) = 2.57, p < .05, \eta^2 = .04; F_{sex}(1,300) = 4.42, p < .05, \eta^2 = .01; F_{immed}(5,300) = 17.87, p < .001, \eta^2 = .23$. The means, reported in Table 3.2, indicate that the combination of close proximity, eye contact, and touch was interpreted as the most dominant, regardless of whether it was enacted by a male or a female, but was especially so for the male initiator. The combinations with no eye contact were seen as the most submissive for both male and female initiators, but again especially so for the male. The second most dominant combination for the male was normal distance with eye contact; for the female, it was close distance with eye contact. The 1 *df* contrasts confirmed that the presence of touch connoted far more dominance than its absence, $F(1,300) = 69.69, p < .0001$, and that the presence of gaze conveyed more dominance than its absence, $F(1,300) = 19.52, p < .0001$. The test of distance effects was nonsignificant.

Overall, the female initiator was also rated as slightly more dominant than the male, but this difference should not be overemphasized when one considers the portion of variance accounted for by gender was 1%, whereas immediacy behavior combination accounted for nearly one-quarter of the variance in dominance ratings.

Initiator gender had no significant impact on interpretations of *immediacy/receptivity* and it did not interact with immediacy behavior combination. Not unex-

TABLE 3.2
Means for Significant Immediacy Behavior by Gender Interaction Effects

Immediacy Behavior Combinations[a]	Male	Female	Behavior Main Effect
(1) Far, Eye Contact	2.97	3.28	3.13
(2) Normal Distance, No Eye Contact	2.59	2.90	2.75
(3) Normal Distance, Eye Contact	3.22	3.13	3.17
(4) Close Distance, No Eye Contact	2.67	2.84	2.76
(5) Close Distance, Eye Contact	2.86	3.46	3.17
(6) Close Distance, Eye Contact, Touch	4.05	3.77	3.19
Gender Main Effect	3.05	3.23	
Immediacy Behavior Combinations[b]			
(1) Far, Eye Contact	2.46	2.66	2.56
(2) Normal Distance, No Eye Contact	2.03	2.18	2.11
(3) Normal Distance, Eye Contact	2.57	2.59	2.58
(4) Close Distance, No Eye Contact	2.24	2.42	2.32
(5) Close Distance, Eye Contact	2.81	2.80	2.80
(6) Close Distance, Eye Contact, Touch	2.10	3.06	2.59
Gender Main Effect	2.37	2.61	

[a]Dominance ($F_{sex \times immed}(5,300) = 2.57, p$ .05, $^2 = .04$).
[b]Similarity/equality/trust ($F_{immed \times sex}(5,300) = 3.23, p$ .01, $^2 = .05$).

pectedly, immediacy behavior combination did have a substantial impact, $F(5,276)$ = 26.27, $p < .0001$, $\eta^2 = .32$. The means, reported in Table 3.3, indicate that the combination including touch was seen as most immediate/receptive, and the two combinations with lack of eye contact were seen as least immediate/receptive. Adding eye contact increased immediacy/receptivity connotations, as did increasing proximity. Thus, the three immediacy behaviors each intensified the perception of immediacy and receptivity.

For messages of *affection/depth*, there was a gender main effect, F_{sex} (1,300) = 4.08, $p < .05$, $\eta^2 = .01$, such that the female initiator was seen as significantly more affectionate than the male. There was also a main effect for immediacy behavior combination, F_{immed} (5,300) = 6.40, $p < .0001$, $\eta^2 = .10$ (see Table 3.3 for means). There was no interaction between gender and immediacy behaviors and, again, the variances accounted for indicate that immediacy behavior combination had a greater impact on relational meaning than did gender. The means reveal that close distance coupled with eye contact, with or without touch, signalled the most affection and depth. Similar to messages of dominance and immediacy/receptivity, the two conditions without eye contact were seen as expressing the least affection and the most superficiality. As with immediacy/receptivity, additions of immediacy behaviors increased perceived affection/depth.

Gender was the only variable to influence interpretations of *composure*, F_{sex} (1,300) = 8.95, $p < .01$, $\eta^2 = .03$. Overall, the female initiator was seen as more composed than the male overall (see Table 3.3), though again, the proportion of variance accounted for was relatively small.

Significant main effects were found for both gender and immediacy behavior combination on messages of *formality*, F_{sex} (1,300) = 11.17, $p < .01$, $\eta^2 = .04$; F_{immed} (5,300) = 4.50, $p < .01$, $\eta^2 = .07$, with no interaction between the two (see

TABLE 3.3
Means for Significant Main Effects for Immediacy Behavior Combination and Gender

Immediacy Behavior Combinations	*Immediacy/ Receptivity*	*Affection/ Depth*	*Formality*
(1) Far, Eye Contact	2.72	2.13	3.33
(2) Normal Distance, No Eye Contact	2.03	1.95	3.16
(3) Normal Distance, Eye Contact	2.76	2.16	3.24
(4) Close Distance, No Eye Contact	2.06	2.03	2.84
(5) Close Distance, Eye Contact	2.96	2.43	3.33
(6) Close Distance, Eye Contact, Touch	3.15	2.53	2.78
Gender Main Effects	*Composure*	*Affection/ Depth*	*Formality*
Male	2.40	2.13	2.95
Female	2.67	2.28	3.27

Note. Immediacy/receptivity: F_{immed} (5,276) = 26.27, $p < .0001$, $\eta^2 = .32$; Affection/depth: F_{immed}(5,300) = 6.40, $p < .0001$, $\eta^2 = .10$; F_{sex} (1,300) = 4.08, $p < .05$, $\eta^2 = .01$; Formality: F_{immed} (5,300) = 4.50, $p < .01$, $\eta^2 = .07$; F_{sex} (1,300) = 11.17, $p < .01$, $\eta^2 = .04$; Composure: F_{sex} (1,300) = 4.08, $p < .05$, $\eta2 = .01$.

Table 3.3). The female was seen as slightly more formal than the male. The behavioral combinations signalling the most formality were both far and close distances with eye contact, followed by normal distance with eye contact. The condition incorporating touch with close distance and eye contact was seen as least formal. Thus, if touch is absent, extremes in distance (far and close) are likely to connote formality. But combining touch with close proximity reverses perceptions, creating a sense of informality.

For messages of *similarity/equality/trust*, an interaction between gender and immediacy behavior combination, $F_{immed \times sex}$ (5,300) = 3.23, $p \leq .01$, $\eta^2 = .05$, and main effects for both obtained, F_{sex} (1,300) = 9.41, $p < .01$, $\eta^2 = .03$; F_{immed} (5,300) = 6.27, $p < .001$, $\eta^2 = .09$. The means indicate similar patterns for both male and female initiators except in the condition involving touch. The female was rated as most similar, equal, and trustworthy to partners when she included touch with close distance and eye contact, whereas the male was seen as most similar/equal/trustworthy when he interacted at a close distance and engaged in eye contact but refrained from touching partners. Close proximity and the presence of eye contact also increased connotations of similarity, equality, and trust relative to normal distances, far distances, or the absence of gaze. Overall, the female was seen as more similar, equal, and trustworthy to partners than the male was.

How well do these results support the hypotheses? Hypothesis 1 posited that close and far conversational distances, touch, and gaze would connote dominance. The hypothesis was largely supported in that the presence of gaze and touch was clearly seen as more dominant than their absence and the combination of close proximity, gaze, and touch was by far the most dominant. The presence of a significant interaction with gender indicated that the dominance or submissiveness connotations were more pronounced with the addition or deletion of gaze and touch for the male initiator and the change in proximity for the female initiator. Although the close and far distances were not interpreted as more dominant when displayed by the male, the pattern of means for the female did fit the hypothesis (see conditions 1, 3, and 5 in which eye contact was present and distance increased from far to close).

Hypothesis 2 posited that these same behaviors would also carry numerous other relational messages. Consistent with H2a, close distance connoted greater immediacy/receptivity, affection/depth, and similarity/equality/trust than did far and normative distances; distance did not affect formality or composure perceptions. Consistent with H2b, combinations with eye contact were also interpreted as more immediate/receptive, affectionate/deep, and similar/equal/trustworthy, but contrary to the hypothesis, were also more formal (at close and far distances). And confirming H2c, touch was seen as more immediate/receptive, affectionate/deep, informal, and, for females only, similar/equal/trustworthy than no touch; only composure failed to show a main effect. Moreover, the combination of close distance, eye contact, and touch conveyed the greatest amount of dominance, immediacy/receptivity, affection/depth, informality, and for females only, similarity/equality/trust over any other behavioral combination.

The remaining hypotheses posited some moderating effects due to gender. Hypothesis 3, that touch coupled with close proximity is more dominant when exhibited by a male than a female, was clearly supported in the gender by immediacy behavior interaction. For males, the high immediacy condition with close proximity and touch present had a mean of 4.05 compared to 3.77 for females. Hypothesis 4, that gaze by an attractive female is seen as less dominant than gaze by an attractive male, was not supported. Not only did attractiveness fail to interact with gender and behavior, females using gaze tended to be rated as more rather than less dominant than males using gaze.

DISCUSSION

The present investigation adds incrementally to a substantial store of knowledge about how women and men compare in their nonverbal communication generally and their expression of power and dominance specifically. What is perhaps most striking about these results is the relative *lack* of differences in the meanings attributed to male and female immediacy behavior. For men and women alike, the immediacy behaviors of touch and gaze, separately or in combination with close proximity, connoted dominance. Additionally, the other relational meanings attributed to these same behaviors were highly similar for both males and females. And the amount of variance accounted for by the nonverbal behaviors themselves far outstripped that due to gender. This overall pattern of findings validates the Social Meaning Model in demonstrating that many nonverbal behaviors have consensually recognized meanings that are fairly invariant across communicators.

Nevertheless, there were some subtle differences due to gender, as had been anticipated from prior research. These differences moderated but did not override the behavioral main effects. Paralleling Henley and Harmon's (1985) findings, when women engaged in the high-immediacy combination of close proximity, eye contact, and touch, they were perceived as less dominant than men exhibiting the same behaviors. At the same time, they were also perceived as expressing far more similarity, equality, and trustworthiness than men with the same combination. Clearly, then, the same behavior pattern is capable of conferring more power on men than women and of having alternative, stereotypical connotations for women, similar to Henley and Harmon (1985) finding that their multiple cue combination was seen as expressing greater sexuality by women.

In the current investigation, it is possible that touch was responsible for the differences in perceptions for this condition. Touch is an ambiguous cue that may range in meanings from intimidation and condescension to consolation, affection, and supportiveness. Although context may often constrain the choice of meanings and heighten the probability that a given meaning is intended or selected, in the present case (as well as Henley and Harmon's study), the use of photographs may have provided insufficient contextual information or cue redundancy to make a single interpretation likely. In line with Expectancy Violation Theory, which postulates that when multiple or ambiguous meanings are possible, communicator characteristics will moderate the choice of interpretation, gender added a stereo-typic patina to the otherwise similar meanings assigned to the touch-inclusive behavior pattern. For the male initiator, the behavior pattern took on more of a dominance lustre, for women, more of a solidarity one. This is consistent with much research showing different imputations of meaning based on gender alone. As but one example, Burgoon et al. (1984) found that men were generally rated as more dominant than women, and women as more immediate and affectionate than men, regardless of their behavior pattern.

However, it must be remembered that the combined touch/gaze/close proximity combination was still the most dominant pattern for the female initiator among the six combinations studied and the absolute dominance ratings were substantially above the neutral point on the scale. Moreover, her behavior was also construed as more dominant when she adopted nonnormative distances, both relative to the male and relative to herself at the normative distance. For the male, distance changes had little impact on dominance perceptions. This implies that women are capable of being perceived as dominant and can influence dominance perceptions through changes in nonverbal behavior. Speculatively, women may be most successful portraying dominance and power by violating distance norms.

Lest we overinterpret gender differences, however, we want to remind the reader that this experiment entailed only one female and one male initiator. Gender differences among the two stimulus people were confounded with whatever unique individual characteristics were evident from the photographs. Conclusions about gender differences need to be bolstered by further research employing multiple male and female encoders and employing interactive as well as observational paradigms. The findings from Burgoon and Hale's (1988) study, which was based on interacting dyads, found that high and low immediacy, which included proxim-ity as one major element, were construed as more dominant than normal immediacy by interaction partners. Burgoon, Newton, Walther, and Baesler (1989) also found in two interactive studies that high degrees of involvement conveyed more domi-nance than low involvement. But those results were not analyzed by gender, leaving us with some uncertainty as to whether subtle gender differences might have emerged.

Apart from the possible gender implications, the current results raise important implications for the study of dominance and power displays. Here, the same behaviors that conveyed dominance (touch, gaze, close proximity) also carried such surplus meanings as immediacy and receptivity (which one often thinks of as a polar opposite of dominance), while the same behaviors that conveyed submis-siveness (gaze aversion, absence of touch) carried meanings of nonimmediacy, superficiality, and lack of affection. And the presence of eye contact simultaneously communicated similarity/equality/trust and slight formality (which is considered most appropriate and polite for showing interest). Contrary to the view promulgated in some quarters (e.g., Mazur, 1985; Ridgeway, Berger, & Smith, 1985; Ridgeway & Diekema, 1989), then, dominant behavior need not be equated exclusively with threat nor even regarded as primarily a negative behavior pattern. As Liska (1988) observed, "dominance is not unidimensional. Dominance may be assessed on a number of dimensions such as aggressiveness, politeness or deference, effectiveness, acceptability/desirability, and so on" (p. 5). Recognizing that dominance is rich in connotations, some of which are socially desirable, rids it of an undeserved (and currently politicized) stigma.

At the same time, it must be understood that because "dominance displays" are multipurpose, it may be easy to mistake a dominance display for some other type of display or to misread immediacy behaviors as dominance attempts. Doubtless some of the confusions regarding what constitutes sexual harassment stem from this conflating of behaviors and meanings. The challenge for scholars and practitioners alike is to identify what accompanying verbal and nonverbal cues can disambiguate a dominance or perceived dominance display, transforming it into an aggressive threat, polite assertiveness, or even deferent involvement.

The investigation reported here is one modest effort at addressing how such cue complexes function. The current results suffer from multiple constraints: the use of still photographs rather than videotapes or actual interaction, the use of single male and female stimulus people, the limitations on the number and kinds of cues that could be depicted through photographs, and even the difficulty of representing the distance factor well with the camera angle used. All of these constraints may have attenuated the gender and immediacy behavior effects. Nevertheless, the substantial effect sizes (in the medium- to-large effect range) associated with the three nonverbal behaviors that were examined points to the value of pursuing nonverbal signals of dominance and relational definitions.

CONCLUSION

To sum up, what have we learned about gender and the nonverbal expression of dominance and power in the 1990s?

1. Touch and eye contact are potent elements in the arsenal of nonverbal dominance signals. Nonnormative distance may also be so, especially for women.

2. There are more commonalities than differences in the dominance interpretations assigned to the immediacy behaviors of women and men. The important implications of this conclusion are that women's nonverbal behavior is as capable of communicating dominance and power as is men's and that men and women may use many of the same behaviors to express dominance.

3. Where gender differences exist, they may take more the form of intensifying or deintensifying a preexisting message, with males' behaviors being given more of a dominance slant and females' behaviors being given more of a solidarity or intimacy slant, in keeping with gender stereotypes.

4. Dominance displays have multiple additional meanings that may transmute them into widely disparate variations on the dominance theme or even into nondominance displays.

5. Concurrent contextual cues are critical for assessing what a given display means. This is doubtless as true for other nonverbal dominance displays as it is for the ones examined here.

REFERENCES

Altman, I., & Vinsel, A. M. (1977). Personal space: An analysis of E. T. Hall's proxemics framework. In I. Altman & J. F. Wohlwill (Eds.), *Human behavior and environment: Advances in theory and research* (Vol. 2, pp. 181–259). New York: Plenum.

Bem, S. L. (1981). Gender schema theory: A cognitive account of sex typing. *Psychological Review, 88*, 354–364.

Burgoon, J. K. (1978). A communication model of personal space violations: Explication and an initial test. *Human Communication Research, 4*, 129–142.

Burgoon, J. K. (1991). Relational message interpretations of touch, conversational distance, and posture. *Journal of Nonverbal Behavior, 15*, 233–259.

Burgoon, J. K. (1993). Interpersonal expectations, expectancy violations, and emotional communication. *Journal of Language and Social Psychology, 12*, 13–21.

Burgoon, J. K., Buller, D. B., Hale, J. L., & deTurck, M. A. (1984). Relational messages associated with nonverbal behaviors. *Human Communication Research, 10*, 351–378.

Burgoon, J. K., Buller, D. B., & Woodall, W. G. (1989). *Nonverbal communication: The unspoken dialogue*. New York: Harper & Row.

Burgoon, J. K., Coker, D. A., & Coker, R. A. (1986). Communicative effects of gaze behavior: A test of two contrasting explanations. *Human Communication Research, 12*, 495–524.

Burgoon, J. K., & Hale, J. L. (1984). The fundamental topoi of relational communication. *Communication Monographs, 51*, 193–214.

Burgoon, J. K., & Hale, J. L. (1987). Validation and measurement of the fundamental themes of relational communication. *Communication Monographs, 54*, 19–41.

Burgoon, J. K., & Hale, J. L. (1988). Nonverbal expectancy violations: Model elaboration and application to immediacy behaviors. *Communication Monographs, 55*, 58–79.

Burgoon, J. K., & Koper, R. (1984). Nonverbal and relational communication associated with reticence. *Human Communication Research, 10*, 601–626.

Burgoon, J. K., & Le Poire, B. A. (1993). Effects of communication expectancies, actual communication, and expectancy disconfirmation on evaluations of communicators and their communication behavior. *Human Communication Research, 20*, 75–107.

Burgoon, J. K., Manusov, V., Mineo, P., & Hale, J. L. (1985). Effects of eye gaze on hiring credibility, attraction, and relational message interpretation. *Journal of Nonverbal Behavior, 9*, 133–146.

Burgoon, J. K., & Newton, D. A. (1991). Applying a social meaning model to relational message interpretations of conversational involvement: Comparing observer and participant perspectives. *Southern Communication Journal, 56*, 96–113.

Burgoon, J. K., Newton, D. A., Walther, J. B., & Baesler, E. J. (1989). Nonverbal expectancy violations and conversational involvement. *Journal of Nonverbal Behavior, 13*, 97–120.

Burgoon, J. K., Pfau, M., Birk, T., & Manusov, V. (1987). Nonverbal communication performance and perceptions associated with reticence: Replications and classroom implications. *Communication Education, 36*, 119–130.

Burgoon, J. K., Walther, J. B., & Baesler, E. J. (1992). Interpretations, evaluations, and consequences of interpersonal touch. *Human Communication Research, 19*, 237–263.

Canary, D. J., & Hause, K. S. (1993). Is there any reason to research sex differences in communication? *Communication Quarterly, 41*, 129–144.

Coker, D. A., & Burgoon, J. K. (1987). The nature of conversational involvement and nonverbal encoding patterns. *Human Communication Research, 13*, 463–494.

Dovidio, J. F., & Ellyson, S. L. (1982). Decoding visual dominance behavior: Attributions of power based on the relative percentages of looking while speaking and looking while listening. *Social Psychology Quarterly, 45*, 106–113.

Dovidio, J. F., & Ellyson, S. L. (1985). Patterns of visual dominance behavior in humans. In S. L. Ellyson & J. F. Dovidio (Eds.), *Power, dominance, and nonverbal behavior* (pp. 129–150). New York: Springer-Verlag.

Eagly, A. H. (1987). *Sex differences in social behavior: A social-role interpretation*. Hillsdale, NJ: Lawrence Erlbaum.

Ellyson, S. L., & Dovidio, J. F. (1985). Power, dominance, and nonverbal behavior: Basic concepts and issues. In S. L. Ellyson & J. F. Dovidio (Eds.), *Power, dominance, and nonverbal behavior* (pp. 1–27). New York: Springer-Verlag.

Exline, R. V. (1972). Visual interaction: The glances of power and preference. In J. K. Cole (Ed.), *The Nebraska symposium on motivation*, 1971 (pp. 163–208). Lincoln, NE: University of Nebraska Press.

Exline, R. V., Ellyson, S. L., & Long, B. (1975). Visual behavior as an aspect of power role relationships. In P. Pliner, L. Krames, & T. Alloway (Eds.), *Nonverbal communication of aggression* (pp. 21–52). New York: Plenum.

French, J. R. P., Jr., & Raven, B. (1959). The bases of social power. In D. Cartwright (Ed.), *Studies in social power* (pp. 150–167). Ann Arbor, MI: Institute for Social Research.

Gallaher, P. E. (1992). Individual differences in nonverbal behavior: Dimensions of style. *Journal of Personality and Social Psychology, 63*, 133–145.

Halberstadt, A. G., & Saitta, M. B. (1987). Gender, nonverbal behavior, and perceived dominance: A test of the theory. *Journal of Personality and Social Psychology, 53*, 257–272.

Hall, J. A. (1984). *Nonverbal sex differences: Communication accuracy and expressive style*. Baltimore: Johns Hopkins University Press.

Hall, J. A., & Halberstadt, A. G. (1986). Smiling and gazing. In J. S. Hyde & M. Linn (Eds.), *The psychology of gender: Advances through meta-analysis* (pp. 136–158). Baltimore: Johns Hopkins University Press.

Hamilton, M. A., & Hunter, J. E. (1988). *Confirmatory factor analysis: A program in Basic*. East Lansing, MI: Michigan State University.

Harper, R. G. (1985). Power, dominance, and nonverbal behavior: An overview. In S. L. Ellyson & J. F. Dovidio (Eds.), *Power, dominance, and nonverbal behavior* (pp. 29–48). New York: Springer-Verlag.

Henley, N. M. (1977). *Body politics: Power, sex and nonverbal communication*. Englewood Cliffs, NJ: Prentice-Hall.

Henley, N. M., & Harmon, S. (1985). The nonverbal semantics of power and gender: A perceptual study. In S. L. Ellyson & J. F. Dovidio (Eds.), *Power, dominance, and nonverbal behavior* (pp. 151–164). New York: Springer-Verlag.

Jaworski, A. (1993). *The power of silence: Social and pragmatic perspectives*. Newbury Park, CA: Sage.

Jones, S. E. (1986). Sex differences in touch communication. *Western Journal of Speech Communication, 50*, 227–241.

Keating, C. F. (1985). Human dominance signals: The primate in us. In S. L. Ellyson & J. F. Dovidio (Eds.), *Power, dominance, and nonverbal behavior* (pp. 89–108). New York: Springer-Verlag.

Le Poire, B. A., & Burgoon, J. K. (1991, November). *I KNEW that you liked me: Nonverbal predictors of relational message perceptions*. Paper presented to the annual meeting of the Speech Communication Association, Atlanta.

Liska, J. (1988, July). *Dominance-seeking strategies in primates: An evolutionary perspective*. Paper presented to the XII Congress of the International Primatological Society, Brasilia, Brazil.

Major, B. (1981). Gender patterns in touching behavior. In C. Mayo & N. M. Henley (Eds.), *Gender and nonverbal behavior* (pp. 15–37). New York: Springer-Verlag.

Marche, T. A., & Peterson, C. (1993). The development and sex-related use of interruption behavior. *Human Communication Research, 19*, 388–408.

Mayo, C., & Henley, N. M. (Eds.). (1981). *Gender and nonverbal behavior*. New York: Springer-Verlag.

Mazur, A. (1985). A biosocial model of status in face-to-face primate groups. *Social Forces, 64,* 377–402.

Mehrabian, A. (1967). Orientation behaviors and nonverbal attitude communication. *Journal of Communication, 17,* 324–332.

Mehrabian, A. (1981). *Silent messages.* Belmont, CA: Wadsworth.

Mitchell, G., & Maple, T. L. (1985). Dominance in nonhuman primates. In S. L. Ellyson & J. F. Dovidio (Eds.), *Power, dominance, and nonverbal behavior* (pp. 49–66). New York: Springer-Verlag.

Mulac, A., Studley, L. B., Wiemann, J. M., & Bradac, J. J. (1987). Male/female gaze in same-sex and mixed-sex dyads. *Human Communication Research, 13,* 323–343.

Omark, D. R. (1980). The group: A factor or an epiphenomenon in evolution. In D. R. Omark, F. F. Strayer, & D. G. Freedman (Eds.), *Dominance relations* (pp. 21–64). New York: Garland.

Ridgeway, C. L. (1987). Nonverbal behavior, dominance, and the basis of status in task groups. *American Sociological Review, 52,* 683–694.

Ridgeway, C. L., Berger, J., & Smith, L. (1985). Nonverbal cues and status: An expectation states approach. *American Journal of Sociology, 90,* 955–978.

Ridgeway, C. L., & Diekema, D. (1989). Dominance and collective hierarchy formation in male and female task groups. *American Sociological Review, 54,* 79–93.

Rosa, E., & Mazur, A. (1979). Incipient status in small groups. *Social Forces, 58,* 18–37.

Sebeok, T. (1972). *Perspectives in zoosemiotics.* The Hague: Mouton.

Staley, C. C., & Cohen, J. L. (1988). Communicator style and social style: Similarities and differences between the sexes. *Communication Quarterly, 36,* 192–202.

Steckler, N. A., & Rosenthal, R. (1985). Sex differences in nonverbal and verbal communication with bosses, peers, and subordinates. *Journal of Applied Psychology, 70,* 157–163.

Stewart, L. P., Cooper, P. J., & Friedley, S. A. (1986). *Communication between the sexes: Sex differences and sex-role stereotypes.* Scottsdale, AZ: Gorsuch Scarisbrick.

Stier, D. S., & Hall, J. A. (1984). Gender differences in touch: An empirical and theoretical review. *Journal of Personality and Social Psychology, 47,* 440–459.

Weisfeld, G. E., & Linkey, H. E. (1985). Dominance displays as indicators of a social success motive. In S. L. Ellyson & J. F. Dovidio (Eds.), *Power, dominance, and nonverbal behavior* (pp. 109–128). New York: Springer-Verlag.

Willis, F. N., Jr., & Briggs, L. F. (1992). Relationship and touch in public settings. *Journal of Nonverbal Behavior, 16,* 55–63.

Chapter 4

Women's Style in Problem Solving Interaction: Powerless, or Simply Feminine?

Anthony Mulac
University of California, Santa Barbara

James J. Bradac
University of California, Santa Barbara

Since the suggestion was first made by Lakoff in 1973, some theorists and researchers have maintained that women's language reflects their position of low power compared to men. Moreover, their use of particular linguistic forms, for example, *tag questions* (It's good, isn't it?) and *hedges* (It's kind of good), reinforces their low power, according to advocates of this position. But there are other possibilities. For example, it may be the case that men are as likely as women to use particular forms indicating tentativeness or uncertainty, at least in some contexts—that is, there may not be a coherent code of powerlessness or "women's language" as Lakoff suggested (1973, 1975, 1990). It may also be the case that whatever linguistic differences do exist are not attributable to differences in power, but rather to differences in socialization unrelated to power. This alternative to the "power–discrepancy" hypothesis, sometimes referred to as the "gender as culture" hypothesis, argues that linguistic differences are the result of the fact that boys and girls grow up in different cultures (Maltz & Borker, 1982; Mulac & Gibbons, 1992; Mulac, Gibbons, & Fujiyama, 1990; Tannen, 1990).

In this chapter we examine the issue of gender and power in the realm of language. Specifically, we examine the question: Can we find evidence supporting the claim that women's language use is attributable to their low power position vis-a-vis men? We search for this evidence in the context of problem-solving interactions conducted by men and women who do not know each other well. Although other contexts could have been exploited to examine this question, we thought that it would be useful to look for evidence in a situation where the interactants were not well known to each other, that is, where idiosyncratic, relationship-specific language patterns were not established. Also we thought that a situation with a clear, external, task-related focus (as opposed to an interpersonal focus) would be desirable in order to minimize linguistic self-consciousness. Finally, the context of problem-solving interaction is an important one in everyday life.

Initially we briefly discuss some conceptions of power and language that inform our work. Then we consider what evidence or pattern of data would support the contention that men display greater power linguistically, in this case in the context of problem-solving interactions. This consideration leads to our research questions, which we use as the basis for discussing previous research on gender, language, and power. We next describe in detail the method of our study of men's and women's language behavior in mixed- and same-gender dyads, and subsequently describe, in equal detail, the results of our research. Finally, we discuss these results, linking them back to the general question of interest in this chapter: Do linguistic differences between men and women reflect differences in their social power?

THE NEXUS OF GENDER, LANGUAGE, AND POWER

A person can have formal authority in a situation, which enables him or her to issue orders, to give commands, and so on, although usually such authority is expressed indirectly, at least in nonmilitary situations (Ng & Bradac, 1993). On the other hand, one can exert influence over others in order to fulfill intentions and to achieve goals. Among other things, the success of attempts to influence hinges on one's style of language (Giles & Coupland, 1991). Influence is informal, not dependent on a person's formal position in an established hierarchy. Influence and formal legitimate power are alike in that they both pertain directly to achieving goals; the achievement of goals or "getting one's way" is often a measure of influence or an indicant of authority.

Or, to make another distinction, a person can impress others as being authoritative or influential, quite apart from whether he or she is genuinely powerful according to some objective criterion. Of course, being perceived as an authoritative or influential person increases the likelihood that one will, in fact, gain compliance, persuade others, or "get one's way"—this is a well known effect of communicator credibility (Burgoon, 1989). There is a good deal of research indicating that an impression of authoritativeness or, more generally, "high power" can be created through the use of particular forms of language and paralanguage. For example, a rapid rate of speech has been positively associated with judgments of communicator competence in a number of studies (e.g., Brown, 1980; Street,

Brady, & Putnam, 1983). Similarly, use of *polite forms* and *intensifiers* may increase ratings of authoritativeness (Bradac & Mulac, 1984b). On the other hand, the use of some linguistic forms may lead to judgments of low power, low competence, and so on, for example, the use of *hesitations* and *hedges* ("sort of" or "kind of") (Hosman, 1989).

To make yet another distinction, which we have implied above, there are two kinds of impressions of power: direct and indirect. That is, one can say: "She is a powerful (strong, dynamic) person"; this is a direct inference about the individual's condition of authority or ability to influence others. In one study that tested this link empirically, a strong, positive relationship was found between *Dynamism* as measured in the present study and judgments of "power" (Bradac & Mulac, 1984b). Or one can say: "He is intelligent"; this is an indirect inference about the person's ability to exert control, because one trait that is related to intelligence is the ability to get others to listen to you (McCroskey, Hamilton, & Weiner, 1974). Or more indirectly still, one can say: "She is warm and friendly"; these are traits possessed by socioemotional leaders in small groups and other collectives (Bales, 1950) and correlated with this kind of leadership is the ability to influence others. In the study reported below, we are concerned with both kinds of impressions of power. Specifically, some of our data represent judgments of individuals' *Dynamism* (direct inferences about power), whereas other data represent judgments of *Socio-intellectual Status* and *Aesthetic Quality* (indirect inferences regarding power).

A number of studies on the effects of noninteractive communication (such as public speeches, oral and written descriptions of landscape photographs, and written essays) have consistently found that in general female communicators are rated higher on *Intellectual Status* and *Aesthetic Quality*, whereas males are rated higher on *Dynamism* (Mulac & Lundell, 1980, 1982, in press; Mulac, Studley, & Blau, 1990). Additional research has also demonstrated that such ratings are attributable to male/female differences in language use (Mulac & Lundell, 1986; Mulac, Lundell, & Bradac, 1986) and has called the phenomenon the "Gender-Linked Language Effect." This effect has been shown to possess a substantial, positive relationship with gender stereotypes, even though it is independent of those stereotypes (Mulac, Incontro, & James, 1985).

Thus, there is actual or real power, where people get what they want, and there is symbolic power, where people are perceived to be authoritative and influential. As suggested above, these two realms of power can interact. The question now becomes: Do men and women differ in the power that they are perceived to have as a result of differences in the kinds of language they use? The related question— Do men and women differ in real power as a consequence of their language use?—is an important and interesting one, and one that is little investigated (Carli, 1990). A part of our data allows us to consider this issue, that which focuses on possible gender differences in interaction partners' mutual influence upon language choices. A more general version of the overall question of interest is: Do differences in men's and women's language both reflect and cause differences in social power?

We will now consider what kinds of evidence are necessary to support the claim that differences in the language used by both men and women are linked to power differences. First and most basically, it must be demonstrated that men's and women's language is, in fact, different. In the case of our research, this difference should manifest itself in problem-solving interactions. There is ample evidence from other contexts supporting the claim of difference, although it should be noted that "difference" here refers to statistical or probabilistic difference rather than to a difference that is absolute. That is, it is not the case that particular lexical items or linguistic forms are used exclusively by men or by women; the term gender "preferential" (as opposed to gender "exclusive") has been used to denote this fact (Smith, 1985).

An example of a linguistic difference between men and women that research has shown to be very consistent across contexts is in the use of *intensifiers*, adverbs that appear, at least, to affirm the speaker's commitment to the proposition being expressed ("It's really good"). A number of studies have shown that women use more *intensifiers* than men do (e.g., Crosby & Nyquist, 1977; McMillan, Clifton, McGrath, & Gale, 1977; Mulac et al., 1986), although a recent study has shown that this may be true primarily in the case of *intensifiers* that are used frequently in the population at large ("really" and "so," for example); men may use less common *intensifiers* more frequently than women do (Bradac, Mulac, & Thompson, in press).

On the other hand, although Lakoff has suggested that women use more *hedges*, an element in "women's language," than men do (1973, 1975, 1990), the empirical evidence is mixed. For example, in two of three studies that sought to test Lakoff's observations, under the rubric of the "female register," Crosby and Nyquist (1977) found that women used more *hedges* than did men. This pattern is consistent with results obtained by Fishman (1983) and by Mulac, Studley, and Blau (1990). On the other hand, Mulac et al. (1986) and Mulac, et al. (1988) obtained a null result for *hedges* in that this linguistic feature did not emerge as a significant predictor variable in discriminant analyses using speaker gender as the criterion variable. Finally, Carli (1990) observed more hedging in female speakers, but only when their interaction partners were males, that is, in mixed-gender dyads. As we can see, no consistent support has been found for a link between speaker gender and use of this form of language that qualifies, or appears to qualify, commitment to an expressed proposition ("It's sort of good"). Thus, as the cases of hedging and intensification illustrate, there is some evidence of statistical differences between men and women in their use of language in some contexts, but not others.

To support the position that linguistic differences linked to gender reflect power differences, the differences in verbal behavior revealed by research should cohere with some explicit conception of high- and low-power language. Lakoff's argument (especially 1973, 1975), which was not driven by data, links particular forms or categories of language to the pivotal concepts "tentativeness" and "uncertainty"; women invoking "women's language" use *hedges, intensifiers, tag questions*, and markers of politeness in order to soften claims or directives, rendering these speech acts more tentative, less assertive, and less direct.

We should point out that the connection between, for example, hedging and tentativeness is usually assumed rather than demonstrated empirically. Conversation analysts would argue that any linguistic form can indicate tentativeness or, contrarily, assertiveness depending on the local conditions of situational context. Indeed, one study suggests that an increased use of *tag questions* can be associated with increased attempts at interpersonal control (Winefield, Chandler, & Bassett, 1989). For us, the truth lies somewhere in between the extremes of rigid linguistic determinism, on the one hand, and radical contextual localism on the other: Politeness tends to be linked to deference, tentativeness, and so on, but this linkage can be severed in special cases, such as with the use of sarcasm.

In contrast to Lakoff, O'Barr (1981) distinguished between "low-" and "high-power" language on the basis of data collected in empirical research. In this case, the communication context was a courtroom in North Carolina. O'Barr and his co-investigators tape recorded many hours of courtroom interaction, including examination of witnesses, judge–attorney exchanges, and questioning of defendants. The researchers then transcribed the tapes and examined the transcription, searching for potentially revealing patterns of communicative behavior. Among other things, they observed that the use of some linguistic forms varied with the status and apparent social power of speakers. Low-status speakers, for example, inexpert witnesses, tended to use more *hedges, intensifiers, tag questions, declaratives with rising intonation, polite forms,* and *hesitations,* whereas high-status speakers tended to avoid these forms. This cluster of linguistic features has been labeled the "low-power style" or "powerless speech" by a number of investigators (Bradac & Mulac, 1984a, 1984b; Erickson, Lind, Johnson, & O'Barr, 1978).

In this case too, the link between specific linguistic forms and social power is less than obvious. Although it is probably true that status and use of various forms are highly correlated in the courtroom and in other contexts, a number of other variables are almost certainly simultaneously correlated as well. One or more of these other variables may be the "true cause" of language variation or may be, at least, more strongly and consistently related to it. For example, low-status speakers may experience high levels of subjective uncertainty in courtrooms and in other contexts, and this cognitive state may produce a tentative or deferential style. The point is that high-status speakers may also experience high uncertainty in some situations and may therefore, also use "low-power" language (Berger & Bradac, 1982).

Thus, there is some basis for claiming that there are linguistic differences between men and women, statistical differences that are variable from case to case. Some of these differences have been related to conceptions of power—there may be a "language of deference" and a "language of tentativeness"—but the links between specific linguistic forms and power are problematic in that they are usually asserted or taken for granted, rather than being demonstrated empirically. Even when some demonstration is made, as in the case of O'Barr's research, alternative causal inferences can be offered.

Another basis for arguing that gender-linked language differences are related to power can be found in associations between specific linguistic forms and the impressions or judgments of naive observers, that is, persons without special expertise in linguistics, sociolinguistics, and so on. As we indicated earlier, there is evidence supporting the hypothesis that *hedges*, *hesitations*, and *tag questions* (for example) produce judgments of low communicator authoritativeness; judgments of sociability are also negatively affected by these linguistic forms (Bradac & Mulac, 1984b). There is other evidence demonstrating that ratings of *Dynamism* (a direct inference about power) are diminished by use of the "low-power style" (Bradac & Mulac, 1984a).

If a person uses language that creates an impression of high or low power, this is likely to have interpersonal consequences. One of the most interesting possibilities is that the person will be treated by others in ways that correspond to his or her language use and to the impression created. Furthermore, this treatment by others may affect the person's subsequent behavior such that he or she will "live up to" the impression. Thus, a person using the "high-power" style may create the impression that he or she is authoritative, which may cause others to behave deferentially. This in turn may cause the person to become more authoritative in fact. Obviously, we are suggesting the possibility of a "Pygmalion effect" (Rosenthal, 1973) in the realm of language and power. As Bradac and Street (1989/1990) suggested:

> In a sense, we are interested in the 'appearance' of power more than in its reality. Nevertheless, in human affairs appearances have a way of becoming real . . . . Thus, unilateral or mutual impressions of power triggered by particular *styles* of language may shape the course of social interaction apart from (or in conjunction with) the *content* or illocutionary force of utterances. (pp. 196–197)

A third basis for claiming that differences in men's and women's language are grounded in power differences involves changes or adjustments in language behavior made during face-to-face interaction. Specifically, there is some evidence that persons who are relatively low in status compared to their interaction partners are more likely to converge to the partner's style of speech; conversely, high-status persons are less likely to converge (Thakerar, Giles, & Cheshire, 1982). Lakoff (1975) supported this expectation that women are more likely to converge to the style of men, stating that because "a girl must learn two dialects, she becomes in effect a bilingual (p. 6)." Thus, if women converge more to the style of language used by their male interaction partners than men converge to the style of their female partners, this would be consistent with the idea of a status or power difference linked to both gender and language. More particularly, it would be consistent with the hypothesis offered by Lakoff and others that women have less power than men do and that this low-power condition is reflected in, and maintained by, their language behavior. As Henley and LaFrance (1984) stated this view, from the companion perspective of nonverbal communication: "We argue that nonverbal behaviors convey much about the status and power distinctions within a culture and further, that nonverbal behaviors are frequently used in the service of maintaining such distinctions" (p. 352).

In fact, there is some reason to believe that women are more likely than men to exhibit convergent behavior in both mixed- and same-gender interaction. Hogg

(1985) compared the language changes made by men and women as they moved from same-gender dyadic interaction to mixed-gender small-group discussions. Men tended to use a "masculine" verbal style in both contexts, although they became somewhat more "masculine" in the presence of women during mixed-gender discussions. On the other hand, women shifted from a "feminine" style to a relatively "masculine" style as they moved from same-gender dyads to mixed-gender discussion groups. Mulac, Studley, Wiemann, and Bradac (1987) examined the sequencing of gaze and talk by men and women interacting in same- and mixed-gender dyads. Among other things they found that women exhibited more mutuality in same-gender dyads than did men (e.g., mutual gaze and mutual silence) and that women were relatively likely to switch to nonmutuality when they moved from same- to mixed-gender dyads. Men were low in mutuality in both contexts—gender of partner did not affect their sequencing of gaze and talk. Mulac et al. (1987) summarized their data, indicating that "the picture that emerges is one of men behaving consistently and inflexibly across situations with regard to gaze and talk, and women adapting their behavior to that of their male and female partners" (p. 339).

However, an entirely different pattern of convergence was found in a study of language behavior of men and women that had many design elements that are common to the present study (Mulac, Wiemann, Widenmann, & Gibson, 1988). In that study, men and women were assigned to either a same- or a mixed-gender dyad and were asked to select and discuss a problem for 10 minutes. Results of linguistic analyses showed that both the men and the women appeared to converge, in similar amounts, to the language of their opposite-gender partner. However that study supported only apparent convergence, because it compared one group of men in same-gender dyads to another group of men in mixed- dyads, and similarly one group of women in one setting to another group in the other. The present study employs a repeated-measure design in which the same men and women are measured in both gender/dyad settings and this design should be more sensitive to gender differences in linguistic convergence.

If women converge to the language of their male partners, or conversely if men converge, this convergence may be perceived by naive observers. Just as other types of language variation affect impressions of speakers, so may shifts in style representing convergence (or divergence, for that matter). In fact, there is evidence that linguistic convergence is perceived by naive observers and used as a basis for evaluating speakers (Giles & Coupland, 1991, chapter 2); for example, one study demonstrated that a speaker who converged to another speaker's relatively low level of lexical diversity was evaluated very favorably along the dimension of *Sociointellectual Status* (Bradac, Mulac, & House, 1988). In terms of the present study, it may be the case that speakers who converge (if convergence indeed occurs) will be judged to be more similar to those persons who are the targets of convergence than will speakers who do not converge; similarity would be perceived along the dimensions of *Sociointellectual Status*, *Aesthetic Quality*, and *Dynamism*. Thus, linguistic convergence may lend to the perception that speakers have converged to the psychological characteristics of their partners. This kind of "psychological assimilation" may be another manifestation of low social power.

The preceding discussion suggests some conditions under which a reasonable claim can be made that relationships exist among gender, language, and power; it also suggests the research questions that motivated the study reported below:

RQ1a: In the context of problem-solving interaction, does men's and women's use of language differ? (The specific language variables investigated will be described below in the Method section.)

RQ1b: If there are differences in language, do they cohere to theoretical conceptions of differences in power of style?

RQ2a: Does linguistic output lead to differences in ratings of men's and women's *Dynamism* (direct, naive inferences about power)?

RQ2b: Does linguistic output lead to differences in ratings of men's and women's *Sociointellectual Status* and *Aesthetic Quality* (indirect, naive inferences about power)?

RQ3a: As men and women move from same- to mixed-gender dyads, do they differ in the extent to which they converge to the *language style* of their partners?

RQ3b: As men and women move from same- to mixed-gender dyads, do outside observers judge them to differ in the extent to which they converge to the *psychological characteristics* of their partners?

If women are less powerful than men, and if their lower power is reflected in their use of language, as Lakoff (1973, 1975, 1990) and others contended, then we would expect that: (a) there will be differences between men and women in their use of language; (b) women will use a "low-power" style (especially when they are interacting with other women); (c) as a result of their language, women will be perceived as relatively low in *Dynamism*, *Sociointellectual Status*, and *Aesthetic Quality*; and (d) women will converge (to some extent) to a "high-power" style when they are interacting with men. In a sense, this is a four-part hypothesis; to the extent that we fail to find evidence for any part, our results will fail to support the idea that men and women speak in different ways as a result of differences in social power.

METHOD

Interactants

Two hundred eight university students enrolled in introductory courses at the University of California, Santa Barbara, participated in the study, which was described as an investigation of "how people solve problems." They were primarily freshmen and sophomores, representing a large number of majors, and ranging from 18 to 24 years of age (*Median* = 19.0, *SD* = 1.3).

Procedure

Between five and eight participants met each hour in the library of a social science research complex where they were: (a) briefed by one of the authors, (b) asked to identify any roommate or close friend in the group, (c) informed that they were free to leave at any time, and (d) asked to sign a consent form.

Participants who spoke English as their first language and who did not know well any of the other students meeting at that hour were randomly selected and paired with a same-gender and an opposite-gender partner. The order of the four interactions in any hour (e.g., M1/M2, F1/F2, M1/F2, and F1/M2) was determined by a 4 × 4 Latin square to balance for the order of gender composition. A student researcher (balanced for gender across sessions) led the participants into the interaction room and instructed them on the problem solving task. They were given two problems designed to favor neither gender, such as, "What are the best ways to relieve school stress?" and "How will life be different in the year 2000?"

At the end of the 8-minute period during which the discussion was recorded, the researcher returned and led the participants back to their individual cubicles. This procedure was followed for the four interactions each hour, during which each individual participated in both a same-gender and a mixed-gender dyad. The topics were different for each of the hour's four dyads.

Transcription of Interactions

The audiotape recordings of the 108 eight-minute interactions were transcribed orthographically by university communication students enrolled in an advanced research course. Each transcript was checked by a second researcher listening to the audiotape, with discrepancies resolved by a third student researcher. The final transcripts were assigned dyad numbers and printed with interactants arbitrarily designated "A" and "B." No indication of interactant gender was given. This process yielded a linguistic corpus of 156,315 words.

Linguistic Analysis of Interactions

A survey of empirical research on gender-linked linguistic features uncovered 20 that were likely to differentiate male from female interactants (see Table 4.1 for a list of the language variables, examples of each, previous studies finding gender differences, and an indication of which gender made greater use of each variable).

Twenty-four advanced communication students, working independently in teams of six individuals, each coded 25% of the 108 transcripts for all 20 language features. The interrater reliability, computed by an intraclass procedure (Winer, 1971, pp. 282–289), indicated generally high agreement among the subsets of coders across the 20 variables (ranging from .76 to .99, with a median reliability of .96).

TABLE 4.1
Descriptions, Examples,[a] and Citations[b] for 20 Language Variables Coded
as Potential Predictors of Interactant Gender

I. SENTENCES

A. *Questions*: ("What is [Communication] 12? What do you do?") But not including directives in question form. 83, 1978, F+ (couple's conversations); Mulac, Wiemann, Widenmann, & Gibson, 1988, F+ (dyadic interactions.)

B. *Tag Questions*: ("It's early Winter, isn't it?") An assertion that is followed immediately by a question asking for support. Crosby & Nyquist, 1977, F+; Dubois & Crouch, 1975, M+ (conference participation); Lapadat & Seesahai, 1978, M+ (informal conversations); Hartman, 1976, F+; McMillan et al, 1977, F+ (problem solving groups); Mulac & Lundell, 1986, F+ (oral descriptions of photographs).

C. *Direct Requests*: ("Think of another.") One interactant telling, in a straight forward manner, the other what to do. Haas, 1979, M+ (interviews); Mulac et al., 1988, M+ (dyadic interactions.)

D. *Indirect Requests*: ("Why don't we put that down?") One interactant asking, in a roundabout manner, the other to do something.

E. *Negations*: ("You don't feel like looking . . .") A statement of what something is not. Mulac & Lundell, 1986, F+ (oral descriptions of photographs); Mulac et al., 1986, F+ (public speeches).

II. CLAUSES AND PHRASES

A. *Sentence Initial Adverbials*: ("Instead of admitting it, he . . . ." "Actually, the best way is . . . .") Beginning a sentence by answering the questions: how?, when?, or where? regarding the main clause. Mulac et al., 1986, F+ (public speeches); Mulac et al., 1988, F+ (dyadic interactions); Mulac & Lundell, in press, F+ (written descriptions of photographs); Mulac, Studley, & Blau, 1990, F+ (fourth grade written essays).

B. *Sentence Initial Conjunctions*: ("And then we decided to take off.") Beginning a sentence with a conjunction. Hunt, 1960, M+ (written essays).

C. *Sentence Initial Fillers*: ("Let's see . ., another good way to get rid of tensions is to . . . ." "Okay, first we can . . . .") Beginning a sentence with a word or phrase used without apparent semantic intent.

D. *Dependent Clauses*: ("I've had jobs like that where you can't do that . . . ." ". . .taking trips every so often which would ease the tension.") A clause that serves to specify or qualify the words that convey primary meaning. Beck, 1978, F+ (oral descriptions of TAT cards); Hunt, 1960, F+ (written essays); Mulac, Studley, & Blau, 1990, F+ (fourth grade impromptu essays); Mulac & Lundell, in press, F+ (written descriptions of photographs) Poole, 1979, F+ (Interviews).

E. *Oppositions*: (". . . we went yesterday, . . no not yesterday." "I think it's awful, but it's so much nicer. . . .") Retracting a statement and posing one with an opposite meaning. Mulac and Lundell, 1986, F+ (oral descriptions of photographs); Mulac et al., 1986, F+ (public speeches).

III. MODIFIERS

A. *Intensive Adverbs*: ("It was really stupid." "I'm so used to getting up . . . .") Crosby and Nyquist, 1977, F+ (dyadic interactions); Lapadat and Seesahai, 1978, F+ (group discussions); McMillan et al., 1977, F+ (group discussions); Mulac and Lundell, 1986, F+ (oral descriptions of photographs); Mulac et al., 1986, F+ (public speeches); Mulac et al., 1988, F+ (dyadic interactions).

B. *Hedges*: ("That would kind of make me pretty mad." "It was sort of unfair.") Modifiers that indicate lack of confidence in, or diminished assuredness of, the statement. Crosby and Nyquist, 1977, F+ (dyadic interactions); Mulac, Studley, & Blau, 1990, F+ (fourth grade impromptu essays).

(Continued)

TABLE 4.1 (Continued)

IV. REFERENCES

A. *References to Emotion*: ("What happened was really frustrating and upsetting.") Any mention of an emotion or feeling. Balswick and Avertt, 1977, F+ (written response to questionnaire); Gleser et al.; 1959, F+ (event descriptions); Mulac & Lundell, in press, F+ (written descriptions of photographs); Mulac, et al., 1986, F +(public speeches); Staley, 1982, F+ (oral descriptions of pictures).

B. *References to Quantity*: ("He'll give you six minutes . . . ," "I lived with three other people.") References to a number or amount. Gleser et al., 1959, M+ (event description); Mulac & Lundell, 1986, M+ (oral descriptions of photographs); Sause, 1976, M+ (interviews); Warshay, 1972, M+ (event description essays); Wood, 1966, M+ (oral descriptions of pictures).

V. MISCELLANEOUS

A. *Fillers*: ("It helped because like, you know, he'll give you . . . .") Words or phrases used without apparent semantic intent. Hirschmann, 1973, F+; Mulac & Lundell, 1986, M+ (oral picture description); Mulac et al., 1986, F+ (public speeches; Mulac, Studley, & Blau, 1990, F+ (fourth grade essays); Mulac et al., 1988, M+ (dyadic interactions).

B. *Vocalized Pauses:* ("So, uhm, I said," "I don't know, ah the first two weeks . . . .") Utterances having no semantic meaning. Frances, 1979, M+ (dyadic interactions); Poole, 1979, M+ (interviews).

C. *Hesitations*: ("Uh . . . I don't know . . . we both . . . .") A period of time during an interactant's turn when he or she is silent.

D. *Interruptions*: (Person A: "I don't really like electrical engineering that much. [By that I mean if you . ." Person B: "[A lot of] people are getting out of that.") Breaking into a person's turn, in an apparent attempt to take over the floor. Mulac et, al., 1988, M+ (dyadic interactions); West & Zimmerman, 1983, M+; Zimmerman & West, 1975, M+ (social interactions).

E. *Obscenities*: ("No shit!") Offensive to general modesty or decency. Selnow, 1985, M+; Simkins & Rinck, 1982, M+ (Written response to questionnaire); Walsh & Leonard, 1974, M+ (Written response to questionnaire).

F. *Back Channels*: (Person B: "She used to play volleyball. . . and," Person A: "Uh huh." Person B: "if she's in a bad mood . . ." Person A: "Uh huh." Person B: "there's no use in staying there." Person A: "Right." A verbal response suggesting that the one interactant is hearing and understanding what the other is saying. Fishman, 1983, F+ (spousal interactions).

[a]Examples were drawn from the transcripts analyzed.

[b]Citations indicate empirical studies in which the variable was found to differ for male and female communicators. Gender distinctions, in terms of whether the variable was more indicative of male or female communicators, are as follows: M+ = Male, F+ = Female. (Note, however, that the linguistic categories were not precisely equivalent across studies.) Communication contexts in which gender differences were found are indicated in parentheses.

The linguistic data for each interactant in each dyad were aggregated across the 6 coders and these scores were transformed into occurrences-per-100-words. Given the proportional nature of the data, arcsine transformations were computed (Winer, 1971, pp. 218–221). These transformed data were arrayed for each interactant for both same- and mixed-gender dyadic interactions. In this form, the data were ready for discriminant analysis to determine whether differences existed between men's and women's use of language.

Untrained Observer Ratings of Interactants

To determine whether observers rated the male and female interactants differently based on their language use, and whether changes in effects took place across time, the transcripts were reprinted to form two time segments: (a) the first 4 minutes, and (b) the second 4 minutes.

Observer impressions of the interactants were measured using the Speech Dialect Attitudinal Scale (SDAS, Mulac, 1975, 1976), a 12-item semantic differential used in a number of earlier studies establishing the Gender-Linked Language Effect in a variety of communication contexts. These and other studies consistently demonstrated a three-factor structure: *Sociointellectual Status*, *Aesthetic Quality*, and *Dynamism*. These factors are in many ways consistent with the three dimensions of Zahn and Hopper's (1985) empirically derived Speech Evaluation Instrument.

Raters were 270 students enrolled in an introductory course in interpersonal and small group communication at the University of California, Santa Barbara. They represented a wide variety of majors and ranged in age from 18 to 29, with a median age of 19.4 years. After receiving instruction in using the SDAS to rate each interactant "as a person," the observers received booklets of four randomly ordered 4-minute dyads: (a) M/M, (b) F/F, (c) M/F, and (d) F/M. In this way, all 108 dyads, in both the first 4 minute and second 4 minute versions, were rated by an average of 5 observers.

Construct validity of the SDAS ratings was assessed through factor analysis of the 2,160 rating forms using common-factor, Varimax procedures. This supported the previously found (Mulac & Lundell, 1980, 1982, in press) three-factor solution: *Sociointellectual Status* (high social status/low social status, rich/poor, white collar/blue collar, literate/illiterate), *Aesthetic Quality* (beautiful/ugly, pleasant/unpleasant, nice/awful, sweet/sour), and *Dynamism* (strong/weak, active/passive, aggressive/unaggressive, loud/soft). The three factors accounted for 66% of the item variance, with primary loadings ranging from .54 to .89, and a median primary loading of .67.

Each rater's judgments were computed by reversing the polarity of negatively loaded items and summing the four item scores to form each dimension. Median intraclass reliability estimates (Winer, 1971, pp. 282–289) indicated acceptable agreement among the raters: *Sociointellectual Status* = .74, *Aesthetic Quality* = .80, and *Dynamism* = .84.

RESULTS

Discriminant Analysis of Language Features

The first research question regarding the ability of the linguistic variables to distinguish between male and female interactants in same- and mixed-gender dyads was tested by means of a step-wise discriminant analysis of the 20 language features. Results (see Table 4.2) indicated gender-linked differences in language

TABLE 4.2
Summary of Step-Wise Discriminant Analysis Predicting Gender on the Basis
of Language Use

Step	Variable	Gender Predicted[a]	Canonical Coefficient[b]	F-to-Remove	Wilks' Lambda
1	Hedges	Male	137.14	18.40	0.92
2	Vocalized Pauses	Male	51.93	12.62	0.86
3	Refer to Emotion	Female	-52.95	8.90	0.83
4	Indirect Requests	Female	-51.71	6.47	0.81
5	Back Channels	Female	-66.04	5.00	0.79
6	Intensifiers	Female	-51.80	4.29	0.77
7	Sentence Initial Fillers	Female	-88.16	3.65	0.76
8	Sentence Initial Conjunction	Male	48.77	2.62	0.75
9	Hesitations	Male	10.41	1.33	0.75
10	Interruptions	Male	20.37	1.12	0.74
11	Negations	Male	136.40	1.09	0.74
12	Sentence Initial Adverbials	Female	-216.06	1.14	0.73

[a] Relatively frequent use of the variable led to this prediction of interactant gender.

[b]Coefficients are not standardized. The designation of male indicators with positive coefficients, and female with negative, is arbitrary.

use (Wilks' Lambda = .73, F [11, 204] = 5.35, $p < .001$, $R^2 = .27$). The language features more indicative of male interactants were, in order of entry into the discriminant function: *hedges, vocalized pauses, sentence initial conjunctions, hesitations,* and *interruptions.* The variables more often used by female interactants were: *references to emotion, indirect requests, back channels, intensifiers, sentence initial fillers,* and *sentence initial adverbials.* On the basis of the discriminant function scores, computed by the discriminant analysis, 70.4% of the interactants (70.4% for men and 70.4% for women) were accurately reclassified as to gender, using the conservative "jackknifed" procedure (Lachenbruch & Mickey, 1968; the reclassification accuracy using standard procedures was 75%).

ANOVA of Discriminant Function Scores

To determine whether gender-linked language differences were greater in same-gender or mixed-gender dyads, a two-way analysis of variance (2 interactant genders × 2 dyad types) was conducted. As a first step, the possibility of a relationship between the partners' discriminant function scores, with its potential for influencing the F ratio (Kraemer & Jacklin, 1979), was assessed by computing Pearson product-moment correlation coefficients for each dyad type. None of these were significant (male/male: $r = .11$; female/female: $r = .21$; male/female: $r = .10$, all p s > .10). In addition, they were of sufficiently low magnitude (< 5% common variance for any dyad pairs) to indicate that the standard analysis of variance procedure was appropriate (Dindia, 1987; Kraemer & Jacklin, 1979).

Results of the analysis of variance showed the expected difference between men's and women's language, without regard to the type of dyad in which they interacted (F [1,106] = 55.46, $p < .001$). However, no differences were found for the statistical interaction between the two dyad contexts and gender (F [1, 106] = 0.06, p > .50). That is, neither the men nor the women changed their use of the 12 gender-distinguishing language features when they interacted in same-gender, versus mixed-gender, dyads. This finding was in conflict with power–discrepancy expectations for research questions 3a and 3b.

Multivariate Analysis of Variance of Untrained Observer Psychological Ratings of Interactants

The possible relationships of partners' ratings on the three SDAS dimensions were assessed through Pearson product-moment correlations. These were nonsignificant and sufficiently low as to be nonproblematic for analysis of variance of psychological ratings by observers (Dindia, 1987; Kraemer & Jacklin, 1979).

The ratings were submitted to a 3-way multivariate analysis of variance (2 interactant genders x 2 dyad types x 2 time segments). This showed a significant main effect for interactant gender (Hotelling T^2 = 25.83, F (3, 249) = 8.54, p < .001). However, no other multivariate effects were found, either for main effects or interactions.

Significant univariate effects were found for the ratings of men and women on all three SDAS dimensions: *Sociointellectual Status* (F [1, 251] = 9.92, p < .01), *Aesthetic Quality* (F [1, 251] = 13.57, p < .001), and *Dynamism* (F [1, 251] = 6.54, p < .05). As Fig. 4.1 shows, the female interactants were generally rated higher on two dimensions that we see as important to indirect power—*Sociointellectual Status* and *Aesthetic Quality*. The male participants, on the other hand, were rated generally higher on the appearance of direct power—Dynamism. In addition, these ratings did not vary as a function of the gender of the partner. The women's

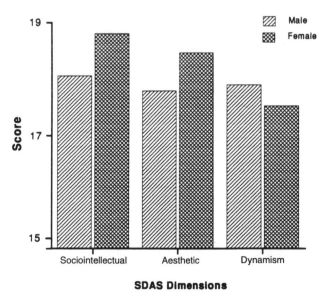

FIG. 4.1.   Mean SDAS dimensions scores for male and female interactants.

language was not affected by whether their partners were men or other women; similarly, the men's language was unvarying in terms of the gender of their partner. Moreover, because each participant was measured in both a same-gender and a mixed-gender dyad, we can see that these men and women failed to modify their language use as a result of their partner's gender. These results are entirely consistent with the Gender-Linked Language Effect found in a number of earlier studies of male and female spoken and written communication.

Multiple Regression Analyses Predicting Psychological Ratings from Language Use

In order to determine the extent to which the gender-discriminating language use by the interactants was implicated in the psychological ratings, a series of multiple regression analyses was conducted. In each case, the criterion or predicted variable was an SDAS dimension, such as *Dynamism*, rated by untrained observers. The predictor variables for the analyses were the 20 potential gender-discriminating language features coded by trained observers. Results of the multiple regression analyses showed that gender-linked language variables were in general implicated, in a predictive sense, in the ratings of all three psychological dimensions: *Sociointellectual Status* (F [3, 212] = 2.68, $p < .05$), *Aesthetic Quality* (F [2, 213] = 3.13, $p < .05$), and *Dynamism* (F [5, 210] = 3.42, $p < .01$). For example, two of the three language features predictive of lower *Sociointellectual Status* ratings, *hedges,* and *vocalized pauses* were more common in male discourse than in female; the third variable implicated in lower scores, *sentence initial fillers*, did not differ for men and women. Similarly for *Aesthetic Quality*, the female indicator, *indirect requests*, was predictive of higher ratings, whereas the male indicator, *hesitations*, led to lower ratings. Finally, the male language feature, *vocalized pauses*, was implicated in higher *Dynamism* ratings, whereas the three female variables, *references to emotion*, *back channels*, and *sentence initial fillers*, were all predictive of lower *Dynamism* ratings. The other variable predictive of higher *Dynamism* ratings, *direct requests*, was not used more by either men or women.

The results of the multiple regression analyses make clear that many of the gender-linked language differences found in the discriminant analysis (see Table 4.2) also help explain, in part, the differences in ratings received by the male and female interactants (see Fig. 4.1). These results provide an empirical link between language use by the participants in the problem-solving dyads and observer ratings of the psychological outcomes of such language use. In this way, these findings help us understand the direct and indirect power implications of differences in male and female speech in ways that go beyond the speculations of Lakoff and others.

DISCUSSION

We proposed initially that in order to find support for the "power-discrepancy hypothesis" in the problem-solving context studied here, our results would have to show the following: (a) differences between men's and women's language use, (b) women's style consistent with "low-power," (c) women rated as relatively low in *Dynamism, Sociointellectual Status*, and *Aesthetic Quality*, and (d) women converging to "high-power" style when interacting with men. To investigate these expectations, we posed the following six related research questions.

(1a) In the context of problem-solving interaction, does men's and women's use of language differ? The results of the discriminant analysis of men's and women's use of 20 language features in both same- and mixed-gender interactions showed that a weighted combination of 12 variables differentiated gender. This difference in male/female language use was both statistically significant and theoretically meaningful. The fact that gender-linked differences in style were found is the first result necessary to support the power-discrepancy hypothesis.

However, the specific language variables that discriminated between men and women were not clearly consistent with the second necessary element, reflected in the next research question: *(1b) If there are differences in language, do they cohere to theoretical conceptions of differences in power of style?* Two of the male-indicative features appear to be consistent with the power-discrepancy hypothesis in that *interruptions* and *hesitations* have been viewed as attempts to exert conversational control (West & Zimmerman, 1983; Zimmerman & West, 1975). It should be noted that some researchers have argued that some types of *interruptions* are not related to power or control, representing instead, for example, enthusiasm or agreement with the speaker's point (Marche & Peterson, 1993). Our global classification scheme for *interruptions* does not allow us to inform the discussion of this issue, but the issue is worth raising because it casts doubt on the *interruption* data as being clearly supportive of the power-discrepancy hypothesis. Men's greater use of *vocalized pauses* (O'Barr used the label "hesitations" for this category, including it as a feature of the "low-power" style) and *hedges* appears to be contrary to the expectations established by the work of Lakoff (1973, 1975) and O'Barr (1981). Bradac and Mulac (1984b) found that *vocalized pauses* (labeled "hesitations") received extremely low ratings for power and effectiveness. In addition, men's slightly greater preference for *negations* is inconsistent with earlier findings (Mulac & Lundell, 1986; Mulac et al., 1986).

Women's greater use of *intensifiers* is in keeping with predictions emerging from the work of Lakoff (1973, 1975) and O'Barr (1981). However, it should be noted that *intensifiers* received high ratings for *Power* and *Effectiveness* in a study by Bradac and Mulac (1984b). The findings of that experimental study of attitudes resulting from use of *intensifiers* were therefore in conflict with Lakoff's (1973, 1975) theoretical and O'Barr's (1981) observational analyses. More generally in studies of language effects, *intensifiers* have produced highly variable results (e.g., Hosman, 1989). This suggests that the link between use of *intensifiers* and low social power is a weak, or even nonexistent, one. Additionally, women's preference for *references to emotion* is consistent with expectations (Balswick & Avertt, 1977; Gleser, Gottschalk, & John, 1959), but once again the link to low power is less than crystal clear. On the one hand, references to one's own negative emotions (for example fear) can increase personal vulnerability; on the other hand, references to another's negative emotions can increase personal control. Further, women's greater use of *back channels* coheres with expectations (Fishman, 1983), as does their preference for *indirect requests*. Use of *back channels* is often viewed as signaling social dependence and use of indirect forms may indicate deference. Still, with regard to indirection, Ng and Bradac (1993) argued that *indirect requests*, for example, can "depoliticize" or mask influence attempts, which can actually enhance the requester's power. Finally, women's preferences for *sentence initial fillers* and *sentence initial adverbials* were not predicted on the basis of power–discrepancy.

Thus, the discriminant analysis findings fail to provide more than weak support for the power-discrepancy hypothesis. Some results are consistent with expectations regarding gender and power of style, whereas others are not. Quite apart from consistency or inconsistency, as we suggested in our opening discussion, one of the difficulties here is that the expectations themselves, whether derived from speculation or from data, are disputable.

The third necessary finding to support power-discrepancy required an affirmative answer to both of the next two research questions: *(2a) Does linguistic output lead to differences in ratings of men's and women's Dynamism (direct, naive inferences about power)? (2b) Does linguistic output lead to differences in ratings of men's and women's Sociointellectual Status and Aesthetic Quality (indirect, naive inferences about power)?* The results of the multivariate analysis of variance of psychological ratings by the untrained observers did affirm the first of these questions—on the basis of their transcribed utterances, women were generally rated as being lower in *Dynamism*, the direct inference regarding power. However they were rated more highly in the two indirect assessments of power, those for *Sociointellectual Status* and *Aesthetic Quality*. Thus only one of the three observer assessments of power, albeit the most direct one, favored the male interactants.

The significant outcomes of the multiple regression analyses indicated that particular language features were implicated in the above-mentioned observer assessments. For example, the "male" feature *hedges* was negatively associated with ratings of *Sociointellectual Status*, while the "female" feature *references to emotion* was negatively associated with ratings of *Dynamism*. One example of the complexity that exists here can be seen in the case of *vocalized pauses*. On the one hand, these semantically meaningless sounds depress ratings of *Sociointellectual Status*, on the other hand, they elevate ratings of *Dynamism*. This means that they may create a positive direct inference regarding a speaker's power, while at the same time creating a negative indirect power inference. An implication is that previous studies reporting negative associations between *vocalized pauses* (or "hesitations") and judgments of power may have led respondents to make indirect inferences.

The last requirement of the power-discrepancy hypothesis was the affirmation of the final research questions dealing with male/female differences in convergence: *(3a) As men and women move from same- to mixed-gender dyads, do they differ in the extent to which they converge to the language style of their partners? (3b) As men and women move from same- to mixed-gender dyads, do outside observers judge them to differ in the extent to which they converge to the psycho-logical characteristics of their partners?* The results of the analysis of variance of discriminant function scores provided a negative answer to the first question—nei-ther men nor women converged toward the language of their opposite-gender partner. This finding is clearly at odds with the power-based expectations of Lakoff (1973, 1975) and others, and does much to weaken their argument for the "bilin-gualism" of women. If these women were indeed bilingual, why did they fail to vary their dialect in conversation with members of the two genders? This finding is also different from results of another empirical study (Mulac et al., 1988), but not in a way that supports the power-disparity argument. Mulac et al. found that both men and women appeared to converge toward the language of their partner, although the comparison was between different groups of men and of women. That finding is also in conflict with the power-based theory, because both genders appeared to converge in a similar amount and therefore to exhibit similar degrees of bilingualism. In the present study, woman again failed to show greater conver-gence to their partner than did men.

Furthermore, the results of the multivariate analysis of variance of observer ratings answered the latter question in the negative—neither men nor women converged toward their opposite-gender partner on any of the psychological judgments of *Dynamism, Sociointellectual Status,* or *Aesthetic Quality.* If women were speaking from a low-power status, as Lakoff and others argued, we would expect that observers (blind to the gender of the communicators) would perceive a shift in the psychological characteristics of women in the two dyad settings. If that argument held true, women would be expected to appear to be different when talking to men than when talking to other women, because men were rated as different from women on all three dimensions.

Thus, the results of this study suggest a pattern that is considerably more complex than that described by the power-discrepancy hypothesis. On the one hand, we found evidence of linguistic differences between the men and women participating in our study, but on the other hand, these differences were not completely consistent with theoretical discussions of gender, language, and power; for example, our male respondents used some ostensibly low-power forms. Further, our female respondents were judged to be relatively high on the dimensions of *Sociointellectual Status* and *Aesthetic Quality.* The former dimension especially has been viewed as strongly linked to power—high-status persons are relatively likely to achieve influence and control (Bradac & Street, 1989/1990), whereas the latter has been associated with effective leadership (Bales, 1950). But the men in our study received high ratings for *Dynamism,* a measure of strength or potency that constitutes a different kind of power, a kind that is relatively basic, perhaps akin to brute force. Finally, neither our male nor our female respondents influenced the language choices of their partners. In other words, we obtained no evidence of a gender-based achievement of influence in the domain of language. Of course, as with any null finding, no strong conclusion can be drawn from this apparent lack of effect.

In summary, we found little evidence favoring expectations for language use that are based on the power-discrepancy hypothesis. That is, the men and women in problem solving pairs in this study used language that differed from what has been described in speculative discussion of gender, power, and language (e.g., Lakoff, 1973, 1975, 1990). Moreover, transcriptions of their interactions yielded ratings that demonstrated dissimilar kinds of, as opposed to different levels of, perceived power. Also inconsistent with power-based explanations, these women failed to converge toward the language behavior of the men.

The most succinct generalization of our findings is that the language style of women in problem solving interactions is both *powerful* and *feminine*. These women apparently did not feel that they had to give up one to get the other. These findings suggest that in any relationship between women and men, both should be aware that they are using different linguistic styles, but that these styles may be similarly effective in exerting influence. Implications are that women do not have to choose between using effective methods of influencing decision making and appearing feminine. In addition, men should not assume that women are any less effective because of their different linguistic style. Disparity of power may exist in the language behavior of men and women in other age groups, in other communication contexts, or those having other relationships. Indeed, Fitzpatrick and Mulac address this issue in this volume, chapter 9, by examining older individuals interacting in two different relational contexts. Nevertheless, what we found in the study reported in the present chapter can only be viewed as failing to support the hypothesis that the differences in men's and women's language are explained by differences in their social power and their intent to exercise that power.

REFERENCES

Bales, R. (1950). *Interaction process analysis: A method for the study of small groups*. Reading, MA: Addison-Wesley.

Balswick, J., & Avertt, C. P. (1977). Differences in expressiveness: Gender, interpersonal orientation, and perceived parental expressiveness as contributing factors. *Journal of Marriage and the Family, 39*, 121–127.

Beck, R. (1978). Sex differentiated speech codes. *International Journal of Women's Studies, 1*, 566–572.

Berger, C. R., & Bradac, J. J. (1982). *Language and social knowledge: Uncertainty in interpersonal relations*. London: Arnold.

Bradac, J. J., & Mulac, A. (1984a). Attributional consequences of powerful and powerless speech styles in a crisis-intervention context. *Journal of Language and Social Psychology, 3*, 1–19.

Bradac, J. J., & Mulac, A. (1984b). A molecular view of powerful and powerless speech styles: Attributional consequences of specific language features and communicator intentions. *Communication Monographs, 51*, 307–319.

Bradac, J. J., Mulac, A., & House, A. (1988). Lexical diversity and magnitude of convergent versus divergent style-shifting: Perceptual and evaluative consequences. *Language and Communication. 8*, 213–228.

Bradac, J. J., Mulac, A., & Thompson, S. A. (in press). Men's and women's use of intensifiers and hedges in problem-solving interaction: Molar and molecular analyses. *Research on Language and Social Interaction*.

Bradac, J. J., & Street, R. S., Jr. (1989/1990). Powerful and powerless styles of talk: A theoretical analysis of language and impression formation. *Research on Language and Social Interaction, 23*, 195–242.

Brown, B. L. (1980). Effects of speech rate on personality attributions and competency evaluations. In H. Giles, W. P. Robinson, & P. Smith (Eds.), *Language: Social psychological perspectives* (pp. 294–300). Oxford, England: Pergamon.

Burgoon, M. (1989). Messages and persuasive effects. In J. J. Bradac (Ed.), *Message effects in communication science* (pp. 129–164). Newbury Park, CA: Sage.

Carli, L. L. (1990). Gender, language, and influence. *Journal of Personality and Social Psychology, 59*, 941–951.

Crosby, F., & Nyquist, L. (1977). The female register: An empirical study of Lakoff's hypothesis. *Language in Society, 6*, 313–322.

Dindia, K. (1987). The effects of sex of subject and sex of partner on interruptions. *Human Communication Research, 13*, 345–371.

Dubois, B. L., & Crouch, I. (1975). The question of tag questions in women's speech: They don't really use more of them, do they? *Language and Society, 4*, 289–294.

Erickson, B., Lind, A. E., Johnson, B. C., & O'Barr, W. M. (1978). Speech style and impression formation in a court setting: The effects of "powerful" and "powerless" speech. *Journal of Experimental Social Psychology, 14*, 266–279.

Fishman, P. M. (1983). Interaction: The work women do. In B. Thorne, C. Kramare, & N. Henley (Eds.), *Language, gender and society* (pp. 89–101). Rowley, MA: Newbury House.

Frances, S. J. (1979). Sex differences in nonverbal behavior. *Sex Roles, 5*, 519–535.

Giles, H., & Coupland, N. (1991). *Language: Contexts and consequences.* Buckingham: Open University Press.

Gleser, G. C., Gottschalk, L. A., & John, W. (1959). The relationship of sex and intelligence to choice of words: A normative study of verbal behavior. *Journal of Clinical Psychology, 15*, 182–191.

Haas, A. (1979). The acquisition of genderlect. In J. Orsanu, M. K. Slater, & L. L. Adler (Eds.), *Language, sex and gender* (pp. 101–113). New York: New York Academy of Sciences.

Hartman, M. (1976). A descriptive study of the language of men and women born in Maine around 1900 as it reflects the Lakoff hypotheses in *Language and Woman's Place.* In B. L. Dubois & I. Crouch (Eds.), *The sociology of the languages of American women* (pp. 81–90). San Antonio, TX: Trinity University Press.

Henley, N. M., & LaFrance, M. (1984). Gender as culture: Difference and dominance in nonverbal behavior. In A. Wolfgang (Ed.), *Nonverbal behavior: Perspectives, applications, intercultural insights* (pp. 351–371). Lewiston, NY: Hogrefe.

Hirschman, L. (1973, December). *Female–male differences in conversational interaction.* Paper presented at the meeting of the Linguistic Society of America, San Diego, CA.

Hogg, M.A. (1985). Masculine and feminine speech in dyads and groups: A study of speech style and gender salience. *Journal of Language and Social Psychology, 4*, 99–112.

Hosman, L. (1989). The evaluative consequences of hedges, hesitations, and intensifiers: Powerful and powerless speech styles. *Human Communication Research, 15*, 383–406.

Hunt, K. W. (1960). *Grammatical structures written at three grade levels.* Champaign, IL: National Council of Teachers of English.

Kraemer, H. C., & Jacklin, C. N. (1979). Statistical analysis of dyadic social behavior. *Psychological Bulletin, 86*, 217–224.

Lachenbruch, P. A., & Mickey, M. R. (1968). Estimation of error rates in analysis. *Technometrics, 10*, 1–11.

Lakoff, R. (1973). Language and woman's place. *Language in Society, 2*, 45–80.

Lakoff, R. (1975). *Language and woman's place.* New York: Harper & Row.

Lakoff, R. (1990). *Talking power.* New York: Basic Books.

Lapadat, J., & Seesahai, M. (1978). Male versus female codes in informal contexts. *Sociolinguistics Newsletter, 8*, 7–8.

Maltz, D. J., & Borker, R. A. (1982). A cultural approach to male–female miscommunication. In J. J. Gumpertz (Ed.), *Language and social identity* (pp. 196–216). Cambridge: Cambridge University Press.

Marche, T. A., & Peterson, C. (1993). The development of sex-related use of interruption behavior. *Human Communication Research, 19,* 388–408.

McCroskey, J. C., Hamilton, P, R., & Weiner, A. N. (1974). The effect of interaction behavior on source credibility, homophily, and interpersonal attraction. *Human Communication Research, 1,* 42–52.

McMillan, J. R., Clifton, A. K., McGrath, D., & Gale, W. S. (1977). Women's language: Uncertainty or interpersonal sensitivity and emotionality? *Sex Roles, 3,* 545–559.

Mulac, A. (1975). Evaluation of the speech dialect attitudinal scale. *Speech Monographs, 42,* 184–189.

Mulac, A. (1976). Assessment and application of the revised speech dialect attitudinal scale. *Communication Monographs, 43,* 238–245.

Mulac, A., & Gibbons, P. (1992, May). *A test of the gender as culture hypothesis: Male and female language differences viewed from an inter-cultural perspective.* Paper presented at the International Communication Association, Miami.

Mulac, A., Gibbons, P., & Fujiyama, S. (1990, June). *Male/female language differences viewed from an inter-cultural perspective: The gender as culture hypothesis.* Paper presented at the International Communication Association, Dublin.

Mulac, A., Incontro, C. R., & James, M. R. (1985). Comparison of the gender-linked language effect and sex role stereotypes. *Journal of Personality and Social Psychology, 49,* 1098–1109.

Mulac, A., & Lundell, T. L. (1980). Differences in perceptions created by syntactic-semantic productions of male and female speakers. *Communication Monographs, 47,* 111–118.

Mulac, A., & Lundell, T. L. (1982). An empirical test of the gender-linked language effect in a public speaking setting. *Language and Speech, 25,* 243–256.

Mulac, A., & Lundell, T. L. (1986). Linguistic contributors to the gender-linked language effect. *Journal of Language and Social Psychology, 5,* 81–101.

Mulac, A., & Lundell, T. L. (in press). Effects of gender-linked language differences in adults' written discourse: Multivariate tests of language effects. *Language and Communication.*

Mulac, A., Lundell, T. L., & Bradac, J. J. (1986). Male/female language differences and attributional consequences in a public speaking situation: Toward an explanation of the gender–linked language effect. *Communication Monographs, 53,* 115–129.

Mulac, A., Studley, L. B., & Blau, S. (1990). The gender-linked language effect in primary and secondary students' impromptu essays. *Sex Roles, 23,* 439–469.

Mulac, A., Studley, L. B., Wiemann, J. W., & Bradac, J. J. (1987). Male–female language differences and effects in same-sex and mixed-sex dyads: The gender-linked differences and mutual influence. *Human Communication Research, 13,* 323–344.

Mulac, A., Wiemann, J. M., Widenmann, S. J., & Gibson, T. W. (1988). Male/female language differences and effects in same-sex and mixed-sex dyads: The gender-linked language effect. *Communication Monographs, 55,* 315–335.

Ng, S., & Bradac, J. (1993). *Power in language: Verbal communication and social influence.* Newbury Park, CA: Sage.

O'Barr, W. M. (1981). *Linguistic evidence: Language, power, and strategy in the courtroom.* New York: Academic Press.

Poole, M. E. (1979). Social class, sex, and linguistic coding. *Language and Speech, 22,* 49–67.

Rosenthal, R. (1973). The pygmalion effect lives. *Psychology Today, 7,* 56–63.

Sause, E. F. (1976). Computer content analysis of sex differences in the language of children. *Journal of Psycholinguistic Research, 5,* 311–324.

Selnow, G. W. (1985). Sex differences in uses and perceptions of profanity. *Sex Roles, 12,* 303–312.

Simkins, L., & Rinck, C. (1982). Male and female sexual vocabulary in different interpersonal contexts. *Journal of Sex Research, 18,* 160–172.

Smith, P. M. (1985). *Language, the sexes, and society.* Oxford: Blackwell.

Staley, C. M. (1982). Sex-related differences in the style of children's language. *Journal of Psycholinguistic Research, 11*, 141–158.

Street, R. L., Jr., Brady, R. M., & Putnam, W. B. (1983). The influence of speech rate stereotypes and rate similarity on listeners' evaluations of speakers. *Journal of Language and Social Psychology, 2*, 37–56.

Tannen, D. (1990). *You just don't understand: Women and men in conversation.* New York: Morrow.

Thakerar, J. N., Giles, H., & Cheshire, J. (1982). Psychological and linguistic parameters of speech accommodation theory. In C. Fraser & K. R. Sherer (Eds.), *Advances in the social psychology of language* (205–255). Cambridge: Cambridge University Press.

Walsh, R. H., & Leonard, W. M. (1974). Usage of terms for sexual intercourse by men and women. *Archives of Sexual Behavior, 3*, 373–376.

Warshay, D. W. (1972). Sex differences in language style. In C. Safilios-Rothchild (Ed.), *Toward a sociology of women* (pp. 3–9). Lexington, MA: Xerox College Pub.

West, C., & Zimmerman, D. (1983). Small insults: A study of interruptions in cross-sex conversations of unacquainted persons. In B. Thorne, C. Kramare, & N. Henley (Eds.), *Language, gender and society* (pp. 102–117). Rowley, MA: Newbury House.

Winefield, H. R., Chandler, M. A., & Bassett, D. L. (1989). Tag questions and powerfulness: Quantitative and qualitative analyses of a course of psychotherapy. *Language in Society, 18*, 77–86.

Winer, B. J. (1971). *Statistical principles in experimental design* (2nd ed.). New York: McGraw-Hill.

Wood, M. M. (1966). The influence of sex and knowledge of communication effectiveness on spontaneous speech. *Word, 22*, 112–137.

Zahn, C. J., & Hopper, R. (1985). Measuring language attitudes: The speech evaluation instrument. *Journal of Language and Social Psychology, 4*, 113–123.

Zimmerman, D., & West, C. (1975). Sex roles, interruptions, and silences in conversation. In B. Thorne & N. Henley (Eds.), *Language and sex: Differences and dominance* (pp. 105–129). Rowely, MA: Newbury House.

Chapter 5

Masculinity and Femininity: Defining the Undefinable

Janet T. Spence
University of Texas at Austin

Camille Buckner
University of Texas at Austin

> *I don't know what good art is but I know it when I see it.*
> —Well-known saying

Massive strides toward equality between men and women have been made in the United States over the past three decades. Yet despite these changes, many inequities remain. From the time they are born, males and females are treated differently in both obvious and subtle ways and are expected to behave differently. With this emphasis on gender, children learn to identify their own biological sex and the sex of others at a very early age and gender quickly becomes a central feature of children's emerging concept of self.[1] They soon acquire knowledge of their

---

[1]The degree to which factors rooted primarily in biology contribute to observed differences in the behaviors and psychological characteristics between men and women is a subject of continued controversy. However, many of these differences can be agreed to arise because of societal expectations and socialization experiences. This has led feminist writers (e.g., Unger, 1979) to suggest that in referring to comparisons of men and women, the term *sex* be used to refer to biological differences between males and females, and the term "gender" be used for those attributes and behaviors acquired as a consequence of being a male or a female in a specific culture. Although this distinction is not without its problems, attempts to observe it have become quite common in the psychological literature and we follow the practice here. However, because of the quite recent origin of the distinction, a certain awkwardness is introduced when we refer to concepts involving roles. For example, the terms *sex-role identification* and *sex-role attitudes* became established some years ago and continue to appear far more frequently than *gender-role identification.* or *gender-role attitudes*, especially when they are attached to measuring instruments that at the time of their development were given the sex-role label. We retain these labels here. As a result, there is a certain inconsistency in our usage of the words sex and gender.

society's stereotypes about differences in the psychological characteristics of men and women and of the different roles that men and women play. As children and adults, people adopt characteristics and behaviors that make them recognizable members of their gender. Masculinity is a quality prized in men and those who are judged to be inadequately masculine or worse, to show signs of femininity, are generally derogated. Men whose personal sense of masculinity is threatened often feel attacked at the core of their being. Similarly, women lacking in femininity are devalued and those who doubt their own femininity often suffer considerable emotional distress.

Masculinity and femininity, then, are qualities of considerable consequence. But what are they? How are they defined? What are their properties? Psychologists have devoted a good deal of attention to the constructs of masculinity and femininity, particularly in recent years, and have devised a number of self-report instruments to measure them. What theories about the organization of gender-differentiating phenomena guided the development of these measures? How do psychologists' conceptions differ from those of people at large? In this chapter, we explore some of these questions.

LACK OF FORMAL DEFINITIONS OF MASCULINITY AND FEMININITY

Masculinity and femininity are well-established terms in the natural language, used freely in everyday discourse. We hear, for example, that John is so secure in his masculinity that he doesn't mind being a house-husband or that Jane's mastectomy has threatened her sense of femininity. Further, when psychologists ask men and women to indicate on a rating scale how much of these qualities they possess, they comply unquestioningly and seemingly without difficulty. Obviously, to most men and women, masculinity and femininity are meaningful concepts. But asking otherwise articulate adults to state what they mean when they use these terms provides little enlightenment. When queried about their own masculinity or femininity, most men and women express confusion and puzzlement about the question itself and if they venture an answer at all, they tend to mention one of their own valued characteristics. Married men, for example, may draw on their role as head of the family or the traits that make them good leaders (Spence & Sawin, 1985). When asked about masculinity and femininity in others, people's answers again are hesitant but they typically refer to observable physical characteristics that distinguish between men and women (Myers & Gonda, 1982; Spence & Sawin, 1985). Paraphrasing the expression about good art, people cannot say what masculinity and femininity are but they know them when they see them.

One might expect the arbiters of the meaning of words, the writers of dictionaries, to do better. However, a search of standard dictionaries fails to yield answers. All dictionaries contain definitions of the adjectives masculine and feminine. In addition to its grammatical meaning, the word *masculine*, dictionaries agree, refers to properties or objects associated with men, objects such as apparel worn by men or properties such as virile, strong, and bold. *Masculinity* appears at the end of the entries for masculine, listed simply as a noun. In like fashion, *feminine* is uniformly defined as referring to objects or properties associated with women, objects such as articles of clothing or properties such as weak, gentle, and delicate, with *femininity* typically appearing at the end of the entry for feminine.

Psychologists' interest in masculinity and femininity as topics of systematic investigation has a long history, and with the rise of the current feminist movement, empirical research devoted to these concepts has come to be highly popular. By way of illustration, a search of the computerized data base for psychological literature (PsycLit) under this pair of headings reveals over 1,100 references during the period from 1974 to 1993. Under these circumstances, one might reasonably expect that definitions of these concepts, although not necessarily in agreement with one another, would abound in the psychological literature. But such is not the case. Although definitions appear in dictionaries of psychological terms (as will be described at a later point), they are not to be found in research publications themselves. Thus, along with the public at large, psychologists appear to regard masculinity and femininity as "real" and as important phenomena but simultaneously, as unnecessary or impossible to define. Psychologists have nonetheless felt free to develop a host of measures of these hypothetical concepts. The first self-report measure of masculinity and femininity appeared some six decades ago (Miles, 1935) and many other measures followed.

Constantinople's Critique

In an article published in 1973 in which she examined the major masculinity–femininity tests in existence at that time and the presumptions that guided their construction, Constantinople also commented on the absence of meaningful definitions of masculinity and femininity. These terms, she observed, "both theoretically and empirically, [are] among the muddiest in the psychologist's vocabulary. A search for definitions related to some theoretical position leads almost nowhere....[I]t seems as if the terms were taken over whole from the public domain with no attempt to explicate them" (p. 390).

Constantinople's analysis led her to suggest that masculinity–femininity tests were based on the tacit assumption that masculinity and femininity are the end points of a single bipolar continuum to which all gender-differentiating phenomena of a psychological nature contribute. The empirical evidence, however, led her to question the validity of this untested tenet as well as the validity of the masculinity–femininity construct itself. Constantinople further noted the complications that were caused by the confusion of the masculinity–femininity concept with such related terms as sex-role adoption, sex-role identity, and sex-role preferences. When concepts remain undefined, she indicated, but are accepted as "real," the necessity of questioning their validity and the possibility of developing alternative conceptions are not recognized. Unfortunately, her article did not receive the attention it deserved.

nople's (1973) critique was published a short time before the appear-
nstruments, the Bem Sex Role Inventory (BSRI; Bem, 1974) and the
Personal Attributes Questionnaire (PAQ; Spence, Helmreich, & Stapp, 1974,
1975). These instruments, which differ in several significant ways from those that
came before, both signaled and stimulated an upsurge of research devoted to
masculinity and femininity and, more generally, to the position of women in society.
Unlike their predecessors, both the BSRI and the PAQ are largely or exclusively
restricted in content to two clusters of desirable personality traits, one cluster
describing self-assertive, instrumental characteristics stereotypically associated
with men and assigned to a separate masculine (M) scale, and the other cluster
describing interpersonally oriented, expressive characteristics stereotypically associated with women and assigned to a separate feminine (F) scale. Although the
two measures have almost completely replaced older tests in investigations of the
masculinity and femininity constructs, the treatment they have received at the hands
of most investigators still suffers from many of the same problems noted by
Constantinople (1973). Included among them is the equation of the terms masculinity and femininity with other gender-related concepts whose meanings often
remain equally unspecified. Added to the terms enumerated by Constantinople,
which we listed earlier, are sex-role orientation, sex typing, and gender schema.

Plan of the Chapter

In this chapter, we address some of the major theoretical and empirical issues posed
by previous research on masculinity and femininity using self-report instruments
and the implicit theoretical models about the organization of gender phenomena
that these instruments reflect. It is in these models and their underlying assumptions
that the meaning of the masculinity and femininity concepts on the part of
investigators are to be found.

We also present an alternative model that provides a better fit to the empirical
data and the preliminary results of a study designed to explore some of its
implications. Before taking up these topics, however, we must first distinguish
between empirical and theoretical usages of the terms masculine and feminine and
masculinity and femininity, and then describe the various alternative terms that
have been used to label the masculinity and femininity constructs.

EMPIRICAL VERSUS THEORETICAL USAGES

As dictionary definitions of the words masculine and feminine make clear, these
adjectives are frequently used as purely descriptive labels to identify the set of
observable phenomena that are, or are believed to be, associated with one gender
more than the other. These terms are typically employed by both psychologists and
lay persons without further explanation. It is assumed that context and a shared
knowledge of societal customs and stereotypes make their referents clear so that
elaboration is unnecessary. For example, we know that labeling occupations as

masculine or feminine signifies that they are dominated by men or by women or are generally thought to be more suitable for one gender than the other. When this year's fashion in women's clothing is described as feminine, we assume that the style is soft rather than tailored and emphasizes the curvaceousness of women's bodies.

As these examples illustrate, the assumption that the empirical referents of the words masculine and feminine do not need to be specified is often justified; that is, it would be possible to demonstrate consensus about what is being implied. But in many instances, there is ambiguity. For example, references often appear in the psychological literature to masculine and feminine personality traits, i.e., traits. But there are many clusters of masculine and feminine personality traits on which the average man and woman differ; some are considered to be socially desirable and others to be undesirable. For example, on self-report measures of conscientiousness, a desirable attribute, women often score higher than men; they also score higher on measures of anxiety, an undesirable attribute. Similarly, men more than women report themselves as being ambitious but also as being arrogant and self-centered. Furthermore, the trait dimensions within the masculine and the feminine categories are not necessarily strongly correlated with one another, if indeed they are correlated at all, and they often have different relationships with other variables. For example, anxiety and conscientiousness are essentially unrelated and have quite different sets of correlates. Unless the particular kinds of masculine and feminine traits and their properties have already been specified (e.g., the desirable instrumental and expressive traits assessed by a particular self-report measure such as the PAQ), the reference simply to masculine and feminine personality traits provides no meaningful information about which traits are under consideration. Even worse, these unqualified terms may falsely imply that it is theoretically or empirically useful to sweep all the traits on which men and women differ into two large categories, masculine and feminine.

In many instances, it is at least clear that the adjectives masculine and feminine are being used to indicate that concrete classes of psychological attributes and behaviors are gender linked (e.g., masculine traits, feminine occupations). There are other instances, however, in which these terms have—or appear to have—the status of theoretical constructs. That is, they refer to abstract properties residing within the person that transcend observable gender-differentiating phenomena.

Occasionally, the nouns "masculinity" and "femininity" are also used in a purely descriptive sense, most usually as a convenient label for identifying an entire class of gender-linked phenomena. A clear-cut example can be found in the dictionary of psychological terms prepared by English and English (1958). They define femininity as "the usual characteristics, *taken collectively*, of women" (p. 205; italics added). More often, however, masculinity and femininity appear to have the status of theoretical constructs. Oddly enough, the English and English definition of masculinity does not parallel that for femininity and is illustrative of a theoretical usage: "*state or condition* of an organism that manifests the characteristic appearance and behavior of a male" (p. 305, italics added). Other dictionaries of psychological terms also specify that masculinity and femininity refer to the quality or the nature of the male or the female sex. As we stated earlier, researchers conducting studies aimed at investigating masculinity and femininity rarely offer a formal definition of the terms. But their treatment makes it clear that they too regard gender-differentiating attributes and behaviors as diagnostic indicators of an underlying condition or quality.

One of our tasks in this chapter is to determine the assumptions that are being made about these abstract constructs and the implicit theoretical models of gender they reveal. Before considering these matters, however, it is necessary to consider briefly the meanings of other terms that have become associated in the psychological literature with the masculinity and femininity constructs.

SEX ROLES, TRAITS, AND OTHER CONSTRUCTS

Sex Roles

The term most commonly linked with the concepts of masculinity and femininity is sex- (or gender-) roles. The word role, which anthropologists, sociologists, and social psychologists have borrowed from the theater, is a general term with a number of components. More specifically, "sex roles" is a collective term referring to normative expectations that members of a given culture or subculture hold about the positions men and women should occupy. "Positions," in this context, stresses the division of labor between the genders within an organized social system, and the associated responsibilities, privileges, and status of the position within the hierarchical power structure of that system. Sex roles also refer to rules of interpersonal behaviors or to scripts, as Schank and Abelson (1977) have labeled them, in informal situations.

As sociologists (e.g., Angrist, 1969) have emphasized, there is not a single sex role. Rather, sex roles are multiple, being made up of sets and subsets. The particular constellations of sex roles that a person plays change over the life span. Furthermore, even within a given period, people may hold a variety of roles associated with gender. A married woman with young children, for example, may occupy the roles of wife, mother, sister, daughter, and daughter-in-law. Even within one of these specific roles, her responsibilities and expected behaviors are diverse. For example, in her role as mother, her actions are not the same in her interactions with her children's teachers, with members of the PTA, or with her children themselves. The latter interactions also vary according to such factors as the age and sex of the children or their physical health. People also occupy roles that are minimally, if at all, related to gender, for example, in their occupational lives. In short, whatever their sex, age, or social circumstances, people play multiple roles at any given period of time, roles that are variable in their demands, the status hierarchy in which they are embedded, the kinds of task responsibilities they entail, and the behavioral rules that govern interactions with particular others.

A pair of presumably complementary roles to which inordinate attention has been paid are those labeled instrumental and expressive. These terms were originally coined by Parsons and Bales (1955) to describe the kinds of behaviors that different people were observed to display in small-group interactions. Some participants assumed what Parsons and Bales called instrumental roles, that is, goal-oriented behaviors directly aimed at accomplishing the purposes of the group. Others assumed what Parsons and Bales described as expressive roles, that is, behaviors aimed at promoting group harmony and cooperation. Parsons (1955) further proposed that this pair of roles parallels those within the traditional family, women taking on expressive functions and men instrumental ones. This gender-linked role distinction, along with the implication that instrumental roles are both more highly valued and more powerful in this society than expressive ones, has taken on major significance in the hands of many investigators. In essence, the contrast between instrumental and expressive roles is often treated as an overall characterization or summary of the different sets of behavioral expectations for males and females. Although the instrumental–expressive distinction has some validity within the family setting, it vastly oversimplifies the complexity of the sex-role structure and the heterogeneous demands associated with particular gender-related roles, even within that limited setting. More specifically, it ignores the fact that within a given set of responsibilities assigned primarily to one gender (for example, child care), their successful accomplishment may require both instrumental and expressive behaviors.

Sex-Role Attitudes, Preferences, and Adoptions

Sex roles exist by virtue of societal consensus about what positions men and women ought to occupy and the behaviors they ought to display. However, especially in societies such as ours in which old sex-role distinctions are breaking down, public opinion about their legitimacy is not unanimous. Thus, people differ in their sex-role *attitudes*: their willingness to endorse conventional beliefs about activities that are more appropriate for one sex than the other. For example, some people believe that married women with young children should not work outside the home, leaving the breadwinner role to their husbands, whereas others disagree. People also differ in their personal *preferences*; for example, a women who believes that even women with small children have a right to work outside the home, may nonetheless prefer to stay at home with her own children. People also differ in their actual role *adoptions*, which may or may not be congruent with their own preferences and sex-role attitudes.

Personality Traits

The content of masculinity–femininity tests are typically diverse but most contain at least a sprinkling of personality traits among their items. The BSRI and PAQ, currently the most popular scales purportedly measuring masculinity and femininity, are almost entirely composed of items describing such traits.

Personality traits are ordinarily considered to be stable predispositions of a socio-affective nature (as opposed to various kinds of cognitive and motor abilities) that influence behavior over a fairly broad range of situations. When assessed by self-report measures, traits can be considered to be aspects of the self-concept. Many standardized self-report measures have been developed, some of them containing single scales devoted to assessing a single personality trait dimension, and others containing multiple scales aimed at assessing a variety of traits dimensions (e. g., instruments such as the California Personality Inventory or the Jackson Personality Research Form). The labels given to the scales on these instruments are typically designed to identify the specific personality attribute that the items are intended to measure. Thus we have self-report measures of such trait concepts as introversion–extroversion, anxiety, achievement motivation, irritability, and dominance, to name but a few. In many instances, the items on these personality inventories have face validity, that is, their content quite directly describes the personality trait being assessed and its concrete manifestations. These comments, of course, are quite standard, as indeed was our discussion of roles.

It would doubtlessly come as a shock to psychologists interested in personality (to say nothing of role theorists) if standardized personality tests were renamed as measures of roles or if well-known theories of personality were referred to as role theories. The Minnesota Multiphasic Role Inventory? Freud's role theory? Yet when the focus is on gender, a pernicious custom has grown up in psychology in which gender-related personality characteristics are identified as sex roles (Angrist, 1969). To cite only relatively recent examples, the term *sex role* is built into the title of Bem's instrument, and both the BSRI and the PAQ are typically identified as measures of sex-role identification or sex-role orientation, despite the fact that the items on these inventories refer to two classes of quite ordinary personality traits—traits such as assertive, independent, tactful, and kind—and have nothing to do with sex-role attitudes, preferences, or adoptions. As Sherif (1982) pungently observed in criticizing the confusion between socially defined sex roles and gender-related personality traits, people are not roles; they *occupy* roles.

It is beyond the scope of this chapter to trace the origins of this practice of equating gender-differentiating traits with sex roles but in some instances, the use of the term *sex role* as a label for traits has become a simple misnomer. In the contemporary literature involving the BSRI, PAQ, and other similar instruments, for example, it is sometimes apparent from a close reading of the text that the investigator using the sex-role term to describe these instruments intends it to refer only to the gender-related instrumental and expressive traits assessed by these instruments. However, the custom of calling traits roles is at best misleading. Not only are the empirical phenomena under consideration unclear, but the sex-role label invites the reader to read theoretical meanings into them that may or may not be intended. The practice is also unnecessary. Alternative labels that are both accurate and fairly concrete are readily available, for example, gender-related instrumental and expressive traits.

In most instances, however, describing personality inventories as sex-role measures reflects an implicit theory about the organization of gender-related phenomena in general. It is not a coincidence, for example, that the gender-differentiating personality dimensions to which the greatest theoretical and empirical attention has been paid, namely self-assertive, goal-oriented attributes associated with males and interpersonally oriented attributes associated with females have been identified as instrumental and expressive. The clear implication is that there is a causal link between the masculine instrumental and feminine expressive roles described by Parsons (1955) and masculine instrumental and feminine expressive traits. Instrumental and expressive roles, it is often implied, constitute complementary sets that capture the essential distinctions between the functions traditionally assigned to men and to women, whereas masculine instrumental and feminine expressive traits constitute the personal attributes that allow men and women to discharge effectively their particular role responsibilities. Frequently, the BSRI and PAQ are not merely labeled as sex-role measures but more elaborately, as measures of sex-role orientation or sex-role identification. Both terms may also reflect the presence of theoretical meanings. In fact, the sex-role identity concept antedates these personality measures and has been employed by a number of investigators interested in sex typing. The meaning of this and related concepts are considered below.

Sex-Role Identification and Related Concepts.

A number of theories have been proffered to explain the development in children of sex-typed characteristics and willingness to adopt the roles assigned to members of their sex (e.g., Block, 1973; Bussey, 1983; Hetherington & Frankie, 1967; Kohlberg, 1966; Langlois & Downs, 1980). Several of these theories, whose origins may be traced to Freudian psychoanalytic theory (Freud, 1927), specify that through the process of identification, children attempt to emulate or model themselves after their own sex or a particular representative of it (such as their same-sex parent). *Sex-role identification* is thus a dynamic concept that concerns the cognitive and motivational processes by which children and adults come to adopt the roles associated with their age and gender. One of the implications of theories employing the sex-role identification concept is that a similar set of processes are responsible not merely for role adoptions, but for the development and the maintenance of the full spectrum of desirable masculine and feminine characteristics, beliefs, and behaviors that men and women are expected to exhibit.

Theories of sex-role identification were initially advanced by developmental psychologists, independently of efforts to measure masculinity and femininity in older groups. The tacit theory embraced by investigators who equate the BSRI and PAQ and other self-report measures of masculinity and femininity in older adolescents and adults with strength of sex-role identification borrows the etiological and motivational features of the sex-role identification concept. That is, by referring to sex-role identification, investigators are implying the kinds of processes by which men and women have developed the abstract qualities of masculinity and femininity (or masculinity–femininity) that they currently manifest.

In contrast, *sex-role orientation* is a term of more recent origin, coming into fashion with the development of the BSRI and PAQ and used to describe these measures. Like sex-role identification, the legitimacy of the term is taken for granted and used without any attempt to justify it or to lay out the presumptions on which it is based. It appears to be a weaker, more static version of the identification concept that lacks its etiological features.

Still another concept that has recently arisen in research using the BSRI and PAQ is that of *gender schema*, one of many types of schemata investigated by cognitive psychologists. As a general proposition, the gender schema concept simply implies that individuals tend to organize and process information about themselves and people, objects, and events in the external world according to the gender, masculine and feminine, with which these stimuli are stereotypically associated. A more specific gender schema theory has been proposed by Bem (1981). According to her theory, individuals vary in the degree to which they employ gender schemata in organizing and evaluating information. Gender schema include gender self-concepts and acceptance of gender stereotypes and traditional ideologies. These individual differences appear early in life, presumably because of variations in strength of sex-role identification, and are responsible for the appearance of gender-linked personality patterns. Sex-typed persons (masculine men and feminine women), as assessed by the personality characteristics on the BSRI , are thus hypothesized to be more schematized than others.

Gender Identity

The final concept that we describe in this section is gender identity. Gender identity is a concept to which most psychologists have paid little attention, not because of any disagreement with it but because it is taken for granted. In contrast, the concept has a central place in the theoretical model we present below. For this reason, we describe it in some detail.

From birth on, one of the most salient characteristics of human beings is their biological sex. When a baby is born, the first announcement of the proud parents is likely to be, "It's a boy!" or, "It's a girl!" Similarly, "What is it?" is the first information that others seek about the newborn. Even as infants, males and females are likely to be dressed differently to make their sex more obvious; they are expected to exhibit different characteristics and are treated in ways that are congruent with these expectations, even when their behavior is in fact identical (e. g., Condry & Condry, 1976; Rubin, Provenzano, & Luria, 1974; Seavey, Katz, & Zalk, 1975). One can thus easily understand that by the age of two or two and a half, children almost universally are able not only to identify their own biological sex but also to identify the sex of other children and adults.

Children's recognition of their biological sex is almost invariably accompanied by the development of what has been called gender identity, a basic, existential sense and acceptance of themselves as male or female (Green, 1974). Gender identity thus becomes one of the earliest, most central, and most enduring aspects of people's self-concept. It emerges before children are linguistically competent and, we suggest, remains fundamentally ineffable—incapable of being put into words.

For the vast majority of children, gender identity is achieved both early and effortlessly. A small group of children exhibit disturbances in gender identity: They are unable to accept their biological sex, insisting that they are members of the other sex, or displaying strong cross-sex preferences in their dress and play activities. It is researchers concerned with these anomalies who have primarily paid attention to the topic of gender identity (e.g., Bates, Bentler, & Thompson, 1973; Green, 1974; Meyer-Bahlburg, 1993). Its generally nonproblematic nature (perhaps reinforced by the fact that, in common with others, investigators' own personal sense of gender identity remains unarticulated and unexamined) may have encouraged investigators interested in normal development to neglect the gender identity concept in favor of such concepts as sex-role identification.

THREE MODELS OF MASCULINITY AND FEMININITY

Having explicated these various conceptual issues, we are now ready to consider the major models of masculinity and femininity that have been entertained in psychological research.

Unifactorial Model

The implicit theory of masculinity and femininity that has dominated the thinking of lay persons and psychologists alike can be characterized as a unifactorial, bipolar model (Constantinople, 1973; Spence, 1985). According to this conception, all of the psychological characteristics that distinguish between the genders in a given society contribute to a single, underlying property, a bipolar continuum with masculinity at one extreme and femininity at the other. Every individual can be assigned a place on this continuum to indicate their degree of masculinity or femininity. Men, of course, are expected to cluster towards the masculine extreme and women are expected to cluster towards the feminine extreme. Reflecting these presumptions, early masculinity–femininity tests varied among themselves in content. Some were made up of a hodge-podge of items describing such thing as roles, traits, and leisure interests, whereas others were more limited in empirical content. Further, items were drawn from various sources, more on the basis of convenience than on the basis of an a priori rationale (Constantinople, 1973). The primary criterion for item selection was an item's capacity to distinguish between the responses of males and females, item content being relatively unimportant. The implicit rationale justifying this procedure was that the general class of traits, interests, attitudes, and behaviors empirically distinguishing between men and women contribute to a single factor in both sexes that could be detected by appropriate statistical analysis. If this assumption is correct, then the content of the particular items chosen from the potential universe of items is of little importance, as is the heterogeneity of content within and between various inventories designed to measure the masculinity–femininity construct.

It was also typically assumed that men and women who did not score close to the gender-appropriate pole suffered from some kind of emotional problem or a disturbance in their sexual orientation. The latter assumption was made explicit in the construction of one well-known measure, the Mf scale on the Minnesota Multiphasic Personality Inventory (MMPI; Hathaway & McKinley, 1943). A criterion for item selection, in addition to the requirement that each item distinguish between men and women, was the item's capacity to distinguish between the responses of homosexual and heterosexual men. Homosexuality in men was thus presumed to be detectable by a large number of "feminine" responses. However, in the last revision of the MMPI, this claim for the Mf scale was abandoned and the only criterion for item inclusion was the distinction between the responses of men and women (Green, 1991).

As we have already described, the BSRI (Bem, 1974) and the PAQ (Spence & Helmreich; Spence et al., 1974, 1975), two similar but independently developed instruments, appeared in the mid 1970s and captured the imagination of the growing number of investigators interested in gender. These questionnaires differ from previous inventories in being largely or wholly confined to the measurement of desirable instrumental and expressive personality traits that stereotypically distinguish between men and women. Further, the two sets of trait items are divided into separate scales, typically identified as measures of masculinity and femininity. The decision to use these labels for the BSRI and PAQ is a theoretical one, reflecting an acceptance of a unifactorial, bipolar model or of the two-factor model, described later.

As an aside, we should note at this point that the theoretical model we espouse rejects the premises on which the masculinity and femininity appellations are based. The more appropriate labels for the PAQ scales, we assert, are Instrumental (I) and Expressive (E); these terms are both empirically accurate and without unwanted theoretical overtones. Naming the BSRI scales is more problematic. Although most of the items describe desirable instrumental and expressive traits, the BSRI also includes other kinds of items (See Spence, 1991). In the present chapter, we have adopted the relatively neutral labels of M and F for scales on the BSRI. We also use M and F when we refer jointly to the scales on both instruments.

In contrast to the theoretical position we have taken, Bem (1974, 1981), along with many other investigators, accepts the validity of the equation between the masculinity and femininity constructs and scores on at least the BSRI. In her initial presentation of the BSRI, Bem (1974) made the then radical claim that contrary to the usual presumption, masculinity and femininity (and its concrete manifestations such as instrumental and expressive personality characteristics) are not psychological opposites. Rather, men and women not only could be both masculine and feminine (androgynous), but substantial numbers of both sexes actually are both masculine and feminine. Thus, for example, being expressive does not preclude being instrumental and vice versa; many members of both sexes possess both sets of attributes.

Bem was explicit in placing this psychological theory in an ideological framework: Her goal, she acknowledged, was to promote an egalitarian society in which gender distinctions were reduced to a minimum and men and women shared equally the roles and the characteristics currently associated with one gender to a greater degree than the other. If this goal is to be achieved, it is necessary to demonstrate that masculinity and femininity are not opposites but can and do coexist.

It has seldom been recognized that in advancing these contentions, Bem was making two incompatible arguments. The first was that masculinity and femininity are independent. Data from both the BSRI and the PAQ (e.g., Bem, 1974; Spence & Helmreich, 1978; Spence et al., 1975) showing that the two scales of each of these instruments are essentially uncorrelated in both men and women appear to confirm this assertion. The second, implicit, proposition was based on the contrary presumption that masculinity and femininity do indeed constitute a single bipolar continuum. Unlike previous investigators, however, Bem called attention to the men and women at the center of the hypothetical masculinity–femininity continuum, those she currently calls non-sex-typed or gender schematic (e. g., Bem, 1981).[2] Also in opposition to prior beliefs, she further contended that lack of sex-typing is more desirable in a number of respects than sex-typing, an argument very much in tune with the rising feminist movement. Bem's version of the bipolar unifactorial model has guided her subsequent theoretical and empirical contributions and has been adopted by a number of other investigators.

The hypothetical masculinity–femininity continuum is essentially a static conception of the organization of gender-related characteristics. As we discussed earlier, association of the concept of sex-role identification with inventories purportedly measuring the masculinity–femininity construct implies the processes by which males high in masculinity and females high in femininity acquire and maintain the attributes and behaviors associated with their gender. Those who are strong in their sex-role identification, it is presumed, engage in an active, though not necessarily conscious, effort to shape themselves in their characteristics, attitudes, and role behaviors to resemble the expected member of their own age and sex, as defined by their culture or subculture. Although this may be the intent of Bem (1974) and others in using sex-role identification to describe what the BSRI and other similar inventories measure, these developmental implications have not been spelled out and are essentially ignored by most investigators.

---

[2]This presumption was implied by Bem's initial procedure of combining the scores from the M and F scales into a single score for each respondent by subtracting one from the other, thus reconstructing a single bipolar dimension. Spence et al. (1975) called attention to the fact that those at the middle of the difference-score distribution are equal in their M and F scores and demonstrated that those scoring high in both differ in significant ways from those low in both. Bem (1977) therefore adopted their suggestion that those scoring high on both scales (androgynous respondents) be treated separately from those scoring low on both scales (undifferentiated respondents). However, she has continued to embrace a bipolar masculinity–femininity model. In this model, both androgynous and undifferentiated men and women are assumed to be gender aschematic and non-sex-typed. As such, these two groups are predicted to be equal to one another and lower than sex-typed persons (masculine men and feminine women) in their endorsement of conventional gender ideologies and their display of other gender-linked characteristics.

The term *sex-role orientation*, which arose as a label for the BSRI and PAQ, is even further shorn of dynamic meanings, serving simply as a rather empty alternative to the terms masculinity and femininity in describing what these questionnaires purportedly measure. In fact, reference to sex-role orientation almost always occurs in conjunction with these instruments.

Two-Factor Model

Prior to the mid 1970s, occasional investigators proposed that masculinity and femininity constitute two independent continua (e.g., Jenkin & Vroegh, 1969). This proposition was essentially ignored until the appearance of the BSRI and PAQ. Studies with each of these instruments have consistently shown that their two gender-linked scales differentiate between men and women in the expected direction (e.g., Bem, 1974; Pedhazur & Tetenbaum, 1979; Spence & Helmreich, 1978; Spence et al., 1975). However, they have also shown that scores on the two scales of each instrument are nonsignificantly correlated. These findings have also been found in elementary school children responding to simpler versions of these instruments (e.g., Boldizar, 1991; Hall & Halberstadt, 1980; Simms et al., 1978; Spence & Hall, 1993). In response to these results, a number of commentators have continued to endorse the global concepts of masculinity and femininity but interpret the data as indicating that masculinity and femininity constitute two unrelated dimensions rather than a single bipolar one. Statements to this effect are quite common in psychology textbooks and other secondary sources.

The claim that masculinity and femininity are two independent constructs implies that all of the attributes and behaviors stereotypically associated with men contribute to a single factor and that all of the attributes and behaviors stereotypically associated with women contribute to another, orthogonal factor. Few researchers have explicitly rejected the unifactorial bipolar model in favor of this two-factor model but the approach of a number of investigators is based on the assumption that masculinity and femininity are independent. That is, after analyzing the separate contributions of the M and F scales to some criterion variable and finding that they are not the same, they draw separate conclusions about the properties of the abstract concepts of masculinity and femininity.[3] This approach is particularly marked in the large number of studies that have been aimed at investigating the

---

[3]Since abandoning the difference-score method of combining M and F scores, Bem and her colleagues in their laboratory experiments have adopted the procedure of preselecting participants to represent the four high -low score profiles on the BSRI (masculine: high M, low F; feminine: low M, high F; androgynous: high M, high F; and undifferentiated: low M, low F). The rationale for this preselection procedure appears to be based on practical considerations and has no theoretical basis.

Instead of preselecting subjects, some investigators use unselected groups with respect to their M and F scores. Under these circumstances, scores on the M and F scales should be treated as continuous and the relationships between the scores and the dependent variable analyzed by regression or other correlational techniques. Unfortunately, for purposes of data analysis, investigators often divide subjects into the four categorical groups post hoc under the mistaken impression that this is a theoretical requirement.

relationships between the M and F scales on the PAQ and BSRI and measures of self-esteem and mental health. Typically, M scores but not F scores are found to be related to these outcome variables. (See, for example, the meta-analytic study of Whitley, 1983). These results are usually interpreted as demonstrating the benefits, not of instrumental personality traits as opposed to expressive traits, but of masculinity as opposed to femininity. In fact, they have sometimes been cited as support for a "masculinity model" of self-esteem.

Current Status of the Bipolar and Two-Factor Models. At the present time, the majority of investigators either implicitly accept the bipolar unifactorial model of masculinity and femininity or simultaneously appear to accept both this and the two-factor model, failing to distinguish between the two theories and to recognize their fundamental incompatibility. When the total body of relevant evidence is considered, however, the data support neither perspective. Nor do they support the presumptions on which each theory is predicated. Instead the many types of observable differences between men and women have been shown to contribute to multiple factors with varying relationships to one another. For example, factor analyses of masculinity–femininity tests of diverse empirical content consistently reveal the presence of a number of factors that are not necessarily the same from one test to another; furthermore, the tests as a whole are not always significantly correlated with one another or with the BSRI or PAQ (e.g., Bernard, 1984; Lunneborg, 1972; Wakefield, Sasek, Friedman, & Bowden, 1976). As a further example, although the desirable instrumental traits and the desirable expressive traits that go to make up the PAQ I and E scales are each unifactorial (e.g., Cota & Fekken, 1988; Helmreich, Spence, & Wilhelm, 1981), the two scales are uncorrelated with each other. In contrast, the BSRI has repeatedly been shown to be multifactorial, due largely to the presence of other kinds of items in additional to desirable instrumental and expressive items (e.g., Pedhazur & Tetenbaum, 1979).

A theoretically important finding is that, despite the nonsignificant correlation between the BSRI M and F scales as a whole in both sexes, significantly negative correlations in both sexes appear between self-ratings on the adjectives masculine feminine, items found on the BSRI M and F scales, respectively (Pedhazur & Tetenbaum, 1979; Spence, 1993; Storms, 1979). A particularly intriguing finding is that self-ratings on these two adjectives tend to be significantly correlated with measures of sex-role attitudes, whereas responses to the instrumental and expressive trait items on the BSRI and PAQ do not (Spence, 1993).

Data disconfirming any simple structural model of gender phenomena had been available well before the current wave of enthusiasm about gender-oriented research and have been accumulating since that time. The continued popularity of the bipolar model, in particular, even in the face of the evidence, undoubtedly has a number of causes. These include the appeal of any simple theory that promises to explain a broad range of phenomena as well as the capacity of the model to fit into the reigning gender ideology of the time (sex typing as desirable in the prefeminist era, non-sex-typing as both possible and desirable in feminist times).

Relatedly, the current preeminence of the BSRI and the PAQ in investigations of masculinity and femininity reflects the role assigned to certain personality dimensions in understanding the fundamental distinction between the sexes. These have been identified as instrumentality and expressiveness and other similar dimensions such as agency and communion (Bakan, 1966) and individualism and collectivism (e.g., Josephs, Markus, & Tafarodi, 1992). These distinctions are, in turn, presumed to be central to masculinity and femininity. But the major contributor to the continued popularity of these simple and sovereign theories of gender may be acceptance of the masculinity and femininity concepts as intuitively real, and simultaneously, the failure to articulate their meanings. This state of affairs may have discouraged critical examination of theories utilizing these monolithic concepts and the presumptions on which they are founded.

Multifactorial Gender Identity Theory

Although the two theoretical models we have just described remain the most common, the multifactorial perspective is slowly gaining adherents as investigators begin to measure independently various categories of observable gender-related characteristics and beliefs and to explore their correlations (e. g., Ashmore, 1990; Downs & Langlois, 1988; Marsh & Byrne, 1991; Orlofsky, 1981; Signorella,1992; Spence & Hall, 1993; Spence & Helmreich, 1978). The relationships are highly variable in degree and direction, but overall there is substantial independence among the various categories within each gender. These data imply that men and women rarely manifest all or even most of the attributes and behaviors associated with their gender. This is true even among those who endorse conventional sex-role attitudes. Thus, the particular constellations of gender-congruent and gender-incongruent characteristics, attitudes, and behaviors that individual men and women display (or fail to display) are diverse; consequently, one can not necessarily use one kind of information about a person to make inferences about his or her standing on another. For example, knowing that a person (man or woman) enjoys cooking tells us little about how much the person likes or dislikes studying math.

Building on the evidence supporting the multifactorial approach, one of us has advanced a theory of gender that focuses on the concept of gender identity (Spence, 1985). Gender identity, we have said, is a basic psychological sense of maleness or femaleness that almost all children develop early in life, an identity that is a central and enduring part of their self-concept. As they mature, children also gain increasing knowledge of their society's gender stereotypes and behavioral expectations and of the different roles played by men and women. Early in life, in an attempt to confirm their emerging sense of gender identity, children typically attempt to adopt the most visible badges of their sex: to dress in the "right" kind of clothes and to play with the "right" kind of toys. But, we assert, children's sense of gender identity does not impel them to adopt all of the behavioral standards for their gender set by society at large or to attempt to mold themselves to fit the stereotypes. The models in children's social environment—peers, older siblings, parents and other significant adults, to say nothing of figures on TV and other media—differ in the degree or the specific ways that they resemble societal stereotypes. The gender-related values and behavioral expectations that parents and other influential adults hold out to children are variable. Furthermore, children differ in their temperaments and their abilities, a function of both experiential and genetic factors (e.g., Mitchell, Baker, & Jacklin, 1989). Consequently, within each sex at any given developmental stage, gender-related phenomena contribute to multiple classes that are not necessarily correlated and have different relationships with one another. At the same time, most adults and children display sufficient numbers of gender-related characteristics and behaviors to make them quite unexceptional members of their gender in their own eyes and in the eyes of others.

According to our theory, by middle childhood, gender identity ceases to have a major role in the development and maintenance of attributes and behaviors that meet societal standards. Other variables, ranging from genetically influenced temperamental factors to systems of ideological beliefs, take over this function. Yet people's gender identity not only endures but also remains central to their sense of self. Social-psychological theories have proposed that people strive to maintain self-consistency and to evaluate themselves positively by emphasizing their desirable characteristics (e.g., Tesser, 1988). In line with these theories, we postulate that, independent of how their characteristics have been acquired, people use the gender-appropriate attributes and behaviors that they happen to possess and the roles that they occupy to define and to protect their gender identity. Similarly, people discount the importance of those gender-congruent characteristics they fail to possess and dismiss the relevance of cross-sex characteristics they actually do possess.

Loss of valued roles or attributes, or even a general lack of self-esteem, may lead men and women to question their sense of adequacy as males or females. For example, a man who loses his job and must rely on his wife's earnings to support his family may experience a threat to his masculinity, whereas a wife whose husband leaves her for a younger woman may experience a threat to her femininity. In response to such events, people respond in various ways in an attempt to restore their feelings of self-worth as males or females; rarely, however, do they question their basic gender identity, let alone try to change it. Gender identity itself remains stable.

For most heterosexuals, sexuality and sexual orientation are extremely important in verifying their own sense of gender identity and are typically important in defining it in others. Adolescence may therefore be a particularly troublesome period as boys attempt to establish their sexual potency and girls attempt to become attractive to members of the other sex. Teenagers, especially males, who are coming to recognize their own homosexuality are likely to experience a good deal of distress and may even question their gender identity. This is particularly likely in the case of boys whose characteristics are considered effeminate or who otherwise stand out in others' eyes as unrepresentative of their gender. However, unlike transsexuals who report that they feel that they are members of one sex trapped in the opposite-sex body, the large majority of homosexuals do not wish to become a member of the other sex and appear to have an appropriate gender identity (Hooker, 1965). Gays and lesbians who are able to acknowledge their own sexual preferences and to establish—or reestablish—their self-esteem and their confidence in their gender identity typically do so by dismissing the negative implications of their same-sex sexual orientation and any cross-sex characteristics they happen to display. They find verification of their gender identity elsewhere.

In summary, the theory we have just outlined basically proposes that gender-related phenomena fall into multiple categories of traits, behaviors, and attitudes whose etiologies are complex and, within each gender, vary from one individual to the next. The result is that men and women are highly variable in the particular patterns of gender congruent and incongruent attributes and behaviors they display, as well as in their gender ideologies. Yet at the same time, the large majority of men and women maintain an unambiguous and stable sense of their own gender identity, their unarticulated existential sense of maleness or femaleness. People verify and defend their personal sense of gender identity by means of the particular sets of gender congruent characteristics they possess, particularly those they consider important.

AN EXPLORATORY STUDY

This multifactorial gender identity theory fits existing data fairly well, certainly better than other major models of the organization of gender phenomena that have been offered. The implications of the theory, however, are just beginning to be investigated in a systematic way. As a start toward filling in some of the gaps, we have recently initiated a study of male and female college students designed to explore a number of the theory's facets.

One major purpose of the study is to gather data on the relationships between several measures of sex-role attitudes and gender stereotypes and measures of a number of other self-reported personal characteristics that differentiate men and women. Included among the latter are the instrumental and expressive traits on the PAQ (Spence & Helmreich, 1978). We anticipated that as suggested by previous research (Spence et al., 1975; Deaux & Lewis, 1984), measures of gender stereotypes and role attitudes would be significantly correlated but that the magnitude of the relationships would be relatively modest. We also expected that the relationships between the measures making up the second set, those assessing other kinds of personal characteristics, would not form any simple, coherent pattern related to gender. Rather the measures would be correlated with one another to the extent that they tapped similar underlying characteristics and properties of a fairly concrete nature. For example, masculine reading preferences and recreational interests might be significantly related to one another but not to self-ratings of masculine abilities. We also predicted that few, if any, significant relationships would occur across the two categories of measures, gender beliefs and gender-related characteristics. Even more specifically, we predicted that contrary to many theories of gender that put a heavy explanatory burden on instrumental and expressive traits, these personality dimensions would not be correlated with measures of gender ideology (Spence, 1993). Within each sex, these traits might be related, however, to other characteristics and self-views that are influenced by these trait dimensions per se. Feelings of self-esteem and self-efficacy are one example. In short, various relationships should appear among the measures, based on properties of the specific characteristics being assessed. Confirmation of these predictions, all of which follow from the multifactorial approach to gender, would add considerable support to this aspect of our theory.

In addition, we are employing three measures that directly assess gender self-concepts. Two of these represent attempts to tap gender identity. We have asserted that for the large majority of males and females for whom it has never been problematic, gender identity is a primitive, unarticulated sense; as such, it may not be possible to assess by means of self-report. Consequently, direct tests of this aspect of the theory may also be impossible to conduct. However, approximate measures of gender identity might be possible to devise. To the extent that our attempts to assess gender identity were successful, we would expect that scores for each sex would cluster at one extreme and that within-group variability would be small.

The third measure asks participants to rate themselves on the adjective masculine and on the adjective feminine. In line with the results of previous studies, we anticipated that the ratings on these two items would be negatively related but only modestly so. We are interested in exploring the relationships of the masculine and feminine self-ratings (and scores on the two gender identity measures) with the two other sets of self-report instruments, gender-related beliefs and personal characteristics.

According to our theory, gender identity at the level of the individual should be associated with the particular gender-related characteristics and beliefs the person values and actually possesses. Although the constellations of attributes people use to protect and maintain their sense of gender identity are variable, the specific characteristics and beliefs making up these constellations tend to be drawn from a common pool about which there is societal agreement. It follows from our theory that at the level of a group of men or women, no single attribute or belief would be strongly associated with our gender measures but that small correlations with these measures would be found across a broad array of gender-related attitudes and attributes.

The measures included in our study, all of them objectively scored self-report instruments, are briefly described below. We also present the results of preliminary analyses, based on the data obtained from the male and female college students we have tested so far.

Self-Report Battery

The various measures are contained in survey booklets, one version for women and another for men. The items on each of the measures are accompanied by a 5-point rating scale. The labels on the points of these rating scales, however, are not always the same for every item within or between measures.

Gender Measures

As one attempt to obtain an approximate measure of gender identity as we define it, we are using a 19-item questionnaire adopted from an inventory designed by

Steven Finn (personal communication, May 1992) and labeled as a measure of gender identity. Finn's primary purpose in developing this instrument was to assess men with an uncertain or a cross-sex gender identity. Using his original scale, Finn found that the scores of a group of transsexuals being evaluated as candidates for a male-to-female sex-change operation strongly clustered at one end of the score distribution whereas men who reported themselves as exclusively heterosexual clustered at the other end. The score distribution for heterosexual men, however, was heavily skewed and had a long tail. Finn also reported that the distribution of men who identified themselves as exclusively or primarily homosexual had a mean that was close to the center of the range of possible scores, with the tails of the distribution overlapping the distribution of scores of heterosexuals at one end and the distribution of scores of transsexuals at the other.

In our version, given to males, several of Finn's items were dropped and several items referring to gender-congruent characteristics were added so that positively worded items would sometimes refer to the possession of masculine characteristics. The majority of items, however, described such things as having feminine characteristics or appearance, feeling different from other men, preferring to play with girls as a child, and having sexual fantasies about being a woman. One item referred to having considered a sex change operation. We also developed a female version whose items parallel those for men. (These male and female gender identity questionnaires are hereafter referred to as Finn.)

A second measure consists of a single item (hereafter referred to as Gender Identity) in which respondents are instructed to rate the strength of their feelings of maleness or femaleness, or gender identity, independently of how much they resemble conventional gender stereotypes in their behaviors and attributes. Slightly different rating scales are used for men and women. For women, the scale runs from *Strong feminine identity* through *Neither* to *More masculine than feminine identity*. For men, the scale interchanges the words *masculine* and *feminine*.

A third measure of gender self-concept consists of ratings on the adjectives masculine and feminine, each of which we anticipated would tap a number of meanings in addition to gender identity. These adjectives were added to the list of items contained on the PAQ Instrumental and Expressive scales. The endpoints of the 5-point rating scale accompanying the masculine item are labeled *Very masculine* and *Not at all masculine*. For the feminine item, the labels are *Very feminine* and *Not at all feminine*.

We refer to this set of questionnaires, the Finn measure of gender identity, the single-item Gender Identity measure, and the adjectives Masculine and Feminine, collectively as *gender measures*.

Measures of Gender Stereotypes and Ideology

The Rules Questionnaire, adopted from Frable (1989), is being used as a relatively non-obtrusive measure of gender-role beliefs. Each item on the questionnaire presents a brief vignette in which a conventional rule (in most instances, related to gender) is being violated. Each vignette is followed by a statement of the rule (e.g., "Jeannie should not join the uncles in telling risque stories."). Two questions accompany each item, one asking how fair the rule is and the other whether it should be changed. (Correlations between the two responses are extremely high and are combined.) Only the gender items are scored.

Two stereotype measures are being administered, one assessing descriptive trait stereotypes and the other assessing prescriptive occupational stereotypes. In the trait measure, 20 desirable personality traits drawn from the BSRI (Bem, 1974) are presented: 8 expressive, 8 instrumental, and 4 gender neutral. Each trait is rated on a scale whose endpoints are labeled *Typical man much more* and *Typical woman much more*; the midpoint is labeled *Sexes equal*. In the second measure, 18 occupations are listed, divided equally into those associated with men, those associated with women, and gender neutral. Respondents are asked to indicate who ought to do each of the jobs on a scale ranging from *Only men*, through *Both equally*, to *Only women*.

Personal Characteristics

Included among this set of questionnaires are measures of reading preferences and recreational interests, each divided into items that are masculine, feminine, and gender neutral. Respondents are asked to indicate how much they like or dislike the reading material or recreational interest each item describes. Another questionnaire lists various activities, masculine, feminine, and neutral, and asks respondents to indicate how skilled they think they are or, with experience could be, in each one. Respondents are also presented with the instrumental and expressive scales on the PAQ.

The last questionnaire in the survey booklet (different versions for males and females) contains several sets of items (scored separately). These items inquire about the respondents' perceptions of their physical attractiveness (Appearance), the attention they pay to how they dress (Clothes), and in the case of males, how much they like athletics (Athletics). Finally, a set of items is included that addresses their interest in sex and in family roles (marriage, children). The last item in this questionnaire, which is separately scored, asks about the respondents' preference for romantic or sexual partners on a scale ranging from exclusively same sex to exclusively other sex.

Only data from the respondents who indicated that their sexual orientation was exclusively heterosexual are reported here (75 men, 94 women). Within the sample tested to date, the absolute numbers of women and men who chose any alternative other than exclusively same sex were too small to make separate analyses feasible.

Preliminary Results

Our preliminary analyses of the data consist primarily of correlations between the measures within each sex. We present only the highlights of these analyses here. We make no reference to gender differences on the several measures that are common to both men and women but it should be understood that, in each case where gender differences were expected, a comparison of the means revealed significant differences. We warn the reader in advance that our theory did not lead us to expect a coherent set of results that would be easy to summarize; in this respect, the data we are obtaining in this exploratory study have not disappointed us. They point the direction, however, to further analyses and to further studies. In presenting the results, we describe first the relationships within each set of measures.

Gender Measures

Especially on the Finn measure of gender identity and on the single Gender Identity item, the scores of both men and women piled up towards the gender-congruent end of the scale. There was, nonetheless, a fair amount of variability within each sex on each of the measures. These characteristics are reflected in the descriptive statistics reported for each measure at the right of Table 5.1.

The correlations between the several gender measures for men and for women are also shown in Table 5.1. Except for the relationship between the Gender Identity and the Feminine item for men, all the correlations were significant but were only of moderate size. These results suggest that the determinants of the several measures of gender self-perceptions overlap but are not identical.

Measures of Gender Ideology

Masculine and feminine occupational stereotypes were substantially correlated (r of .76 and .75 for men and women, respectively) and were similarly correlated with other variables. For purposes of data reduction, they were therefore combined to form a single occupational stereotypes measure. Masculine and feminine trait stereotypes were also significantly related but the r's were notably lower than in the case of occupations (r's of .47 and .25 for men and women, respectively) and were therefore not combined.

The two trait stereotype measures were nonsignificantly related to responses to the Rules Questionnaire but all other comparisons yielded significant correlations of moderate magnitude (r in the .30s and .40s for both sexes). We conclude that although these various gender-related beliefs might turn out to contribute to a single higher order factor, there would be substantial independence between its various components.

Measures of Personal Characteristics

The pattern of relationships with these variables can be broken down into three sets: those involving the PAQ scales; those involving abilities, interests, and reading preferences; and those involving the remaining measures. Because of the special attention paid to instrumental and expressive traits, the data from these scales are reported in more detail at a later point.

In women, the correlations between masculine abilities, interests, and reading preferences were all significant, as were the correlations between feminine abili-

TABLE 5.1
Mean, Standard Deviation, and Range for Each Sex on the Gender Measures and the Correlations Between the Measures

					Description Statistics						
	Correlations				Men			Women			
	Finn	GI	Masc	Fem	Mean	SD	R	Mean	SD	R	
Finn	–	61	−53	49	83.92	7.84	57–95	81.90	9.13	44–95	
GI	40	–	−41	43	4.04	0.83	2–5	4.33	0.82	1–5	
Masc	33	34	–	−45	3.75	0.90	1–5	2.00	0.93	1–4	
Fem	−53	−14	−30	–	1.73	0.76	1–4	4.02	0.77	1–5	

Note. Finn = Finn Gender Identity Questionnaire; GI = single Gender Identity item; Masc = adjective masculine; Fem = adjective feminine. High scores indicate gender-congruent responding on the Finn and GI measures and higher rating on the adjectives masculine and feminine. Women are above the diagonal and men are below. Decimals are omitted. For men: $r_{.05} = 22$ and $r_{.01} = 29$. For women: $r_{.05} = 20$ and $r_{.01} = 26$.

127

ties, interests, and reading preferences (r's ranging from .34 to .66). These results might seem to suggest the operation of a masculine factor and a feminine factor that encompasses abilities, reading preferences, and recreational interests. However, within each of the pairs of masculine and feminine ratings, the correlations were also positive. The relationship between masculine and feminine abilities was particularly high ($r = .44$). These latter findings, the abilities outcome in particular, suggests the operation of a general activity or self-confidence factor that to some degree transcends the link of the items with gender. These results were not unique to women: The pattern of results obtained from men were comparable in all respects. For example, the correlation between masculine and feminine abilities was .50.

In women, none of this set of measures (abilities, interests, reading preferences) was significantly related to the remaining scales, that is, those addressed to sex and romantic attachments, physical appearance, and interest in dressing attractively. The latter scales, however, were all modestly but significantly correlated with one another in a positive direction. In men, sex and romantic attachments, physical appearance, and interest in athletics were also modestly related to one another, but interest in clothes was not. Several other significant correlations, all positive in sign, were also found in men: physical attractiveness was related to both masculine and feminine abilities, and interest in sex and romance was related to masculine interests.

We turn next to the correlations between the gender measures and the other two sets of questionnaires.

Relationships Between the Gender Measures and the Other Measures

Correlations with the Gender Ideology Measures.   The values of the correlations of the several gender measures with the Rules Questionnaire and the two stereotype measures (instrumental and expressive traits, occupations) are shown in Table 5.2. Inspection of the table indicates that a number of significant but modestly sized correlations emerged. The findings are not easy to summarize, especially since the results from women and men differed in several respects. Several patterns, however, are worthy of note. In both sexes, the Finn measure was significantly correlated with endorsement of conventional rules of behavior (Rules Questionnaire) and occupational stereotypes, two measures concerned with gender roles. The same was true for the Gender Identity item, except for occupational stereotypes in men.

The most interesting set of findings, however, involved self-ratings on the adjectives masculine and feminine. Women who rated themselves as masculine tended to reject conventional rules, trait stereotypes, and occupational stereotypes. (All r's but that for masculine traits were significant). Conversely, women who scored high on the adjective feminine were more likely to endorse feminine trait stereotypes and occupational stereotypes. A pattern that was approximately the mirror image of these findings occurred in men. Here it was men rating

TABLE 5.2

Correlations Between the Gender Measures and the Measures of Gender-Role Attitudes and Beliefs

	Women				Men			
	Finn	*GI*	*Masc*	*Fem*	*Finn*	*GI*	*Masc*	*Fem*
Rules	25*	23*	− 22*	08	48	21*	14	− 39
Trait St								
Masc I	16	01	− 10	05	− 05	− 04	− 03	− 28
Fem E	37**	07	− 39**	36**	− 02	− 01	18	− 07
Occup St								
Masc + Fem	34**	20*	− 27*	27*	28**	− 03	10	− 30

Note. Rules = Rules Questionnaire; Trait St = Trait Stereotypes, Masc I = Masculine Instrumental, Fem E = Feminine Expressive; Occup St = Occupational Stereotypes, Masc + Fem = masculine and feminine combined. Decimals are omitted. High scores on the gender ideology measures and on the Finn and GI measures indicate more conventional or gender congruent responses. High scores on the adjectives masculine and feminine indicate higher endorsement.

*p ≤ .05. **p ≤ .01.

themselves high on the adjective feminine who rejected conventional rules, masculine trait stereotypes, and occupational stereotypes. Men's self-ratings on the adjective masculine, however, were not significantly related to any of the belief measures.

It is tempting to interpret these data as indicating that "masculine" women and "feminine" men are less committed to conventional beliefs about men and women than others. It is, in fact, the type of conclusion that is frequently reached in this area of research. However, this interpretation presumes, a priori, that self-ratings on these gender adjectives reflect some quality or series of qualities that are different from conventional gender-related beliefs in the same sense, for example, that a measure of academic aspirations is not the same thing as a measure of academic achievement. Not only can it not be assumed that self-ratings on these adjectives are independent of gender beliefs but our theoretical position suggests that it may be otherwise. People's scores on these gender adjectives, we suggest, represent peoples' summary judgments about themselves. Thus it is possible that, among a group of men and women, gender beliefs are one of the factors that contribute to these summary judgments. If this were the case, then a correlation between the summary judgment and each of its components would automatically follow. The challenge is to distinguish between these two possibilities: gender beliefs as one of the contributors to people's global rating of being masculine or feminine versus people's self-perceptions of being masculine or feminine as independent of gender beliefs but as causally linked, one leading to the other.

Correlations with Other Personal Characteristics. The relationships between the gender measures and the measures of personal characteristics are shown in Table 5.3. Because of the large number of measures and the relatively few correlations of any magnitude that were found, only significant values ($p < .05$) are reported in the table. Attention is called to several findings. First, more

TABLE 5.3

Correlations Between the Four Gender Measures and Measures
of Other Personal Characteristics

	Women				Men			
	Finn	*GI*	*Masc*	*Fem*	*Finn*	*GI*	*Masc*	*Fem*
Abil Masc		28				26		−24
Fem	27	30	27	28		29	28	
Inter Masc								
Fem					−25			23
Read Masc						22		−30
Fem	31	22	−30					
Sex/Rom	30	21				37	31	
Appear				23		25	30	
Clothes	53	29	−24	30		−26	−35	
Athletics	−	−	−	−	26		37	
PAQI		29				32		
PAQE								

Note. Finn = Finn Gender Identity Questionnaire; GI = single Gender Identity item; Masc = adjective masculine; Fem = adjective feminine. Rules = Rules Questionnaire; Trait St = Trait Stereotypes, Masc I = Masculine Instrumental, Fem E = Feminine Expressive; Occup St = Occupational Stereotypes, Masc + Fem = masculine and feminine combined. Only *r*s with $p \leq .05$ are reported. Decimals are omitted.

significant correlations were found with the Gender Identity item than with the other gender measures. Second, significant positive correlations were found between the Gender Identity item and self-reports of masculine and feminine abilities and instrumental traits on the PAQ not only in men but also in women. The finding that women with higher gender-congruent scores on the Gender Identify item are also higher on traits identified as masculine is quite contrary to usual views of gender.

Finally, women who paid attention to their dress tended to rate themselves higher on the two gender identity measures and the adjective feminine, as we had anticipated. The correlation with the adjective masculine, however, was significantly negative, a plausible outcome. Conversely, men who admitted to paying attention to their clothes tended to score lower on the Gender Identity and masculine items (*r*'s of −.26 and −.35, respectively). These findings again suggest the complex meanings that accrue to our gender measures.

Relationships with Instrumental and Expressive Traits. We have already noted that the PAQ Instrumental scale was significantly related to the Gender Identity measure in both men and women, as reported in Table 5.2. This was the only significant finding involving the gender measures and the two PAQ scales. The PAQ scales also failed to be significantly related to the set of measures tapping gender ideology, a result confirming the outcomes of previous studies (e.g., Spence, 1993; Spence & Hall, 1993; Spence et al., 1975). However, inspection of the correlations between the PAQ scales and other personal characteristics, shown in

Table 5.4, reveals an interesting pattern of relationships. In both sexes, higher scores on the PAQ Instrumental scale were significantly associated with higher self-ratings of both masculine and feminine abilities. (The correlations with masculine abilities were higher than those for feminine abilities, in part because of a fairly obvious association between instrumental attributes and several of the masculine items, for example, "taking charge of situations"). In both sexes, the PAQ Instrumental scale was also significantly related to masculine interests and reading preferences and with the items concerning a physically attractive appearance. Items related to athletic interests (asked of men only) were also positively related to instrumental traits. These findings appear to be brought about by a combination of two factors. First, as we have already noted, responses to the PAQ Instrumental scale (but typically not the Expressiveness scale) are substantially correlated with measures of self-esteem. Men and women high in instrumentality thus have a high regard for themselves in a number of respects. Second, activities stereotyped as masculine are often more involving and challenging than those considered feminine and therefore are more appealing to persons of both sexes who possess such instrumental characteristics as active, independent, adventuresome, and able to stand up under pressure (e.g., Spence & Hall, 1993). The results, then, suggest the importance of desirable instrumental traits in and of themselves, traits that happen to be somewhat more characteristic of men than women.

Fewer significant results were observed with the Expressiveness scale. In women, those high in PAQ E rated themselves higher in feminine abilities, interests, and reading preferences, all suggesting that the person-oriented characteristics tapped by this scale are expressed in these sets of activities. Similarly, men high on

TABLE 5.4

Correlations Between PAQ Instrumental and Expressive Scales and Self Reports of Other Personal Characteristics

	Women		Men	
	PAQ I	*PAQ E*	*PAQ I*	*PAQ E*
Abil Masc	64**	09	51**	− 30**
Fem	26**	41**	29**	15
Inter Masc	23**	− 02	27**	− 00
Fem	14	35**	− 02	39**
Read Masc	24**	− 02	26*	01
Fem	08	34**	00	30**
Sex/Rom	00	07	18	15
Appear	32**	13	31**	− 09
Clothes	14	14	− 05	− 20
Athletics	—	—	29**	− 02

Note. Finn = Finn Gender Identity Questionnaire; GI = single Gender Identity Item, Masc = adjective masculine; Fem = adjective feminine. Rules = Rules Questionnaire; Trait St = Trait Stereotypes, Masc I = Masculine Instrumental, Fem E = Feminine Expressive; Occup St = Occupational Stereotypes, Masc + Fem = masculine and feminine combined. Decimals are omitted.

*p ≤ .05. **p ≤ .01.

the E scale rated themselves higher in feminine interests, and reading preferences. Unlike the women, they did not rate themselves significantly higher on feminine abilities. Unexpectedly, they did rate themselves significantly lower on masculine abilities.

Discussion

Clearly, much remains to be done in the way of both additional data collection and more sophisticated data analyses. But even at this early point, it is abundantly apparent that a variety of patterns of findings are buried among the mass of data yielded by our battery of measures of gender ideology and gender-related personal characteristics. It is significant in several respects that for the measures that were parallel or the same for men and women, the results for the two sexes were often highly similar. Among other things, the fact that a significant finding in one sex was basically replicated in the other minimizes the possibility that a given outcome was due to chance. More important, the similarity of outcomes suggests that, within the limits of our test battery, there is nothing unique about being male or female. In this connection, we should note that many, if not most, of the psychological characteristics differentiating the genders not only do so quantitatively rather than qualitatively but also that the differences between the means of men and women are frequently small in comparison to the variability within each sex. In short, the amount of the total variance accounted for by gender is often quite minor.

It is also clear that the patterns we have uncovered do not lend themselves to any simple empirical or theoretical statements about the organization of gender-differentiating phenomena. In some instances, the findings do not even yield to explanations in terms of gender as opposed to other variables, for example, the relationships of the PAQ Instrumental scale with other personal characteristics. These latter results suggest the importance of instrumental attributes per se, buttressed by their accompanying higher self-esteem.

Overall, the results from the measure of gender beliefs and gender-linked personal characteristics suggest not only that a multidimensional approach to gender is called for but also that understanding the implications of the concrete gender-related findings may often have to be considered in their own terms rather than in term of abstract gender constructs.

Turning to the results obtained with the gender measures, inspection of the total set of results obtained with the Finn inventory suggests that although it may be satisfactory as a method of assessing marked disturbances in gender identity, this questionnaire is only partially successful for our purposes. The marked skew in the distributions of both men and women, with a pile-up of scores at the gender-congruent pole, implies that the Finn taps gender identity to a large extent. However, in both sexes, the score distributions revealed a fair amount of variability. Although a number of men and women earned the maximum score, the mode fell short of this value in both sexes and, as reflected in the size of the standard deviation, the tail of the distribution was quite long. Finn reported a similar outcome for his sample of heterosexual men. Inspection of the items suggests a reason for the variability among respondents: A number of items describe others' reactions to the person's behavior, the person's resemblance to others of his or her sex, and so forth. Those who fail to correspond to socially dictated gender expectations in these respects could be expected to score lower in their total scores, even if they had a firm, unambiguous gender identity. This may explain the shape of the distribution reported by Finn for male homosexuals: approximately symmetrical with a mean near the center of the possible range of scores. Although the stereotype of the male homosexual is a man who displays a number of physical and psychological characteristics associated with women, gay men are variable in these respects. Some homosexual men are conspicuously effeminate in their overt behaviors or possess some of the gentler characteristics associated with women but others are stereotypically masculine in all but their sexual orientation.

It is also notable that in the present group of heterosexuals, high scores on the Finn, that is, scores indicating a strong gender-congruent identity, are also associated in both men and women with more stereotyped beliefs about appropriate gender roles, suggesting that those who subscribe to these beliefs are more likely to deny being like or feeling like members of the other sex.

Like the Finn, the single item Gender Identity measure produced distributions of scores that clustered at the gender appropriate end of the scale for both sexes but at the same time, had long tails. The two measures had somewhat different correlates, however. The Gender Identity measure was correlated with self-ratings of personal characteristics more often than the Finn and less often than the latter with stereotyped beliefs. Perhaps the safest conclusion is that both measures are heavily saturated, but not exclusively, with self-perceptions of gender identity. That is, the responses of men and women are also influenced by other elements that are not identical for the Finn and Gender Identity measures but for both, are major contributors to the variability in responses within each sex. Pure measures of people's existential sense of gender identity may be impossible even to approximate closely, except perhaps in those who manifest a troubled or cross-sex identity.

We anticipated that self-ratings on the adjectives masculine and feminine would be even more heavily influenced by factors other than gender identity. More specifically, we regarded people's responses to each of these items as a kind of weighted summary statement of the ways in which they perceived themselves as possessing stereotypically masculine and feminine characteristics and attitudes that they considered important. It was therefore not surprising to find that the means on these adjectives tended to be further from the extreme pole than the Gender Identity measure. Further, although the ratings were negatively related, the correlations were quite modest (r of $-.45$ and $-.30$ for women and men, respectively). Other findings also suggest that these two adjectives are not primarily perceived by respondents as mirror images of one another. For example, women's self-ratings on the feminine item were unrelated to their endorsement of conventional gender rules but those with high scores on the item masculine were significantly more likely to reject these rules. For men, the pattern was reversed, no correlation being found with the rules measure for masculine but a negative correlation for feminine.

In summary, each of the gender measures tapped a common factor or set of factors in each sex but at the same time, had nonidentical sets of correlates. Each, then, had complex and somewhat different meanings that we are only beginning to understand.

DEFINING THE UNDEFINABLE: SUMMARY AND CONCLUSIONS

We return to the questions with which we began this chapter. What are masculinity and femininity? How are they defined? As scientists, psychologists are free, within reason, to define psychological terms as they please, as long as they make their definitions explicit. When this is done, the question becomes, not whether a given verbal or operational definition is correct or superior to another, but whether the definition is useful or accounts for the phenomena it purports to explain better than its rivals. However, as Constantinople observed more than two decades ago, although they have presumed to measure them, psychologists have not offered definitions of the terms masculinity and femininity and apparently have not appreciated the need to do so. They share this lapse with the public at large. Thus, when we ask what masculinity and femininity mean (along with the meanings of the adjectives masculine and feminine), we have had to cast ourselves into the role of semantic detectives, trying to ferret out from various sources of evidence the meanings that people have given to them.

We suggest that their meanings are multiple. People tend to endow many objects and events with gender significance. In everyday parlance, gender terms are attached to many phenomena that are not necessarily human or even compatible with biological fact (e.g., among animals, cats are stereotypically regarded as "feminine" and horses are "masculine"). When gender labels are used in connection with human beings, they sometimes refer to concrete behaviors and attributes that are believed to differentiate between males and females of a given age or culture or to objects (such as articles of clothing) that are associated with one gender more than with another. These instances represent empirical usages. But lurking behind most usages of the nouns masculinity and femininity is the assumption that there is some single internal quality or pair of qualities of profound significance in understanding the mysteries of gender.

The properties that psychological theorists have attributed to these hypothetical qualities have to be inferred, often from the instruments they use to diagnose them and from the presumed correlates of these instruments. Although there is universal agreement that masculinity and femininity or masculinity–femininity in their theoretical senses are somehow real and important, there is no implicit consensus about what their properties are or what implications they have for observable gender-linked characteristics and behaviors. Failure to offer explicit definitions of gender terms has obscured recognition of the nature of these disagreements and has sometimes led investigators simultaneously to advance contradictory theories.

We have examined two theoretical models of masculinity and femininity and their underlying presumptions. The several versions of one of these models implicitly propose that there is a single masculinity–femininity continuum to which all gender-differentiating attributes and behaviors adhere (or at least all those attributes and behaviors that are expected by society at large to distinguish between males and females). The second of these models proposes instead that masculinity and femininity are separate constructs, attributes and behaviors associated with males contributing to the former and those associated with females contributing to the latter. The evidence, however, supports neither of these models.

The multifactorial model we advanced in their place is centered around the concept of gender identity, the basic, unarticulated conviction of one's maleness or femaleness, a psychological sense that parallels one's knowledge of one's biological sex. To the extent that at the phenomenological level, masculinity and femininity have an intuitive reality that most people experience, we suggest that they refer to gender identity, men's psychological sense of being male and women's psychological sense of being female. We further postulate (although we cannot supply direct evidence in favor of the contention) that for the vast majority, gender identity is essentially dimorphic: Males have an ineffable and indivisible sense of maleness and females have a similar sense of femaleness.

Gender-related psychological characteristics, whatever their etiological roots, do not, however, share this etiological feature. Both men and women tend to possess, though in different proportions and intensities, an assortment of both masculine and feminine characteristics, that is, characteristics that exist along a continuum and tend to be exhibited to a greater degree by one sex than the other. In this sense, dualistic theories postulating that both sexes possess both masculine and feminine qualities appear to have validity (Carlson, 1972). In older, dualistic theories, such as Jung's theory of animus and anima or Bakan's theory of agency and communion, these male and female qualities are postulated to be logical and psychological opposites. In contemporary two-factors theories, they are assumed to be essentially orthogonal. When applied to particular sets of characteristics, both notions may have merit. These very different ideas, on the one hand, masculinity and femininity as gender identity, essentially categorical variables that are almost always isomorphic to one's knowledge of one's biological sex, and on the other hand, masculinity and femininity (or masculine and feminine) as collective labels for concrete behaviors and attributes that exist along a continuum, have become conflated. Two very different conceptions have been labeled with the same set of terms.

We concur, then, with Constantinople's (1973) indictment: Both theoretically and empirically, masculinity and femininity are among the muddiest in psychologists'—and lay persons'—vocabulary. Because of the multiple meanings that masculinity and femininity have come to possess and the variety of tacit presumptions in which they have become enmeshed, a question arises about the utility of these terms in scientific discourse. To avoid the mischief caused by becoming tangled up in unintended meanings and the vagueness of current usages, it might be well for scholars to abolish the nouns masculinity and femininity from their scientific vocabulary. In their stead, investigators should substitute defined terms that more specifically identify the particular observable qualities or theoretical constructs to which they are referring. This approach would not only minimize confusions about meanings but would also make more obvious the presumptions underlying gender theories. Only when these presumptions are recognized and subjected to objective scrutiny will it become possible to make theoretical progress.

ACKNOWLEDGEMENT

Thanks are due to Jennifer Baer who assisted in the collection and analysis of data from the study reported in this chapter.

REFERENCES

Angrist, S. A. (1969). The study of sex-roles. *Journal of Social Issues, 15,* 215–232.

Ashmore, R. D. (1990). Sex, gender, and the individual. In L. A. Pervin (Ed.), *Handbook of personality: Theory and research.* (pp. 486–526). New York: Guilford.

Bakan, D. (1966). *The duality of human existence.* Chicago: Rand-McNally.

Bates, J. E., Bentler, P. M., & Thompson, S. K. (1973). Measurement of deviant gender development. *Child Development, 44,* 591–598.

Bem, S. L. (1974). The measurement of psychological androgyny. *Journal of Consulting and Clinical Psychology, 42,* 155–172.

Bem, S. L. (1977). On the utility of alternate procedures for assessing psychological androgyny. *Journal of Consulting and Clinical Psychology, 46,* 196–205.

Bem, S. L. (1981). Gender schema theory: A cognitive account of sex typing. *Psychological Review, 88,* 354–364.

Bernard, L. C. (1984). The multiple factors of sex roles: Rapproachment of unidimensional and bidimensional assessment. *Journal of Clinical Psychology, 40,* 986–991.

Block, J. H. (1973). Conceptions of sex roles: Some cross-cultural and longitudinal perspectives. *American Psychologist, 28,* 512–526.

Boldizar, J. P. (1991). Assessing sex typing and androgyny in children: *The Children's Sex Role Inventory.* Developmental Psychology, 27, 505–513.

Bussey, K. (1983). A social-cognitive appraisal of sex-role development. *Australian Journal of Psychology, 35,* 135–143.

Carlson, R. (1972). Understanding women: Implications for personality theory and research. *Journal of Social Issues, 28,* 17–32.

Condry, J., & Condry, S. (1976). Sex differences: A study of the eye of the beholder. *Child Development, 47,* 813–819.

Constantinople, A. (1973). Masculinity–femininity: An exception to the famous dictum? *Psychological Bulletin, 80,* 389–407.

Cota, A. A., & Fekken, C. K. (1988). Dimensions of the Personal Attributes Questionnaire: An empirical replication. *Journal of Social Behavior and Personality, 3,* 135–140.

Deaux, K., & Lewis, L. L. (1984). Structure of gender stereotypes: Interrelationships among components and gender label. *Journal of Personality and Social Psychology,* 46, 991–1004.

Downs, A. C., & Langlois, J. H. (1988). Sex typing: Construct and measurement issues. *Sex Roles, 18,* 87–100.

English, H. O., & English, A. B. (1958). *A comprehensive dictionary of psychological and psychoanalytical terms.* New York: Longmans Green.

Frable, D. E. S. (1989). Sex typing and gender ideology: Two facets of the individual's ideology that go together. *Journal of Personality and Social Psychology, 56,* 95–108.

Freud, S. (1927). Some psychological consequences of the anatomical distinction between the sexes. *International Journal of Psychoanalysis, 8,* 133–142.

Green, R. (1974). Sexual identity conflict in children and adults. New York: Basic Books.

Green, R. L. (1991). *The MMPI–2/ MMPI: An interpretive manual.* Needham Heights, MA: Allyn and Bacon.

Hall, J. A., & Halberstadt, A. G. (1980). Masculinity and femininity in children: Development of the Children's Personal Attributes Questionnaire. *Developmental Psychology, 16,* 270–280.

Hathaway, S. R., & McKinley, J. C. (1943). The Minnesota Multiphasic Personality inventory. New York: Psychological Corporation.

Helmreich, R. L., Spence, J. T., & Wilhelm, J. A. (1981). A psychometric analysis of the Personal Attributes Questionnaire. *Sex Roles, 7,* 1097–1108.

Hetherington, E. M., & Frankie, G. (1967). Effects of parental dominance, warmth, and conflict on imitation in children. *Journal of Personality and Social Psychology, 6,* 119–125.

Hooker, E. (1965). An empirical study of some relations between sexual patterns and gender identity in male homosexuals. In J. Money (Ed.), *Sex research: New developments* (pp. 24–52). New York: Holt, Rinehart and Winston.

Jenkin, N., & Vroegh, K. (1969). Contemporary concepts of masculinity and femininity. *Psychological Reports, 25,* 679–697.

Josephs, R. A., Markus, H. R., & Tafarodi, R. W. (1992). Gender and self-esteem. *Journal of Personality and Social Psychology, 63,* 391–402.

Kohlberg, L. A. (1966). A cognitive developmental analysis of children's sex-role concepts and attitudes. In E. E. Maccoby (Ed.), *The development of sex differences* (pp. 82–173). Stanford, CA: Stanford University Press.

Langlois, J. H., & Downs, A. C. (1980). Mothers, fathers, and peers as socialization agents of sex-typed play behaviors in young children. *Child Development, 51,* 1237–1247.

Lunneborg, P. W. (1972). Dimensionality of MF. *Journal of Clinical Psychology, 28,* 313–317.

Marsh, H. W., & Byrne, B. M. (1991). Differentiated additive androgyny model: Relations between masculinity, femininity and multiple dimensions of the self-concept. *Journal of Personality and Social Psychology, 61,* 811–828.

Meyer-Bahburg, H. F. L. (1993). Gender identity development in intersex patients. *Child and Adolescent Clinics of North America, 2,* 501–512.

Miles, C. C. (1935). Sex in social psychology. In C. Murchison (Ed.), *Handbook of social psychology* (pp. 683–797). Worcester, MA: Clark University Press.

Mitchell, J. E., Baker, L. A., & Jacklin, C. N. (1989). Masculinity and femininity in twin children: Genetic and environmental factors. *Child Development, 60,* 1475–1485.

Myers, A. M., & Gonda, G. (1982). Utility of the masculinity–femininity construct: Comparison of traditional and androgyny approaches. *Journal of Personality and Social Psychology, 43,* 514–522.

Orlofsky, J. L. (1981). Relationship between sex role attitudes and personality traits and the Sex Role Behavior Scale–1: A new measure of masculine and feminine role behaviors and interests. *Journal of Personality and Social Psychology, 40,* 927–940.

Parsons, T. (1955). Family structure and the socialization of the child. In T. Parsons & R. F. Bales (Eds.), *Family, socialization, and interaction process* (pp.35–151). Glencoe, IL: Free Press.

Parsons, T. & Bales, R. F. (Eds.). (1955). *Family, socialization, and interaction process.* Glencoe, IL: Free Press.

Pedhazur, E. J., & Tetenbaum, T. J. (1979). Bem's Sex Role Inventory: A theoretical and methodological critique. *Journal of Personality and Social Psychology, 37,* 996–1016.

Rubin, J., Provenzano, R., & Luria, Z. (1974). The eye of the beholder: Parents' views on sex of newborns. *American Journal of Orthopsychiatry, 44,* 512–519.

Schank, R., & Abelson, R. (1977). *Scripts, plans, goals, and understanding*. Hillsdale, NJ: Lawrence Erlbaum Associates.

Seavey, C. A., Katz, P. A., & Zalk, S. R. (1975). Baby X: The effect of gender labels on adult responses to infants. *Sex Roles, 1*, 103–109.

Sherif, C. W. (1982). Needed concepts in the study of gender identity. *Psychology of Women Quarterly, 6*, 375–398.

Signorella, M. L. (1992). Remembering gender-related information. *Sex Roles, 2*, 143–156.

Simms, R. E., Davis, M. H., Foushee, H. C., Holahan, C. K., Spence, J. T., & Helmreich, R. L. (1978, April). *Psychological masculinity and femininity in children and their relationships to trait stereotypes and toy preferences*. Paper presented at annual meeting of Southwestern Psychological Association, Houston, Texas.

Spence, J. T. (1985). Gender identity and implications for concepts of masculinity and femininity. In T. B. Sonderegger (Ed.), *Nebraska Symposium on Motivation: Psychology and Gender* (Vol. 32, pp. 59–96). Lincoln: University of Nebraska Press.

Spence, J. T. (1991). Do the BSRI and PAQ measure the same or different concepts? *Psychology of Women Quarterly, 64*, 624–635.

Spence, J. T. (1993). Gender-related traits and gender ideology: Evidence for a multifactorial theory. *Journal of Personality and Social Psychology, 64*, 624–635.

Spence, J. T., & Hall, S. K. (1993). *A multidimensional approach to children's gender-related self-perceptions and stereotypes*. Manuscript submitted for publication.

Spence, J. T., & Helmreich, R. L. (1978). *Masculinity and femininity: Their psychological dimensions, correlates, and antecedents*. Austin: University of Texas Press.

Spence, J. T., Helmreich, R. L., & Stapp. J. (1974). The Personal Attributes Questionnaire: A measure of sex-role stereotypes and masculinity and femininity. *JSAS: Catalog of Selected Documents in Psychology, 4*, 43–44.

Spence, J. T., Helmreich, R. L., & Stapp, J. (1975). Ratings of self and peers on sex-role attributes and their relations to self-esteem and conceptions of masculinity and femininity. *Journal of Personality and Social Psychology, 32*, 29–39.

Spence, J. T., & Sawin, L. L. (1985). Images of masculinity and femininity: A reconceptualization. In V. O. Leary, R. Unger, & B. Wallston (Eds.), *Sex, gender, and social psychology* (pp. 35–66). Hillsdale, NJ: Lawrence Erlbaum Associates.

Storms, M. D. (1979). Sex-role identity and its relationship to sex role attributes and sex role stereotypes. *Journal of Personality and Social Psychology, 37*, 1779–1789.

Tesser, A. (1988). Toward a self-evaluation maintenance model of social behavior. In L. Berkowitz (Ed.), *Advances in Experimental Social Psychology* (Vol. 21) (pp. 181–227). New York: Academic Press.

Unger, R. K. (1979). Toward a redefinition of sex and gender. *American Psychologist, 34*, 1085–1094.

Wakefield, J. A., Jr., Sasek, J., Friedman, A. F., & Bowden, J. D. (1976). Androgyny and other measures of masculinity–femininity. *Journal of Consulting and Clinical Psychology, 44*, 766–770.

Whitley, B. E. (1983). Sex-role orientation and self-esteem: A critical meta-analytic review. *Journal of Personality and Social Psychology, 44*, 765–778.

Part III

Women and Men Together

Chapter 6

Sexual Discourse and Sexual Intercourse: How the Way We Communicate Affects the Way We Think About Sexual Coercion

Rhonda K. Reinholtz
University of Kansas

Charlene L. Muehlenhard
University of Kansas

Joi L. Phelps
University of Kansas

Arthur T. Satterfield
University of Kansas

Newspapers, television programs and advertisements, movies, academic journals, popular music, literature, personal conversations—all are modes of communication. All serve to communicate ideas, both explicitly and implicitly, and in so doing they simultaneously reflect and shape cultural beliefs and values.

Communication about sexuality, through these modes as well as others, creates and perpetuates cultural assumptions about sexuality. These assumptions are communicated both explicitly and implicitly because the language we use conveys more than the obvious content of its message—it also expresses cultural values. These assumptions about sexuality influence our thinking about sexual coercion: the extent to which sexual coercion is visible or invisible, our perspectives on the victim and the perpetrator, and many subtle notions about what constitutes sexual coercion.

In this chapter we explore the role of communication in supporting existing power relations and perpetuating sexual coercion. First, we discuss previous research on sexual coercion and why that research has steered us toward an examination of communication issues. Then, we outline our understanding of language and discourse and their roles in both expressing and shaping cultural understandings of human sexuality and sexual coercion. Next, we discuss how grammatical structures can influence thinking about sexual coercion. Finally, we present examples of common themes about sexuality and sexual coercion.

PREVALENCE OF SEXUAL COERCION

The prevalence of sexual coercion in America has been demonstrated by numerous researchers. Several studies have found that 15% of college women have been raped by men (Koss, Gidycz, & Wisniewski, 1987; Muehlenhard & Linton, 1987; see Muehlenhard, Powch, Phelps, & Giusti, 1992, for a discussion of definitions of rape). Even higher prevalence rates have been found in nonstudent populations: Koss, Woodruff, and Koss (1990) found 21%, and Russell (1984) found 24%. When sexual behaviors other than penetration are included, prevalence rates are even higher (Koss et al., 1987; Muehlenhard & Linton, 1987). Men are also raped, although less frequently than women (Burnam et al., 1988; Groth & Burgess, 1980; Kaufman, DiVasto, Jackson, Voorhees, & Christy, 1980; Sarrel & Masters, 1982).

Verbal sexual coercion is also common. Koss et al. (1987) found that 25% of college women reported engaging in unwanted sexual intercourse, and 44%, in other unwanted sexual activities, due to being overwhelmed by a man's continual arguments and pressure. Muehlenhard and Cook (1988) found that 34% of college women and 27% of college men reported engaging in unwanted sexual activity, and 11% of women and 13% of men, in unwanted sexual intercourse, due to verbal coercion by a partner.

People sometimes engage in unwanted sexual activity for reasons other than being pressured by a partner. People have reported engaging in unwanted sexual activity due to peer pressure (45% of women & 52% of men); fear of appearing shy or afraid, unfeminine or unmasculine, homosexual, or inexperienced (49% of women & 48% of men); and a desire to be more popular (13% of women & 18% of men) (Muehlenhard & Cook, 1988). Other sources of pressure to engage in unwanted sexual activity include expectations that everyone should be heterosexual and that marriage should include sex (Muehlenhard, Goggins, Jones, & Satterfield, 1991; Muehlenhard & Schrag, 1991; Russell, 1990). In these cases of unwanted sexual activity, the pressure comes not from the partner per se, but from others' or one's own expectations about how one should behave sexually.

Clearly, then, sexual coercion is not solely due to a few deviant individuals. The high frequency of physical and verbal sexual coercion suggests implicit cultural support for such coercion, if not explicit support. And the high frequency of unwanted sexual activity due to expectations about how one should behave sexually suggests cultural support for such expectations. This highlights the need to focus on aspects of our culture that underpin—either explicitly or implicitly—sexual coercion. In this chapter, we will address how communication about sex creates and perpetuates common cultural themes that support sexual coercion.

Language and Discourse

Language does more than just describe our viewpoints and experiences; it forms our ideas at the same time that it expresses them (Hellinger, 1984; Rubin, 1988). "Language not only *expresses* ideas and concepts but actually *shapes* thought" (Moore, 1976/1992, p. 331). This idea has been summarized in the Whorfian hypothesis: "The Whorfian hypothesis, or *linguistic determinism*, states that the structure of language influences the structure of thought. Furthermore, the Whorfian hypothesis argues that a person speaking Language A might carve up the conceptual world differently from a person speaking language B" (Matlin, 1992, p. 294). Although the strong form of the Whorfian hypothesis—that language determines thought—is no longer generally accepted, the weak form—that language influences thought—is generally agreed upon (Matlin, 1985).

An important implication of the Whorfian hypothesis is that our way of thinking and communicating is not the reflection of "the one true" reality. Fiorenza (1986) suggested that language, "as interpretation and legitimization, is the key concept in the social construction of reality" (p. 23). The socially constructed nature of reality is one of our own central assumptions. The word "reality" is often used to imply that the way we behave and the meaning we attribute to our behavior is somehow objective and free of human influence. A central tenet of this chapter is that this is not, in fact, the case. Instead, language serves a highly influential role in the creation of a mutually agreed upon reality. Our conceptualization of human sexuality, for example, is a product of our culture and language and reflects but one way of understanding human sexual experience. As Tiefer (1992) noted, "What is 'known' about sexuality, particularly about one's own sexuality, results from an interaction of learned concepts and categories, perceived bodily experiences, memory, expectations, and the appraisal of the momentary situation" (p. 1).

Related to an understanding of the function of language in communication is an understanding of discourse, defined as "an interrelated system of statements which cohere around common meanings and values . . . [that] are a product of social factors, of powers and practices, rather than an individual's set of ideas" (Hollway, 1983, cited by Gavey, 1989, pp. 463–464). Discourses, according to Gavey, are more than words. They may include gestures, images, and cultural norms, as well as spoken and written words. Language and discourse, themselves inextricably intertwined, construct the meaning that we assign to our experience, including our sexual experience.

Resistance to the belief that human sexuality is socially constructed is prevalent (Schur, 1988). Such resistance may be understood as a result of dominant sexual discourse as well as indicative of American cultural beliefs more broadly. In his book, *The Americanization of Sex*, Schur noted that American culture is replete with media images, personal interactions, and cultural traditions that shape human sexuality. Yet, Americans still resist the idea that their sexuality may be socially constructed. Two factors contribute to this resistance. The first is the notion that heterosexual sex is natural, and the second is the American emphasis on individuality. This resistance to the idea that sexuality is socially constructed stands in the way of analyzing dominant discourse and understanding the impact of this discourse on human sexuality and sexual coercion.

Resistance, however, can also produce work in favor of deconstructing previously held beliefs about sexuality—it can take the form of resistance to the ideas conveyed through dominant discourse. Gavey (1992) noted the importance of this type of resistance and cited women who described socially condoned sexual interactions and experiences as "undesired, unwanted, and not enjoyed" (p. 346) as evidence of resistance on an individual level. This type of resistance is evidenced in the present chapter as we attempt to use language to make explicit the implicit assumptions in discourse about sex and sexual coercion, with the ultimate goal of reducing sexual coercion.

Language, Discourse, and Power

Language and discourse play an integral role in the perpetuation of existing power relations. They serve to convey prevalent power structures, and in so doing they perpetuate the dominance of the ruling group. Lerner (1986), in her work on the creation of patriarchy, noted that words "are socially created cultural constructs" (p. 232) that represent ideas espoused by the culture at large. She discussed the role of language in perpetuating women's marginality and observed that our language expresses the patriarchal thought whence it originated. Gavey (1989) also linked the notion of the social construction of reality with the maintenance of power in positing that knowledge and dominant conceptions of reality are socially constructed to preserve male power. She noted that dominant discourses appear "natural" and thus act to preserve existing conditions and beliefs by appealing to common sense. In this way, power differentials are maintained through their continual re-creation in discourse. Discursive positions provide meaning and constitute experience in such a manner that existing power structures are perpetuated rather than questioned or challenged.

A similar idea was expressed by Richardson (1990) in her discussion of cultural stories. She observed that "participation in a culture includes participation in the narratives of that culture" (p. 24), of which cultural stories are one type. Cultural stories are told from the point of view of the "ruling interests," or the dominant group. These stories perpetuate the status quo and serve the interests of the dominant group. Richardson specifically highlighted the role of cultural stories in the preservation of gender inequality. As one example she discussed adultery and suggested that "the storyline blames the minor characters, the women" (p. 25) for breaking up a family, because it is told from the perspective of the major characters, the men.

Harrison (1985) further underscored the relationship between language and power, writing that language

> conveys our sense of personal-relational power, or lack of it. Language encodes our sense of how we are positioned in our basic relations to and with others who make up our social world. This means that language teaches us, below the level of consciousness and intentionality, our sense of power-in-relation. It also functions either to reproduce and reinforce existing social relations, thereby teaching us to accept the legitimacy of what is given, or to enable imaginative reappropriation or transcendence of the given. . . . The potential of language, then, is either to expand human possibility or to function as a transmitter of subtle, and not so subtle, patterns of human oppression and domination. (p. 24)

This understanding of power and its perpetuation via language and discourse is central to our exploration of how dominant discursive positions frame our culturally negotiated understanding of sexual coercion.

Language, Discourse, and Sexual Coercion

Language plays a powerful role in shaping our ideas about sexual experience, including sexual coercion. Language shapes our understanding of where the responsibility for sexual coercion lies. It can make the victim appear to be at fault for the sexual coercion, as if the victim elicited the coercive behavior from someone—the perpetrator—who was helpless to act otherwise. It can shift the focus from the perpetrator to the victim so that the perpetrator becomes imperceptible. Language can render sexual coercion inconsequential or even invisible by concealing the coercive nature of an act so that it is seen only as a "normal" sexual encounter. The ascription of normality to a sexual behavior plays a role in the visibility of sexual coercion, in that a behavior thought of as "natural" will not readily be defined as criminal, coercive, or otherwise unacceptable.

Beneke (1982) suggested that "every man who grows up in America and learns American English learns all too much to think like a rapist, to structure his experience of women and sex in terms of status, hostility, control, and dominance" (p. 16). Similarly, women who grow up in America learn to think of themselves as the potential victims of male rape; they learn to structure their experience with men in terms of status, control, and power relations. "In some instances, rapes literally 'don't exist' because the victim sees the coercive sexual experience as natural and legitimate in the context of a structured power relationship between a man and a woman" (Cherry, 1983, p. 252).

In this chapter, we will illustrate how language serves to conceal or to trivialize sexual coercion. Our hope is that our examination of some of the explicit and implicit results that language may effect will lead readers to examine further the implications of their own and others' communication about human sexuality.

It is important that we make explicit our understanding of the association between gender and sexual victimization. One of our goals in this chapter is to point out ways in which communication about human sexuality obscures male victims and female perpetrators of sexual coercion in both other- and same-sex incidents. However, although persons of either sex can be victims or perpetrators, the vast majority of forcible rapes involve male perpetrators and female victims. At times our language will refer explicitly to male rape of females, which we will do to emphasize this dominant cultural pattern. Whenever possible, however, our language will remain gender neutral to reflect how what is being discussed can be applied to more than just male perpetrators and female victims.

GRAMMAR AND WORD CHOICE

Passive Constructions

One aspect of language that renders the perpetrators of sexual coercion invisible and therefore reinforces status quo power relations between women and men is passive voice. "The rhetorical impact of the passive voice—the art of making the creator or instigator of action totally disappear from a reader's perception—can be devastating" (Greenfield, 1975, p. 146). Often the passive voice is used in talking about sexual coercion: for example, "24 percent of the women had been raped at least once" (Harney & Muehlenhard, 1991, p. 7); "one out of every four women will be raped" (Resick, 1983, p. 129); "15–22% of women have been raped" (Koss & Burkhart, 1989, p. 27); "women who have been battered say . . ." (Glazer, 1993, p. 172). In such constructions only the victim is visible, and there is no apparent agent, no individual responsible for coercing or violating.

Penelope (1990) referred to use of passive voice as "the process of agent-deletion" (p. 146) and noted that this has the effect of accentuating the objects—the victims—with the end result that we forget that a human being is responsible for the act. Daly (1978) similarly stressed the impact of passive voice and discussed agent deletion as disguising the agents of "androcracy" (p. 324). She also suggested, to use her own terminology, that passive voice has the effect of pacifying/passivizing its victims, hiding the agents—men—and rendering the objects—women—passive.

Passive voice can reinforce victim blaming. Phrases such as "women get raped" imply that "women get *themselves* raped" (Penelope, 1990, p. 116). Adjectives, in phrases such as "abused children" and "battered women," similarly shift the focus away from the individuals committing the abuse and onto the victims as if the characteristic of being abused resides in the victims (Penelope, 1990). Often the victims are explicitly identified as female, in phrases such as "battered women," but the gender of the perpetrators is not identified. Once these phrases are integrated into our communication, they shape our ideas about sexual coercion and abuse. Women and children, the most frequently identified victims, take on the quality of being abused or abusable; the identity of the perpetrators remains concealed; the possibility of men as victims becomes virtually inconceivable. Language, then, has the power to obscure the perpetrator and make the victim the visible, and implicitly responsible, party.

Another form of passive construction that omits the agent of the abuse is illustrated in a discussion of child sexual abuse. Murphy (1991) stated that having experienced child sexual abuse was associated with "a present dating or marital relationship that was physically and/or sexually abusive" (p. 85). Here again, there is no agent, no perpetrator of the abuse; rather, the relationship itself is abusive.

Euphemisms and Pronouns

The April 12, 1993, issue of *People Weekly* included an article about the Spur Posse—a group of male high school students accused of multiple acts of sexual coercion. The author referred to the boys' sexual activity as "exploits" ("The Body Counters," 1993, p. 36). By using this word, which denotes "notable or heroic acts" (G. & C. Merriam Co., 1981), the author framed the debate by portraying the boys as spirited and adventurous rather than as criminal.

Sexual coercion is often referred to by euphemisms that conceal coerciveness, violence, and even specific acts. Penelope (1990) discussed the use of the word "it" to refer to a father's raping his daughter. She quoted a victim who stated that "*it* started when I was ten" (p. 139) and a reporter who asked, "Why does *it* keep happening?" (p. 139). Referring to "it" in these examples conceals the rape, obscuring the fact that the father raped his daughter. (Furthermore, the passive construction of the reporter's question, in which "*it* keeps happening," obscures the responsibility that the father bears for continuing to rape his daughter. This question suggests that the raping just kept happening on its own, outside the father's control.)

Sexist Language

Sexist language is an example of how language conveys power relations. Words such as "chairman," "freshman," and "mankind" create images of men in certain roles and construct men as representative of all people. Ng (1990), discussing the generic "he" and other masculine words, cited several studies showing that "individuals interpret the generics to be male-specific" (p. 456). "The use of masculine terms perpetuates the morphological and psychological invisibility of women, whereas morphological marking of female referents often implies semantic derogation" (Hellinger, 1984, p. 139). Diminutive forms for females (e.g., "authoress," "heroine") also serve to maintain status quo power relations. Similarly, the common Western practice of referring to married couples by the husband's name (e.g., "Mr. and Mrs. John Smith") constructs men as more powerful and important than women and renders women invisible. Constructing men as more powerful than women conveys to both women and men the notions that men's needs take precedence over women's needs and that men are entitled to be sexually satisfied and women's role is to satisfy them. Sexual coercion against women is rendered inconsequential (it becomes "natural" for the more powerful to coerce the less powerful) or even invisible (if people regard complying as women's natural role, they might not even question men's sexual demands).

COMMON THEMES IN COMMUNICATION
ABOUT SEXUALITY

In this section we discuss prevalent cultural notions about human sexuality, focusing on cultural norms and beliefs that affect contemporary understandings of sexual coercion.

Male Sexuality as Uncontrollable

One common theme, conveyed both explicitly and implicitly throughout communication about human sexuality, is that male sexuality is uncontrollable. There are at least two components to this idea. One is that men are overwhelmingly sexual beings who inevitably respond with sexual arousal to even the slightest provocation or innuendo. The other is that once a man is sexually aroused, there is no stopping his progress to orgasm—he cannot slow down or control his sexual behavior but is compelled by forces beyond his control to achieve sexual gratification via orgasm.

A 1990 Billboard chart hit illustrates an explicit expression of this theme. Billy Idol, in "Cradle of Love," sings, "my love starts a rolling train/you can't stop it/it ain't in vain." Earlier examples include Rod Stewart's 1976 hit, "Tonight's the Night" ("come on angel, my heart's on fire/don't deny your man's desire, you'd be a fool to stop this tide/spread your wings and let me come inside/cause tonight's the night . . . ain't nobody gonna stop us now") and Lou Christie's 1966 hit, "Lightnin' Strikes" ("when I see lips beggin' to be kissed, I can't stop . . . nature's taking over my one-track mind . . . if she gives me a sign that she wants to make time, I can't stop, I can't stop 'cause that lightning's striking again!"). These train, tide, and lightning metaphors all portray male sexuality as inevitable and uncontrollable, and in each case the implication is that women either cannot or should not stop men's sexual advances. Popular music artist Ice-T expressed this idea succinctly when he stated in an MTV interview that the only way to stop sexism would be to "castrate every boy at birth. *We can't help it* [emphasis added]" (Kirchner, 1993, p. 71).

An implicit illustration of this theme comes from advice columnist Dr. Joyce Brothers (1981). She suggested that a woman "who wants her man to feel that he is cock of the walk" (p. 165) can accomplish this by measuring his penis and reassuring him that it is large. She suggested that the woman begin by measuring his limp penis and "finish your measuring when he gets an erection, *which should be almost immediately* [emphasis added]" (p. 165). Depending on the results of the measuring, she continued, women may be able to "expect a great performance that night" (p. 165). The implicit message is that any act involving a man's penis should produce an erection and that men's erections indicate sexual arousal and desire. The word "should" suggests the normalcy of automatic, unstoppable male sexual arousal and intimates that if the man does not become aroused in this circumstance, there is something wrong with him.

At times the idea that men are sexually uncontrollable is conveyed in subtle ways. The May, 1993, issue of *Glamour* magazine carried a column entitled "sex & health" (Lever & Schwartz, 1993, p. 87). One female reader wrote saying that she *and her boyfriend* wanted to wait until they were married to have sex and asking whether they were the "only ones who think like this" (p. 87). The columnists' response began with statistics on the percentage of *women* ages 20 to 24 who are virgins—but gave no mention of the percentage of men. Has no one researched the percentage of men who are virgins? Did it not occur to the columnists to check? Did they assume the number would be so small it would be insignificant? The columnists next listed some reasons that women and men may decide to postpone sex until marriage and then devoted most of their answer to discussing "women who choose to remain virgins" (p. 87). The subtle message conveyed by this column—by its emphasis on female virgins in response to a letter about a couple in which both partners are virgins—is that female virgins do exist and male virgins do not. Males are implicitly surmised to be sexually experienced. Male sexual behavior is assumed—the columnists even referred to generic boyfriends' "constant demand to 'go all the way'" (p. 87)—as if all boyfriends invariably and incessantly pressure their girlfriends for penile–vaginal intercourse.

These examples have important implications for sexual coercion; by making male sexuality appear "naturally" uncontrollable, they render sexual coercion invisible or inevitable. The message is that because men are naturally overwhelmed by their own sex drive, their advances toward women—even those advances that are unwanted and constitute a violation of the women—are normal and expected. An American expression that exemplifies this theme—"boys will be boys"—is used to explain and excuse unsolicited male sexual behavior. The author of the Spur Posse article discussed previously provided an illustration of this expression: "Parents . . . as well as [students] . . . take the position that boys will be boys, arguing that the youths have been persecuted for doing only what comes naturally" ("The Body Counters," 1993, p. 35). One parent stated, "nothing my boy did was anything that any red-blooded American boy wouldn't do at his age" (p. 36). Sexual coercion, according to this view, is not a crime or an inappropriate act for which males ought to be condemned but is rather a natural expression of males' biological drives.

The idea that male sexuality is uncontrollable also implies that men cannot be sexually coerced. The implication is that when a man gets an erection, he wants to have sex culminating in orgasm. The idea that erections must inevitably lead to orgasm leaves no room for erections resulting from unwanted physical stimulation, and the idea that men always want sex leaves no room for the possibility of sex against a man's will. Together, these ideas make the notion of a man or a woman sexually coercing a man virtually inconceivable.

Female Responsibility for Male Sexuality

Related to the idea that male sexuality is uncontrollable is the idea that women are responsible for men's sexual behavior. One powerful conduit for this notion is language that characterizes women as "doing something to men" to which the men can only respond with uncontrollable sexual arousal. In "Lightnin' Strikes," the popular song discussed earlier, the words, "when I see lips beggin' to be kissed," suggest that the woman's lips beg the man to kiss them, and his response, "I can't stop," conveys the inevitability of this interaction. Colloquial expressions convey the same idea; phrases such as "she bowled me over," "she's striking," and "she's a knockout" suggest that the woman affects the man in ways he cannot mediate or control.

This message may be conveyed in the briefest and most subtle phrases. A shoe advertisement in the February, 1993, issue of *Glamour* magazine pictured a woman's body from the torso down, with the caption, "For feet that turn heads" (p. 148). The feet themselves "turn heads," causing men to look; there is no agent, no volition, and no self-responsibility for the act of looking. It is as though women's bodies force a reaction in men for which the men themselves are not responsible. An advertisement for a woman's fragrance, in the November, 1992, issue of *Glamour*, stated the message more directly: "The power of a woman" (p. 196). It is a power that men cannot resist, a power that draws men uncontrollably and that is ultimately used against women when female victims rather than male perpetrators are held responsible for sexual coercion. Such messages are often so indirect and subtle that they may not even be noticed, yet they serve as a powerful influence on how readers understand sexual interactions.

The "gatekeeper theory," which holds that women are the gatekeepers of both women's and men's sexual behavior, is also an expression of this notion. Allgeier and Allgeier (1991), describing this theory, noted that "women are expected to be the 'gatekeepers'—that is, to take responsibility for setting the limits on the extent of sexual intimacy" (p. 190). Similarly, Lips (1991) noted that women have "traditionally been told, through the double standard, that they must be responsible for acting as gatekeepers and holding back men's sexual advances" (p. 132). The implication of this theory is that women are responsible for men's sexual behavior, and that a woman who is raped is responsible for failing to control the perpetrator's behavior.

Romance

American cultural notions about romance also hold important implications for sexual coercion. The ideal romance is a natural, blissful progression in which two people "fall" in love. It is not a rational, controlled, or directed process; instead, it "sweeps one off one's feet." Although this may seem unrelated to sexual coercion at first glance, it is one element of sexuality discourse that serves to obscure sexual coercion.

Sexual coercion is obscured to the extent that consent and nonconsent are obscured. Within the world of romance, there is no such thing as either acknowledging consent or stopping the progression of sexual interaction. It is not romantic to break the mood and discuss one's feelings about sexual activity; instead, one is to go with the feeling of being "carried away."

Attitudes toward birth control emphasize romance and de-emphasize explicitly talking about sex. Ad copy for the Today brand vaginal sponge contraceptives conveys that romance requires not disturbing the natural progression of sexual activity: "Let's face it, interruptions spoil the mood"; "Prevent the pregnancy, preserve the mood"; "All you'll turn off is the light" (*Glamour*, February, 1993, p. 118). The implicit message to women is that they are responsible for providing a birth control method that will not "turn off" their male partners. The sponge allows them to "preserve the mood" by never having to acknowledge or discuss birth control—or, implicitly, any other aspect of sexual interaction. To maintain romance, they are to go along with the progression of sexual activity.

Another example regarding romance may be seen in an ad for Narcisse™ perfume by Chloé. The ad in the October, 1992, issue of *Glamour* showed a man and a woman kissing, with the caption, "then I was in his arms and reality faded away" (p. 66). This caption implies that romance and sexuality are not "reality" experiences and do not involve rationality or deliberate consent. Thus men and women, when under the spell of romance with reality faded away, are no longer responsible for their actions.

Sex as a Force of Nature

Sex is often constructed as a natural force, inevitable and free from social influence. An ad for men's cologne, Gravity,™ depicted a man and a woman wearing swimsuits and embracing passionately on a rocky coast. The ad reads, "More than a fragrance/it's a force of nature . . . you couldn't resist it, even if you tried" (*McCall's*, December, 1993). An ad for women's perfume, Spellbound,™ depicted a man and a woman, looking closely at one another, with the sole caption "SPELLBOUND" (*Glamour*, November, 1992). Both ads imply that it is impossible to resist the force of sexual attraction.

The popular music discussed earlier also conveys the sense that sex is a force of nature; the sexual metaphors include lightning and the force of the tide. Such metaphors underscore the notion that sex is as powerful and uncontrollable as the forces of nature.

If sexual attraction is an irresistible force of nature, resisting it would be to defy nature. Thus, sexual coercion becomes merely the expression of inevitable natural forces, and the appropriate response is not to resist, but to embrace it.

Men as Untrustworthy

The idea that men are not trustworthy makes male sexual coercion seem normal and natural. Sexually coercive men, rather than being viewed as unusual or inappropriate, are viewed as normal and even desirable partners. An ad for Lady Foot Locker stores, which may at first seem unrelated to sexuality, consists of text in which a woman lists all of the activities she does with men and then concludes in boldface letters, "but I trust women" (*Glamour*, December, 1992, pp. 72–73). Wojtyla (1981), currently known as Pope John Paul II, wrote that, "a man does not have to fear female sensuality as much as a woman must fear the sensuality of the male" (p. 177). When women are told that they cannot trust men, they learn to expect not to trust men, and they learn to accept a society in which they form relationships with partners whom they cannot rely upon to honor their own wishes. Sexually coercive male behavior becomes normative and acceptable rather than aberrant and unacceptable.

This theme is taken further by Silhouette Books' advertisements for romance novels. They explicitly characterize the male protagonists as dangerous and un-trustworthy—and it is these very traits that are understood to make them attractive to women. One ad begins by noting, "He drives a car fast, a bargain hard and women to distraction" (*Glamour*, May, 1993, p. 147); another, "You wouldn't call him Prince Charming. Not right off the bat, anyway . . . . If he's got any armor, it's around his heart" (*Glamour*, December, 1992, p. 137); and a third, "TO DIE FOR. He's handsome. He's smart. He's passionate. Could he also be fatal? . . . in Silhouette Shadows, books that flirt with the darker side of love" (*Glamour*, March, 1993, p. 283). The "darker side of love," which in this case includes potential fatality, is portrayed as appealing and desirable to women. Sexual coercion, rather than being understood as inappropriate or harmful to women, by implication becomes attractive and characteristic of normative masculine behavior. The implicit message is that rape is not rape when it is the behavior of desirable men.

Women Ask For It

The idea that women "ask for it"—that women evoke or elicit sexual contact, including rape—is another common theme. A fragrance advertisement in the May, 1993, issue of *Glamour* relied on this notion; it depicted a woman wearing high heels and a mini-skirt, presumably wearing the advertised fragrance, with the words "Make a statement without saying a word!" (p. 125). A clothing ad in the April, 1993, issue of *Glamour* pictured a woman dressed in a bra and short skirt with the caption, "REQUEST JEANS." Again, the implication is that the woman is making a sexual request merely by wearing Request™ clothing. The message is that a woman's appearance—and even her scent—communicate her sexual intent. There need be no explicit communication of desire, intent, or consent.

This notion that women elicit or request sexual advances from men simply by appearing a certain way supports victim blaming. According to this notion, sexual coercion is not against the woman's will; rather, it occurs in response to her appearance, which conveys her sexual intent.

The belief that women "lead men on" by their behavior or appearance is one aspect of the theme that women "ask for it." Muehlenhard and MacNaughton (1988) investigated the salience of this theme by having college women rate a date rape scenario. Compared with other women, women who believed that "leading a man on" justifies rape rated the victim more negatively, viewed her as more responsible for the rape, and considered the rape more justified. Women who were moderate and high in their belief in the "leading men on" theme were more likely than low-belief women to have experienced verbal sexual coercion. These women apparently considered themselves responsible for their partner's sexual arousal and therefore felt obligated for their partner's sexual satisfaction. "Leading a man on" may take many forms. For example, college students—especially men with traditional gender role attitudes—interpreted a woman's going to a man's apartment, asking him out, or letting him pay for a date as indicating that the woman wanted sex and as making rape more justifiable (Muehlenhard, 1988).

Advice columnist Ann Landers explicitly advanced this idea. A reader wrote the following, which Landers (1985, Aug. 12) supported:

> Women should be made aware of the ways *they invite trouble* [emphasis added]. Here are just a few: Telling raw jokes and using street language. Bouncing around (no bra) in low-cut sweaters and see-through blouses. Wearing skirts slit to the city limits up the sides, back or front. Most males will be as sexually aggressive as their partners allow them to be . . . . it's the female who calls the signals and decides whether she wants to hold that line. (p. B6)

Sex as Coitus

American discourse about human sexuality is virtually ubiquitous in its characterization of "sex" as coitus—as penile–vaginal intercourse. Haas and Haas (1990), in their human sexuality text, explained that when "people touch, caress, and kiss—physically and psychologically preparing for coitus—it is called foreplay. This preliminary pleasurable sexual stimulation leads to the dilation and lubrication of the vagina and the erection of the penis so that coitus can take place" (p. 115). Feldman's (1993) introductory psychology textbook defined the "excitement phase" as "a period during which the body prepares for sexual intercourse" (p. 388) and defined the vagina as "the female canal into which the penis enters during sexual intercourse" (p. 388). Defining the vagina in terms of sexual intercourse is a particularly powerful conduit for the equation of sex with coitus. Significantly, Feldman did not define male bodies in such terms; his definition of the penis was "the primary male sex organ," p. 388. This imbalance, in which the vagina is defined as a receptacle for the penis, but the penis is defined in relation only to itself, underscores the tendency to define women in terms of their ability to service men sexually.

If sex means penile–vaginal intercourse, then other forms of sexual contact are merely preliminary or substitutive; they are not the real thing. If sex means penile–vaginal intercourse, then rape means forced penile–vaginal intercourse, and other sexual behaviors—such as fondling a person's genitals without her or his consent, forced oral sex, and same-sex coercion—are not considered rape. Although some other forms of forced sexual contact are included within the legal category of sodomy (e.g., anal penetration and oral–genital contact), many unwanted sexual contacts have no legal grounding as rape in some states.

Koss and Harvey (1991) addressed the emphasis on penile–vaginal penetration found in traditional rape laws. However, even within their criticism of this emphasis on penile–vaginal penetration, they stated that "rape is a penetration offense; the victim is penetrated by the offender" (p. 4). Sexual coercion between two women, which cannot involve penile penetration and may or may not involve other forms of penetration, is concealed by this emphasis. Male victims who are not penetrated but who are forced to participate in coitus are also concealed by the emphasis on penetration of the victim.

The issue of the invisibility of male rape victims is controversial. Estrich (1987) discussed the implications of defining and thinking of rape as a gender-neutral crime. She noted that "the empirical reality is that men rape, not women" (p. 82). Her point was that making rape a gender-neutral crime may further perpetuate status quo power relations by de-emphasizing the gender-related nature of most sexual offenses. Defining rape as a crime only against women, however, implies that men cannot be sexually coerced or violated, and this is not the case.

The emphasis on coitus may also be instrumental in the pervasiveness of rape, as Schnarch (1991) discussed. Writing about sexual–marital therapy and sexual dysfunction in dyadic systems, he noted that "coitus-focused sexuality, with its inherent emphasis on male erectile functioning, invariably perpetuates male insecurity and fear of female sexuality and elicits corresponding attempts to subjugate and control women" (p. 228).

Equating sex with penile–vaginal intercourse may also lead to sexual coercion by implying that other forms of sexual activity are merely preliminaries to "the real thing." A woman may engage in other forms of sexual activity because to her they constitute a satisfying sexual encounter in and of themselves. The idea that sex must equal penile–vaginal intercourse, however, can lead to the assumption that when a woman engages in sexual contact with a man, she has "led him on," and thus he has the right to expect intercourse. Ann Landers, in her October 14, 1985, advice column, summarized this idea when she responded to a female reader who preferred to engage in sexual activities other than intercourse: "It is foolish to take such chances. Going to bat with the intention of stopping at third base may prove hazardous to a woman's health" (p. 3A).

Men as Dominant, Women as Submissive

The theme that men are dominant and active, whereas women are submissive and passive, is virtually ubiquitous in American culture. The December, 1992, issue of *Glamour* ran an ad in which a woman lay on her back, a man hovering above her stroking her chin, with the words, "How I longed for him to hold me, to be in his arms . . . [ellipsis in original]" (p. 47). Rather than holding him in her arms, she would merely wait and long for him to hold her. The man was constructed as active; the woman, as passive.

Fairy tales and nursery rhymes provide countless examples of this imbalance (Hammond, 1987). Cinderella, Sleeping Beauty, Snow White—all were rescued or saved by men. More recently, Walt Disney's movie, *The Little Mermaid*, has carried on the tradition of these stories. Once again, a female is portrayed as the passive romantic, yearning for her prince, without any life direction of her own. A familiar nursery rhyme insidiously portrays girls as helpless and incompetent: Jack and Jill went up the hill to fetch a pail of water; Jack fell down and broke his crown and Jill came tumbling after. As Hammond (1987) pointed out, Jill is apparently unable either to help Jack or to fetch the water, let alone walk back down the hill. She simply collapses and follows his lead. These ubiquitous images serve to reinforce boys' and girls' ideas about the roles they are expected to play in relationships.

Male dominance in marriage is explicitly prescribed in the *Bible*. Passages such as I Corinthians 11:3 ("the husband is supreme over his wife"), I Corinthians 11:10 ("a woman . . . is under her husband's authority"), and Ephesians 5:21–24 ("Wives, submit yourselves to your husbands as to the Lord. For a husband has authority over his wife just as Christ has authority over the church . . . and so wives must submit themselves completely to their husbands just as the church submits itself to Christ") have been employed to reinforce existing power differentials and to justify male dominance.

Male dominance is not restricted to American culture. Unger and Crawford (1992) pointed out that cross-cultural research has shown a multinational tendency for women to be associated with submissiveness and for men to be associated with forcefulness and independence.

This theme relates to sexual coercion by implying that men's role is to make sexual advances, even if his partner shows no signs of sexual interest. Thus, some sexually coercive behaviors may be construed as normative male sexual advances rather than as coercive.

Objectification of Women

The objectification of women is the practice of viewing women as objects valued for their appearance, sexual services, or other functions rather than for their humanity. Objectification of women is perhaps most evident in advertising, where women's bodies are used to sell virtually everything from cars to jewelry to beer. Often the objectification is implicit in the ad when the woman appears along with the product with no rationale for her presence or her alluring appearance. At times, however, her role as object of adornment is made explicit. An underwear ad in the May, 1993, issue of *Ladies' Home Journal* featured a woman wearing only underpants and a bra standing atop a canyon, with the heading, "Help Keep America Beautiful" (p. 93). A similar idea was conveyed in a swimsuit ad in the December, 1992, *Glamour*, in which a bikini-clad woman on a beach was pictured with the caption, "Keep our *beaches* beautiful" (p. 249). According to these ads, women's role is to appear beautiful and thus to adorn their surroundings. The progression from women's objectification as attractive sex objects to sex outlets is all too easy.

An article in the November, 1990, issue of *Ladies Home Journal* also conveyed this theme. The article's title asked, "What makes a woman sexy?" (Cohen, 1990, p. 116) and followed that query with the further question, "Is it her breasts, her lips, her legs—or something far more mysterious and subtle?" (p. 116). The author eventually concluded that a combination of physical beauty, self-assuredness, humor, and interest in sex are what make a woman sexy, but she initially addressed physical beauty. She suggested that women who are sexy "have learned to play up their best features" (p. 116), and after quoting a man's praise for his girlfriend's ability to "display [her legs] to their best advantage" (p. 121), she asked, "what other features do men find attractive?" (p. 121). Here again, women's bodies are objects—collections of sexual features—for men's sexual approval.

If women are valued for their sexuality, their appearance, and their ability to satisfy others sexually, then sexual coercion becomes not a violation of a person but an appropriate use of an object. Straight and lesbian women alike may internalize the notion that their role is to sexually satisfy others, which may make them less likely to construe their relationships as sexually coercive. Thus, sexual coercion might be regarded as trivial or even flattering rather than problematic. Furthermore, if women are objects, they can be owned.

Women as Property

Another common theme in American culture is that women are owned by men, and that this ownership implies women's responsibility to be sexually available and faithful to their male partners. Spousal rape exemptions, which maintain that husbands cannot rape their wives because sexual activity is their marital right, evidence this theme. Estrich (1987) provided an insightful discussion of spousal exemption in rape law. She pointed out that the origin of spousal exemptions lies in English common law and directly reflects the notion that a wife is the property of her husband and that by marrying him she has given him unmitigated consent for sexual activity. Laura X (personal communication, December 15, 1993), director of the National Clearinghouse on Marital Rape in Berkeley, CA, stated that as of 1993, only 20 American states had eliminated spousal exemptions completely. Thirty states had partial exemptions that defined rape more narrowly between married persons than between unmarried persons. Five states had partial exemptions for cohabiting persons, and one state even provided a partial exemption for dating partners.

Biblical interpretation also contributes to the notion that husbands cannot rape their wives. The *Bible* includes several passages that have been used to support spousal exemptions: "Wives, submit yourselves to your husbands, for that is what you should do as Christians" (Colossians 3:18); "woman was created for man's sake" (I Corinthians 11:9); and a reference to spouses' marital duties toward one another: "each should satisfy the other's needs . . . do not deny yourselves to each other, unless you first agree to do so for awhile in order to spend your time in prayer; but then resume normal marital relations" (I Corinthians 7:3–5).

The idea that women are men's property is also manifested in rape during war. "In war, women like so many plots of land become with renewed clarity the disputed possessions of men, their bodies an inevitable part of the battleground" (TePaske, 1982, p. 14). "Stemming from the days when women *were* property, access to a woman's body has been considered an actual reward of war" (Brownmiller, 1975, p. 28).

Discourse implying that women are men's property, then, may serve two functions with regard to sexual coercion. In cases where a man sexually victimizes "his own woman," sexual victimization becomes invisible because the man rightfully has dominion over his own property. In cases where men rape "other men's women," rape becomes a weapon that men use against other men.

Sex as a Commodity

Indecent Proposal, a recent Hollywood movie about a billionaire who offers one million dollars to a couple in order to have sex with the wife, illustrates the idea of sex as a commodity. In an ad for this movie, the male billionaire is pictured with the words, "I buy people every day. It's naive to think it can't be done" (*Glamour*, April, 1993, p. 93).

Schur (1988) discussed the commoditization of sex and related it to the objectification of women; he noted that "once sexuality and sexual partners are objectified, it is but a small step further to make them into commodities . . . [including] the exchange of sex for money, status, or security" (p. 11). Furthermore, Schur argued, once sex is commoditized, it is but another small step to take sex—a commodity—by force.

The commoditization of sex is conveyed by the language we use to discuss sexuality. *Glamour* magazine's "sex & health" column discussed earlier stated that some women "believe it [virginity] makes them more attractive in the marriage market" (Lever & Schwartz, 1993, p. 87). Men who have sex are sometimes said to "get some." Women who have sex without getting enough in exchange are said to be "cheap."

Sex Privatization

"Sex privatization," a phrase coined by Firestone (1993), is "the process whereby women are blinded to their generality as a [sexual] class which renders them invisible as individuals to the male eye" (p. 449). Sex privatization, in which women learn to value themselves for their generic sexual appeal rather than for their intellect or personality, is communicated through many of the examples we have previously cited. Advertisements portraying women as sex objects, advice columns discussing women's role as sexual servicers, movies conveying the commoditization of sex—all contribute to a mind set in which women come to think of themselves as valuable for their sexuality. Sex privatization results in women's feeling complimented by comments and gestures that glorify female sexuality but that do not necessarily refer to individual women (e.g., feeling flattered by unsolicited touches, catcalls, and "generalized male horniness taken as a sign of personal value and desirability," Firestone, 1993, p. 450).

Kuster (1992) argued that women who feel complimented by such attention feel that way only because they have been socialized to do so. She quoted Callie Khouri, screenwriter of *Thelma and Louise*: "a woman who enjoys being yelled at on the street is a woman who has been socialized to think that she is valued and defined by her sexuality" (pp. 309–310). Kuster's article concluded with a series of suggestions for how women can respond to sexual harassment. Although this is an important topic for women who will continue to experience harassing remarks and gestures, the focus is once again on women's responsibility for handling the comments and actions of men.

Compulsory Heterosexuality

Compulsory heterosexuality was defined by Rich (1980) as "the enforcement of heterosexuality for women as a means of assuring male right of physical, economical, and emotional access" (p. 647). Heterosexuality is enforced for men as well as for women (Pharr, 1988). Heterosexuality is enforced in numerous ways, many involving communication. Perhaps most important is the invisibility of homosexual relationships in the media—in advertisements, television shows, and so forth (e.g., in the magazines we examined, we found no ads depicting homosexual relationships). When homosexuality is mentioned, it is often in a negative context. For example, the phrase "admitted homosexual" implies that homosexuality is a fault to which one must admit. The term "homosexual" is often used in negative contexts in which the term "heterosexual" is not used in comparable situations. For example, the term "homosexual killer" is sometimes used, whereas the term "heterosexual killer" is not. Many jokes about homosexuals perpetuate negative stereotypes.

Compulsory heterosexuality perpetuates sexual coercion in several ways. Women and men are pressured to engage in heterosexual activity, even if they would prefer to engage in homosexual activity (Muehlenhard & Cook, 1988; Rich, 1980). Sanday (1990) suggested that social prohibitions against homosexual behavior lead to fraternity gang rape: Because fraternity men, even heterosexual men, feel a need to bond with each other but are prohibited by social norms from being physically or emotionally intimate, they bond with each other by taking turns having sexual intercourse with the same nonconsenting woman. In addition, when same-sex relationships are rendered invisible, then sexual coercion in these relationships is also rendered invisible, and lesbian, bisexual, and gay individuals may be less likely to define their coercive experiences appropriately and to seek legal and emotional services and support (Waterman, Dawson, & Bologna, 1989).

CONCLUSIONS

Language and discourse, as primary modes of communication, both reflect and shape cultural notions about human sexuality. These notions, in turn, influence our understanding of sexual coercion, often obscuring sexually coercive acts or making sexual victimization seem inconsequential.

When we use passive constructions, euphemisms, pronouns, and sexist language, we either inadvertently or intentionally obscure the perpetrators of sexual coercion and maintain a focus on the victims. Attending closely to communication about sexuality is one way to counteract this tendency; using active forms that give responsibility to the perpetrators and recognizing phrasing and vocabulary that contribute to victim blaming are important steps to take.

Common themes about human sexuality perpetuate males' sexual victimization of females, while simultaneously obscuring male victims. These themes are conveyed by cultural images, idioms, and stories. Many of the themes we have discussed are interrelated. The notion that male sexuality is uncontrollable is similar to the idea that sex is a force of nature. The objectification of women, women as property, and sex as a commodity are all founded on valuing women for their ability to service men sexually. The belief that "women ask for it" relies on the notion that women are responsible for male sexuality. The idea that sex equals coitus perpetuates compulsory heterosexuality. The convergence of these themes forms a powerful overarching cultural norm regarding human sexuality. As a whole, they convey a message that perpetuates sexual victimization.

The problems that arise from contemporary sexuality discourse may be addressed in a number of ways. First, individuals can respond to media images and messages directly by writing the companies that perpetuate sexual stereotypes and harmful images in their advertisements. Sometimes the company's address or phone number appears on the product itself. If not, one can phone or visit a local library, where reference collections provide the addresses of U.S. companies. If the trade name of the product is known, but not the company name, the *Standard Directory of Advertisers Tradename Index* will supply the company name and address. If the company name is known, the *Standard Directory of Advertisers* will provide the company's address as well as information about their advertising policies and agencies.

Second, citizen voting power may be used in favor of representatives and legislation that appropriately address sexual coercion and against individuals and proposals that perpetuate the invisibility of sexual violence. Being informed during local and national elections and becoming involved in local politics allows individuals to exercise their power as citizens and to influence the governmental policies that affect sexual coercion.

Third, parents can raise their children to be critical participants in the sexuality discourse. Children can be taught to think critically about the images and messages in the world around them. Rather than censoring television entirely or restricting the books and magazines that children read, parents can share their reactions to the discourse and teach their children to question what they see and hear. Children can be raised to view women and men as equally competent, effectual, and important. This way, girls and boys will be less apt to internalize media images depicting women as passive recipients of male sexuality and men as sexually driven predators of women.

There are efforts to use language in positive ways to promote sexual autonomy and gender equality. Children's books are an important avenue of positive change. Although the majority of books for children continue to perpetuate sexual stereotypes, there are those that actively oppose traditional gender roles and work to promote gender equality. *Father Gander's Nursery Rhymes for the Nineteen Nineties* (Gander, 1989) is an example of such a work. Although most films continue to perpetuate the themes discussed in this chapter, occasionally an individual creates a work that combats those themes. For example, *Thelma and Louise* portrays the pain of sexual coercion while refusing to perpetuate the themes that obscure male perpetrators' responsibility for their sexual violence and sexual harassment. Books written by feminists, such as Dale Spender's (1990) *Man Made Language* and Julia Penelope's (1990) *Speaking Freely: Unlearning the Lies of the Father Tongues*, critique language usage and suggest changes. Such efforts can also be seen in the mass media. *Los Angeles Times* editor Shelby Coffey III recently issued new guidelines suggesting alternatives to language that may be offensive to different ethnic, racial, gender, and sexual minorities (Kathy Gosnell, *Los Angeles Times*, personal communication, December 16, 1993; Kurtz, 1993). The guidelines recommend against using sexist terms such as "mailman" and heterosexist terms such as "admitted homosexual." Some staff members (see Kurtz, 1993) as well as commentators (e.g., Schorr, 1993) have criticized this policy as "boneheaded" or trivial. But language is power, and working to use language in ways that promote sexual autonomy and discourage sexual coercion is an important step toward creating a society in which sexual choice is respected and sexual activity is freely chosen.

REFERENCES

A billionaire [Movie advertisement]. (1993, April). *Glamour*, p. 93.

Allgeier, E. R., & Allgeier, A. R. (1991). *Sexual interaction* (3rd ed.). Lexington, MA: D. C. Heath.

Beneke, T. (1982). *Men on rape: What they have to say about sexual violence*. New York: St. Martin's Press.

The body counters. (1993, April 12). *People Weekly*, pp. 34–37.

Brothers, J. (1981). *What every woman should know about men*. New York: Ballantine Books.

Brownmiller, S. (1975). *Against our will: Men, women and rape*. New York: Bantam Books.

Burnam, M. A., Stein, J. A., Golding, J. M., Seigel, J. M., Sorenson, S. B., Forsythe, A. B., & Telles, C. A. (1988). Sexual assault and mental disorders in a community population. *Journal of Consulting and Clinical Psychology, 56*, 843–850.

Cherry, F. (1983). Gender roles and sexual violence. In E. R. Allgeier & N. B. McCormick (Eds.), *Changing boundaries: Gender roles and sexual behavior* (pp. 245–260). Palo Alto, CA: Mayfield.

Cohen, S. S. (1990, November). What makes a woman sexy? *Ladies Home Journal*, pp. 116, 121–123.

Daly, M. (1978). *Gyn/ecology: The metaethics of radical feminism*. Boston: Beacon Press.

Estrich, S. (1987). *Real rape*. Cambridge: Harvard University Press.

Feldman, R. S. (1993). *Understanding psychology*. New York: McGraw–Hill.

Fiorenza, E. S. (1986). *In memory of her: A feminist theological reconstruction of Christian origins*. New York: Crossroad.

Firestone, S. (1993). The culture of romance. In A. M. Jaggar & P. S. Rothenberg (Eds.), *Feminist frameworks: Alternative theoretical accounts of the relations between men and women* (3rd ed.) (pp. 448–453). New York: McGraw–Hill.

G. & C. Merriam Co. (1981). *Webster's new collegiate dictionary*. Springfield, MA: Author.

Gander, P. (1989). *Father Gander's nursery rhymes for the nineteen nineties: The alternative Mother Goose*. New York: Oleander Press.

Gavey, N. (1989). Feminist poststructuralism and discourse analysis. *Psychology of Women Quarterly, 13*, 459–475.

Gavey, N. (1992). Technologies and effects of heterosexual coercion. *Feminism and Psychology, 2*, 325–351.

Glazer, S. (1993, February). Violence against women. *CQ Researcher*. Washington, DC: Congressional Quarterly.

Greenfield, T. A. (1975, April). Race and passive voice at Monticello. *The Crisis*, pp. 146–147.

Groth, N., & Burgess, A. W. (1980). Male rape: Offenders and victims. *American Journal of Psychiatry, 137*, 806–810.

Haas, A., & Haas, K. (1990). *Understanding sexuality*. St. Louis: Times Mirror/Bosby.

Hammond, D. B. (1987). *My parents never had sex: Myths and facts of sexual aging*. Buffalo, NY: Prometheus Press.

Harney, P. A., & Muehlenhard, C. L. (1991). Rape. In E. Grauerholz & M. A. Koralewski (Eds.), *Sexual coercion: A sourcebook on its nature, causes, and prevention* (pp. 3–15). Lexington, MA: Lexington Books.

Harrison, B. W. (1985). *Making the connections: Essays in feminist social ethics*. Boston: Beacon Press.

Hellinger, M. (1984). Effecting social change through group action: Feminine occupational titles in transition. In C. Kramarae, M. Schulz, & W. M. O'Barr (Eds.), *Language and power* (pp.136–153). Beverly Hills, CA: Sage.

Kaufman, A., DiVasto, P., Jackson, R., Voorhees, D., & Christy, J. (1980). Male rape victims: Noninstitutionalized assault. *American Journal of Psychiatry, 137*, 221–223.

Kirchner, J. (1993, July). Are women's images changing on MTV? *Glamour*, p. 71.

Koss, M. P., & Burkhart, B. R. (1989). A conceptual analysis of rape victimization. *Psychology of Women Quarterly, 13*, 27–40.

Koss, M. P., Gidycz, C. A., & Wisniewski, N. (1987). The scope of rape: Incidence and prevalence of sexual aggression and victimization in a national sample of higher education students. *Journal of Consulting and Clinical Psychology, 55*, 162–170.

Koss, M. P., & Harvey, M. R. (1991). *The rape victim: Clinical and community interventions* (2nd ed.). London: Sage.

Koss, M. P., Woodruff, W. J., & Koss, P. G. (1990). Relation of criminal victimization to health perceptions among women medical patients. *Journal of Consulting and Clinical Psychology, 58*, 147–152.

Kurtz, H. (1993, November 29). You don't say . . . L.A. Times banishes words that can wound. *The Washington Post*, pp. D1, D9.

Kuster, E. (1992, September). Don't "hey, baby" me: How to fight street harassment. *Glamour*, pp. 308–311, 332–334.

Landers, A. (1985, August 12). Many actions tend to invite trouble: Women should convey right messages to their dates. *Kansas City Star*, p. B6.

Landers, A. (1985, October 14). Sexual teasing leads to trouble. *Bryan-College Station Eagle*, p. 3A.

Lerner, G. (1986). *The creation of patriarchy*. New York: Oxford University Press.

Lever, J., & Schwartz, P. (1993, May). "Sex & health." *Glamour*, p. 87.

Lips, H. M. (1991). *Women, men, and power*. London: Mayfield.

Matlin, M. W. (1985). Current issues in psycholinguistics. In T. M. Shlechter & M. P. Toglia (Eds.), *New directions in cognitive science* (pp. 217–241). Norwood, NJ: Ablex.

Matlin, M. W. (1992). *Psychology*. New York: Harcourt Brace Jovanovich.

Moore, R. B. (1992). Racism in the English language. In P. S. Rothenberg (Ed.), *Race, class, and gender in the United States: An integrated study* (2nd ed.). New York: St. Martin's Press. (Reprinted from *Racism in the English language*, 1976, New York: Council on Interracial Books for Children)

Muehlenhard, C. L. (1988). Misinterpreted dating behaviors and the risk of date rape. *Journal of Social and Clinical Psychology, 6*, 20–37.

Muehlenhard, C. L., & Cook, S. W. (1988). Men's self–reports of unwanted sexual activity. *Journal of Sex Research, 24*, 58–72.

Muehlenhard, C. L., Goggins, M. F., Jones, J. M., & Satterfield, A. T. (1991). Sexual violence and coercion in close relationships. In K. McKinney & S. Sprecher (Eds.), *Sexuality in close relationships* (pp. 155–175). Hillsdale, NJ: Lawrence Erlbaum Associates.

Muehlenhard, C. L., & Linton, M. A. (1987). Date rape and sexual aggression in dating situations: Incidence and risk factors. *Journal of Counseling Psychology, 34*, 186–196.

Muehlenhard, C. L., & MacNaughton, J. S. (1988). Women's beliefs about women who "lead men on." *Journal of Social and Clinical Psychology, 7*, 65–79.

Muehlenhard, C. L., Powch, I. G., Phelps. J. L., & Giusti, L. M. (1992). Definitions of rape: Scientific and political implications. *Journal of Social Issues, 48*, 23–44.

Muehlenhard, C. L., & Schrag, J. L. (1991). Nonviolent sexual coercion. In A. Parrot & L. Bechhofer (Eds.), *Acquaintance rape: The hidden crime* (pp. 115–128). New York: Wiley.

Murphy, J. E. (1991). An investigation of child sexual abuse and consequent victimization: Some implications of telephone surveys. In D. D. Knudsen & J. L. Miller (Eds.), *Abused and battered: Social and legal responses to family violence* (pp. 79–87). New York: Aldine de Gruyer.

Ng, S. H. (1990). Androcentric coding of *man* and *his* in memory by language users. *Journal of Experimental Social Psychology, 26*, 455–464.

Penelope, J. (1990). *Speaking freely: Unlearning the lies of the fathers' tongues.* New York: Pergamon.

Pharr, S. (1988). *Homophobia: A weapon of sexism.* Inverness, CA: Chardon Press.

Resick, P. A. (1983). The rape reaction: Research findings and implications for intervention. *Behavior Therapist, 6*, 129–132.

Rich, A. (1980). Compulsory heterosexuality and lesbian existence. *Signs: Journal of Women in Culture and Society, 5*, 631–660.

Richardson, L. (1990). *Writing strategies: Reaching diverse audiences.* Newbury Park, CA: Sage.

Rubin, D. L. (1988). Introduction: Four dimensions of social construction in written communication. In B. A. Roforth and D. L. Rubin (Eds.), *The social construction of written communication.* Norwood, NJ: Ablex Publishing.

Russell, D. E. H. (1984). *Sexual exploitation: Rape, child sexual abuse, and workplace harassment.* Beverly Hills, CA: Sage.

Russell, D. E. H. (1990). *Rape in marriage* (rev. ed.). Bloomington: Indiana University Press.

Sanday, P. R. (1990). *Fraternity gang rape: Sex, brotherhood and privilege on campus.* New York: New York University Press.

Sarrel, P. M., & Masters, W. H. (1982). Sexual molestation of men by women. *Archives of Sexual Behavior, 11*, 117–131.

Schnarch, D. M. (1991). *Constructing the sexual crucible: An integration of sexual and marital therapy.* New York: Norton.

Schorr, D. (1993, November 30). Commentary. *All Things Considered.* National Public Radio.

Schur, E. M. (1988). *The Americanization of sex.* Philadelphia: Temple University Press.

TePaske, B. A. (1982). *Rape and ritual: A psychological study.* Toronto: Inner City Books.

Tiefer, L. (1992, August). *A kiss is not a kiss: Sexual experience and social constructionism.* Paper presented at the meeting of the American Psychological Association, Toronto.

24 Hours of protection, and all you'll turn off is the light. [Advertisement for Today Sponge[TM]]. (1993, February). *Glamour,* p. 118.

Unger, R., & Crawford, M. (1992). *Women and gender: A feminist psychology.* New York: McGraw-Hill.

Waterman, C. K., Dawson, L. J., & Bologna, M. J. (1989). Sexual coercion in gay male and lesbian relationships: Predictors and implications for support services. *Journal of Sex Research, 26*, 118–124.

Wojtyla, K. (1981). *Love and responsibility.* New York: Farrar, Straus, and Giroux.

Chapter 7

Negotiating Safer Sex: The Dynamics of African-American Relationships

Lynn Carol Miller
University of Southern California

Diane M. Burns
University of Alabama

Sadina Rothspan
University of Southern California

Sex. Arguably, no arena of relations between men and women is so fraught with inequities. From ancient Greece to more recent times, when women were in short supply, they were often highly "valued"; still, men often controlled whom women would marry, whether they could be sold into slavery, divorced, or forced into prostitution. At other times, when women were in overabundance, they tended to be "devalued." In such times, Guttentag and Secord (1983) argued, men tend to be less committed to a single relationship, more likely to de-emphasize love and marriage, and more likely to engage in transient sexual relationships.

At least one current American population exhibits this type of sex ratio imbalance: African Americans. Since 1960, the ratio of men to women among African Americans has been low (Guttentag & Secord, 1983), especially among those who are young (16 to 42 years old) and unmarried. And, in line with Guttentag and Secord's argument, with an overabundance of women, there appear to be corresponding differences in the sexual attitudes and behaviors of African American men and women (Fullilove, Fullilove, Haynes, & Gross, 1990). Men are more likely than women to endorse premarital sexual relations (Belcastro, 1985; Reiss, 1964), to have more sexual partners, and to engage in more extramarital affairs than women (Anderson & Dahlberg, 1992; Weinberg & Williams, 1988).

In light of AIDS, these behaviors may have fatal consequences since, sadly, these sexual behaviors are not associated with safer sexual practices. Condom use among African American men and women is less likely than in other ethnic groups (DiClemente, 1991; Weinstock, Lindan, Bolan, Kegeles, & Hearst, 1993). These dangers are compounded by negative attitudes regarding safer sexual practices. African-American men are more likely than African American women to report negative and angry reactions to the use of condoms (Johnson et al., 1991). And, as Weinstock et al. (1993) found, African-American and Hispanic women are especially unlikely to use condoms when their partners respond negatively to their use. Some have suggested that with relatively few available men, African-American women may be more likely to acquiesce in using unsafe sexual practices rather than risk losing the relationship (Mays & Cochran, 1988).

Such acquiescence could significantly enhance the spread of disease. Unfortunately, sexually transmitted diseases, particularly syphilis and gonorrhea, have increased markedly among African Americans, compared to other ethnic groups (CDC, 1990). The rates of HIV (human immunodeficiency virus) transmission in the African-American population, the population focused on here, are among the fastest rising in the nation. Although African Americans are only 12% of the population in the United States, they comprise 27% of the reported AIDS cases (CDC, 1991). Furthermore, a higher percentage of African Americans AIDS cases are via heterosexual transmission (12%) compared to Caucasians (2%) or Hispanics (6%). Perhaps, not surprisingly, among AIDS cases, African-American women (52%) and children (53%) greatly outnumber their Caucasian (26%, 21%), and Hispanic (20%, 25%) peers. An earlier onset of sexual activity among African Americans (Weinberg & Williams; 1988; Wilson, 1986), and lower rates of condom use (DiClemente, 1991; Jemmott & Jones, 1993), may explain the much higher rates of sexually transmitted diseases and unintended pregnancies (Hernandez & Smith, 1990) among African Americans compared to Whites.

What are the intrapersonal and interpersonal dynamics that may shed some light on why some individuals—despite the risks—fail to successfully negotiate safer sexual practices? Are there inequities in the relationships between African-American men and women that affect individual vulnerability to AIDS? Do these dynamics suggest that one gender may take a more instrumental role in controlling their likelihood of contracting this disease?

The goal of the current work is to explore the interpersonal dynamics that affect the use of safer sexual practices in lower class and lower middle class, heterosexual African-American relationships. Before we discuss several of our own studies examining some of these dynamics in both committed and uncommitted relationships, we will elaborate one of the most promising theoretical frameworks for thinking about power differentials among African Americans (Guttentag & Secord, 1983). That work, dovetailing with a dynamic goal-based approach to negotiation processes (Miller, Bettencourt, DeBro, & Hoffman, 1993; Miller & Read, 1987; 1991; Read & Miller, 1989), suggests that power inequities may result not only in different sexual behaviors for men versus women, but may also affect goals in sexual relationships, and the process by which men and women negotiate safer sex.

After presenting our own work, we conclude by discussing the implications of this work for understanding sex and power in heterosexual relations among African Americans in an era of AIDS.

SEX RATIOS, POWER, AND SEXUAL BEHAVIORS OF MEN AND WOMEN

Sex Ratios

What Causes Imbalances? Over historical time, Guttentag and Secord (1983) argued the ratio of men to women has often been unbalanced, with either a shortage of men (more than 100 women for every 100 men or low sex ratios) or an overabundance of men (fewer than 100 women per 100 men or high sex ratios). There are a variety of reasons for such imbalances. For example, war, disease and plagues, poverty, and famine all seem to disproportionately affect male compared to female mortality rates. During wars and plagues, women and children were often sent away to safer locations. Although it is unclear why, restraints on diets due to poverty and famine tend to disproportionately affect male compared to female births, and have more deleterious consequences for male childhood survival rates. On the other hand, other factors, such as infanticide and fatalities of women in childbirth could reduce the number of females generally, and migration and immigration patterns would reduce the number of women to men in a given locality. Typically, female offspring are more likely to be killed at birth than male offspring. And, until modern times, death in childbirth was a significant threat. Because men often migrated, leaving the women behind, there was often a shortage of women in areas such as frontier towns and other sites of migration.

Guttentag and Secord (1983) argued that to understand the relationships between men and women, ratio imbalances also need to be considered in terms of "local" conditions for acceptable marriageable or dating partners. That is, the available pool of men is usually constituted of those who are a few years older than the women and who have certain characteristics (e.g., social status, higher educational levels, income, belonging to a particular race or religion, etc.). For African Americans, there has been an imbalance between men and women in such "local populations" since the 1960s. At present there are 92 African-American men per 100 African-American women (Johnson, 1993). Perhaps due to dietary restrictions, there are fewer males than females born in this population, and "available" males are further depleted compared to females by activities such as gang warfare, prison terms, and generally higher accidental death and homicide rates. According to Johnson (1993), "When we consider the proportion of African-American men who are incarcerated, addicted to drugs, homosexual, select white women as partners, or who are uneducated and unemployable, it becomes very clear that there is a real shortage of African-American men" (p. 52).

What are the Implications for Heterosexual Relationships? When sex ratios are high and there is an overabundance of men, Guttentag and Secord (1983) argued, women, in certain cultural contexts, might subjectively perceive greater power in their relationships and more control over their outcomes. This is more likely to be the case, they argued, when women are able to choose their marriage partners. Their relative sense of control would be directed within traditional institutions of society, marrying into higher socioeconomic classes, rather than attempting to advance careers and actively seek broader political and personal rights. Sexual morality during such periods would be stressed, especially for women, with virginity prized. Although there might be a "double standard" in these societies, the culture would emphasize male, as well as female, commitment in a single, long-term relationship. With a significant voice in mate choice, women, as well as men, would tend to be committed to ideals of romantic love.

On the other hand, when sex ratios are low and there is an overabundance of women, Guttentag and Secord (1983) argued that women

> in such societies would have a subjective sense of powerlessness and would feel personally devalued by the society...more likely to be valued as mere sex objects...[women] would find it difficult to achieve economic mobility through marriage. More men and women would remain single or, if they married, would be more apt to get divorced. [Sexual] options would be greater for men than for women. Sexual relationships outside of marriage would be accepted...brief liaisons would be usual. Women would more often share a man with other women. Adultery would be commonplace...men would have opportunities to move successively from woman to woman or to maintain multiple relationships with different women...The culture would not emphasize love and commitment, and a lower value would be placed on marriage and the family. Instead, transient relationships between men and women would become important. (pp. 20–21)

Exploring the available historical record in high and low sex ratio societies from those of classical Greece, early and latter Middle Ages, through the British colonial and frontier period, to more contemporary subcultures in the United States, Guttentag and Secord provided intriguing suggestive evidence that sex ratios may play an important role in shaping the prevailing relationships between men and women in a given era and within a given culture.

Dyadic and Structural Power

Guttentag and Secord (1983) argued that in order to understand couples' relationships, the relationships between dependency and power must be examined. To the extent that one party's satisfaction is more dependent on the other, that individual has less power and is "in a weaker position for negotiating or obtaining satisfaction in the relationship. For our purposes...a crucial feature that determines the balance of dependency and power in a relationship is the level of outcomes that is perceived to be obtainable in *alternative* relationships" (p. 21).

Guttentag and Secord argued that the perceived availability of partners would be high when members of the alternative gender were in overabundance. When outcomes in alternative relationships are perceived to be relatively high and those relationships are readily available, dependency within a current relationship is low, resulting in what Guttentag and Secord referred to as *dyadic power*. When sex ratios are high, and there are more men available than women, individual women have dyadic power; when the sex ratios are low, and there are more women available than men, individual men have dyadic power.

How do individuals with low dyadic power respond to limitations in the number of available partners? Perhaps, in a variety of ways. Some might compromise and settle for a less desirable partner, or choose to be a "weaker" partner in a relationship, making more sacrifices, being unusually tolerant of inappropriate behavior, and catering more to the partner's needs. Some may stress "working on" the relationship and developing and using strategies to enhance its satisfaction; they may attempt to maximize the desirability of the current relationship for their partner compared to alternatives. Or, they might spend more time with same sex individuals, or turn to other activities, such as advancing their own careers. Over an extended time frame, those lacking dyadic power may organize various consciousness-raising groups and attempt to change the prevailing norms regarding relationships between men and women. When the low dyadic power group is women, this may include advocating enhanced freedom and independence for women. When the low dyadic power group is men, they might enhance their efforts to appear more romantic and exert greater effort wooing potential mates. But, in a more organized way, they might push for changes in social norms that devalue promiscuity for women, favor monogamy, and value virginity before marriage. All of these changes would place constraints on the power women might have to leave relationships with men.

The consequences for men and women of high and low sex ratios, Guttentag and Secord (1983) argued, are not the same. That is, in addition to dyadic power, men–but not women–can bring to bear a second type of power that can be used to constrain and control the power women might derive from being in short supply. Guttentag and Secord argued that historically, in virtually all societies, men, and not women, held *structural power*, or power derived from "their superior economic, political, and legal position in society, as well as the sheer weight of the social values and practices that implement these powers" (pp. 153–154). As the level of men's structural power varied from low to high and absolute across time and cultures, there was apt to be a corresponding decrease in the extent to which women could take advantage of the power that they derived from the imbalance of sex ratios.

For example, Guttentag and Secord (1983) referred to the Bakweri, a West African tribe, studied by anthropologists in the 1950s. There, the sex ratio was 236 (236 men for every 100 women). Due to the imposition of a British justice system, Bakweri men had little structural power. Under these circumstances, relationships were highly unstable with high divorce rates. Women's families demanded high "bride-wealth" prices from prospective husbands, and women—both married and not—engaged in numerous extramarital affairs, in part to have an independent income derived from these activities that they could use to free themselves of their husbands. Without strong structural controls, although men were displeased by these affairs, men were unable to impose traditional roles on the women. In contrast, among Chinese Americans in the American West of the late 1800s, the sex ratio was 2,000, a state of affairs that would normally afford the women considerable dyadic power. This, however, was overwhelmed by the powerful controls and enormous structural power imposed by the Chinese-American men; women were either deceived into a life of prostitution in brothels or kept as virtual prisoners by wealthy Chinese-American men.

Thus, the level of both dyadic power and structural power of men and women in a particular cultural group would seem important in making predictions about the potential impact of sex ratio imbalances on the sexual relationships of men and women. How might these two factors "play out" in the contemporary relationships between African-American men and women?

Implications for African-American Men and Women.   Given that there is a low sex ratio among African-American men and women in the United States, given Guttentag and Secord's analysis, African-American men would have dyadic power in their relationships with women. This suggests that African-American men should be more likely to (a) have more sexual partners and more extramarital affairs than women, and (b) perceive greater power in negotiating what they might want in relationships. For example, if men wanted to avoid AIDS, they might be more likely to broach the topic of using condoms, or be more likely to initiate the use of condoms. Women might be relatively unlikely to respond negatively to these attempts to influence the partner to allow the use of a condom. On the other hand, given that many African-American men tend to view condoms negatively (Johnson et al., 1991), their desire to avoid discomfort might be sufficiently salient, especially in the "heat of the moment" (Miller et al., 1993), that they might perceive more obstacles to safer sex, and give more negative responses to women who attempt to persuade them to use a condom. Furthermore, consistent with Guttentag and Secord's (1993) argument, African-American men may be less interested in commitment, love, and working on the relationship than women.

Women may respond to men's dyadic power in a variety of ways. Coupled with a perceived imbalance in power caused by economic or *structural* dependence, some may feel powerless to control their outcomes with respect to AIDS and passively acquiesce (Wilson, 1986). Consistent with this possibility, for example, Weinstock, Lindan, Bolan, Kegeles, and Hearst (1993) found that African-American women cite lack of power and inability to assert condom use as explanations for a failure to use condoms. This difference may be exacerbated with increasing education and age, as the sex ratios become even more pronounced (Wilson, 1986). Some women might attempt to deal with these inequities, by emphasizing the importance of love, commitment, and working on the relationship, compared to men, trying to make their current relationship a close one and better than the alternatives the men might seek.

On the other hand, some women might refuse to have their health outcomes dependent on men who might be prone to numerous affairs and infidelity. They might become quite vocal and instrumental both in talking about condoms with their partners as well as insuring that their partners use condoms. Another study investigating gender-role stereotypes of African Americans did *not* find support for culturally based roles involving "male dominance and female submissiveness" (Kline, Kline, & Oken, 1992). Furthermore, in that work, the authors found that focus groups of African-American and Hispanic women, all IV drug users, included many quite independent women: These women were often adamant about the use of condoms, and reported abstaining from sex to avoid contracting and transmitting HIV.

It seems likely that compared to their White counterparts, African-American men, especially those in the lower ends of the socioeconomic spectrum might enjoy relatively little structural power. Thus, local fluctuations in sex ratios might be particularly important in affecting gender differences in sexual behavior patterns and communication patterns related to the process of negotiating safer sex.

One important additional factor that may tend to be overlooked in past research, is the nature of the relationships men and women have with one another. Individuals who are in more committed relationships (married or living with someone) may differ considerably from those individuals who are not in committed relationships (e.g., single individuals). Although there may be similar patterns for men and women in both types of relationships regarding some variables (e.g., their relationship goals), it seems reasonable to assume that individuals may differ considerably regarding their communicated behaviors in committed relationships compared to those not in such relationships. For example, there may generally be less need for discussion and negotiation regarding safer sex in the former type of relationships, in which these issues may have been previously "hammered out." Thus, examining these groups separately would seem prudent.

DYNAMICS OF SAFER SEX NEGOTIATION

As Miller, Bettencourt, Hoffman, and DeBro (1993) argued, to address what keeps individuals from using safer sexual practices, we need to understand the complex, intrapersonal and interpersonal dynamics within which safe or unsafe sexual behaviors are embedded. Miller and Read (1987; 1989; Read & Miller, 1989) argued that critical dynamic units for understanding such complexities include individuals' goals, their plans and strategies for goal achievement, resources necessary for successfully carrying out those strategies, and beliefs that affect, for example, what goals and strategies are selected.

Goals are simply something the individual desires or wants to attain (Miller & Read, 1987; 1991; Read & Miller, 1989); the strength of these differ across individuals and over time. Discrepancies between what an individual wants and has achieved are viewed as driving strategic actions. However, as Wilensky (1983) noted, an individual's goals are not always complementary or unrelated; they may conflict (intrapersonal goal conflict). Likewise, these goals may conflict with the perceived goals of others (interpersonal goal conflict).

In our earlier work, exploring the dynamics of negotiating safer sex, we were interested in the goals of individuals in sexual relationships, and how these goals may relate to the obstacles that they perceive in negotiating safer sex (Miller & Bettencourt, 1989; Miller et al., 1993), as well as their strategies for negotiating safer sex (DeBro, 1993) and the place of goals in the plans and sexual scripts of individuals in different types of sexual relationships (Burns, Monahan, & Miller, 1993). For example, Miller and Bettencourt (1989; Miller et al., 1993) identified three dating goal composites for White college students: (a) wanting to avoid conflict in relationships; (b) wanting to maintain emotional intimacy and closeness with one's partner; and (c) wanting to achieve narcissistic goals, such as wanting sexual intimacy, making a positive impression, keeping fit, and avoiding pain. There were, however, no sex differences. In other work, DeBro and Miller (1992) found that individuals in different types of sexual relationships (e.g., one night stands, affairs, "bed buddy" relationships, long-term relationships, etc.), have different salient goals. For example, in long-term relationships individuals are particularly concerned with being close to and accepted by their partner, being themselves with their partner, and being comfortable and being able to communicate openly. In other relationships, especially those not involving commitment, leading goals include avoiding AIDS and sexually transmitted diseases (STDs), being physically attractive, and being in control over what happens. Again, among White college students, for whom there were not marked sex ratio imbalances, there was little support for gender differences in relationship goals.

Individuals' important goals were found, in turn, to be predictive of the obstacles individuals perceive to safer sex. Miller and Bettencourt (1989) also identified a set of 101 obstacles to safer sex for college students, most of which fell into one of ten categories, including, obstacles associated with the "heat of the moment," "talking about safe sex," the act of "buying and presenting the condom," "perceiving that condoms are unromantic," and "pressure" to have sex without the condom. Interestingly, different goal configurations predicted different obstacles to safer sex. For example, those with narcissistic goals, including desiring physical intimacy, report that perceptions that condoms are unromantic and being in the heat of the moment, are their most problematic obstacles to safer sex. Again, there were few sex differences in the perceived obstacles to safer sex.

However, individual differences in goals were predictive of perceived obstacles to safer sex. Although both men and women rate avoiding AIDS consistently as their most important goal in relationships, their desire for sexual excitement, especially in the heat of the moment, might cause an *intrapersonal* goal conflict, making negotiating safer sex problematic. On the other hand, when one partner wants to use a condom, but they believe that their partner doesn't, this creates an *interpersonal* goal conflict. Those who wish to avoid such conflicts report that obstacles to safer sex are more likely to involve problems talking about safer sex, buying or presenting condoms, or offending their partners (Miller & Bettencourt, 1989; Miller et al., 1993).

Some have argued that the goals of men and women are often quite different. Some have argued that these differences are rooted in our ancient past, and have a biological basis (Buss & Schmitt, 1993). We did not find such gender differences in relationship goals in our own work. Others, including Guttentag and Secord (1983) might argue that the goals of men and women depend on the particulars of their local "situation," such as when sex ratios are imbalanced. This latter position is closer to our own. We would argue that although individuals might differ considerably in their goals in relationships, there should *normally be few sex differences* in the goals of men and women. However, when sex ratios are imbalanced, as in the case of some African-American populations, the gender in overabundance, in that case women, may respond to these inequities by emphasizing commitment, love, and working on the relationship.

To explore the role of sex ratio imbalances on relationship goals, sexual behavior, and safer sex negotiation processes, we chose a sample from a working class and middle class sample of African-American men and women living in Los Angeles, California. In this group, we would expect there to be a sex ratio imbalance in that there would be fewer available men for the available women within the same "dating pool." In this group we examined the following hypotheses:

H_1: Men should be more likely than women to have more sexual partners, have an earlier age of first intercourse, engage in more extramarital affairs, and have more sexually transmitted diseases than women.

H_2: Women should be more likely than men to stress such relationship goals as wanting to love and be loved, wanting commitment, and wanting to work on a close relationship. This would be true for individuals both in committed relationships and not in committed relationships.

H_3: Although men and women may be equally concerned about avoiding AIDS, men should be more likely to engage in behavior consistent with that goal, broaching the topic of using condoms more frequently, and being more likely to initiate the use of condoms. This would be more likely to be the case among singles than committed individuals because presumably those individuals have a longer history with one another and might have either resolved these issues earlier or feel more comfortable discussing these issues than individuals who are less familiar with one another.

H_4: Women should be relatively unlikely to respond negatively to these attempts to influence the partner to allow the use of a condom.

On the other hand, the negative views of some men regarding condoms might suggest an additional hypothesis. Although men may be in an easier position to initiate safer sex, especially during the heat of the moment, other goals (e.g., good sex, being in control) may become more salient. Men might perceive more obstacles to using safer sex than women and be more resistant to condom use.

H_5: Women should get more negative responses from men when women attempt to persuade men to use condoms.

H$_6$: Men should perceive more obstacles to safer sex than women.

H$_7$: Men should perceive that they are more instrumental and in control of the probability that they will contract AIDS. After all, they are the ones who could more readily initiate and use condoms.

In addition to investigating these hypotheses, we were also interested in the nature of the safer sex topics, individuals talked about and the extent to which those were discussed. Furthermore, because earlier researchers had found that men tended to lie more about their sexual histories (Cochran & Mays, 1990), we wanted to know if African-American men who were in committed relationships and those who were not were more likely than women to lie.

METHOD

Participants

The majority of the participants (M = 27 years old) were sexually active, heterosexuals (95%) and lived in a low to middle income and working class area. Of the 426 participants (216 men and 210 women), 416 identified themselves as African American and were retained for further analysis. Although there was considerable variability in condom use in this sample, average use of condoms was a little more than half of the time (differing substantially from college samples). Twenty five percent of the sample had been diagnosed in the past as having a sexually transmitted disease (STD); almost 50% reported problems with condoms (e.g., slipping, breaking, and tearing during intercourse). Because patterns of findings might differ considerably for married individuals and those living with someone versus single individuals, we typically performed analyses separately for these different groups. Data are presented, collapsed across dating status, when this variable made little difference to the pattern of findings. There were 149 single men and 136 single women; of those living with someone or married, there were 63 men and 68 women. Sample sizes fluctuated by variable however, since not all participants filled out all measures.

Procedures

Participants were recruited from two shopping malls in predominately African-American sections of Los Angeles, California, and paid $5.00 each to complete the survey. Researchers explained the study, handed out questionnaires, helped participants with any questions that they had regarding the questionnaire, debriefed participants, and paid each $5 for approximately 1 hour of their time. In addition to inquiring about demographic information, participants were asked a series of questions about their goals in sexual relationships, their perceived obstacles to safer sex, their communication patterns generally and in their last sexual relationship, (e.g., whether they had ever given or received negative responses to using a condom and if so what was the nature of that response and how did it affect their subsequent response), items pertaining to feelings about AIDS and relationships, and their history of sexually transmitted diseases, sexual relationships, and condom use (including the incidence of condom slips, tears, etc.).

Materials

Demographic and Sexual History Measures.   Participants indicated their gender, age, income, ethnicity, age at first intercourse, number of sexual partners in the past year, their sexual preference (including a series of questions regarding who they were attracted to and had sex with, as well as questions concerning how they perceive themselves), their dating status (e.g., single, living with someone, married, divorced, etc.), the frequency of condom use during sexual intercourse (e.g., from "I never use a condom during sex" to "Every time I have sex I use a condom"), and the frequency of sexual activity.

Sexual Negotiation Measures.   Remembering their last sexual encounter, we asked participants to indicate whether they talked to their partner about using a condom or not. If they had, we asked them who first brought up the topic, and asked them to indicate which of a series of topics they discussed (e.g., buying condoms, the type of condoms preferred, if you or your partner likes condoms, birth control and condoms, diseases and condoms, who has a condom, etc.), as well as the extent to which they had discussed important issues, and the extent to which the partner was willing to use a condom. Then we asked participants whether they discussed, and the extent to which they talked about (separately), their own sexual history (as well as their partner's sexual history) and the extent to which the individual was truthful or not. We also asked them whether they had talked about a series of topics such as the number of their past sexual relationships, whether they were seeing someone else, how long they dated their last partner, how far they went sexually with their last partner, whether they ever had a sexually transmitted disease, what their past relationships were like, their IV drug use history, their past homosexual relationships, whether they took an AIDS test and their HIV status.

We also asked them whether they used a condom or not in this encounter and whether they had ever received (or had given) a negative response when they asked to use (or were asked to use) a condom. They were asked to indicate which of a series of negative responses they gave or received (e.g., the person became angry, violent, refused to have sex, walked out, ended our relationship, forced sex anyway, said, "Don't you love me?," told me not to worry, questioned my loyalty, insulted me, told me they didn't have a disease, was disappointed, was disgusted, and so forth). We also asked if they asked (or were asked by) this person to use a condom again afterwards.

Relationship Goals.   To measure relationship goals, subjects were asked to imagine that they were about to start a new sexual relationship. They were asked, to indicate on a scale from 0 (extremely unimportant) to 7 (extremely important) to what extent each of a series of relationship goals might be important to them in their social interactions with this dating partner. The 86 goals included such things as wanting to be loved and to love, wanting commitment, being accepted, wanting physical intimacy, being respected by others, being able to communicate openly, and so forth.

Obstacles to Safer Sex.   Subjects were asked to indicate for a new sexual relationship, the extent to which each of the 54 obstacles, derived from prior pilot work with African-American focus groups, would keep them from using safer sex. For example, participants were presented with items such as, "If I talk about using a condom I will upset my partner. This will keep me from using a condom." They were then asked to indicate how much they agreed or disagreed with each statement on a scale from 1 (strongly agree) to 7 (strongly disagree). We recoded this variable for ease of discussion: Thus, *high* scores indicated that the individual perceived greater obstacles to safer sex.

AIDS and Relationship Beliefs Measure.   Participants were asked to indicate the extent to which they strongly agreed (1) to strongly disagreed (7) with each of a series of questions about AIDS and relationships such as "I think it is necessary to get to know my partner well before I have sex," "I refuse to have sex unless a condom is used," "I am fearful about the possibility of getting AIDS," "There's no point in taking precautions regarding AIDS. It's all a matter of luck anyway," "I make using a condom fun," "I'm real good at persuading my partner we need to use a condom," and so forth. We recoded this variable, for ease of discussion, such that high scores indicated that individuals strongly agreed with the item.

SEXUAL PATTERNS AND BEHAVIORS OF AFRICAN-AMERICAN MEN AND WOMEN

We hypothesized that men should be more likely than women to have an earlier age of first intercourse, more sexual partners in the past year, more sexual partners currently, engage in more extramarital affairs, and have more sexually transmitted diseases than women. For both committed (married and living together) and single individuals, men reported a significantly earlier (p's < .05) age of first intercourse (M's = 14.7, 13.9) than women (M's = 17.1, 15.8), as well as a significantly (p's < .05) more sexual partners in the past year (M's = 5.8, 9.8 for men; 2.0, 3.2 for women). Although men also reported more sexual partners currently both in and out of marriage (M's = 3.2; 1.9) than women (M's = 1.0, .8), perhaps due to sample size differences and greater variability for the married men, this difference was statistically significant only for the singles (p < .05). Thus, this pattern of findings generally suggests that men appear to be more sexually active on average than women within this sample. Men appear more likely to have multiple partners generally, including married men.

Among the single individuals, 26.7% of the men and 26% of the women reported having had an STD. Among the committed individuals, 30% of the men and 15.2% of the women reported having had an STD: This difference was significant, $\chi^2 = 4.01, p < .05$. These findings seem to support the first hypothesis and are consistent with prior work on African-American men (Anderson & Dahlberg, 1992; Weinberg & Williams, 1988).

GOALS OF AFRICAN-AMERICAN MEN AND WOMEN

Our second hypothesis was that women should be more likely than men to stress such relationship goals as wanting to love and be loved, wanting commitment and wanting to work on a close relationship. In order to address this issue, an overall MANOVA was performed separately for committed individuals and single individuals, examining differences across 86 goals for men and women. The overall MANOVA was significant ($F(86, 55) = 1.57, p < .05$) for singles but not for the committed individuals. Although the overall MANOVA was not significant for committed individuals, the patterns of goal differences for both committed and single individuals involved considerable overlap. Examining the univariates, among the committed individuals, men and women differed significantly ($p < .05$) on 23 of the 86 goals; for the singles, they differed significantly ($p < .05$) on 24 of the 86 goals. For *both* groups, women were significantly more likely than men to view the following goals as important that are related to our initial hypothesis: To be loved by the partner, to make the relationship last, to be accepted by my partner, to accept my partner, to date only that partner and to have them date only me, to be able to communicate openly with my partner, and to have a partner who is able to communicate openly with me.

Of the singles, women were also significantly more likely than men to view the following goals as important that are related to our hypothesis: being comfortable with my partner and having my partner be comfortable with me, having a partner who is able to be themselves, having a partner who feels close, having a partner who is nurturant and supportive of me, and being nurturant and supportive of my partner. Among the committed individuals, goals women viewed as more important included the following relevant to our hypothesis: having a partner who is good at working out problems in the relationship, having a partner who is willing to commit to the relationship, being willing to commit myself to the relationship, loving my partner, and sharing my life with my partner. Thus, there would appear to be considerable support for a tendency of women in this sample to be more likely than men to emphasize goals having to do with being committed to and working on the relationship.

Other goals on which men and women differed included a greater emphasis by both single and committed women on respect (from their partner for both groups; for their partner for single women; and for themselves for committed women), on being themselves and on having partners who can offer financial security. Single women were also concerned with avoiding a variety of relationship outcomes (e.g., not giving someone a sexually transmitted disease, avoiding a partner who is violent, avoiding becoming violent with one's partner, avoiding pregnancy); committed women were more likely to focus on achieving their own goals and being in control over what happens to them compared to men, whereas single women were more concerned than men about having a partner who can achieve their goals. Interestingly, men and women were *equally* and highly concerned about avoiding giving and receiving AIDS, and having physical intimacy.

USE OF SAFER SEXUAL PRACTICES

Our third hypothesis was that although men and women may be equally concerned about avoiding AIDS, men should be more likely to engage in behavior consistent with that goal, broaching the topic of using condoms more frequently, and being more likely to initiate the use of condoms. Fifty-three percent of men and 62% of women reported talking about using a condom in their last sexual encounter. Consistent with this hypothesis, more men reported that they were the one to broach the topic of using a condom (37%) compared to women (26%) and this difference was significant ($p < .05$).

There were no significant differences generally in the rate of condom use reported by men and women, with both single and married individuals reporting using condoms about 50% of the time, and similar percentages of men and women reporting using a condom the last time that they had sex (55% versus 53%). Regarding who initiated the use of the condom the last time the person had sex, our hypothesis was not confirmed: There were *no* significant differences between men and women overall or for single individuals. Furthermore, for committed individuals, *women* were more likely than men to agree that "the last time I had sex, I initiated the use of a condom" ($F(1, 64) = 4.8, p < .05$).

Related to this work was our fourth hypothesis: Women should be relatively unlikely to respond negatively to these attempts to influence the partner to allow the use of a condom. We asked participants to indicate whether they had *ever* received or given a negative response to their partner regarding using a condom, and if so, what was the nature of the response. Overall, a marginally higher percentage of women (36%) than men (28%) reported receiving a negative response in the past from their partners regarding using a condom ($\chi^2(1) = 2.92, p = .08$). Furthermore, there was a tendency for more men (22%) than women (15%) to report giving a negative response ($\chi^2(1) = 3.7, p = .05$). This pattern of gender differences, however, was stronger for single individuals. Therefore we will discuss these findings in detail only for single individuals.

We had argued that some men do not wish to use condoms and typically report more negative attitudes about condom use (Johnson et al., 1991). Thus, men should report giving more negative responses than women (our fourth hypothesis) and women may get more negative responses from men than men report getting from women (our fifth hypothesis). As indicated in Table 7.1, for single individuals, more men (25%) than women (15%) reported having given a negative response to their partner regarding the use of a condom ($\chi^2(1) = 3.74$, $p < .05$), and more women (44%) than men (24%) reported having received a negative response from their partner ($\chi^2(1) = 12.85$, $p < .001$). Thus, the fourth and fifth hypotheses, although marginal for the overall group, were confirmed for single men and women.

As is indicated on Table 7.1, although men were more likely to say that they *gave* negative responses, of those who gave negative responses, there were no gender differences in the type of response reported. Some of the responses reported by at least 10% of both women and men were becoming angry (19% men, 11% women), forcing sex anyway (23% men, 11% women), saying "don't worry" (30% men, 24% women), questioning loyalty (23% men, 11% women), and saying, "I don't have a disease!" (25% men, 14% women).

Among those men and women who reported *receiving* a negative response, some of the most frequent responses include the partner becoming angry, saying, "Don't worry," questioning loyalty, saying, "I don't have a disease!," and being disappointed. There were sex differences regarding two responses: Women (42%) more frequently than men (18%) received responses involving disappointment ($\chi^2(1) = 4.49$, $p < .05$). Men (18%) more frequently than women (3%) received responses involving disgust from their partners ($\chi^2(1) = 4.48$, $p < .05$).

TABLE 7.1
Percentage of Negative Responses to the Use of Condoms Given and
Received by Single Individuals

	Partner Gave Negative Response		I Gave Negative Response	
	Men	Women	Men	Women
Overall	24[a]	44[b]	25[a]	15[b]
Types of Responses				
Became Angry	25	20	19	11
Became Violent	9	3	6	9
Refused Sex	19	8	15	5
Walked Out	9	3	11	3
Ended Affair	4	3	6	3
Forced Sex	14	9	23	11
"Don't love?"	23	12	15	8
"Don't worry"	33	40	30	24
Questioned Loyalty	21	22	23	11
Insulted	7	5	0	3
"Don't have disease"	28	39	25	14
Disappointed	18[a]	42[b]	7	9
Disgusted	18[a]	3[b]	10	9
Ask to use a condom again?	59[a]	80[b]	64	58

Note.   Different lettered superscripts within a *response* category indicate significant differences between men and women, $p < .05$.

In addition, we asked participants if they had attempted to persuade their partners again to use a condom after the negative response. A greater percentage of women (80%) than men (59%) said that they had done so ($\chi^2(1) = 11.35, p < .001$).

It is striking to us that such a large percentage, 25%, of all single men reported giving a negative response to a partner who wanted to use a condom. However, others might take a very different perspective, arguing that perhaps such figures suggest that there is relatively little resistance to using condoms (Edgar, 1992).

Although there were not any sex differences regarding what individuals did the last time that they had sex, 17.6% of single individuals reported giving a negative response the very last time that they had sex. Given that individuals may be more likely to remember details such as these that are more historically recent, one wonders if the overall figures for giving or receiving negative responses underrepresent the negative responses that individuals actually give one another in their sexual interactions. Furthermore, such negative responses do seem to suppress—at least somewhat—the use of condoms, at least with that partner, in the future. Thus, although this figure may be less than our "worst case scenario," we continue to view negative responses by partners or perceived by partners as a significant problem affecting condom use.

OBSTACLES TO SAFER SEX: DIFFERENCES BETWEEN MEN AND WOMEN

Our sixth hypothesis was that men might generally perceive more obstacles to safer sex than women. We examined this question two ways. First, we did a general MANOVA examining differences for men and women across 54 obstacles to safer sex. Patterns for committed and single individuals were similar, so the data were collapsed. For the overall sample of 390 individuals (194 men and 196 women), there was a significant multivariate effect for gender ($F(54, 335) = 1.45, p < .05$). For the vast majority of these obstacles, 50 of the 54, there was a significant univariate effect as well, and for all but one of the remaining obstacles was the univariate effect marginal. The pattern throughout was the same. Whether the obstacles referred to problems with condoms, per se, problems in the heat of the moment, problems buying or using condoms, problems offending one's partner, being embarrassed, and so forth, men generally perceived more obstacles to safer sex than women.

A second way of looking at this question involved first factor analyzing the obstacle measure. Rothspan and Miller (1994) performed an orthogonal factor analysis on this data, using a varimax rotation. They found that the patterns of factors were cleaner when the data were analyzed separately by gender. Three factors emerged for women and three similar factors emerged for men. For men, the factors involved (a) perceptions that condoms interfered with pleasure, (b) condoms caused embarrassment, and (c) concerns regarding partners' judgments of them. For women, the factors involved (a) concerns regarding partners' judgments of them—similar to factor c for men, (b) miscellaneous excuses about condoms (not pleasurable, not convenient), and (c) issues involving comfort using condoms and not wanting condoms to "alter the feeling." Internal reliability's were high for each composite (e.g., alpha = .90 or higher). Analyses, examining gender differences were performed separately for each set of factors, yielding significant overall differences for men and women on the three factors derived from the men's data as well as for the three factors derived from the women's data. Every univariate analysis resulted in a highly significant effect ($p < .001$) such that men perceived more obstacles to safer sex than women. Thus, these findings were in line with the hypothesis.

PERCEIVED CONTROL AND INSTRUMENTALITY WITH RESPECT TO AIDS: GENDER DIFFERENCES

We also predicted that men would perceive that they are more instrumental and in control of the probability that they will contract AIDS. After all, since a condom is used on male anatomy, men could presumably more readily initiate and use condoms. In order to examine this issue, we performed a factor analysis of individuals' perceptions of their interactions with others. Because the factors were similar for men and women the data were combined: There were three factors. The first factor, labeled responsiveness, included items tapping into being at ease using condoms in a particular relationship and skill, such as "The last time I had sex, my partner was very comfortable talking to me about using a condom," "The last time I had sex, I responded pretty positively to my partner when my partner wanted to use a condom," "I have pretty good communication skills in dating situations." The second factor, labeled instrumentality included items that tapped into a fear of AIDS (e.g., "I am fearful about the possibility of getting AIDS"), a determination to take steps to reduce that possibility (e.g., "I make sure a condom will be available if it looks like I'm going to have sex," "I refuse to have sex unless a condom is used," "There's a lot I can do to keep myself from getting AIDS," "I think it's necessary to get to know my partner well before I have sex"), and a tendency to make using condoms easier in the interaction (e.g., "I make using a condom fun," "I make using a condom pretty exciting (sexually)"). The third factor, labeled "helplessness" taps into items that suggest that the person does not perceive that anything that they do will affect whether they get the disease or not, thus, "There's no point in taking precautions regarding AIDS: It's all a matter of luck anyway," and "I have too much 'other stuff' to worry about, to worry about taking precautions about getting AIDS." The internal reliability of these subscales was acceptable (alpha = .81 to .90).

We separately examined differences between men and women for single versus committed individuals. For committed individuals there were no significant gender differences. For single individuals however, men perceived themselves as much more "helpless" or not in control over getting AIDS compared to women ($F(1,175) = 15.66$, $p < .001$). Similarly, women were more likely to report attitudes and behaviors that were more instrumental in reducing their chances of contracting HIV $(F(1,175) = 6.25, p < .05)$.

SAFE SEX TALK AND LIES: GENDER DIFFERENCES?

We were also interested in the extent to which individuals, with the last partner that they had sex with, felt that they had talked about important issues related to AIDS, such as their own and their partner's sexual histories, whether and what they had talked about with respect to condoms, who was more likely to broach the topic of using safer sex, and whether they felt that they and their partners were truthful. For both single and committed individuals, there were few gender differences with respect to whether partners felt that they had talked about important issues related to AIDS, although among both single and committed men and women a high percentage of individuals (40% for committed individuals; above 50% for uncommitted individuals) reported that they had talked about their sexual history with this person.

The only consistent difference of note concerned whether individuals talked about having an AIDS test and their HIV status. A higher percentage of women (50%) than men (30%) said they discussed this issue, and these differences were significant, such that women tended to perceive that they talked about this issue with respect to the partner's sexual history more than men in both committed relationships (60% versus 27.6%; $\chi^2(1) = 5.77, p < .02$) and uncommitted relationships (45.8% versus 31.1%; $\chi^2(1) = 3.69, p = .05$). In committed relationships, a similar pattern emerged for talking about the partner's history regarding whether they had an STD (56% of the women versus 27.6% of the men; $\chi^2(1) = 4.49, p < .05$) and what their sexual relationships were like (48% of the women versus 20.7% of the men; $\chi^2(1) = 4.51, p < .05$). However, relatively few individuals discussed their IV drug use history or past homosexual relationships, two factors that would seem important in evaluating a partner's risk factors.

Regarding talking about condoms, among single individuals, but not among committed individuals, a higher percentage of women (73.5% versus 59.7%; $\chi^2(1) = 6.06, p < .02$) reported talking about condoms. However, there were no significant gender differences in what individuals talked about regarding condoms, although single women more frequently reported talking about the type of condom that they prefer compared to men (37.1% versus 25.4%, $\chi^2(1) = 3.77, p < .05$). In contrast to prior work (Cochran & Mays, 1990), men were not more likely to say that they lied to their partners in this sample.

RELATIONSHIPS AMONG MEASURES?

How are some of these variables related to one another for men and women? To explore this question, Rothspan and Miller (1994) considered some of the correlations among these measures below, many of which are provided in Table 7.2. Let us begin with the correlations between some of our measures of communicative responsiveness and control. Because there were *no gender* and *no relationship differences* in the patterns of correlations, we collapsed over gender and relationship type. As is indicated, individuals who were high in instrumentality had a higher rate of condom use, were more likely to use condoms during the last sexual encounter, talked with their partner about using condoms and perceived fewer obstacles to safer sex. Those individuals who reported greater responsiveness on their part and on the part of their partner reported a similar pattern of condom use, talking about condoms, and perceived obstacles to safer sex. Individuals who seemed "helpless" or lacking control in getting AIDS, were more likely to perceive more obstacles to safer sex. In addition, there was one interesting gender difference regarding these variables: Men who were more "helpless" about getting AIDs, saying that they couldn't control their chances of AIDS, reported giving more negative responses to their last sexual partner who wanted to use a condom ($p <$ .05) whereas women reported receiving more negative responses ($p < .05$).

Rate of condom use (which was significantly related to STD rate, $r = .13, p <$ .05), was also significantly related to perceived obstacles to safer sex for both men and women. As indicated in Table 7.3, men who reported higher rates of condom use were those less likely to perceive obstacles to safer sex involving pleasure reduction, embarrassment, and concerns regarding partners' judgments. As indicated in Table 7.4, women who reported higher rates of condom use were those less likely to perceive obstacles to safer sex involving concern for partner's judgments, miscellaneous excuses, and issues involving comfort in using condoms and not wanting to alter the feeling. Weaker but similar findings emerged for the

TABLE 7.2
Correlations Between Condom Use and Communicative Responsiveness and Control Measures

| | Communicative Responsiveness and Control | | |
	Instrumentality	Responsiveness	Lack of Control
Rate of condom use	.30*	.34*	.05
Condom use during last sexual encounter	.25*	.31*	.08
Talks with partner about using condoms	.30*	.32*	.05
Men's Obstacles to Safer Sex			
Pleasure reduction	− .35*	− .33*	.26*
Embarrassment	− .26*	− .27*	.44*
Concern for other's judgments	− .31*	− .38*	.35*
Women's Obstacles to Safer Sex			
Concern for other's judgments	− .26*	− .37*	.40*
Miscellaneous	− .33*	− .35*	.32*
Condoms alter feeling	− .36*	− .32*	.25*

*$p < .01$.

TABLE 7.3
Correlations Between Men's Obstacles to Condom Use and Sexual History

| | Obstacles to Safer Sex | | |
	Pleasure Reduction	Embarrassment	Concern for Other's Judgments
History of an STD	.05	−.02	.01
Number of sexual partners	.01	.00	.05
Rate of condom use	−.40**	−.22**	−.25**
Condom use during last sexual encounter	−.30**	−.15*	−.10
Talks with partner about sexual history	−.05	.00	−.03
Perceived ability to deny sexual relations	−.10	−.18*	−.17*
History of receiving a negative response to the use of condoms	.05	.14	.16*
History of giving a negative response to the use of condoms	.29**	.12	.16*
Experienced problems when using condoms (e.g., breaks, slips, etc.)	.28**	.27**	.12

*p < .05. **p < .01.

TABLE 7.4
Correlations Between Women's Obstacles to Condom Use and Sexual History

| | Obstacles to Safer Sex | | |
	Concern for Other's Judgments	Miscellaneous	Condoms Alter Feeling
History of an STD	.05	.11	.19**
Number of sexual partners	.05	.18*	.17*
Rate of condom use	−.28**	−.38**	−.39**
Condom use during last sexual encounter	−.14	−.24**	−.25**
Talks with partner about sexual history	−.09	−.19**	−.17*
Perceived ability to deny sexual relations	−.26**	−.30**	−.28**
History of receiving a negative response to the use of condoms	.11	.06	.02
History of giving a negative response to the use of condoms	.29**	.31**	.31**
Experienced problems when using condoms (e.g., breaks, slips, etc.)	.01	.06	.04

*p < .05. **p < .01.

last sexual encounter. Thus, perceived obstacles to safer sex are related to being less likely to use condoms.

As indicated in Table 7.3, men who perceived obstacles involving pleasure reduction were less likely to talk to their partners about condoms, and had a history of giving a negative response to their partners when their partners attempted to persuade them to use a condom. These men also reported more problems using condoms. Men concerned with embarrassment are less likely to perceive that they can deny their partners sex if they do not want to use a condom and are also more likely to report experiencing problems with condoms in the past. Men concerned with their partner's judgments talked less to their partners about condoms, were less likely to perceive that they could deny sex when their partner did not want to use a condom, and also had a history of giving more negative responses to their partners when their partners wanted to use a condom. Still, these men do not have a higher rate of STDs or sexual partners.

As indicated in Table 7.4, women who view condoms as altering the feeling, and this is an obstacle to safer sex, may have a high number of risk factors associated with contracting HIV. These women have a history of STDs, more sexual partners, lower rates of condom use, are less likely to talk to their partners about condoms or their partner's sexual history, feel less able to deny their partners sex if their partner does not want to use a condom, and report a history of giving negative responses to partners who want to use condoms. These women seem to be "playing with fire." Significant correlations also emerge on some of these variables for the other two obstacle measures as well.

Interestingly, women with higher incomes perceived fewer obstacles to safer sex across the board ($p < .05$). Perhaps as women become less economically dependent upon men they may be less apt to be influenced by a host of concerns, including power differentials, in engaging in behaviors consistent with their goals (e.g., avoiding AIDS).

Individuals who have had a large number of partners, are currently seeing a large number of partners, and have had an STD in the past might all be considered individuals more at risk for HIV. For women, but not for men, these tendencies reveal a particularly disconcerting picture. The number of partners now for women is positively correlated with past number of partners ($r = .21, p < .01$), age at first intercourse ($r = -.31$), and having had an STD ($r = .19, p < .01$). Sadly, the more partners currently, the less these women perceive that they can deny sex to their partners if they want to ($r = -.17, p < .05$), the less instrumental they are in getting their partners to use condoms ($r = -.25, p < .01$), the less likely they were to have used condoms the last time they had sex ($r = -.19, p < .05$), and the more likely they got a negative response the last time that they tried to get their partner to use a condom ($r = .21, p < .05$). As mentioned earlier, these women perceive significantly ($p < .05$) more obstacles to safer sex pertaining to miscellaneous issues regarding condoms and comfort losing the feeling when using condoms (r's = .18; .25, p's $< .05$).

Women who have had an STD perceive that they are less instrumental in getting their partners to use condoms ($r = -.21, p < .05$), less likely to have talked about using a condom the last time they had sex ($r = -.23, p < .01$), less likely to have used a condom the last time ($r = -.26, p < .01$) or asked about their partner's history relevant to AIDS ($r = -.21, p < .01$). As mentioned earlier, they perceive more obstacles in terms of losing the feeling when using condoms ($r=.19, p<.01$), were significantly younger at first intercourse, and have had more partners in their lifetimes and more partners now. Thus, these correlations suggest that those women

perhaps most at risk for contracting HIV may feel relatively powerless in controlling their outcomes.

SUMMARY OF GENDER DIFFERENCES IN
NEGOTIATING SAFER SEX: POWER,
INEQUITY, AND INSTRUMENTALITY

Men tend to have a general pattern of greater sexual promiscuity. It is striking that
committed men are not necessarily engaging in safer sexual practices, and that they
are often clearly not monogamous, compared to women in these relationships.
Thus, committed relationships between men and women are highly inequitable
with men less likely to honor sexual fidelity commitments compared to women and
more likely to place their partners unwittingly at risk.

How do women respond to a shortage of available men? Clearly, at least some
women are more likely, as Guttentag and Secord (1983) suggested, to stress
working on the relationship and commitment. This was true for both women in
committed relationships and those who were not. Single men report being more
"helpless" than single women. Furthermore, a substantial number of the women in
our sample report being instrumental in using condoms (e.g., they make condom
use fun and incorporate condom use into the sexual activity), and in spite of
receiving negative responses from their partners, report asking their partners to use
condoms in a subsequent sexual encounter.

On the other hand, whereas some women within this sample are adamant about
and report being very instrumental in getting their partners to use condoms, other
women, particularly those perhaps, with fewer financial resources or who are
particularly "needy" in terms of having relationships, may find themselves more
likely to simply focus on the sexual experience, seemingly ignoring risks for
contracting HIV and putting themselves at greater risk for contracting the virus.
Thus, the current set of findings suggests that different women may respond quite
differently to sex ratio imbalances in African-American subsamples. Although men
appear to have more dyadic power in relationships, this does not mean that they
use that power to insure the use of safer sex in their sexual negotiations. On the one
hand, men in general were more likely to say that they initiated the topic of using
condoms, but, this was not the case in committed relationships. Women in committed relationships who presumably have more power in these more secure
relationships, were more likely to broach the topic of using condoms. Still, neither
in uncommitted nor committed relationships was one gender more likely to actually
initiate the *use* of condoms. Interestingly enough, single men perceive that they
have less control over AIDS outcomes than women. In uncommitted relationships,
women are significantly more likely to report engaging in more instrumental behaviors
and feeling more in control over whether they get AIDS compared to the men.

Men instead appear to provide more roadblocks to using condoms in their
relationships with women. Men are more likely to give more negative responses to

using condoms, perceive more problems with the use of condoms such as slips, tears, and breaks, and perceive more obstacles to using condoms, than women.

Generalizing Across African-American Samples

A look at a Very Low Socioeconomic Status Sample. In one of our additional projects involving African-American populations, we went into a low socioeconomic area in an inner city community and collected data from over 100 individuals. In contrast with the findings of main study reported here, there were few goal differences between men and women, few differences in the perceived obstacles to safer sex, and generally few sex differences on other measures.

Instead, individual differences in the goals of men and women, rather than sex differences, seemed to be predictive of negotiation processes. For example, men and women who had goals associated with being "safe and avoiding AIDS" *and* having a close relationship were significantly more likely to report that in their most recent relationship, they discussed safer sex, felt comfortable initiating condom use, and perceived their partner as responsive. These individuals, although not afraid of getting AIDS, were most adamant about getting to know their partners before sex and refusing sex without a condom, and perceived no particular obstacles to safer sex. In contrast, "needy" individuals, those concerned with avoiding conflict and embarrassment, yet wanting acceptance and physical intimacy, were significantly more likely to perceive a host of obstacles to safer sex, particularly when those obstacles involved risking the loss of their partner and risking talking about safer sex. Thus, in many respects, the lack of gender differences here paralleled earlier findings in our Caucasian, upper middle class sample.

Why? One gender difference in the present sample stood out and provided a key to guide subsequent research. Unlike past research with African Americans, women reported significantly more sexual partners in the past year than men: 51.5% of the women in our sample reported having five or more partners; 31.2% of the men reported that many partners. The median number of partners for women, 5, was substantially higher than the median number of partners for men, 2.

How, however, might structural and dyadic power issues, along with goal considerations, play out in *different* African-American populations? Whereas there is generally a sex ratio imbalance among African Americans, with an overabundance of women, this would be most pronounced among those groups of men who were considered the most "acceptable" partners. To the extent that men had more economic or other structural power (e.g., greater economic status), these power differentials between men and women might be especially pronounced (that is, more women would be interested in a relatively smaller group of men). But, at the low end of the socioeconomic spectrum, fewer men might be considered "acceptable" partners; thus, perhaps, greatly reducing men's power in their relationships with women. Meanwhile, women in this low socioeconomic status group, perhaps having fewer resources with which to compete for the more desirable men, might adopt a more "short-term" sexual strategy, in which sex might be part of an economic bargaining process, to achieve greater financial security, because long term dependence upon a particular man might seem less prudent. Women might use whatever resources they had to attract a greater number of male partners. This might result in women, in this lower economic group, having more sexual partners than men in this sample.

If we were right, among those men with more sexual partners (suggesting more economic resources perhaps), we might see more perceived obstacles to using safer sex, especially concerning negative views of condoms. This was the case: Men, but not women, with more partners viewed problems surrounding condoms as more problematic obstacles to safer sex compared to those with few partners. Curiously, although there were no sex differences in goals overall: women who had more sexual partners reported that being physically attractive was an important goal, whereas men who had more partners viewed it as a relatively unimportant goal. Perhaps, women in this group may have viewed attractiveness as one of their few resources for attracting partners and enabling them some measure of control, whereas for men, having more partners may have been associated with very different resources (e.g., economic).

It is important to note that tendencies among some subsamples of African Americans may be the result of factors that may have less to do with African-American historical and cultural factors generally, and more to do with sex ratio imbalances, economic factors, and the dynamic emergence of behavioral tendencies that result from such factors, regardless of the population examined. In taking into account differences in different African-American populations, it is important to consider the relative power of individuals in those populations in terms of male–female sex ratios in their "local population" of "acceptable men," and the structural power women may glean from their own resources and personal determination (e.g., increased income, political and social status, and so forth).

ACKNOWLEDGEMENT

This work was supported by the California University wide AIDS Research Program (Grant number R90USC021) to the first author; both of the second authors were also funded on a California University wide AIDS Research Program Training Grant, funded to the first author as the Director of that training grant. The authors would like to thank Stephen John Read for comments on an earlier draft of this manuscript. We extend special thanks to the editors for their diligent assistance, support, and patience, without which this manuscript would not have emerged.

REFERENCES

Anderson, J. E., & Dahlberg, L. L. (1992). High-risk sexual behavior in the general population. *Sexually Transmitted Diseases, 19*, 320–325.
Belcastro, P. (1985). Sexual behavior differences between black and white students. *Journal of Sex Research, 21*, 56–67.

Burns, D., Monahan, J., & Miller, L. C. (1993). [Sexual scripts and goals in different types of sexual relationships]. Unpublished raw data.

Buss, D. M., & Schmitt, D.P. (1993). Sexual strategies theory: An evolutionary perspective on human mating. *Psychological Review, 100,* 204–232.

Centers for Disease Control. (1990). *Acquired immunodeficiency syndrome (AIDS) weekly surveillance report, United States AIDS activity.* Atlanta: Author.

Centers for Disease Control. (1991). *Acquired immunodeficiency syndrome (AIDS) weekly surveillance report, United States AIDS activity.* Atlanta: Author.

Cochran, S. D., & Mays, V. M. (1990). Sex, lies, and HIV. *The New England Journal of Medicine, 322* (11), 774–775.

DeBro, C. S. (1993). *Men's and women's dating goals in different types of sexual relationships as predictors of condom influence strategies.* Unpublished doctoral dissertation, Claremont Graduate School, Claremont, California.

DeBro, C. S., & Miller, L. C. (1992). [Identifying different sexual relationships]. Unpublished raw data.

DiClemente, R. J. (1991). Predictors of HIV-preventive sexual behavior in a high-risk adolescent population: The influence of perceived peer norms and sexual communication on incarcerated adolescents' consistent use of condoms. *Journal of Adolescent Health, 12,* 385–390.

Edgar, T. (1992). A compliance-based approach to the study of condom use. In T. Edgar, M. A. Fitzpatrick, & V. S. Freimuth (Eds.), *AIDS: A Communication Perspective* (pp. 47–67). Hillsdale, NJ: Lawrence Erlbaum Associates.

Fullilove, M. T., Fullilove, R. E., Haynes, K., & Gross, S. (1990). Black women and AIDS prevention: A view towards understanding the gender rules. *The Journal of Sex Research, 27,* 47–64.

Guttentag, M., & Secord, P. F. (1983). *Too many women? The sex ratio question.* Beverly Hills, CA: Sage.

Hernandez, J. T., & Smith, F. J. (1990). Racial targeting of AIDS programs considered. *Journal of the National Medical Association, 83,* 17–21.

Jemmott, J. B., & Jones, J. M. (1993). Social psychology and AIDS among ethnic minority individuals: Risk behaviors and strategies for changing them. In J. Pryor & G. Reeder (Eds.), *The Social Psychology of HIV Infection* (pp. 183–224). Hillsdale, NJ: Lawrence Erlbaum Associates.

Johnson, E. H. (1993). *Risky sexual behaviors among African-Americans.* Westport, CT: Praeger.

Johnson, E. H., Grant, L., Hinkle, Y. A., Gilbert, D., Willis, C., & Hoopwood, T. (1991). Do African-American men and women differ in their knowledge about AIDS, attitudes about condoms, and sexual behaviors? *Journal of the National Medical Association, 84,* 49–64.

Kline, A., Kline, E., & Oken, E. (1992). Minority women and sexual choice in the age of AIDS. *Social Science Medicine, 34,* 447–457.

Mays, V. M., & Cochran, S. D. (1988). Interpretation of AIDS risk and risk reduction activities by Black and Hispanic women. *American Psychologist, 43,* 949–957.

Miller, L.C., & Bettencourt, B.A. (1989). *Self-consciousness, interpersonal goals, and intimate negotiations: Predicting 101 obstacles to safer sex.* Unpublished manuscript.

Miller, L. C., Bettencourt, B. A., DeBro, S., & Hoffman, V. (1993). Negotiating safer sex: An interpersonal process. In J. Pryor & G. Reeder (Eds.), *The social psychology of HIV infection* (pp. 85–123). Hillsdale, NJ: Lawrence Erlbaum Associates.

Miller, L. C., & Read, S. J. (1987). Why am I telling you this? Self-disclosure in a goal-based model of personality. In V. Derlega & J. Berg (Eds.), *Self-disclosure: Theory, research, and therapy* (pp. 35–58). New York: Plenum.

Miller, L. C., & Read, S. J. (1991). Inter-personalism: Understanding persons in relationships. In W. Jones & D. Perlman (Eds.), *Perspectives in interpersonal behavior and relationships.* (Vol. 2, pp. 69–99). Hillsdale, NJ: Lawrence Erlbaum Associates.

Monahan, J. L, Rothspan, S., & Miller, L. C. (1994, November). *The roles of sexual expertise and safer sex expertise in negotiating sexual encounters.* Presented at the Commission on Health Communication of the Speech Communication Association Conference, New Orleans.

Read, S. J., & Miller, L. C. (1989). Inter-personalism: Toward a goal-based theory of persons in relationships. In L. Pervin (Ed.), *Goal concepts in personality and social psychology* (pp. 413–472). Hillsdale, NJ: Lawrence Erlbaum Associates.

Reiss, I. L. (1964). Premarital sexual permissiveness among Negroes and whites. *American Sociological Review, 29,* 688–698.

Rothspan, S., & Miller, L. C. (1994). Unpublished raw data.

Weinberg, M. S., & Williams, C. J., (1988). Black Sexuality: A test of two theories. *The Journal of Sex Research, 25,* 197–218.

Weinstock, H. S., Lindan, C., Bolan, G., Kegeles, S. M., & Hearst, N. (1993). Factors associated with condom use in a high-risk heterosexual population. *Sexually Transmitted Diseases, 20,* 14–20.

Wilensky, R. (1983). *Planning and understanding: A computational approach to human reasoning.* Reading, MA: Addison-Wesley.

Wilson, P. M. (1986). Black culture and sexuality. Special Issue: Human sexuality, ethnoculture, and social work. *Journal of Social Work and Human Sexuality, 4,* 29–46.

Chapter 8

Power and Equality in Mentoring Relationships

Pamela J. Kalbfleisch
University of Wyoming

Joann Keyton
University of Memphis

Why do we keep losing talented young women?
—a senior manager quoted in Parker and Kram (1993)

Being a mentor with young adults is one of the most significant relationships available to a man in middle adulthood.
—Levinson (1978, p. 253)

Relationships between mentors and their proteges have been chronicled throughout human history and mythology. The term "mentor" takes its origin from the "original" mentor described in the mythical account of Odysseus who trusted the instruction of his son Telemachus to his perceptive and trusted adviser, Mentor (Homer, 1960). This form of helping, guiding relationship reemerges in mythology in the form of the magician Merlin and his protege King Arthur (Mallory, 1969), and more recently in the pairing of the deceased but still present, Obe Wan Kenobe and the young Luke Skywalker in the movie, *Star Wars*.

In history, United States president's have had mentors and proteges. In fact, two of President Thomas Jefferson's proteges, James Madison and James Monroe, became United States presidents themselves (Bushardt, Fretwell, & Holdnak, 1991). Other prominent mentor–protege relationships include famous psychologists, Sigmund Freud and Carl Jung; civil rights lawyers Charles Hamilton Houston and Thurgood Marshall; Daytona 500 race car drivers Dale Earnhart and Ernie

Irvan; and basketball coaches Bobbie Knight (Indiana University) and Joby Wright (University of Wyoming).[1]

Specifically, mentors can be best portrayed as people who provide advice, support, information, and professional sponsorship to their proteges; share their values; and help their proteges gain access to powerful networks (Olian, Carroll, Giannantonio, & Feren, 1988). Proteges, on the other hand, "receive guidance from their mentors and may in turn support them as their knowledge grows and the mentoring relationship develops" (Kalbfleisch & Davies, 1993, p. 339). The relationship between a mentor and a protege is unique in nature, and as it develops it becomes a relationship in which neither participant can be substituted without changing the characteristics of this mentoring relationship (Kalbfleisch & Davies, 1993). In other words, each evolving mentorship is a unique personal relationship between a mentor and a protege. Further, these relationships are alliances with the potential of benefiting the career advancement of both the mentor and the protege.

Researchers have documented the direct financial and career benefits to individuals who have a mentor (e.g. Fagenson, 1989; Whitely, Dougherty & Dreher, 1991,1992). In his advice to young men, Levinson (1978) advocated finding a mentor for career advancement, and noted to aging men that mentoring another can be a satisfying opportunity and chance to pass on knowledge to a younger generation. Other benefits of mentoring include enhanced power and prestige of the mentor, increased social support, assistance with tasks, and additional network integration (Kalbfleisch, in press).

Because, historically well-known men have had great success with mentoring relationships, and demographically participants in mentoring relationships (especially the proteges) benefit financially and promotionally from mentorships, mentoring has been heralded as a means through which women can find equality in the workplace and career success. Unfortunately, women have not had the same success as men have had in forming these mentoring relationships. Keyton and Kalbfleisch (1993b) noted that although women are faced with exhortations from trade periodicals and popular press magazines, to *Get ahead! Find a mentor!*, they experience difficulty finding someone to mentor them. In their essay, Keyton and Kalbfleisch highlighted an example of a career women who has been continually frustrated in her attempts to find a mentor.

In explaining perhaps some of the frustrations experienced by similar career women, Kalbfleisch and Davies (1991a) found a significant pattern in both academic and business settings where men engaged in mentoring relationships with other men, but were much less likely to form mentoring relationships with women. Kalbfleisch and Davies further found that for both the university and the business settings, men were consistently more likely to be part of a mentoring relationship than were women. Other researchers such as Brown (1985), Burke (1984), Farris and Ragan (1981) and Hall and Sandler (1983) also found that the mentoring relationships in their samples were predominately male relationships.

---

[1]These pairs were found through a library search for references to mentors and proteges in the popular press periodicals and academic journals.

One interpretation of this pattern of male mentoring may be that there are simply more males in the workplace than females, and that eventually women will find themselves in mentorships as their numbers grow. However, if mentoring is a way to "break the glass ceiling" and rise professionally, and women are proportionately not establishing these relationships, then such a future would appear to be one in which increasing numbers of women are trapped in the lower ranks of an organization or profession and are not progressing up to senior organizational or professional positions.

Additionally, Kalbfleisch and Davies (1991a) found that when women were able to establish mentoring relationships, these relationships were most often established with other women. They found the mentoring relationships that were the least likely to form were those between women and men. Other researchers have also discovered similar patterns of sex preferences in mentoring relationships with females more likely to mentor other females, and males more likely to mentor other males (e.g., Kram 1985; Ragins 1989).

Because women in general are particularly facile at establishing and maintaining interpersonal relationships such as friendships (cf. Kalbfleisch, 1993), this difficulty in establishing mentoring relationships is at first somewhat puzzling. However, when one examines descriptions of traditional mentoring relationships, what becomes apparent is that these relationships have been modeled as male to male relationships with masculine characteristics and interaction values. It may be that women do not have a referent for this type of relationship, and they may need a mentoring relationship with different characteristics (cf. Ragins, 1989). This chapter examines women's experiences in finding mentors and describes gender differences in the mentoring process. An alternative model for women's mentoring relationships is developed and tested, and the implications of this model are discussed.

WOMEN'S MENTORING RELATIONSHIPS

From an organizational perspective, Kram (1986) identified two broad categories of functions the mentor provides: (a) *career functions* (preparation for organizational advancement), and (b) *psychosocial functions* (provision of a sense of self worth, identity, and effectiveness). Noe (1988) validated Kram's two mentoring functions and further suggested that the primary components that distinguish mentoring relationships from other organizational relationships (such as supervisor/subordinate) are (a) the relative power of the mentors, (b) the strong degree of identification between mentors and proteges, and (c) the intensity of emotional involvement.

Whereas intimate friendships may help women develop socially and interpersonally, women need mentoring relationships to help them develop professionally and advance their careers. Mentors can provide advice, visibility, empathy, and support (Collins, 1983). In its most basic form, mentoring is the relationship between junior and senior colleagues that provides a variety of developmental functions for both partners in the relationship. Collins (1983) specified that a mentor should be (a) high up on the organizational ladder, (b) an authority in the field, (c) influential, (d) interested in the protege's growth and development, and (e) willing to commit time and emotion to a mentoring relationship.

Whereas the traditional male-to-male mentoring models rely on an acceptance of hierarchy and focus on task activity, females appear to desire more psychosocial and emotional support in their organizational relationships than do their male counterparts. In fact this support is so important to women, that they often rely on their peers for "mentoring" rather than looking further up in the organization for a mentoring relationship (Kram & Isabella, 1985). Consequently, these peer relationships provide essential psychosocial and emotional support, but lack the growth and development available from an influential mentor. Nevertheless, understanding these peer relationships and friendships may provide a new access point or building block for females who want to develop relationships with higher ranking women mentors.

One important aspect that women may not recognize is the importance of mentoring relationships in achieving their professional goals. Nieva and Gutek (1981) noted that women may believe that hard work, perseverance, and talent are the determinants of organizational success and are less likely to form ties with influential superiors. Whereas males have long acknowledged the crucial nature of being mentored for professional success, women have only recently acknowledged this fact of organizational life. To make matters more complex, even when women identify the importance of these relationships they may face extreme difficulty in establishing such relationships (Brown, 1985; Burke, 1984; Farris & Ragan, 1981; Shapiro, Haseltine, & Rowe, 1978) and in using such relationships to their full potential.

The difficulties females experience in developing mentorships are contrary to their experience in establishing friendships. In general, females are able to establish intimate friendships that are useful to them in examining their own motives, needs, and desires (Sherrod, 1989). It seems that women do not transfer their experience in developing and using friendships to the development and use of mentorships. This could be because the traditional mentoring relationship exhibits stereotypical male characteristics.

Women may also need a different model for mentoring because they develop their careers and enter the work force in different patterns than males. Thus, a woman's individual career stage and chronological age may be out of sync with the traditional mentoring model (cf. Kram, 1986). Typically, this occurs as women make career decisions in relation to their marital and family situations. A female mentor may be more sensitive to these problems of professional advancement and role conflict than a male mentor. Whereas balancing personal and professional roles is an issue for both males and females, females take greater responsibility (socially and culturally) for marital and family issues. Nelson and Quick (1985) pointed out that role stress and extraorganizational duties of marriage and children are common stressors for professional women and that mentoring can be an effective antidote.

Further, whereas men can serve as general mentors to women, they may not be able to provide a model for the myriad of roles that women must learn to execute in order to effectively accomplish personal and professional goals (Jeruchim & Shapiro, 1992).

Females mentoring other females avoid many of the problems associated with cross-gender mentoring. Kram (1986) identified several of these problems: (a) confusion and anxiety about how to work closely with someone of the opposite gender; (b) the effect of sex role socialization on relationship dynamics; and (c) cross-gender mentoring alliances are more likely to attract notice and scrutiny adding negative pressures to already complex situations. Bowen's (1985) comparison of male–female mentoring dyads to female–female mentoring dyads clearly shows that male mentors and female proteges perceive many problems specifically attributable to the fact that the relationship is cross-gender (jealous spouse, office gossip, family resentment, and others). In addition, women mentors are also somewhat better equipped to help women deal with issues of sexual discrimination and sexual harassment.

Hardesty and Jacobs (1986) provided further argument for females to develop mentoring relationships with females. Beyond the sexual themes that can occur in a male–female mentoring relationship, women cannot develop the father–son characteristics of the traditional male mentoring model. Attempts to develop this type of relationship often result in the female protege becoming overly dependent upon the male mentor thereby obscuring her ability to make her own decisions. Even though every male–female mentoring relationship does not become sexual, a "sexual undercurrent, however repressed, is virtually always present" (Hardesty & Jacobs, 1986, p. 123).

Jeruchim and Shapiro (1992) articulately argued the need for a female defined model for mentoring:

> We found that the male model did not mesh with the contemporary woman's needs or with her unique place in the work force. Women wished for a female perspective on surviving and thriving in the predominantly male work environment. They longed for a female role model to show them how to combine their career and family responsibilities. In essence they yearned for a broader, more eclectic perspective on mentoring. (p. 192)

Thus, women in organizations may seek a different mentoring model, one that includes women's unique developmental paths, their affinity for relationships, and their minority status in a predominantly male work environment. Jeruchim and Shapiro (1992) believe that women can be effective mentors because, "Women possess within themselves the strength to become mentors. They know intimacy well from their personal relationships. If women use their power and their understanding of intimacy, they can restructure the mentoring relationship to keep pace with women's evolving position in our changing society" (p. 201).

GENDER DIFFERENCES IN THE MENTORING PROCESS

Research has documented many of the gender differences in male and female mentoring. For example, Jeruchim and Shapiro (1992) reported that male mentors give more instrumental assistance and sponsorship whereas female mentors give more emotional support and personal advice. These researchers attributed this lack of instrumental assistance and sponsorship to the less powerful positions of women in organizations. In comparing males to females, Reich (1985, 1986) found that females more frequently reported mentors as being responsible for information about company politics, career moves, and personal weakness. Reich (1985, 1986) further found that females more frequently reported their mentors as being responsible for improvements in self-confidence.

After reviewing the mentoring literature, Ragins concluded that "male proteges may not only receive different treatment from their mentors, but they may also use their mentors more effectively than female protegees" (Ragins, 1989, p. 5). Perhaps this is reflective of the uncomfortable fit of women trying to use male mentoring strategies. The lack of fit may also be responsible for women not seeking female mentors and mentors not selecting female proteges. The development of an alternative model of mentoring that is productive and satisfying for the female mentor and female protege is critical. This is especially true when one considers that a survey of 500 female managers revealed that half of them perceived minimal or no support from more senior women in their organizations (Warihay, 1980).

FRIENDSHIP CHARACTERISTICS IN MENTORING RELATIONSHIPS

Sherrod's (1989) research on same-sex friendships suggests that each gender differentially perceives and establishes same-sex friendships. Whereas females use their friendships to talk about feelings and problems, they may also require discussion of feelings and problems in the work place as well as socially. When examined in this light, comparing female friendships to female mentorships may help in developing a more appropriate mentoring model for females than the traditional male model.

In addition, female friendships have been reported as providing a high degree of support that results in greater emotional and physical well being (Sherrod, 1989). This type of support may be precisely the help women need in the work place, because as Ball (1989) suggested "a good mentor . . . is more than a good role model. . . [a mentor is] a teacher, a sounding board, a cheerleader . . . a friend" (p. 135).

There is some evidence that the female friendship is an appropriate developmental model for female mentoring relationships. A recent survey at Honeywell Corporation found that women saw "personal relationships as the key element in upward mobility" ("Welcome to the woman-friendly," 1990, p. 53). Likewise, Sands, Parson and Duane (1991) found that a factor identified as "friend" accounted for the most variance in their mentor definition and encompassed socioemotional, personal, and interpersonal qualities.

There has been little research that examines why more women do not actively pursue mentorships. Some suggest that females have not developed mentoring relationships because they have been socially and culturally conditioned to believe that it is their role to provide support and nurturance rather than to accept that behavior from others (Phillips-Jones, 1982). Instead of relying on this justification for explaining the posit of female mentoring relationships, it may be that this same nurturing characteristic can be used as base of the female-to-female mentoring relationship. Specifically, if female friendships are characterized by closer emotional intimacy and conversation (Sherrod, 1989), the ideal female mentorship may also be characterized by similar components.

Currently females fail as they try to develop mentoring relationships that parallel the male network. Because few women have ever been accepted in this institutionalized form of male bonding and mentoring, women may be trying to emulate an experience for which they have no referent. Simply put, females may be trying to copy a male experience for which there is no female correlate. If gender plays a role in accounting for differences in friendships (e.g., Sherrod, 1989), it is likely that the mentoring experience will be different as well.

INITIAL DEVELOPMENT OF A FEMALE MENTORING MODEL

The specific objectives of the study presented in this chapter are: (a) explore how the communication variables of intimacy and informality characterize female–female friendships, and female–female mentorships, (b) explore what sets of relational needs are met in both types of relationships, and (c) explore how those needs are met. These three objectives are an initial attempt to develop a model for female mentoring relationships.

Scope of the Study. We believe it is necessary to examine mentorships in relation to friendship for two reasons. First, because there are fewer women in positions to be mentors, females may have to rely on one person to serve both mentor and friend roles. Kram (1985) noted that over time some mentorships become friendships. Reich (1986) found that "more women than men noted that their relationships with mentors (67% versus 42%) and proteges (63% versus 44%) developed into close friendships" (p. 54).

Second, it may be possible that some of the same communication variables are important in both mentorships and friendships, with differences only in levels of formality and intimacy. In friendships, the qualities of formality and intimacy are expected from both partners (Leatham & Duck, 1990). In a mentoring relationship, it is likely that these qualities are complementary. For example, the mentor may expect the protege to reveal enough information about herself so that the mentor can provide advice. However, the mentor may retain her more formal position by withholding intimate information.

Women in specific one-on-one female–female mentoring relationships are examined in this study for several reasons. First, there is little systematic research documenting this type of relationship (cf. Hunt & Michael, 1983). Second, by asking respondents to focus on one specific relationship, the study avoids the problem of subjects responding to mentoring in general instead of a specific mentoring relationship (cf. Dreher & Ash,1990). Third, it is time that attention is directed toward the female–female mentorship. As more women enter the workforce, newcomers will find more senior women available to them as mentors. Kram (1986) and Hardesty and Jacobs (1986) reported that those females who experience a positive mentoring alliance in their early career years are more likely to mentor junior members of their organization or profession. We would like to capitalize on this cycle of mentoring. And, as Hardesty and Jacobs (1986) argued: "The time has come for women to take the next step and help one another as women, recognizing they must support members of their own sex before they can expect to gain anything approaching the power or influence men in the corporation have obtained" (p. 375). This is especially important if women are to break the barrier between the visible and invisible organizational structure. One aspect of this barrier is the male-dominated corporate culture ("The gains are slow," 1992; "The view from the trenches," 1990). By virtue of their gender and minority status, women are not part of the political shadow of the organization—the arena where action occurs (Jeruchim & Shapiro, 1992). Although still not equally placed in the work force, women have made significant gains. Statistics from the Bureau of Labor Statistics indicate that women represented 43% of the overall labor force in 1981 and 46% in 1991. Whereas females were only 27% of the managers in 1981, this figure rose to 41% in 1991 ("Corporate women," 1992). It is crucial that women in the position to mentor other females take more positive steps to help erase this invisible internal glass ceiling ("The gains are slow," 1992).

Fourth, the type of mentoring most needed by women may be a relationship with other woman. Worell and Remer (1992) underscored the therapeutic nature of relationships that can form between women. It is possible that women may receive ancillary benefits from forming female–female mentoring relationships beyond those that normally accrue through the mentoring process.

Finally, female interaction models in organizations are not atypical or unrealistic. Dowd (1991) reported that top executives are noticing a second generation of women in management today that does not use traditional male styles of leadership.

Because our ultimate goal is to provide a mentoring model that is more accessible to females, we believe it is important to describe the interaction that exists in that type of relationship and compare it to a familiar female–female relationship of friendship. Crucial to building a model are the basic relational elements such as positive feelings toward the relational partner, satisfaction of relational needs, emotional intimacy, and supportive communication. Each of these variables will be considered in this mentoring model.

Model Components

Relational Adjectives. Collins (1983) reported that proteges used the following adjective to describe how they felt about their mentors. In order, they are: respect, admiration, trust/confidence, loyalty, support, friendship, appreciation, awe, and resentment. In general, these characteristics represent an index of primarily positive feelings about the relational partner.

Themes of Relational Communication. Burgoon and Hale's (1987) relational theme scale should provide a framework for understanding and comparing the relational needs of friendships and mentorships. Previously, Burgoon and Hale (1984) proposed 12 interrelated message themes that were central to defining interpersonal relationships. Burgoon and Hale's (1987) revised measurement instrument consisted of 41 items representing eight dimensions in this measure. This scale is broken into eight subscales: immediacy, similarity, receptivity, composure, formality, dominance, equality, and task. This scale should provide an ideal base from which to describe and compare mentoring relationships to friendships because, as Burgoon and Hale (1987) suggested "Variations in the actual communication behavior of dyadic participants produce different relational interpretations by partners on multiple dimensions" (p. 39). Burgoon and Hale further indicate that this scale could be useful for studying relational communication in several types of human relationships.

Emotional Intimacy. Frequently, women's relationships are characterized by intense emotional intimacy, certainly more than expected in male friendships (Williams, 1985). Intimacy expressed in same-sex friendships emphasizes expressiveness and person-oriented qualities (cf. Kalbfleisch, 1993). Williams (1985) hypothesized and found that femininity is positively related to emotional intimacy in same-sex friendships. She found that females were more likely to confide in their close friends, openly express feelings of vulnerability, demonstrate affection, emphasize mutual understanding and responsibility, and discuss personal issues with their female friends. Williams measured emotional intimacy with a 20-item unidimensional measure; 19 of these items were retained for this study.

Emotional intimacy should also be apparent in female–female mentoring relationships as identification between mentor and protege should generate intimacy and bonding. In comparing male-to-female and female-to-female mentoring relationships, Jeruchim and Shapiro (1992) noted that the affective, or emotional quality is more vital for women than for men. More importantly, developing intimacy in a female mentoring relationship yields increased levels of productivity and development for the relationship while avoiding the negative effects of sexual overtones as gauged by those outside the relationship if the relationship was male–female (Burke & McKeen, 1990).

Kram (1986) argued that an individual's attitude toward intimacy is an important factor in successful mentoring. Kram suggested that this characteristic influences the extent to which the dyad will develop an open and enhancing relationship. Greater intimacy, based on sharing, self-disclosure, listening, and building rapport, is more likely to build strong mentor/protege alliance.

Organizational Communication Support. From their study of mentoring in the academic environment, Kogler Hill, Bahniuk, Dobos, and Rounder (1989) developed a measure of organizational communication support. This measure represents both the formal and informal structures and processes that occur in the organizational setting. In this operationalization, mentoring is an informal organizational communication process that is part of the larger organizational communication support domain. Two dimensions make up this measure. The *support behavior* subscale represents the conventional definition of mentoring. The second subscale, *collegial social*, represents reciprocal interaction between colleagues (e.g., giving advice, sharing confidences). A third subscale of *collegial task* reflects work-related communication support that would not apply to interaction outside of the academic context and was not included in this study.

In developing scale items, Kogler Hill and her associates (1989) stated that "care was taken to include one-way, nonreciprocated behaviors as well as two-way, reciprocated behaviors" (p. 360). Factor analysis confirmed that communication support behavior is informal and multidimensional. Whereas the first factor captured the traditional mentoring relationship as a one way-complementary relationship, the second factor was a separate dimension of informal communication support. The two subscales produced a correlation of .56.

Relational Outcomes. Five general relational outcomes were developed as semantic differential scales to form a composite relational outcome measure. Four outcomes are indicative of mentorships and friendships (happiness–sadness, support–lack of support, helpful–not helpful, respect–lack of respect). The fifth outcome (professional advancement–no professional advancement) was included to test the effect of the mentoring relationship.

Research Questions

Given the paucity of research focusing on female mentors interacting with female proteges, this study was designed to explore how that interaction is characterized in relationship to female friendships. Thus, the framework questions are:

RQ1: How do women characterize their feelings toward their partners, the satisfaction of their relational need, their level of emotional intimacy, level of communication support, and relational outcomes in their mentoring relationships?

RQ2: How do women characterize their feelings toward their partners, the satisfaction of their relational need, their level of emotional intimacy, and their relational outcomes in their friendships?

Additionally, in order to explore the development of a female–based mentoring model based on an existing female relationship,

RQ3: What variables provide a model of similarities/ differences between female mentoring relationships and female friendships?

METHOD

The method of obtaining data for this project was a population directed questionnaire. To compare mentorships to friendships it was necessary to find a sample of females who were involved in both types of relationships.

Research Participants

Because friendships were assumed to be a general population variable, the first step was to identify samples of women who were likely to have participated in a mentoring relationship. The mailing lists of several professional women's organizations were used to locate these participants. A total of over 2,300 professional women were contacted in three midwestern and southern metropolitan areas. Out of this group 200 women responded that they had been involved in mentoring relationships with a female mentor or a female protege.

These research participants were asked to identify themselves as either a mentor or a protege. Subjects identifying themselves as a mentor in one relationship and a protege in another were asked to choose only one relationship. Participants were further asked to supply the name and address of their mentoring relational partner. Questionnaires were mailed to each partner of the mentoring relationship in coded format to retain the pair-wise comparison. A cover letter explained the project and requested participation in the mentoring portion of the study specifically referencing the respondent's mentor or protege and requesting their responses based on their relationship. Of the 200 mentoring partners solicited, 56 mentors and proteges returned questionnaires to be matched with their partners in the subject pool. Data were also collected from respondents who did not identify their partners in their mentorship and from respondents who indicated that they had never had a mentor nor been a protege (this additional data is not included in demographic or inferential analysis).

Questionnaire

To allow the direct comparison of mentor and protege responses, a cover letter accompanying the questionnaire reminded the respondent of the specific individual she selected as her mentoring partner and indicated she should fill out the mentoring portion of the questionnaire with her relationship with that person in mind. This format was used to allow participants to respond to a particular mentoring relationship and not to mentoring relationships in general.

The questionnaire was composed of two parts. One part requested information on a female–female friendship. To provide a characterization of the friendship relationship, four measures were used: a list of adjectives that characterize the positive nature of the relationship (Collins, 1983); a 19-item emotional intimacy scale (Williams, 1985); a 41-item relational need scale (Burgoon & Hale, 1987); and a 5-item relational outcome measure.

A second part of the questionnaire contained data requests on a female–female mentoring relationship. There were two versions of this portion of the questionnaire (a mentor version and a protege version). Respondents were asked to respond to an 8-item questionnaire to identify the roles (Phillips-Jones, 1982) the mentor provided. Subjects responded to the Collins (1983), Williams (1985), and Burgoon and Hale (1987) scales listed above as well as an organizational communication support measure developed by Kogler Hill, Bahniuk, Dobos, and Rouner (1989).

Personal and professional demographic and relational characteristics data were collected for both the friendship and the mentoring relationship. Order of the two parts of the questionnaire (mentoring, and friendship) were varied during the questionnaire administration.

RESULTS

Mentoring Relationship Demographic Variables

Of the 56 pairs of female mentors and female proteges that were included in this study, 85% of the mentors were Caucasian, and 81% were employed full time in the middle (40%) and upper (55%) levels of their organizations. Sixty percent of the mentors made more than $40,000 annually; the mean age was 49.375. Proteges were also Caucasian (82%), and employed full time (91%) in the middle (46%) and upper (37%) levels of their organizations. More than 90% made less than $60,000 annually; the mean age was 37.464.

Approximately 80% of mentoring relationship partners were within the same profession. Although matched pairs were sought for the study, subjects did not perceive their mentoring relationship partner similarly in terms of in/out organizational status. Mentors reported that 87% of their proteges were in their organization while 75% of the proteges reported that their mentors were in their organization. This can be explained by different perceptions of organizational definitions. For example, a protege mentored by someone in the same parent organization who works in a separate office facility may perceive the mentor outside their immediate organization, whereas the mentor perceived her protege within the organization.

There was also some discrepancy regarding perceptions about the currency of the mentoring relationship. Approximately 60% of the mentors perceived the relationship as current, whereas 77% of proteges perceived the relationship as current. There was greater agreement regarding how frequently the mentoring relationship partners talked to one another. Approximately 70% of the mentoring pairs talked on a daily or weekly basis.

There was some evidence that proteges benefitted from the mentoring relationship as most began the relationship subordinate to their mentors, whereas approximately half ended the relationship in (or was currently in an) equal position to their mentor. Mentors had more tenure in their profession (19.375 years) than proteges (10.353 years), more years in the organization (13.826 years) than proteges (7.843 years), and more years in the current job position (9.152 years) than proteges (3.980 years).

Mentor Roles

Using Phillips-Jones (1982) mentor role definitions, mentors' and proteges' perceptions of the mentor role are shown in Table 8.1. Role 1 is described as the traditional mentor role in which the protege follows the mentor up the organizational ladder. Role 2 is one in which the mentor acts as a teacher, guide, or coach. Role 3 represents the mentor who is part of the top echelon of management. Role 4 represents the type of mentor proteges hire to help them. Role 5 represents the mentor who provides access to power and material clout. Role 6 is the mentor who helps plan and implement career goals. Finally, Role 7 represents the mentor who does favors for her protege and others in similar positions in the organization. There appears to be agreement among mentors and proteges in the roles the mentor played in their relationships; the only significant difference occurred for the rating of Role 5 as mentors perceived they had more power and material clout than that perceived by proteges. The teacher, guide, coach description of mentor role was more commonly described; the mentor as a hired agent was least commonly described.

Friendship Demographic Variables

Subjects reported on current friendships (90%) in which they interacted on a weekly (37%) and daily (22–33%) basis. The friendships reported by mentors had lasted an average of 17 years, whereas the proteges reported being in their friendships for an average of 10 years.

TABLE 8.1
Perceptions of Mentor Role

Role	Mentor Perceptions	Protege Perceptions
Role 1	3.852	3.808
Role 2	4.407	4.327
Role 3	3.611	3.538
Role 4	1.481	1.192
Role 5	3.241	3.152
Role 6	3.778	3.962
Role 7	3.444	3.462

TABLE 8.2
Means of Communication Variables

Variable	Mentoring Relationships		Friendships	
	Mentors	Proteges	Mentors	Proteges
Relational Adjectives	38.764	39.981	40.019	40.982
Emotional Intimacy (abc)	65.472	69.340	79.925	77.553
Relational Need (b)	136.074	138.170	146.519	136.303
Immediacy	36.370	37.075	37.760	35.464
Similarity	19.037	19.415	20.278	19.089
Receptivity	26.204	25.774	26.204	23.911
Composure (b)	18.444	19.641	21.815	19.375
Formality (bc)	8.630	8.906	12.185	11.125
Dominance	16.574	16.207	15.481	15.018
Equality	10.815	11.151	12.796	12.321
Outcome (a)	21.148	22.865	20.889	22.345
Supportive	45.151	44.481		
Traditional	33.528	32.308		
Social	11.846	12.173		

Note. Italics indicate subscales.

a = significant difference between mentors & proteges. b = significant difference between mentors' perceptions of protege & friendship. c = significant difference between proteges' perceptions of mentor & friendship.

Communication Characteristic Variables

The interaction variables of positive relational adjectives, relational need, emotional intimacy, and organizational communication support are shown in Table 8.2 with the outcome variable for both mentoring relationships and friendships. The table displays means and standard deviations, identifies significant differences between mentor and protege perceptions, and identifies differences between perceptions of mentoring and friendship relationships.

Relational Adjectives

The relational adjective scale demonstrates how positively mentors and proteges perceived their relationships. In the mentoring relationship, the internal reliability for mentors was .787 and .899 for proteges; for the friendship, reliabilities were .706 and .797. Relatively, all subjects perceived their mentoring relationships and friendships positively; no differences were found.

Relational Themes

The relational needs measure is presented as a composite index and as its eight subscales. For the composite measure, internal reliabilities were high, ranging from .913 to .959. At the composite level, a significant difference was found for mentors' perceptions of their mentoring relationship and their friendships, with their friendships meeting higher relational needs. Of the subscales, internal reliabilities were generally moderate to high (.615 to .983). On the subscales, there were no differences between mentors and proteges as they rated their mentoring relationships. Mentors reported significant differences between their mentoring relationships and friendships on the composure and formality subscales. The friendships were perceived as having higher levels of formality and composure. Proteges reported significant differences between their mentoring relationships and friendships on the formality scale; the friendship was more formal than the mentoring relationship.

Emotional Intimacy

In Williams' (1985) original study, females delivered mean scores of 57.29 (cross-sex typed females) and 63.53 (sex typed females). In comparison, this sample reported significantly higher values of emotional intimacy in both mentoring relationships and friendships (65.472 to 79.925) with reliabilities ranging from .809 to .904. Subjects reported differences in emotional intimacy at each of the three comparisons. Mentors were less emotionally intimate in their mentoring relationships than proteges. Both mentors and proteges reported being more emotionally intimate with their friends than their mentoring relationship partner.

Organizational Communication Support

Reliabilities for this measure were high ranging from .816 to .916. No differences were reported between mentors and proteges. While Kogler Hill et al.'s (1989) study did not differentiate on gender, they did report means for each of the subscales. The mean for mentors on the traditional mentoring scale was 29.00 and 19.77 for proteges, which are significantly lower than the values reported here. The means for mentors on the social/collegial scale was 13.41 and 10.40 for proteges, which are similar to the values reported here.

Relational Outcomes

The outcome measures reported internal reliabilities of .622 to .864. There was a significant difference between mentors' and proteges' perceptions of relational outcomes in the mentoring relationship.

Predicting Relational Outcomes

Because mentoring relationships are typically established to assist the protege, we regressed the communication characteristic measures against the proteges' relational outcome measure. Using proteges' measures of relational adjectives, relational need, emotional intimacy, and supportive communication, no significant equation was obtained. Using the same measures of the mentors to predict protege relational outcome did not produce a significant equation.

With the friendship data, measures of relational need and emotional intimacy predicted relational outcome for mentors ($F = 5.544, p = .007, r^2 = .149; F = 6.202, p = .001, r^2 = .228$). No significance was found for proteges.

Comparing Mentor and Protege Perceptions

Canonical correlation was performed between the set of mentor variables and the set of protege variables with SAS. Both the mentor and protege sets included their respective measures of relational adjective, relational need, emotional involvement, and supportive communication. Increasingly large numbers reflected more positive reports of the relationship, greater satisfaction of relational need, greater emotional involvement, and more supportive communication.

The first canonical correlation was .592 (35.0% of variance). The remaining three canonical correlations were effectively zero. With all four canonical correlations included $F = 1.868, df = 16, p = .030$. Subsequent tests were not significant. The first pair of canonical variates accounted for the significant relationship between the two sets of variables. Data on the pair of canonical variates appear in Table 8.3. Shown in the table are correlations between the variables and the canonical variates, standardized canonical variate coefficients, within-set variance accounted for by the canonical variates (percent of variance), redundancies, and canonical correlations. Total percentage of variance and total redundancy indicate that the canonical variates were minimally related.

With a cutoff of .3, the variable in the mentor set that was correlated with the protege canonical variate was supportive communication. Of the protege set, supportive communication correlated with the first canonical variate. The first pair of canonical variates indicate that mentors perceiving the mentorship as being high

TABLE 8.3
Canonical Correlation of Mentor and Protege Perceptions

	Correlation	Coefficient
Mentor Set		
Relational need	.238	−0.035
Emotional involvement	.046	0.086
Supportive communication	.997	1.008
% of variance	.351	
Redundancy	.118	
Protege Set		
Relational need	.187	0.021
Emotional involvement	.131	0.134
Supportive communication	.990	0.988
% of variance	.344	
Redundancy	.115	
Canonical Correlation	.579	

Note. $F = 2.921, df = 9, p = .004$.

TABLE 8.4
Canonical Correlation of Mentors' Perceptions of Mentoring Relationships
and Friendships

	Correlation	*Coefficient*
Mentoring Relationship		
Relational need	.995	1.036
Emotional involvement	.297	−0.105
% of variance	.539	
Redundancy	.239	
Friendship		
Relational need	.974	0.898
Emotional involvement	.526	0.739
% of Variance	.613	
Redundancy	.272	
Canonical Correlation	.666	

Note. $F = 8.097$, $df = 4$, $p = .001$.

in supportive communication (.974) also tended to report the same finding by the protege (.978).

Comparing Mentors' Perceptions of Mentoring Relationship with Friendship

Canonical correlation was performed between the set of mentor's perceptions of the mentoring relationship and the set of mentor's perceptions of the friendship. Sets included respective measures of relational adjective, relational need, and emotional involvement. The first canonical correlation was .673 (45.3% of variance). The remaining two canonical correlations were effectively zero. With all three canonical correlations included $F = 3.543$, $df = 9$, $p = .0007$. Subsequent tests were not significant. The first pair of canonical variates accounted for the significant relationship between the two sets of variables. Data on the pair of canonical variates appear in Table 8.4. Total percentage of variance and total redundancy indicate that the canonical variate was moderate.

With a cutoff of .3, all of the variables in the mentoring relationship set were correlated with the friendship canonical variate. The first pair of canonical variates indicate that mentors perceive their mentoring relationship as (a) positive (.422), (b) satisfying their relational needs (.997), and (c) emotionally involving (.301), and mentors perceive their friendship as (a) positive (.429), (b) satisfying their relational needs (.976), and (c) emotionally involving (.492).

Comparing Proteges' Perceptions of Mentoring Relationship with Friendship

As before, canonical correlation was performed between the set of protege's perceptions of the mentoring relationship and the set of protege's perceptions of the friendship. The first canonical correlation was .612 (37.5% of variance); the second was .439 (19.3% of variance). The remaining canonical correlation was effectively zero. With all three canonical correlations included $F = 4.306$, $df = 9$, $p = .0001$ with the first canonical correlation removed $F = 3.17$, $df = 4$, $p = .0173$. Subsequent tests were not significant. The first two pairs of canonical variates accounted for the significant relationship between the two sets of variables. Data on the pair of canonical variates appear in Table 8.5. Total percentage of variance and total redundancy indicate that the relationship between the canonical variates was low.

With a cutoff of .3, the relational adjective and relational need variables in the mentoring relationship set were correlated with the relational need and emotional involvement variables of the friendship canonical variate. The first pair of canonical variates indicate that proteges perceiving their mentoring relationship as positive (.898) and their relational needs as satisfied (.610) also reported their friendship as satisfying relational need (.733), and negatively emotionally involved (−.452). The second pair indicate that proteges perceiving their relational needs met (.386) and high emotional involvement (.780) in the mentoring relationship also reported high relational need satisfaction (.678) and high emotional involvement (.722) in the friendship. Taken as a pair, these variates suggest that relational need is the most constant variable of the proteges' perceptions of these two important personal relationships.

DISCUSSION

These data are a first step in uncovering a female model of mentoring by characterizing existing female mentoring relationships and female friendships and then

TABLE 8.5
Canonical Correlation of Proteges' Perceptions of Mentoring Relationships and Friendships

	Factor 1	
	Correlation	Coefficient[a]
Mentoring Relationship[a]		
Relational need	.508	0.762
Emotional involvement	.650	.591
% of variance	.538	
Redundancy	.157	
Friendship[b]		
Relational need	.999	1.002
Emotional involvement	.065	− 0.026
% of variance	.502	
Redundancy	.147	
Canonical Correlation	.541	

Note. $F = 5.569$, $df = 4$, $p = .001$.
[a]Total percentage of variance = .655; total redundancy = .199. [b]Total percentage of variance = .618; total redundancy = .169.

comparing the nature of interaction in the two relationships. Paired t-tests revealed few differences in the communication variables measured. As expected, emotional intimacy was significantly greater in friendships than in mentoring relationships and significantly greater for proteges than mentors in the mentoring relationships. Although greater emotional intimacy is achieved in friendships, the reported values for the mentoring relationships were moderately high. There were surprising significant differences on the formality subscale of the relational need measure. Both mentors and proteges reported higher degrees of formality in their friendships than they reported in their mentoring relationships. This suggests that the female mentoring relationship may be more relaxed and casual than previously thought. Finally, proteges achieved higher relational outcomes in their mentoring relationships than did their mentors. These few differences indicate that the underlying nature of mentoring relationships and friendships may not be that different and it may be worthy of exploring in building a female mentoring model. Both relationships are characterized by positive feelings, emotional intimacy, meeting relational needs, and providing satisfying relational outcomes.

Thus, in answering research questions 1 and 2, we find that these variables may be worthy of exploration in building a female model for mentoring. As a first step toward that effort, we tested three canonical correlations. The first canonical correlation tested the set of mentor variables with the protege variables. Although the overall structure was significant, redundancy (the degree to which the two sets of variables overlap) was very low. It should be noted that supportive organizational communication was the highest loading variable in the variate structure for both mentors and proteges.

More promising were the canonical correlations testing how mentors and proteges perceived their mentoring relationships in comparison to their friendships. For the mentors, a significant structure was uncovered and there was moderate shared variance, yet the redundancy between the two sets of variables was low. Similar results were found for the proteges. The redundancy values were higher in these two tests than in the test between mentors and proteges suggesting some overlap in how females perceive their mentoring and friendship interaction and partners. We did not expect that these redundancy values would be high as we were not trying to predict perceptions of mentors or proteges from perceptions of friendships.

Of more value to this study is the variate structure. From the mentors' point of view, relational need loads high with moderate loadings for both relational adjectives and emotional intimacy in both mentoring and friendship relationships. It appears that both types of relationships satisfy the relational needs and emotional intimacy needs of these women. A more complex variate structure resulted from proteges' perceptions. On the first factor, relational adjectives and relational need of the mentoring relationships loaded highly with relational need of the friendship. Interesting here is the negative moderate loading of emotional involvement. The second factor loads highly for relational adjectives in the mentoring relationship and relational need in the friendship. Once again, emotional intimacy in the friendship has a moderately high negative loading. This could be interpreted as satisfaction of relational need that accompanies some risk in level of emotional intimacy.

Implications

Admittedly, the framework presented in this chapter is a modest attempt to model the dynamics of the female mentoring relationship. With the bulk of mentoring research based on male mentoring relationships, the study presented in this chapter is an attempt to examine the female version of these helping relationships. This study provided some initial evidence that the nature of female mentoring relationships closely reflects the model for female friendship. Both of these female relationships appear to be different than the more hierarchical and task-oriented male mentorships (eg., Hardesty & Jacobs, 1986), and the more task and activity-oriented male friendships (eg., Sherrod, 1989; Weiss & Lowenthal, 1975).

Hopefully, this study provides some insight into how women structure their helping relationships. The problems women face when forming mentoring relationships are twofold: a) men are less likely to initiate mentoring relationships with women than with men, whereas conversely women are more likely to form mentoring relationships with other women than with men, and b) the traditional model of mentoring that appears to fit many male–male mentoring relationships does not appear to fit female–female mentoring relationships, and is not likely to fit male–female mentoring relationships either. This situation ultimately places women in the position of having fewer high-ranking or desirable mentors with which to form relationships (until more women are able to become upwardly mobile in organizations) and leaves them with a traditional model for mentoring relationships that may not fit successful female relationships.

The model presented in this chapter should provide a glimmer of hope for women who are trying to find desirable mentors or who are trying to develop competent proteges. It suggests that one way for women to gain empowerment in the workplace and in their professions is to adapt the familiar friendship model to their professional relationships. Although this may not be the only solution to the problem of seeking sources of social support in the workplace, it is a place to begin as women strive to develop the power and equality that can result from and be a part of a successfully advancing career and professional life.

However, a question that remains concerns women and men working together. If women and men are more likely to mentor members of their own sex rather than form cross–sex mentoring relationships, then what does this say about the future of women and men working together? Are women and men forever doomed to avoid one another? Although the model presented in this chapter suggests an alternative for women attempting to achieve power and equality in the workplace, the development of this model also implies that other alternative mentoring models may exist for mentoring relationships between women and men (cf. Kalbfleisch & Davies, 1991b).

For example, a primary barrier to women and men working together has traditionally been sex itself. Specifically, women and men working together in close mentoring relationships have often been the subject of sexual innuendo and rumor (eg., Bowen, 1985). Whether or not the members of the partnership are actually involved sexually, comments from co-workers, increased scrutiny by management and other members of the profession, as well as jealousy voiced by spouses and loved ones can make the formation and maintenance of these relationships distressing (Kalbfleisch, in press). If mentoring relationships are partnerships that involve some professional and personal risk as Kalbfleisch and Davies (1993) suggested, then the additional pressure resulting from cross-sex alliances would pose an even greater risk and deterrent to the formation of such mentorships.

It would seem that eventually enough women and men will work together that this problem could be resolved. However, waiting for this change is similar to the logic of waiting for women to advance up the ranks of the organization. Both changes may eventually occur, but the wait will be unnecessarily protracted and many talented people will become frustrated and fail in the interim if we do not look at facilitating this process.

It is likely that one of the problems women and men face when working together is the existing frameworks that persist for modeling male and female relationships. Perhaps by examining these frameworks we can understand how to smooth the difficulties encountered by women and men in helping relationships (Kalbfleisch, in press). For example, while some women have found the father–daughter format for male–female working relationships to be helpful (Kalbfleisch, in press), others complain that this form of relationship can be too restrictive (Hardesty & Jacobs, 1986). The problem appears to be that the person in the role of "father" can become overly restrictive and protective of the person in the role of the "daughter." This difficulty appears to be more of a problem for the father–daughter style of mentoring, than the father–son style that many male mentorships model.

The second "traditional" female–male relationship is that of husband–wife or of lovers. Women and men working together may find themselves falling into this relational framework because it is one for which they can easily find a referent in their personal relationships (Kalbfleisch, in press). In point, mentoring relationships between women and men sometimes do develop into love relationships, such as that of Auther Stiglitz and Virginia O'Keefe (artists), or they can originate from love relationships themselves such as John and Bo Derek (director/actor). Nevertheless, it would seem that for the most part, basing mentoring relationships on this framework could lead to misunderstandings and potential problems.

It would be easy to see why co-workers would talk, other professionals would scrutinize, and spouses would be jealous if the "lover" framework is the model chosen for a female–male mentoring relationship. It would also be easy to see how "friendly" cues could be misinterpreted as "flirting" or "seductive" behavior by the members of such mentoring relationships (cf. Koeppel, Montage-Miller, O'Hair, & Cody, 1993). The implications for issues of sexual harassment or minimal discomfort in such situations should be readily apparent.

It seems that there must be other models for women and men to use in forming strong enduring mentoring relationships. The study presented in this chapter suggests that an alternate model is available that may be more appropriate for women. It would follow, that alternative satisfactory models may also exist for women and men.

Minimally, it may be enough at the start for women and men to recognize that a sexual undercurrent may be a part of their mentoring relationships. Perhaps, this realization alone may help women and men be more sensitive to the appropriateness of their behavior in their working and helping relationships. Alternately, Heinrich (1991) suggested transforming the underlying sexuality of these relationships. She suggested that instead of acting on this sexuality in a physical sense, we should instead use awareness of this sexuality to fire the creativity and energy of this working relationship. Heinrich suggested that perhaps such inspired relationships may be the most productive and invigorating of them all.

In sum, this chapter may actually raise more questions than it answers. Although offering an alternative for empowering women, it does not provide a similar alternative for empowering women and men working together. Two common frameworks for the professional relationships of women and men are discussed; however other models for these relationships could also apply. It is evident that much is yet to be learned about the women and men who work together and who work apart.

ACKNOWLEDGEMENT

This research was supported by a grant to the first author from the Office of the Vice President for Research and Graduate Study at the University of Kentucky, and by a University Research Grant to the second author from Baylor University. Earlier versions of this manuscript were presented at professional conventions as Kalbfleisch (1991; 1994) and Keyton and Kalbfleisch (1993a).

REFERENCES

Ball, A. L. (1989, October). Mentors & proteges: Portraits of success. *Working Woman*, pp. 134–142.

Bowen, D. D. (1985, February). Were men meant to mentor women? *Training and Development Journal, 39*(2), 30–34.

Brown, D. A. (1985). The role of mentoring in the professional lives of university faculty women. *Dissertations abstracts international, 47*(1), 160A.

Burgoon, J. K., & Hale, J. L. (1984). The fundamental topoi of relational communication. *Communication Monographs, 51*, 193–214.

Burgoon, J. K., & Hale, J. L. (1987). Validation and measurement of the fundamental themes of relational communication. *Communication Monographs, 54*(1), 19–41.

Burke, R. J. (1984). Mentors in organizations. *Group and Organization Studies, 9*(3), 353–372.

Burke, R. J., & McKeen, C. A. (1990). Mentoring in organizations: Implications for women. *Journal of Business Ethics, 9*(4–5), 317–332.

Bushardt, S. C., Fretwell, C., & Holdnak, B. J. (1991). The mentor/protege relationship: A biological perspective. *Human Relations, 44*(6), 619–639.

Collins, N. W. (1983). *Professional women and their mentors: A practical guide to mentoring for the woman who wants to get ahead.* Englewood Cliffs, NJ: Prentice Hall.

Corporate women: Progress? Sure. But the playing field is still far from level. (1992, June 8). *Business Week*, pp. 74–83.

Dowd, M. (1991, November). Power: Are women afraid of it—or beyond it? *Working Woman*, pp. 98–99.

Dreher, G. F., & Ash, R. A. (1990). A comparative study of mentoring among men and women in managerial, professional, and technical positions. *Journal of Applied Psychology, 75*(5), 539–546.

Fagenson, E. A. (1989). The mentor advantage: Perceived career/job experiences of proteges versus non-proteges. *Journal of Organizational Behavior, 10,* 309–320.

Farris, R., & Ragan, L. (1981). Importance of mentor–protege relationships to the upward mobility of the female executive. *Mid-South Business Journal, 1*(4), 24–28.

The gains are slow, say many women. (1992, June). *Business Week*, p. 77.

Hall, R. M., & Sandler, B. R. (1983). Academic mentoring for women students and faculty: A new look at an old way to get ahead. *Project on the Status and Education of Women*, Association of American Colleges: Washington, DC.

Hardesty, S., & Jacobs, N. (1986). *Success and betrayal: The crisis of women in corporate America.* New York: Franklin Watts.

Heinrich, K. T. (1991). Loving partnerships: Dealing with sexual attraction and power in doctoral advisement relationships. *Journal of Higher Education, 62*(5), 514–538.

Homer (1960). *The odyssey of homer,* (E. Rees, Trans.). New York: Random House.

Hunt, D. M., & Michael C. (1983). Mentorship: A career training and development tool. *Academy of Management Review, 8*(3), 475–485.

Jeruchim, J., & Shapiro, P. (1992). *Women, mentors, and success.* New York: Fawcett Columbine.

Kalbfleisch, P. J. (1991, November). *Gender Issues and Academic Mentoring.* Paper presented at the Seminar Series on Mentoring at the annual conference of the Speech Communication Association, Atlanta.

Kalbfleisch, P. J. (1993). Public portrayals of enduring friendships. In P. J. Kalbfleisch (Ed.), *Interpersonal communication: Evolving interpersonal relationships.* (pp. 189–212) Hillsdale, NJ: Lawrence Erlbaum Associates.

Kalbfleisch, P. J. (1994, February). *The Mentoring Relationships of Women and Men.* Paper presented at the annual meeting of the Western States Communication Association, San Jose, CA.

Kalbfleisch, P. J. (in press). *Mentoring as a personal relationship.* New York: Guilford Press.

Kalbfleisch, P. J., & Davies, A. B. (1991a, April). *Mentors and proteges: Choices in partnership.* Paper presented at the annual meeting of the Southern States Communication Association (Top Three Paper), Tampa, FL.

Kalbfleisch, P. J., & Davies, A. B. (1991b). Minorities and mentoring: Managing the multicultural institution. *Communication Education, 40*(3), 266–271.

Kalbfleisch, P. J., & Davies, A. B. (1993). An interpersonal model for participation in mentoring relationships. *Western Journal of Communication, 57*(4), 399–415.

Keyton, J., & Kalbfleisch, P. J. (1993a, April). *Building a Normative Model of Woman's Mentoring Relationships.* Paper presented at the annual meeting of the Southern States Communication Association, Lexington, KY.

Keyton, J., & Kalbfleisch, P. J. (1993b). *Mentoring: From a female perspective. Mentor, 5,* 1–10.

Koeppel, L. B., Montagne-Miller, Y., O'Hair, D., & Cody, M. J. (1993). Friendly? flirting? wrong? In P. Kalbfleisch (Ed.), *Interpersonal communication: Evolving interpersonal relationships,* (pp. 13–32). Hillsdale, NJ: Lawrence Erlbaum Associates.

Kogler Hill, S. E., Bahniuk, M. H., Dobos, J., & Rouner, D. (1989). Mentoring and other communication support in the academic setting. *Group and Organization Studies, 14*(3), 355–368.

Kram, K. E. (1985). *Mentoring at work.* Glenview, IL: Scott Foresman and Company.

Kram, K. E. (1986). Mentoring in the workplace. In D. T. Hall and Associates (Eds.), *Career development in organizations* (pp. 160–201). San Francisco: Jossey-Bass Publishers.

Kram, K. E., & Isabella, L. A. (1985). Mentoring alternatives: The role of peer relationships in career development. *Academy of Management Journal, 28*(1), 110–132.

Leatham, G., & Duck, S. (1990). Conversations with friends and the dynamics of social support. In S. Duck (Ed.), *Personal relationships and social support* (pp. 1–29). Newbury Park, CA: Sage.

Levinson, D. J. (1978). *The seasons of a man's life*. New York: Ballantine Books.

Mallory, T. (1969). *King Arthur and his knights*, (E. Vinaver, Trans.). New York: Houghton Mifflin.

Nelson, D. L., & Quick, J. C. (1985). Professional women: Are distress and disease inevitable? *Academy of Management Review, 10*(2), 206–216.

Nieva, V. F., & Gutek, B. A. (1981). *Women and work*. New York: Praeger.

Noe, R. A. (1988). An investigation of the determinants of successful assigned mentoring relationships. *Personnel Psychology, 41*, 457–479.

Olian, J. D., Carroll, S. J., Giannantonio, C. M., & Feren, D. B. (1988). What do proteges look for in a mentor? Results of three experimental studies, *Journal of Vocational Behavior, 33*, 15–37.

Phillips-Jones, L. (1982). *Mentors & proteges*. New York: Arbor House.

Ragins, B. R. (1989). Barriers to mentoring: The female manager's dilemma. *Human Relations, 42*(1), 1–22.

Reich, M. H. (1985). Executive views from both sides of mentoring. *Personnel, 62*(3), 42–46.

Reich, M. H. (1986). The mentor connection. *Personnel, 63*(2), 50–56.

Sands, R. G., Parson, L.A., & Duane, J. (1991). Faculty mentoring faculty in a public university. *Journal of Higher Education, 62*(2), 174–193.

Shapiro, E. C., Haseltine, F. P., & Rowe, M. P. (1978). Moving up: Role models, mentors, and the "patron system." *Sloan Management Review, 19*, 51–58.

Sherrod, D. (1989). The influence of gender on same-sex friendships. In C. Hendrick (Ed.), *Close relationships* (pp. 164–186). Newbury Park, CA: Sage.

The view from the trenches. (1990, August). *Business Week*, p 54.

Warihay, P. D. (1980). The climb to the top: Is the network the route for women? *Personnel Administrator, 25*(4) 55–60.

Weiss, L., & Lowenthal, M. F. (1975). Life-course perspectives on friendship. In M. F. Lowenthal, M. Thurnher, & D. Chiriboga (Eds.), *Four stages of life* (pp. 48–61). San Francisco: Jossey-Bass.

Welcome to the woman-friendly company: Where talent is valued and rewarded. (1990, August). *Business Week*, pp. 48–55.

Whitely, W., Dougherty, T. W, & Dreher, G. F. (1991). Relationship of career mentoring and socioeconomic origin to managers' and professionals' early career progress. *Academy of Management Journal, 34*(2), 331–351.

Whitely, W., Dougherty, T. W., & Dreher, G. F. (1992). Correlates of career-oriented mentoring for early career managers and professionals. *Journal of Organizational Behavior, 13*, 141–154.

Williams, D. G. (1985). Gender, masculinity–femininity, and emotional intimacy in same-sex friendship. *Sex Roles, 12*(5–6), 587–600.

Worell, J., & Remer, P. (1992). *Feminist perspectives in therapy: An empowerment model for women*. New York: Wiley.

Chapter 9

Relating to Spouse and Stranger: Gender-Preferential Language Use

Mary Anne Fitzpatrick
University of Wisconsin-Madison

Anthony Mulac
University of California-Santa Barbara

It has long been our concern that much of the research on sex differences in the communication practices of men and women ignores the contexts in which communication takes place. Of particular concern in this chapter is the relational context. In other words, the relationship between given male and female communicators is expected to exert a strong influence on their linguistic and communicative practices. By directly comparing men and women as they interact with both strangers and spouses, we present a more nuanced view of gender differences in social interaction.

We begin with a discussion of the gender-linked language effect and the empirical support this effect has received in a number of contexts. We then turn to the issue of gender preferential language and present data on social interaction in mixed-sex dialogues.

THE GENDER-LINKED LANGUAGE EFFECT

The Gender-Linked Language Effect refers to the attributional consequences of using clusters of linguistic features found to differentiate male from female speech. These linguistics features may include, for example, intensive adverbs, adverbials beginning sentences, and negations (Mulac & Lundell, 1986; Mulac, Lundell, & Bradac, 1986). In studies of this effect, printed transcripts of naturally occurring language samples (none indicating the speaker's gender) are rated by untrained observers using semantic differential scales. In general, female communicators are rated higher on *Sociointellectual Status* and *Aesthetic Quality*, whereas male communicators are rated higher on *Dynamism*. Because the observers in these studies are unable to guess accurately the gender of the speakers, the differences in ratings appear to be the result of gender-linked language differences rather than the raters' sex-role stereotypes.

Mulac and Lundell (1980) demonstrated this linguistic effect using brief oral descriptions of landscape photographs (made in the presence of a researcher, balanced for gender) by speakers from four age groups ranging from 11–12 to 50–69 years of age. In this study, the *Aesthetic Quality* ratings favored the older female speakers more than the younger ones. The effect had earlier been shown in a study of regional dialect in which transcripts of adults' descriptions of landscape photographs favored females on *Aesthetic Quality* and males on *Dynamism* (Mulac & Rudd, 1977). Further support for the effect on all three attributional dimensions (i.e., sociointellectual status, aesthetic quality, and dynamism) was found by Mulac and Lundell (1982) using transcripts of university students' first classroom speeches in an introductory public speaking course.

Evidence of the Gender-Linked Language Effect has also been reported for written descriptions of landscape photographs by university students (Mulac & Lundell, in press), with female writers rated higher on *Sociointellectual Status* and *Aesthetic Quality* and male writers higher on *Dynamism*. The same pattern of effects was also obtained for fourth grade boys' and girls' impromptu essays on the topic, "Is it ever all right to tell a lie?" (Mulac, Studley, & Blau, 1990). For that study's eighth and twelfth graders, the only differences favored the male writers on *Dynamism*.

A comparison of the Gender-Linked Language Effect and sex-role stereotypes was undertaken in a recent study (Mulac, Incontro, & James, 1985). Results demonstrated that the patterns of effects resulting from the two were strongly and positively related ($r = .93$). The language and stereotype effects, however, were also shown to be independent of each other, in that they could be produced separately, added together, or subtracted from each other.

The evidence for the Gender-Linked Language Effect has been generally consistent in monologic communication. Mulac, Wiemann, Widenmann, and Gibson (1988) expanded the domain of the effect by studying social interactions in both same-sex and mixed-sex groups. As usual, linguistic forms easily indentified male and female speech patterns and the sex-stereotyped attributional effects occurred in same-sex dialogues. Curiously, however, in mixed-sex dyads it was men who were rated as high on Aesthetic Quality and women who were rated as high on Dynamism. The study reported in this chapter examined mixed-sex dyads in greater detail. In the next section, we consider mixed-sex groups and discuss how partner influence may modify language behavior.

INTERACTION IN MIXED-SEX GROUPS

Substantial attention in recent years has been directed to the ways in which members of different social groups interact and with what consequences. This work has been based on the assumption that social group members use a variety of linguistic and nonlinguistic devices that are peculiar to their own group and distinguish them from other groups. Speech accent, for an obvious example, differs among ethnic groups (Giles & Powesland, 1975). Less obviously, the extent of use of linguistic features such as *intensive adverbs* (Crosby & Nyquist, 1977; Hiatt, 1978; Lapadat & Seesahai, 1978; McMillan, Clifton, McGrath, & Gale, 1977; Mulac & Lundell, 1986; Mulac, Lundell, & Bradac, 1986) and *personal pronouns* (Koenigsknecht & Friedman, 1976; Mulac & Lundell, 1986; Poole, 1979) distinguishes between males and females. These sorts of distinctions are not merely sociolinguistic curiosities. Rather, they are frequently of consequence to those involved in intergroup interactions. Thus, accented speech potentially marks one as an outsider (Giles, Scherer, & Taylor, 1979). Furthermore, linguistic patterns typical of women are argued to be less powerful than those associated with men (Kramarae, 1981; Lakoff, 1975).

A considerable body of research treats these linguistic and nonlinguistic behaviors as traits of individuals that are inherently related to their membership in a particular social group. Such treatment overlooks that fact that there can be a great deal of linguistic variation within individual communicators from context to context. People vary their speech production, consciously or unconsciously, for reasons related to both their internal state (for example, mood) and the constraints of the situation in which they find themselves (for example, their interaction partners: see Forgas, 1983). In this study, we wanted to determine how linguistic forms differed for men and women during interaction in mixed-sex groups. We know from extensive previous research by Mulac and his associates that the use of gender preferential language has particular attributional consequences. Because of the possible consequences of such variations, gender-linked linguistic variation may be a strategy for either emphasizing or moderating social group-related differences.

Strategic use of linguistic devices in this way has been extensively investigated by Giles and his colleagues (for example, Giles & Powesland, 1975; Giles & Smith, 1979; Street & Giles, 1982; Thakerar, Giles, & Cheshire, 1982) under the rubric of Speech Accommodation Theory. This work has shown that people often do vary specific linguistic and prosodic features of speech (for example, speech rate or pronunciation) in order to converge toward the behavior of a member of their own social group. In addition, Cappella's Discrepancy-Arousal model (Cappella, 1983; Cappella & Greene, 1982) provides a rationale for the often-reported findings that interaction partners tend to mirror the nonverbal behavior of the other, establishing a relationship that can be described as one of partner influence. Males and females can be seen as constituting two different social groups of sociolinguistic communities (Ashmore, 1981, Ashmore & De Boca, 1981; Maltz & Borker, 1982) for which accommodation and mutual influence might be important from an intergroup perspective.

But it is also true that there are identifiable linguistic patterns that have been associated with members of particular social groups. Not only has the language of males and females been shown to differ (Smith, 1985, Thorne, Kramarae, & Henley, 1983), the effect of those differences, which we call the Gender-Linked Language Effect, has been documented in a variety of settings and communicational tasks by Mulac and his associates (Mulac & Lundell, 1980, 1982; Mulac, Studley, & Blau, 1990; Mulac & Rudd, 1977).

Partner Influence

Although it can hardly be denied that partners influence one another in interaction (compare Cappella, 1983; Giles, Mulac, Bradac, & Johnson, 1987; Patterson, 1984), the mechanism through which this influence occurs is still open to debate. We do not have the space to examine these various theoretical positions in detail (see Anderson & Anderson, 1984, for a comparison of several influence models) but the theoretical work agrees that partners in conversation can influence one another to behave similarly or dissimilarly.

When interacting with someone from a different speech community, communicators often try to diminish differences by matching the behaviors of their partners. For example, nonverbal response matching occurs in a large number of interpersonal encounters and for a large number of interpersonal variables. Latencies, intensities, simultaneous speech, talk/silence states, vocalizations, pauses, switching pauses, proximity, and gaze tend to match across partners (Cappella, 1983; Cappella & Greene, 1982; Cappella & Planalp, 1981; Mulac, Studley, Wiemann, & Bradac, 1987). These results are important because matching is taken as a sign of involvement and responsiveness and consequently leads to positive interpersonal outcomes. Perhaps matching is a reflection of a speaker's need for identification with another (Giles et al., 1987). Thus, in cooperative interactions where maintenance of in-group identity is not salient, we would anticipate that participants would tend to converge their speech styles, a premise that is supported by a wealth of empirical research (see Giles et al., 1987; Street & Giles, 1982; and Thakerar et al., 1982, for recent comprehensive reviews).

In contrast to the convergence predictions, it is possible to state a theoretical case for increased sex-role stereotypical (i.e., divergent), behavior in mixed-sex interaction. Some early research in small group behavior (see e.g., Strodtbeck & Mann, 1956) has been interpreted as supporting greater stereotypical mixed-sex behavior. In a direct test of the stereotypical hypothesis, however, Piliavin and Martin (1978) failed to find any evidence for this view in male, female, and mixed-sex groups. Hammen and Peplau (1978) did find that women who interacted with a man in a waiting room reported more traditional (that is, stereotypical) attitudes toward sex-roles than did women who interacted with a woman; men showed no difference. In this study, however, the behavioral differences between men and women for distance, looking, and talking failed to favor either the stereotypical or the convergence prediction consistently.

In the majority of recent investigations, there is general agreement that people adjust, verbally and nonverbally, in order to mirror the behavior of others they like, whom they wish to have like them, or whom they see as rewarding them in some way. Further, these adjustments are typically positively evaluated by the partner as long as the partner perceives them and evaluates them as being within acceptable levels (that is, for example, not too intimate, intrusive, or arousing).

Empirical support for convergence in mixed-sex dyads comes from the work of Mulac, Wiemann, Widenmann, and Gibson (1988), who found that the language of male and female speakers permits more accurate discrimination of interactant gender in same-sex, than in mixed-sex, dyads. Furthermore, the attributional consequences of speech in mixed-sex dyads were that males were perceived as more aesthetically pleasing and females were perceived as more dynamic. Our prediction is that in mixed-sex groups both males and females will converge in their gender preferential language in that men will be more feminine and women will be more masculine in their linguistic styles in conversations with one another.

What prediction do we make for married couples? As a relational unit, married partners are an "in-group." Thus, we would expect even more convergence in language use than that which occurs in stranger dyads. Whereas, we predict linguistic convergence in all mixed-sex dyads, we expect the greatest convergence between married partners.

GENDER PREFERENTIAL LANGUAGE USE

Men and women use language in different ways and achieve different effects. Across a wide array of linguistic choices, male and female talk can be recognized. When asked to describe interesting or dramatic life experiences, men made more references to destructive actions, space, time, and quantity, whereas women made more reference to feelings, emotions, motivations, and the self. These male and female differrences appear in the language choices of even young children. One study found girls as young as 4 employing more reflective and emotional language than boys of the same age (Staley, 1982). Such gender-based differences have been reported in both dyadic and group intereaction situations (Crosby & Nyquist, 1977; Martin & Craig, 1983; McMillian et al., 1977; Poole, 1979; Price & Graves, 1980; Sause, 1976).

In Table 9.1, we present descriptions of 32 linguistic variables coded in this study, many of which have been shown to be predictive of speaker gender. A consideration of the discriminating language provides insights into the conscious or unconscious stylistic strategies that appear to operate for both men and women. Following Smith (1985), we believe that these indicators should be thought of as

TABLE 9.1
Description, Examples, and Citations[a] for 32 Language Variables Coded as Potential Predictors of Interactant Gender

I. Elements

A. Words: The number of printed elements, separated by spaces, having semantic meaning. Price & Graves, 1980, M+ (spoken) and F+ (written); Wood, 1996, M+.
B. *Pauses*: ("...") Nonvocalized hesitations in the flow of speech.
C. *Vocalized Pauses*: ("ah," "uhm.") Utterances having no semantic meaning; Frances, 1979, M+, Mulac, Wiemann, Widenmann, & Gibson, 1988, M+; Poole, 1979, M+.
D. *Fillers*: ("you know," "like.") Words or phrases used without apparent semantic intent. Hirschman, 1973, F+ Mulac & Lundell, 1986, M+; Mulac et al., 1986, F+, Mulac, Studley, & Blau, 1990, F+ ; Mulac et al., M+.
E. *Back Channels*: ("Unhuh," "Right.") Utterances showing apparent interest in having the partner continue talking.
F. *Interruptions*: (Person A: "I don't really like electrical engineering that much. [By that I mean if you]" Person B: "[A lot of] people are getting out of it." Breaking into a person's turn [not including back channels such as "yeah"], in an apparent attempt to take over the floor.) Mulac et al., 1988, M+; West & Zimmerman, 1983, M+; Zimmerman & West, 1975, M+.
G. *Interruption Words*: The number of overlapping words uttered while apparently trying to take over the conversational floor from the partner.
H. *Mean Length Sentence*: The number of words divided by the number of sentences (defined as sequences of words beginning with a capital letter and ending with a period). Hunt, 1965, F+; Mulac et al., 1986, F+; Mulac & Lundell, 1986, F+; Mulac & Lundell, in press, F+, Mulac, Studley, & Blau, 1990, M+; Poole, 1979, F+.

II. Sentences

A. *Questions*: ("What is expected of us?" "What do you do?") but not including directives in question form. Fishman, 1978, F+ Mulac et al., 1988, F+.
B. *Tag Questions*: ("It's early Winter, isn't it?") An assertion that is followed immediately by a question asking for support. Crosby & Nyquist, 1977, F+; Dubois & Crouch, 1975, M+, Lapadat & Seesahai, 1978, M+; Hartman, 1976, F+; McMillan et al., 1977, F+; Mulac & Lundell, 1986, F+.
C. *Directives*: ("Think of another," "Why don't you put that down?") Haas, 1979, M+; Mulac et al., 1988, M+.
D. *Affirmations*: ("I think you're right on that one.") Statements indicating apparent agreement (but not counting back channels).
E. *Negations*: ("You don't feel like looking . . .") A statement of what something is not. Mulac & Lundell, 1986, F+; Mulac et al., 1986, F+.
F. *Opposition*: ("The snow must have fallen fairly recently, but it has been a while ...;" ". . . Very peaceful, yet full of movement. . .") Retracting a statement and posing one with an opposite meaning. Mulac & Lundell, 1986, F+; Mulac et al., 1986, F+.
G. *Justifiers*: ("It's winter because there's snow. . .") A reason is given for the assertion made. Mulac & Lundell, 1986, M+; Mulac et al., 1988, F+.
H. *Modals*: ("I would say that it's . . .," "It could be. . . ") A model verb form is used that suggests doubtfulness. McMillan et al., 1977, F+.

III. Sentence Initial Elements

A. *Sentence Initial Adverbials*: ("Instead of being the light blue. . ., it is. . .;" "Because the trees still have snow. . ., it looks like. . .") Answers questions regarding the main clause such as: How?, When?, or Where? Mulac et al., 1986, F+; Mulac et al., 1988, F+; Mulac & Lundell, in press, F+; Mulac, Studley, & Blau, 1990, F+.
B. *Sentence Initial Fillers*: ("Okay, the first thing we should do is . . . .") Mulac et al., 1988, M+.
C. *Sentence Initial Conjunctions*: ("And then I thought about. . . .") Mulac et al., 1988, M+.

(Continued)

218

TABLE 9.1 (*Continued*)

IV. Modifiers

A. *Intensive Adverbs*: ("very," "really," "quite.") Modifiers that apparently increase the strength or intensity of a statement. Crosby & Nyquist, 1977, F+; Lapadat & Seesahai, 1978, F+; MCMillan et al., 1977, F+; Mulac & Lundell, 1986, F+; Mulac et al., 1986, F+; Mulac et al., 1988, F+.
B. Hedges: ("possibly," "somewhat," "maybe," "rather.") Modifiers that indicate lack of confidence in, or diminished assuredness of, the statement. Crosby & Nyquist, 1977, F+; Mulac, Studley, & Blau, 1900, F+.

V. Personal Pronouns

Words that stand for beings. Gleser et al., 1959, F+; Haslett, 1983, F+; Koenigsknecht & Friedman, 1976, F+; Mulac & Lundell, 1986, F+; Mulac & Lundell, in press, M+; Mulac et al., 1988, F+; Poole, 1979, F+; Westmoreland et al., 1977, F+.

A. *"I"*: ("I think it's better to . . . .") Mulac & Lundell, in press, M +; Mulac, Studley, & Blau, 1900, M+.
B. *"me"*: ("If it's up to me, . . .")
C. *"we"*: ("We wanted to . . . .")
D. *"us"*: ("How can anyone expect us to do that?")
E. *"you"*: ("You should know that . . . .")
F. *"him"* or *"her"*: (". . . give it to him.")
G. *"they"*: ("They said. . . . ")
H. *"he"* or *"she"*: ("She's the one who. . . .")
I. *"them"*: ("Just give it to them.")

VI. Miscellaneous

A. *References to Emotion*: ("happy," "enticing," "depressing.") Any mention of an emotion or feeling. Balswick & Avertt, 1977, F+; Gleser et al., 1959, F+; Mulac & Lundell, in press, F+; Mulac, et al., 1986, F+; Staley, F+.
B. *Obscenities*: ("fucking," "shitty.") Words that offend accepted standards of decency.

Note. From Fitzpatrick, Mulac, and Dindia (1995). Reprinted by permission of Sage Publications, Inc.
[a] Citations indicate empirical studies in which the variable was found to differ for male and female communicators. Gender distinction, in terms of whether the variable was more indicative of male or female communicators, are as follows: M+ = Male, F+ = Female. (Note, however, that the linguistic categories were not in all cases precisely equivalent across studies.)

gender preferential rather than *gender distinct*. The differences in these language strategies are not only subtle but also dynamic in that they can change with the social context of the interaction.

Beside failing to take into account possible changes in group behavior depending on context (e.g., sex of the partner), the majority of research on male/female language differences has viewed individual language variables in isolation, rather than in combination. We chose instead to study the gender-predicting efficacy of a cluster of variables in the form of a weighted combination of language variables in discriminant function scores. These weighted scores represent the unique contributions of the various language variables. These combinations represent natural conversations. Furthermore, these scores have been found capable of predicting gender in interviews (Poole, 1979), storytelling tasks (McLaughlin, Cody, Kane, & Robey, 1981), photograph descriptions (Mulac & Lundell, 1986), and public speeches (Mulac et al., 1986).

In addition to examining a range of linguistic behaviors that discriminate male and female speech, we broaden our discussion of mixed-sex groups to include married partners.

METHOD

Subjects

Mailings were sent to all couples in a local church requesting them to complete a questionnaire and to participate in the study. Participants were told that $1 would be donated to the church for each questionnaire completed. In addition, a free marital communication workshop was conducted for members of the church at the completion of the experimental sessions. The church community included 100 couples and 58 questionnaires were returned. In general, questionnaires were completed by wives. Twenty married couples were voluntarily recruited from among the 58 couples who completed the questionnaires. These couples received $30.00 at the end of their participation in three laboratory sessions.

The questionnaire contained demographic questions and the Locke–Wallace Marital Adjustment Scale (1959). The husbands and wives in this study were about 36 years old and the majority had completed college. On average, couples had been married about 10 years and had three children. Fifty percent of wives worked outside the home. There were no differences in any of the demographic measures nor in the level of marital happinesss and adjustment experienced by the couples who participated in the study in contrast to those who merely completed the questionnaire. There were no male–female marital satisfaction differences in participant ($t(19) = .242$; ns) or nonparticipant samples (t(44) = −1.64; ns).

Procedures

The 20 couples were divided into five groups of four couples each. Each group of four couples came to the video laboratory three times. Letters were sent to the couples describing the procedures and the amount of time each session was expected to last. When they reached the laboratory, couples were greeted by members of the research team. We had four laboratories designed to look like living rooms. We randomly scheduled the participants to engage in seven, 10-minute conversations. In other words, each man and woman would, at some point in the evening, speak with his or her spouse and all of the other participants. Research assistants escorted particpants from room to room. We wanted to insure that the research particpants did not speak with one another outside the laboratory.

Subjects were given a list of topics to choose from to discuss for each of their conversations. The topics concerned important aspects of marriage. These topics were chosen because the subjects were married and because we thought these topics would stimulate intimate interaction. The 15 topics were taken from the Dyadic Adjustment Scale (Spanier, 1976). They were: handling family finances; matters of recreation; religious matters; demonstrations of affection; friends; sex relations; conventionality; philosophy of life; dealing with in-laws; aims, goals, and things believed important; amount of time spent together; making major decisions; household tasks; leisure time; and career decisions.

The procedure was repeated on three separate occasions. Each session was approximately 1 week apart. Because it was extremely important that no data be lost in this design, participants were reminded via telephone of their appointments each week. No participant dropped out of the study. Our design was a round robin design in which all possible pairs of subjects in a group interacted with one another on each occasion. Thus, for each group, eight subjects (four married couples) conversed with each of seven other participants on each of three separate occasions. Thus, we collected and transcribed, 420 conversations (28 conversations x 3 sessions x 5 groups). Because of the labor intensive nature of this linguistic coding task, only conversations from the first session were analyzed in this study.

A small church was selected to avoid the "stranger on the train" phenomenon. Theory and research suggests (Berger & Roloff, 1982) that initial interaction between strangers who know they will not meet again is not generalizable to the more typical situation of strangers interacting who know they will or may see each other again. Subjects in this study knew there was a chance they would see each other again (at church or church-related functions) after the study was completed. We tried to assign couples to groups such that all the couples in a given group were strangers, however, this was not always possible. Thus, some of the couples were acquaintances ("we met once or twice") and two couples were friends.

Coding Scheme

Survey of the literature on gender-linked language differences suggested a relatively large number of language features that might conceivably differentiate between male and female interaction (see Mulac, Wiemann, Widenmann, & Gibson, 1988).

Thirty-two linguistic variables were coded in this study (see Table 9.1), either because they had been found in previous research to differ for men and women (e.g., *intensive adverbs*) or because they had the potential for differing in the relational setting tested here (e.g., "*We*"). These language features can be divided into six groups. The first group may be considered elements of speech such as *words* and *interruptions*. The second group involves sentence forms such as *questions* and *directives*. The third includes ways of beginning sentences, such as *sentence initial adverbials*. The fourth contains two common modifiers, *intensive adverbs* and *hedges*. The fifth group is made up of different personal pronouns such as "*I*" and "*us*." The final group includes two important miscellaneous forms, *references to emotion* and *obscenities*.

Previous research on same-sex and mixed-sex stranger dyads has demonstrated, for example, that a weighted combination of eight of these types of linguistic variables could discriminate male from female speech. Male speech has been shown to be marked by *interruptions*, *directives*, and *sentence initial conjunctions/fillers*, whereas female speech is marked by *questions*, *justifiers*, *intensive adverbs*, *personal pronouns* and *sentence initial adverbials* (Mulac, Wiemann, Widenmann, & Gibson, 1988).

In this study, we had 140 10-minute conversations to analyze. The first step involved transcribing these transcripts. Coders were then trained to code the transcripts for the presence of the 32 linguistic variables of interest (see Table 9.1). Three teams of nine undergraduate majors met weekly for 8 weeks for their 2-hour training session. Coders practiced coding the week's new variables on transcripts from previous studies. Training continued until consensus was reached, and coders were then given transcripts and coding sheets to code independently. The realiability for the 32 variables, in the form of agreement among coders, was determined by an intraclass procedure (Winer, 1971). Consistently high across variables, the coefficients ranged from .82 to .99.

How did we begin the computations of the dependent variable for this study? First, we computed the mean number of occurrences of each variable for each speaker across the coders. Then, we transformed this data. Because the number of words generated by each speaker were not the same, the counts for each person were converted to occurrences per 100 words. Arcsin transformations were computed on these proportions.

Discriminant Analysis

A discriminant analysis was conducted to see if a subset of the linguistic variables could differentiate male and female speech, and if so, what the weighted discriminant function score was for each individual. This weighted discriminant function score could then be used in the subsequent round-robin analysis of variance to test the difference between marital communication and communication in mixed-sex dyads.

Results of the direct discriminant analysis (all variables forced into the equation) showed that the 32 variables correctly predicted the gender of the speaker in all but one case. This justified a subsequent stepwise discriminant analysis to determine the weighted combination of variables best able to predict gender. This stepwise analysis indicated that 20 variables were entered into the discriminant equation before reaching the predetermined cut-off point. Table 9.2 gives the canonical discriminant function coefficients, along with the final F-to-remove ratios, for each of the 20 variables making up the discriminating cluster. Four variables were shown to be indicative of male interactants: *Vocalized pause*; use of "*he*" or "*she*"; *pausing*;

TABLE 9.2

Linguistic Variables Selected by Stepwise Discriminant Analysis Predicting Gender
for All Interactants

Step	Variable	Gender Predicted[a]	Canonical Coefficient[b]	F-to-Remove	Wilks' Lambda
1	Vocalized Pause	Male	-.73	41.87	.87
2	Intensifiers	Female	.53	31.62	.81
3	Interruptions	Female	.40	26.55	.78
4	"Them"	Female	.56	23.90	.74
5	Conjunctions begin sentence	Female	.31	20.76	.73
6	"He" or "She"	Male	-.29	18.44	.71
7	Fillers begin sentences	Female	.20	16.93	.70
8	"Us"	Female	.25	15.32	.69
9	Questions	Female	.24	13.96	.68
10	Pauses	Male	-.12	12.75	.68
11	Affirmations	Female	.14	11.77	.67
12	References to emotions	Female	.14	10.93	.67
13	"Me"	Female	.18	10.21	.67
14	Words	Female	.28	9.71	.66
15	Interruption words	Female	.21	9.24	.66
16	Negatives	Male	-.14	8.81	.65
17	Modals	Female	.14	8.37	.65
18	"We"	Female	.13	7.97	.65
19	Directives	Female	.12	7.61	.64
20	Fillers	Female	.15	7.28	.64

Note. From Fitzpatrick, Mulac, and Dindia (1995). Reprinted by permission of Sage Publications, Inc.
[a] Relatively frequent use of this variable led to this prediction of interactant gender.
[b] Coefficients are not standardized. The designation of male indicators with negative coefficients, and female with positive, is arbitrary.

and the use of the *negative*. The other 16 variables, in weighted combination, characterized female speech.

The Social Relations Model: Case of the Mixed-Sex Dyads

The Social Relations Model assumes that people are both social stimuli and producers of social responses. To study both aspects simultaneously, one needs data generated from dyadic social interaction. A round-robin research design must be employed in which each person in a group interacts dyadically with every other person in the group.

In this chapter, we are interested in exploring the use of gender preferential language by males and females in conversations with married partners and with opposite sex strangers. In order to examine the effect of the relationship on the use of gender preferential language, we compared males speaking to females with husbands speaking with wives as well as females speaking to males with wives speaking to husbands.

Interestingly, we found no significant differences [$t(4) = .21$] in the use of female language markers for women when speaking to either their husbands ($M = .65$) or to other men ($M = .62$). Women did not converge toward either their husbands or other men during these dialogues. Rather, women maintained the same gender preferential linguistic style in both types of interactions. The differences that did occur were for men when speaking to both their wives and other women. When men were engaging in casual conversations with other women, they tended to use significantly more [$t(4) = 2.28\ p < .09$] masculine language forms ($M = -.78$) than these same men did when speaking to their wives ($M = -.30$). Men converged toward their wives' feminine style. Husbands appear to try to decrease the interaction distance between themselves and their wives by adopting a more feminine gender-preferential style than they do in conversations with women in general.

Why do men use more masculine language when speaking with women they have only met? A number of sources of variation may account for these findings. Men may use this masculine language form in the presence of a variety of different female partners (i.e., the actor effect). Men may elicit a given language behavior from a variety of different partners (i.e., the partner effect). Or, men may behave toward a particular other women in a specific manner, above and beyond any actor or partner effect.

Only males displayed any actor effect in this study. Sixty-nine percent of the variance in masculine talk (reliability = .89) can be accounted for by a stable dispositional trait of these male speakers. In an initial conversation with a woman, men tend to use masculine forms of language without any concern for particular characteristics of the female conversational partner. Men may be trying to differentiate themselves from women by maintaining a linguistic distance from them. In contrast, in the female data, no variation was accounted for by an actor effect.

This masculine use of language appears to have a strong conversational effect. For mixed-sex stranger dyads, there is a high actor–partner correlation ($r = .65$): men who use masculine language forms with women tend to elicit masculine language from women. In other words, by differentiating from women with whom they are interacting for the first time, men may be drawing from these women a convergent response. The actor–partner correlation suggests that men who use the masculine gender preferential style draw such a style from the women with whom they interact.

DISCUSSION

This study demonstrates that there are objectively measured gender differences in linguistic use. By designing a weighted combination of 20 different language variables, we were able to predict the gender of a speaker. Developing a weighted combination of linguistic variables that can separate male from female speech is a useful research technique. It helps us to see that language differences between males and females are subtle and multifacted. This technique reminds us that it is naive to think in univarate terms as "males used more a, b, or c than females." Rather, we need to think multivariately about these differences. And, because the scores are not based on dyad composition but rather on samples of speaking styles with a variety of different conversational partners (i.e., same-sex, opposite-sex, and spouse), this index gives us more confidence that it is tapping into actual differences in male and female language use.

Our hypotheses of linguistic convergence received only limited support. In other words, across stranger mixed-sex dyads, both males and females retained their gender preferential linguistic use. Wives did not converge toward husbands and maintained the same feminine gender preferential language in marital as in stranger dialogues. The only sign of convergence in these data was for husbands. Husbands who used masculine gender preferential language with women, converged toward their wives' feminine preferential style when interacting with her.

When interacting with a spouse, both husbands and wives used the female gender preferential linguistic style. We may find in future research that the female style is the language of relationships for both males and females. Interestingly, it is males who converge toward their wives in adopting this style.

Our research indicates that men and women demonstrate objective linguistic differences in their conversations. We find not only gender-linked differences but partner influence on that use, albeit not in the direction we predicted. In future research, we intend to explore the question of spouse and stranger interaction more fully and to elaborate the factors that might help us predict conditions under which divergence as well as convergence in gender preferential language use will occur.

SPECULATION ON POWER AND EQUALITY IN MARITAL RELATIONSHIPS

We began this chapter with a discussion of the gender preferential language use in mixed-sex dyads. The gender-linked language effect, in which male talk is rated as dynamic and female talk is rated as high on sociointellectual status and aesthetically pleasing, has been supported in a number of studies. Interestingly, this effect has been shown to diminish in mixed-sex dyadic conversations. In other words, men used masculine preferential talk in conversations with other men, women used female preferential talk in conversations with other women, but men and women converged toward the other person's style.

In our study, we took up the issue of the mixed-sex dyad and compared conversations in two different relational states: spouses and strangers. In other words, we compared the use of gender preferential language in discussions between spouses to those between unacquainted men and women. Research on gender differences in communication must take into account the relationship that communicators have to one another. When we did, we found that women used the female preferential style regardless of whether the listener was their husband or another man. In contrast, men used the masculine preferential style in conversations with women but adjusted their style to a more feminine preferential one with their wives.

Wives appear to maintain a female preferential style with both their husbands and male strangers. It is husbands who change their style when interacting with their wives. Husbands appear to accommodate their linguistic style when interacting with their wives. In situations of low conflict, feminine preferential language may be *the language of relationships* for both males and females. Why, then, would women use this style across relational types whereas men reserve this style for their wives?

One possible explanation comes from the theoretical work on male and female differences in concerns for relationships versus autonomy. Husbands and wives who reside in the same household have been described as living in "his and Her marriages" (Bernard, 1974), as speaking in different ethical voices (Gilligan, 1982), and as sending messages across cultures in different tongues (Tannen, 1990). Many current stereotypes about gender differences in marital communication support that notion that women are more interested than men in establishing and maintaining intimate relationships (e.g., Chodorow, 1989; Gilligan, 1982; Rubin, 1983). Compared to men, women are more likely to value connectedness, to devalue autonomy, and to adopt nurturant roles. In contrast, men emphasize the importance of preserving separateness as it defines and empowers the self.

Interestingly, the research on attachment styles does not necessarily support any particular pattern of gender differences (Fitzpatrick, Fey, Segrin, & Schiff, 1992). That is, men are as capable as women of achieving secure (or insecure) attachment relationships with loved ones. Although it appears that insecurely attached people avoid marital conflict, these people are no more nor less likely to be men (Kobak & Hazan, 1991). What accounts for these very different pictures of male and female relational connections?

Our data support the idea that women value connection in that they use the feminine gender preferential style with spouses and strangers. Males do appear to maintain a dynamic distance and autonomy from women who are strangers, yet not from their wives. In these martial conversations, husbands converge toward their wives' feminine preferential style, implying they are comfortable in the relationship. It is important to note, however, that these conversations were very low key and casual. There was no conflict among partners. Gender differences in marital communication are significantly more likely to appear during conflict (Baucom, Notarius, Burnett, & Haefner (1990). Scholars, popular writers, clinicians (e.g., Forgarty, 1976), and novelists (e.g., Stegner, 1987) tell us that when the emotional atmosphere heats up, men distance themselves from conflict as women pursue intimacy. Thus, husbands are capable of engaging in relational talk but are more likely to do so when the conversation is not emotionally conflictual or tense.

Do husbands always retreat during heated marital conflict? Our answer is an emphatic "No." In empirical research spanning 20 years, Fitzpatrick (1988) found that women who have a separate marital orientation are as likely as male separates to retreat from marital conflict. In addition, males with an independent orientation to marriage are significantly more likely to engage in open conflict, bargaining and negotiation with their wives. Burggraf and Sillars (1987) found that relational ideology and not the sex of the communicator was predictive of use of avoidance, cooperation, or competition in marital conflict. Thus, conflict avoidance is a personality disposition rather than a gender-defined characteristic.

Second, we cannot discuss conflict avoidance without considering "whose issue" is at stake. Thus, during conflicts about issues that are important to them, women may be more likely to bring up issues and to pursue their discussion even risking more conflict, rejection, or criticism from their husbands as they pursue their goal. Take a conflict between a husband and wife about the domestic division of labor. Sociologists tell us that married women who work outside the home also do the majority of the housework (Thompson & Walker, 1989). Consequently, the wife is likely to bring us this issue in order to renegotiate the domestic division of labor. For this issue, it is within the husband's best interest to limit the breadth and emotional intensity of the discussion of this issue, lest he end up doing more housework. Women may be more demanding in relationships because overall wives may have more problems in marriages than do husbands. Generally more satisfied with the marital situation, husbands have less to lose by withdrawing from marital conflict when the wives want to discuss their issues (Noller & Fitzpatrick, 1988).

Finally we are left with the issue of the relationship between avoidance, gender, and power in marital dialogue. We have no definitive answer to this question but two perspectives offer promise. An intriguing approach to conflict avoidance in personal relationships is presented by Roloff and Cloven (1990). These authors argue that retreating from conflict is related to power in relationships: The person with the least power in the relationship may be particularly unlikely to even bring up grievances or complaints. Their "chilling effect" specifies that the more dependent the person is on the relationship, the less likely that person is to even bring up problems. For these authors, the less powerful person is not always, nor exclusively, the wife. In contrast, Thorne (1982) argued that conflict avoidance in marital dialogues surrounding problems represents a masculine perspective, intended to preserve the established, male-dominated structure of most American marriages. To compare these two perspectives, we would like to consider husbands and wives interacting with one another over two separate issues: one issue of great salience to him and the other of great salience to her.

We began this chapter by proposing a more nuanced and subtle view of gender and communication. We think that to understand gender and communication, we need to be very aware of the context for that communication. The sex of the partner, the relationship between partners, and the topic under discussion are contextual factors that must be evaluated before we can make any statements about male and female communication.

ACKNOWLEDGMENT

This research was supported by NIH (Biomedical Research Division, University of Wisconsin 141207) to Mary Anne Fitzpatrick. The authors would like to thank Kathryn Dindia for her help on this manuscript.

REFERENCES

Andersen, P. A., & Andersen, J. F. (1984). The exchange of nonverbal intimacy: A critical review of dyadic models. *Journal of Nonverbal Behavior, 8*, 327–349.

Ashmore, R. D. (1981). Sex stereotypes and implicit personality theory. In D. L. Hamilton (Ed.), *Cognitive processes in stereotyping and intergroup behavior* (pp. 37–81). Hillsdale, NJ: Lawrence Erlbaum Associates.

Ashmore, R. D., & Del Boca, F. K. (1981). Conceptual approaches to stereotyping. In D. L. Hamilton (Ed.), *Cognitive processes in stereotyping and intergroup behavior* (pp. 1–35). Hillsdale, NJ: Lawrence Erlbaum Associates.

Balswick, J., & Avertt, C. P. (1977). Differences in expressiveness: Gender, interpersonal orientation, and perceived parental expressiveness as contributing factors. *Journal of Marriage and the Family, 39*, 121–127.

Baucom, D. H., Notarius, D. I., Burnett, C. K., & Haefner, P. (1990). Gender differences and sex-role identity in marriage. In F. D. Fincham & T. N. Bradbury, (Eds.), *The psychology of marriage: Basic issues and applications* (pp. 150–171). New York: Guilford.

Berger, C. R., & Roloff, M. E. (1982). Thinking about friends and lovers: Social cognition and relational trajectories. In M. E. Roloff, & C. R. Berger, (Eds.), *Social cognition and communication* (pp. 1–32). Beverly Hills, CA: Sage.

Bernard, J. (1974). *The future of marriage.* New York: World.

Burggraf, C. S., & Sillars, A. L. (1987). A critical examination of sex differences in marital communication. *Communication Monographs, 54*, 176–294.

Cappella, J. N. (1983). Conversational involvement: Approaching and avoiding others. In J. M. Wiemann & R. P. Harrison (Eds.), *Nonverbal interaction* (pp. 113–148). Beverly Hills, CA: Sage.

Cappella, J. N., & Greene, J. O. (1982). A discrepancy-arousal explanation of mutual influence in expressive behavioral for adult and infant–adult interaction. *Communication Monographs, 49*, 89–114.

Cappella, J. N., & Planalp, S. (1981). Talk and silence sequences in informal conversations: III. Interspeaker influence. *Human Communication Research, 7*, 117–132.

Chodorow, N. J. (1989). *Feminism and psychoanalytic theory.* New Haven. Yale University Press.

Crosby, F., & Nyquist, L. (1977). The female register: An empirical study of Lakoff's hypotheses. *Language in Society, 6*, 519–535.

Dubois, B. L., & Crouch, I. (1975). The question of the tag questions in women's speech: They don't really use more of them, do they? *Language in Society, 4*, 289–294.

Fishman, P. M. (1978). Interaction: The work women do. *Social Problems, 25*, 397–406.

Fitzpatrick, M. A. (1988). *Between husbands and wives: Communication in marriage.* Newbury Park, CA: Sage.

Fitzpatrick, M. A., Fey, J., Segrin, C., & Schiff, J. (1993). Attachment styles and internal working models of relationships. *Journal of Language and Social Psychology, 12*, 103–131.

Fitzpatrick, M. A., Mulac, A., & Dindia, K. (1995). Gender-preferential language use in spouse and stranger interaction. *Journal of Language and Social Psychology, 14*(1–2), 18–39.

Forgarty, T. F. (1976). Marital crisis. In P. Buerin (Ed.), *Family Therapy: Theory and Practice* (pp. 27–36). New York: Gardner Press.

Forgas, J. P. (1983). Language, goals and situations. *Journal of Language and Social Psychology, 2,* 267–293.

Frances, S. J. (1979). Sex differences in nonverbal behavior. *Sex Roles, 5,* 519–535.

Giles, H., Mulac, A., Bradac, J. J., & Johnson, P. (1987). Speech accommodation theory: The first decade and beyond. In M. L. McLaughlin (Ed.) *Communication yearbook 10* (pp. 13–48), Newbury Park, CA: Sage.

Giles, H., & Powesland, P. F. (1975). *Speech style and social evaluation.* London: Academic Press.

Giles, H., Scherer, K. R., & Taylor, D. M. (1979). Speech markers in social interaction. In K. R. Scherer & H. Giles (Eds.), *Social markers in speech* (pp. 343–381). Cambridge: Cambridge University Press.

Giles, H., & Smith, P. (1979). Accommodation theory: Optimal levels of convergence. In H. Giles & R. N. St. Clair (Eds.), *Language and social psychology* (pp. 45–65). Oxford: Blackwell.

Gilligan, C. (1982). *In a different voice: Psychological theory and women's development.* Cambridge, MA: Harvard University Press.

Gleser, G. C., Gottschalk, L. A., & John, W. (1959). The relationship of sex and intelligence to choice of words: A normative study of verbal behavior. *Journal of Clinical Psychology, 15,* 182–191.

Haas, A. (1979). The acquisition of genderlect. In J. Orsanu, M. K. Slater, & L. L. Adler (Eds.), *Language sex and gender* (pp. 101–113). New York: New York Academy of Sciences.

Hammen, C. L., & Peplau, L. A. (1978). Brief encounters: Impact of gender, sex–role attitudes, and partner's gender on interaction and cognition. *Sex Roles, 4,* 75–90.

Haslett, B. J. (1983). Children's strategies for maintaining cohesion in their written and oral stories. *Communication Education, 32,* 91–105.

Hartman, M. (1976). A descriptive study of the language of men and women born in Maine around 1900 as it reflects the Lakoff hypothesis in Language and Woman's Place. In B. L. Dubois & I. Crouch (Eds.), *The sociology of the languages of American women* (pp. 81–90). San Antonio, TX: Trinity University Press.

Hiatt, M. P. (1978). The deminise style: Theory and fact. *College Composition and Communication, 29,* 222–226.

Hirschman, L. (1973, December). *Female-male differences in conversational interaction.* Paper presented at the meeting of the Linguistic Society of America, San Diego, CA.

Hunt, K. W. (1965). *Grammatical structures written at three grade levels.* Champaign, IL: National Council of Teachers of English.

Kobak, R. R., & Hazan, C. (1991). Attachment in marriage: The effects of security and accuracy of working models. *Journal of Personality and Social Psychology, 60,* 861–869.

Koenigsknecht, R. A., & Friedman, P. (1976). Syntax development in boys and girls. *Child Development, 47,* 1109–1115.

Kramarae, C. (1981). *Woman and men speaking.* Rowley, MA: Newbury House.

Lakoff, R. (1975). *Language and women's place.* New York: Harper & Row.

Lapadat, J., & Seesahai, M. (1978). Male versus female codes in informal contexts. *Sociolinguistic Newsletter, 8,* 7–8.

Maltz, D. N., & Borker, R. A. (1982). A cultural approach to male-female miscommunication. In J. J. Gumperz (Ed.), *Language and social identity* (pp. 196–216). Cambridge: Cambridge University Press.

Martin, J. N., & Craig, R. T. (1983). Selected linguistic sex differences during initial social interactions of same-sex and mixed-sex student dyads. *Western Journal of Speech Communication, 47,* 16–28.

McLaughlin, M. L., Cody, M. J., Kane, M. L., & Robey, C. S. (1981). Sex differences in story receipt and story sequencing behaviors in dyadic conversation. *Human Communication Research, 7,* 99–116.

McMillan, J. R., Clifton, A. K., McGrath, D., & Gale, W. S. (1977). Women's language: Uncertainty or interpersonal sensitivity and emotionality? *Sex Roles, 3,* 545–559.

Mulac, A., Incontro, C. R., & James, M. R. (1985). Comparison of the gender-linked language effect and sex-role stereotypes. *Journal of Personality and Social Psychology, 49,* 1098–1109.

Mulac, A., & Lundell, T. L. (1980). Differences in perceptions created by syntactic-semantic productions of male and female speakers. *Communication Monographs, 47,* 111–118.

Mulac, A., & Lundell, T. L. (1982). An empirical test of the gender-lined language effect in a public speaking setting. *Language and Speech, 25,* 243–256.

Mulac, A., & Lundell, T. L. (1986). Linguistic contributors to the gender-linked language effect. *Journal of Language and Social Psychology, 5,* 81–101.

Mulac, A., & Lundell, T. L. (1990, June). *Male/female language differences and their attributional consequences in university student impromptu essays: The gender-linked language effect.* Paper presented at the annual meeting of the International Communication Association, Dublin, Ireland.

Mulac, A., & Lundell, T. L. (In Press). Effects of gender-linked language differences in adults' written discourse: Multivariate tests of language effects. *Language and Communication.*

Mulac, A., Lundell, T. L., & Bradac, J. J. (1986). Male/female language differences and attributional consequences in a public speaking situation: Toward an explanation of the gender–linked language effect. *Communication Monographs, 53,* 115–129.

Mulac, A., & Rudd, M. J. (1977). Effects of selected American regional dialects upon regional audience members. *Communication Monographs, 44,* 185–195.

Mulac, A., Studley, L. B., & Blau, S. (1990). The gender-linked language effect in primary and secondary students' impromptu essays. *Sex Roles, 23,* 439–469.

Mulac, A., Studley, L. B., Wiemann, J. M., & Bradac, J. J. (1987). Male/female gaze in same-sex and mixed-sex dyads: A test of gender-linked differences and mutual influence. *Human Communication Research, 13,* 323–343.

Mulac, A., Wiemann, J. M., Widenmann, S. W., & Gibson, T. W. (1988). Male/female language differences and effects in same-sex and mixed-sex dyads: The gender-linked language effect. *Communication Monographs, 55,* 315–335.

Noller, P., & Fitzpatrick, M. A. (Eds.), (1988). *Perspectives on marital interaction* (Vol. 1 in Monographs in the Social Psychology of Language). Clevedon, England: Multilingual Matters.

Patterson, M.L. (1984). Nonverbal exchange: Past, present and future. *Journal of Nonverbal Behavior, 8,* 35–39.

Piliavin, J. A., & Martin, R. R. (1978). The effects of the sex composition of groups on style of social interaction. *Sex Roles, 4,* 281–296.

Poole, M. E. (1979). Social class, sex, and linguistic coding. *Language and Speech, 22,* 49–67.

Price, B. G., & Graves, R. L. (1980). Sex differences in syntax and usage in oral and written language. *Research in the Teaching of English, 14,* 147–153.

Roloff, M., & Cloven D. (1990). The chilling effect in interpersonal relationships. In D. Cahn (Ed.), *Intimates in Conflict* (pp. 49–76). Hillsdale, NJ: Lawrence Erlbaum Associates.

Rubin, L. B. (1983). *Intimate strangers.* New York: Harper and Row.

Sause, E. F. (1976). Computer content analysis of sex differences in the language of children. *Journal of Psycholinguistic Research, 5,* 311–324.

Smith, P. M. (1985). *Language, the sexes and society.* Oxford: Basil Blackwell.

Spanier, G. B. (1976). Measuring dyadic adjustment: New scales for assessing the quality of marriage and similar dyads. *Journal of Marriage and the Family, 38,* 15–28.

Staley, C. M. (1982). Sex-related differences in the style of children's language. *Journal of Psycholinguistic Research, 11,* 141–158.

Stegner, W. (1987). *Crossing to safety.* New York: Penguin.

Street, R. L., Jr., & Giles, H. (1982). Speech accommodation theory: A social cognitive approach to language and speech behavior. In M. E. Roloff & C. R. Berger (Eds.), *Social cognition and communication* (pp. 193–226). Beverly Hills, CA: Sage.

Strodtbeck, F. L., & Mann, R. D. (1956). Sex role differentiation in jury deliberation. *Sociometry, 19,* 3–11.

Tannen, D. (1990). *You just don't understand: Women and men in conversation.* New York: William Morrow & Co.

Thakerar, J. N., Giles, H., & Cheshire, J. (1982). Psychological and linguistic parameters of speech accommodation theory. In C. Fraser & K. R. Sherer (Eds.)., *Advances in the social psychology of language* (pp. 205–255). Cambridge: Cambridge University Press.

Thompson, L., & Walker, A. J. (1989). Women and men in marriage, work, parenthood. *Journal of Marriage and the Family, 51*, 845–872.

Thorne, B. (1982). Feminist rethinking of the family: An overview. In B. Thorne with M. Yalom (Eds.), *Rethinking the family: Some feminist questions* (pp. 1–24). New York: Longman.

Thorne, B., Kramarae, C., & Henley, N. (1983). Language, gender and society: Opening a second decade of research. In B. Thorne, C. Kramarae, & N. Henley (Eds.), *Language, gender and society* (pp. 7–24). Rowley, MA: Newbury House.

West, C., & Zimmerman, D. H. (1983). Small insults: A study of interruptions in cross-sex conversations between unacquainted persons. In B. Thorne, C. Kramarae, & N. Henley (Eds.), *Language, gender and society* (pp. 102–117). Rowley, MA: Newbury House.

Westmoreland, R., Starr, D. P., Shelton, K., & Pasadeos, Y. (1977). New writing styles of male and female students. *Journalism Quarterly, 54*, 599–601.

Winer, B. J. (1971). *Statistical principles in experimental design* (2nd ed.). New York: McGraw Hill.

Wood, M. M. (1966). The influence of sex and knowledge of communication effectiveness on spontaneous speech. *Word, 22*, 112–137.

Zimmerman, D. H., & West, C. (1975). Sex roles, interruptions, and silences in conversations. In B. Thorne, & N. Henley (Eds.), *Language and sex: Difference and dominance* (pp. 105–129). Rowley, MA: Newbury House.

Chapter 10

Managing Conflict and Anger: Investigating the Sex Stereotype Hypothesis

William R. Cupach
Illinois State University

Daniel J. Canary
Pennsylvania State University

Researchers often assume that sex differences provide information about the way people behave (Deaux & Major, 1990). Presumed sex differences are often accompanied by a second belief, that is that people's sex differences reflect traditional, conventional stereotypic portraits of men and women. The stereotypic woman is kind, nurturing, relationally sensitive, warm, and expressive; the stereotypic man is dynamic, assertive, competitive, task-oriented (or agenic), and competent (Deaux & Lewis, 1984).

It is also commonly believed that men and women exhibit significantly different behaviors that reflect these stereotypes when managing interpersonal conflict. That is, because men are more competitive and less relationally sensitive than women, men more likely engage in competitive or avoidant conflict management behaviors, whereas women more often rely on cooperative and engaging conflict management behaviors. In this chapter, we combine such views on men and women and label them the *sex stereotype hypothesis*. If this hypothesis is true, it presents important implications for the ways in which heterosexual couples (romantically or otherwise involved) negotiate their differences, and how they ultimately manage their relationships.

Although researchers often assume there are sex differences that affect social interaction, recent reviews and meta-analyses on interaction behavior in various contexts cast doubt on the generalizability and strength of sex differences. For example, in a review of 15 meta-analyses on sex differences relevant to social interaction, Canary and Hause (1993) found that only approximately 1% of the variance was explained by sex differences, and all studies reported factors that significantly moderated each reported sex difference. Given that men and women act similarly about 99% of the time, the presumption that sex differences affect most social behavior is clearly unfounded. However, given the conceptual correspondence between sex stereotypes and generic approaches to managing conflict, it is possible that conflict is one domain of behavior wherein sex differences remain robust.

The purpose of this chapter is to assess the validity of the sex stereotype hypothesis in the context of interpersonal conflict between men and women. We begin by selectively reviewing self-report and observational research regarding sex differences in conflict management. Then we summarize the literature on sex differences in anger and its behavioral correlate, aggression. Next we present some original data regarding sex differences from our research on conflict communication among married couples. In the final section, we assess the status of the sex stereotype hypothesis, taking into account the existing literature as well as our own data.

Our interests here are circumscribed to ordinary everyday disputes that inevitably arise from incompatibilities and misunderstandings in personal relationships. We are not concerned in this chapter with phenomena such as acquaintance or date rape (e.g., Parrot & Bechhofer, 1991), sexual harassment (e.g., Junger, 1987; Pryor, 1987), physical abuse or violence (e.g., Levy, 1991; Marshall, 1994; Scheff & Retzinger, 1991), the influence of media on aggressive behavior (e.g., Roloff & Greenberg, 1979), or criminal behavior in general. These extreme forms of behavior are each worthy of careful consideration, and understanding of them cannot be generalized from ordinary conflict behavior.

SEX DIFFERENCES I: MANAGING INTER-PERSONAL CONFLICT

Reported Sex Differences in Conflict Management

Research under the rubrics of conflict strategies, tactics, or styles bears on the issue of behavioral differences between the sexes. This section summarizes survey research on reported sex differences in conflict behaviors. Kelley and colleagues (1978) investigated the *stereotypes* regarding what men and women do and say in their interpersonal conflicts, and they examined sex differences in *behaviors* reported by members of close heterosexual couples. The consistent sex differences were summarized as follows: "The female member is expected and reported to cry and sulk and to criticize the male for lack of consideration of her feelings and insensitivity to his effect on her. The male shows anger, rejects the female's tears, calls for a logical and less emotional approach to the problem, and gives reasons for delaying the discussion" (Kelley et al., 1978, p. 487). The authors interpret these findings as reflecting an interaction pattern whereby males find emotional display to be uncomfortable or upsetting, and are therefore conflict avoidant; whereas females, who find such avoidance to be frustrating and want feelings to be considered, are confrontational. This pattern is apparently consistent with the sex stereotype hypothesis. However, some additional findings attenuate the significance of these sex differences. First, only about half of the behaviors included in this study were expected more often by one sex or the other. Just as many behaviors characterize similarity between men and women as characterize differences. Second, the behaviors that did *not* differentiate men and women exhibited higher ratings of likelihood than those that did differentiate. As Kelley et al. pointed out, "the larger portion of the conflict interaction is carried (or is thought by our subjects to be carried) by actions *common* to the two sexes rather than by ones that the sexes tend to use differentially" (p. 488).

Fitzpatrick and Winke (1979) explored sex differences in conflict between same and opposite sex partners. Respondents rated how often they used each of 44 influence tactics in the past few months with their closest friend of the opposite sex, and their closest friend of the same sex. Although males and females exhibited differences in their same-sex friendships, no differences were found in the conflict behaviors reported by men and women in their opposite-sex relationships.

Other research seems to support the sex stereotype hypothesis. Berryman-Fink and Brunner (1987), for instance, discovered male students were more likely than female students to report that they compete in conflict, and female students were more likely than male students to report that they compromise. Other studies, however, run contrary to the belief that men are more competitive or antisocial compared to women in conflict episodes (e.g., Canary, Cunningham & Cody, 1988). Several investigations have found men and women to be largely similar in their conflict management tactics (e.g., Bell, Chafetz, & Horn, 1982; Renwick, 1977; Sternberg & Soriano, 1984; Zammutto, London, & Rowland, 1979). Although these findings come primarily from survey data, it is noteworthy that the experimental (games) literature also is equivocal with respect to whether women are more or less cooperative than men (Terhune, 1970).

Gayle-Hackett (1986) performed a meta-analysis of 13 studies that specifically examined sex differences in conflict management practices. She concluded that the average effect size for sex differences across all the studies was very small. Further, the sex effect diminished with increasing age. Whereas studies using high school students showed a moderate effect, studies using college students exhibited only. a small sex effect, and studies using managers, workers, and married couples demonstrated no sex effect.

Observational Analyses of Sex Differences in Conflict Management

Perceived stereotypical differences between men and women (such as those found by Kelley et al., 1978), probably outweigh any actual behavioral differences (Fisher, 1983). One's recall of conflict behavior in self-reports is probably biased by one's expectations for men and women, which may include stereotypic beliefs.

Observational studies are not as easily affected by such biases. Unfortunately, the conflict literature contains relatively few observational analyses. Nevertheless, the small number of studies indicate that there are few sex differences, and they often do not conform to the stereotype of men and women (e.g., Burggraf & Sillars, 1987). Moreover, situational considerations often obliterate "real" sex differences. Three studies illustrate these conclusions.

Margolin and Wampold (1981) observed married couples, relying on the Marital Interaction Coding Scheme (MICS). These authors found that wives are more likely to smile/laugh, complain, and criticize the partner, whereas husbands offer more excuses. Also, distressed husbands showed less "tracking" (i.e., more withdrawing from the conversation). Margolin and Wampold also found that a couple's satisfaction affects conflict sequences; specifically, dissatisfied couples reciprocated negative affect whereas satisfied couples did not reciprocate negative affect (see also Gottman, 1979; Ting-Toomey, 1983). However, it should be noted that husbands and wives did *not* differ on 75% of the codes, including the major categories of problem-solving, positive verbal comments, negative verbal comments, and negative nonverbal behaviors. Nonetheless, the study suggests a "demand/withdrawal" pattern, where the wife seeks to engage the partner in conflict and the husband withdraws.

Christensen and Heavey (1990) sought to test two alternative explanations for the demand/withdrawal pattern. The first explanation is that, based on socialization processes, men are more independent than women and women seek more intimacy than men. This explanation reflects the conventional stereotypes of men and women. Gottman and colleagues (e.g., Gottman, 1990; Gottman & Carrere, 1994), however, have reported that men withdraw because of their relatively higher and sustained negative arousal to conflict. The second explanation is that women are underbenefited in most marriages, hence they are more likely to seek to improve their condition by approaching their husbands on problematic issues. Because husbands are said to gain more rewards than wives in most marriages, husbands do not want to change the status quo, and hence they withdraw from discussion of the problematic issues. The latter explanation is situational, insofar as whoever is less benefited would likely be the one to make demands from the partner. Christensen and Heavey rated the interactions of men and women on topics where one partner wanted to change the other. They found a crossed interaction effect, where wife demand/husband withdrawal occurred most often when the wife wanted to change the husband. However, husband demand/wife withdrawal occurred more often than wife demand/husband withdrawal in conversations where the husband wanted to change the wife. Christensen and Heavey interpreted these findings as evidence for the situational explanation, which could not be explained by stereotypic behaviors or observers' expectations based on stereotypes.

Finally, Burggraf and Sillars (1987) examined the effects of sex on marital conflict behavior in addition to the effects due to couple type (cf. Fitzpatrick, 1988) and partner's communication. They found that the partner's antecedent conflict behavior and couple type were stronger predictors of the communicator's conflict behavior than was the communicator's sex. Specifically, conflict behaviors were often reciprocated by both spouses, overriding the effects due to sex.

Sex Differences in Responses to Relational Dissatisfaction

The studies reviewed thus far have examined conflict management at the episodic level; that is, conflict behaviors are studied within the confines of a situation presumably identifiable as a conflict. However, relational problems and dissatisfaction are not always overtly manifested in discrete episodes of conflict interaction. Responses to relational dissatisfaction may be passive or indirect and may emerge over a considerable period of time. Thus, Rusbult and colleagues (Rusbult, 1987; Rusbult & Zembrodt, 1983; Rusbult, Zembrodt, & Gunn, 1982) have developed a more global typology of responses to dissatisfaction in close relationships. The four general responses are: (1) *exit*—actively destroying the relationship; (2) *voice*—actively repairing the relationship; (3) *loyalty*—passive waiting for the relationship to improve; and (4) *neglect*—passively allowing the relationship to deteriorate. Consistent with the sex stereotype hypothesis, Rusbult et al. predicted that men would exhibit greater exit and neglect compared to women, and that women would show greater voice and loyalty compared to men. The only consistent finding across studies has been that men tend to be more neglectful than women, though there is also some indication that women may engage in more voice than men. However, summarizing their program of research, Rusbult (1993) conceded that "these results tend to be rather weak and inconsistently observed" (p. 43).

Healey and Bell (1990) adapted the items developed by Rusbult and colleagues and applied the Exit–Voice–Loyalty–Neglect model to dissatisfaction in friendship relationships. In examining the preferred responses of men and women, Healey and Bell uncovered only one sex difference: Men were slightly more likely than women to report using loyalty. This pattern is opposite of that reported by Rusbult et al. (1986) for heterosexual romantic relationships. Healey and Bell (1990) conclude that "there is little evidence that friends' responses to dissatisfaction are shaped in any significant way by their gender" (p. 42).

Summary

Although men and women may exhibit *some* differences in conflict management behavior, these differences are found inconsistently. Both reported and observed studies on conflict fail to support the sex stereotype hypothesis. Sex differences are exaggerated and do not conform to patterns implied by conventional stereotypes. Moreover, other qualifications of the research findings are noteworthy. Sex differences in conflict tend to be small in magnitude and are often greatly overshadowed by other contextual, personal, and relational factors. Most notably, Christensen and Heavey (1990) found that whomever was the target of proposed change in a conflict episode, whether male or female, engaged in withdrawal behavior. Second, the Burggraf and Sillars (1987) study demonstrates the powerful effects of interaction patterns, suggesting that people's behaviors are more influenced by the partner's preceding behavior than by their own sex during interaction. Finally, the meta-analysis reported by Gayle-Hackett (1986) is significant because it suggests that the sex stereotype effect attenuates with age. As with other behaviors, sex differences in conflict management may be most apparent among children. Such differences seem to greatly diminish with emotional and physical development. Research using aging cohorts would shed more definitive light on this issue.

SEX DIFFERENCES II: COPING WITH ANGER

Given the centrality of affect in the experience and expression of conflict, researchers are increasingly paying attention to the role of emotions in conflict episodes (e.g., Gottman, 1990; Zillmann, 1990), especially the emotion of anger. Being provoked to anger is likely to initiate an episode of conflict, and one's use of particular conflict behaviors may in turn trigger anger in the partner. Zillmann (1990) described how a conflict episode can involve a cascade effect of emotional escalation, where parties experience more and more anger toward their partner. Betancourt and Blair (1992) similarly illustrated that the experience of anger during conflict likely mediates one's reactions to an instigation such that increasing anger disposes one to exhibit aggressive behavior.

It is commonly assumed that men and women differ significantly in the experience and expression of anger in ways consistent with sex stereotypes. For example, women are expected to control the experience and display of anger more than men (e.g., Smith, Ulch, Cameron, & Cumberland, 1989) and are presumed to anticipate condemnation when they fail to do so (Campbell & Muncer, 1987). It is also argued on biological grounds that males are more prone to angry aggression than females (see Averill, 1982). If significant sex differences exist in interpersonal conflict, they ought to be most apparent and robust in conflict situations involving anger. We concede that the literature on aggression is copious and has been reviewed extensively elsewhere (e.g., Averill, 1982; Baron, 1977; Felson & Tedeschi, 1993); we focus our attention solely on the issue of sex differences in anger and aggression.

Sex Differences in Aggression

Rohner (1976) examined ethnographic records from numerous societies in order to discern the cross-cultural generality of sex differences in aggressive behavior. Based on the 31 societies for which separate ratings of aggression were available for men and women, Rohner determined that men and women were equally aggressive in 20 societies, men were more aggressive in six, and women were more aggressive in five. Moreover, the differences in aggression between cultures were substantially greater than sex differences within cultures.

Examining several dozen studies in social psychology, Eagly and Steffen (1986) performed a meta-analysis and concluded that men both exhibited and received aggressive behavior more than women. It is noteworthy, however, that the effect sizes were small to modest, and that a host of contextual factors moderated such sex differences (e.g., setting, type of aggression, etc.). Similarly, Frodi, Macaulay, and Thome (1977) thoroughly reviewed the experimental literature on aggressiveness and found that men are not consistently more aggressive than women. Indeed, "of 72 studies that involved a measure of some form of aggressive behavior (excluding studies of general hostility), 61% did not show the expected higher male than female aggressiveness across all conditions" (Frodi et al., 1977, p. 634). Nor was support indicated for the conclusion that women display indirect or displaced aggression. The authors demonstrate that observed sex differences in aggression are moderated by such factors as nature of the provocation, sex of the instigator, sex of the victim, empathy with the victim, and aggression anxiety.

We should emphasize that virtually none of the experimental research on aggression is in the context of close interpersonal relationships. Thus, survey research on aggression in dating and marital relationships is important to consider. Stets and Henderson (1991) surveyed a nationally representative sample of persons who date and found that women were more likely than men to report using physical aggression in their relationships, and men were more likely than women to report receiving severe aggression. Similarly, in a nationally representative sample of over 5,000 married couples, it was found that men and women engage in approximately equal amounts of verbal/symbolic aggression against their partners (Straus & Sweet, 1992).

Because the sex stereotype hypothesis is widely believed, and because males tend to be physically bigger and stronger than their female partners, the mere threat of male aggression may be sufficient in many cases to obviate the need for men to display aggressive behavior. Individuals endowed with power often do not have to resort to power tactics. Men, therefore, may be less aggressive in their actual relational behavior than is generally expected. Similarly, women may engage in aggressive, distributive behaviors to a greater extent than generally is expected, in an effort to exert power. Women may feel justified in behaving aggressively to the extent such behavior is less likely to inflict serious harm compared to male aggression.

It is important to realize that anger is not tantamount to aggression. The experience of anger may or may not be manifested in aggressive behavior, and aggression is often exhibited in the absence of anger. Therefore, inferences about anger made from the general literature on aggressive behavior must be made with caution. We now summarize literature that deals specifically with situations involving anger.

Sex Differences in the Everyday Experience of Anger

Despite the popularity of the sex stereotype hypothesis, numerous studies have failed to find significant sex differences in the likelihood of experiencing, expressing, or suppressing anger (Averill, 1982; Burrowes & Halberstadt, 1987; Kopper & Epperson, 1991; Spielberger, Jacobs, Russell, & Crane, 1983; Stoner & Spencer, 1987; Tavris, 1984; Thomas, 1989). In summarizing their extensive research, Frost and Averill (1982) concluded that "when all the data are considered, it is remarkable that the observed sex differences were so few in number and (with the exception of crying) small in magnitude. As far as the everyday experience of anger is concerned, men and women are far more similar than dissimilar" (p. 297).

Ironically, observed sex differences in aggressive behavior are partially attributable to sex differences in what provokes anger. When studying aggression, experimenters typically present men and women with the same provocation stimulus. To the extent men and women differ in how angered they are in response to a particular stimulus, sex differences in aggression will appear. Frodi (1978) conducted a study in which she provoked male and female subjects in a sex-appropriate way; that is, with a provocation that was shown in prior research to be effective for each sex. Under these conditions, men and women became equally angry, exhibited parallel elevations in physiological arousal, and showed equal amounts of aggressive behavior.

Sex Differences in What Provokes Anger

One source of sex differences in episodes involving anger may inhere in the antecedent conditions that provoke anger. Campbell and Muncer (1987) studied accounts of anger episodes and identified the following reasons for anger:

1. Integrity threat. Attack on competence in role or status as a spouse, lover, professional, parent or friend.
2. Jealousy.
3. Threat of or actual physical harm or violation of personal space.
4. Loyalty. Fighting to protect the integrity or safety of another person.
5. Incompetence of another person.
6. Impotence. Inability to gain the compliance of another person. (Campbell & Muncer, 1987, pp. 493–494).

For both men and women, the majority of anger episodes concerned the issue of personal integrity. Among women, the second most common reason for anger was jealousy, whereas men were split between physical harm and others' incompetence (Campbell & Muncer, 1987, p. 495). Campbell and Muncer suggested that the distinction between a minor annoyance and outright anger may depend on whether or not an incident is perceived to contain an integrity threat. They indicated that "post-conflict rumination leading to increased anger often seems to involve the addition of just this component to the initial source of annoyance" (p. 506). Thus, the annoying behavior of another would seem to become offensive and anger-provoking when it is seen as particularly face threatening. Men and women may have different thresholds for perceiving face threat and/or may differ in what they find face threatening.

Both condescension and aggression are likely to arouse anger in men and women alike, though women appear to be especially angered by condescension. In a survey conducted by Frodi (1977), women were most provoked by condescending treatment from men or women. Men were most often provoked by condescending treatment from a women, or physical or verbal aggression from a man. Buss (1989) discovered that men were more upset by women being moody, physically self-absorbed, and sexually withholding, whereas women were more upset by treatment that was condescending, inconsiderate, neglecting or rejecting, and emotionally constricted. Harris (1993) found that males were more angered than females by a female displaying physical aggression or a male hurting another person. Females, on the other hand, were more angered than males by condescending or insensitive treatment from either sex, verbal aggression from a female, and physical aggression from a male. Harris also found differences in anger due to the sex of the instigator. Physical aggression and hurting another were more anger producing when instigated by a male rather than a female; dishonesty by a female was more anger provoking than dishonesty by a male. Additionally, females perceived condescending or insensitive behavior to be worse when coming from a male than from a female (cf. Frodi, 1977).

Sex Differences in Liability for Being the Target of Anger

In an episode containing anger, the roles of expressing anger and being subjected to it associate with different subjective perceptions that likely influence behavior. Baumeister, Stillwell, and Wotman (1990), for example, studied and compared autobiographical accounts of being angered and of angering another. They discovered that perpetrator accounts tended to portray provoking behavior as meaningful, comprehensible, isolated, and without long-term implications. On the other hand, victim accounts portrayed the event as arbitrary, gratuitous, incomprehensible, and carrying lasting implications of harm, loss, and grievance.

In general, men are more often the target of anger and/or aggression than are women (Eagly & Steffen, 1984). This finding is moderated, however, by the relationship between the angry person and the target. Averill (1982) found that men are more often the target of anger when they are not well known (i.e., stranger or acquaintance). When the target is a loved one, men tend to get angry at women and women tend to get angry at men.

Sex Differences in Manifestations of Anger

One clear behavioral difference in the manifestation of anger is found in the reports of men and women: women's anger is much more likely than men's to be accompanied by tears (Crawford, Kippax, Onyx, Gault, & Benton, 1992; Frost & Averill, 1982; supported also in the conflict literature, e.g., Kelley et al., 1978). Crying is not considered by women to be an alternative to anger, nor is it a consequence of misplaced or suppressed feelings of anger. Crawford et al. (1992) explained that crying in this case "is a message used to communicate to others the strength and seriousness of the anger; it contains a strong element of the feeling of being a victim, and in particular is interpreted by the actor as a plea for understanding in the face of being disbelieved or misunderstood" (p. 173). Thus, for women, crying does not replace anger; rather, it can be a behavioral manifestation of anger.

Because of the belief that anger is associated with aggressive behavior, a woman's anger may be easily misconstrued when it includes crying (Campbell & Muncer, 1987; Crawford et al., 1992). Focussing on the tears, men may misinterpret the woman's anger as hurt, depression, helplessness, or incapacity. If a woman expresses anger through tears, the male partner may fail to recognize the anger and respond accordingly. The woman may then interpret the man's response as condescension and become even more angry (perhaps crying even more as a consequence). Moreover, if the woman's tearful anger is in response to the man's anger, then he may interpret the tears in a fashion opposite of what was intended; he may construe the crying as remorse or capitulation, which validates his sense of justice for being angry in the first place. Obviously, such a sequence results in miscoordination, misunderstanding, and escalation or repression of conflict.

Summary

The literature suggests that women and men become angry for various issues, and they share some of these reasons, although women consistently find condescending treatment especially nettlesome. There is little difference, however, when considering how experiences of anger translate into interaction behaviors. Both sexes appear to be capable of aggression during interpersonal conflict. Of the many interaction behaviors, crying is the only one that clearly varies according to sex.

In the next section we briefly overview our own program of research on communication in interpersonal conflict. Employing a competence model of conflict communication, we present empirical evidence pertinent to the sex stereotype hypothesis.

CONFLICT COMMUNICATION AND COMPETENCE EVALUATIONS

The Competence Model as a Frame for Understanding Sex Differences in Conflict

Our own research, which has primarily concerned how people evaluate conflict tactics and strategies in terms of communication competence (Canary & Cupach, 1988; Canary & Spitzberg, 1989, 1990), has also examined the issue of sex differences. More precisely, Canary and Spitzberg (1987) proposed that women and men differ in the way conflict strategies are judged according to appropriateness and effectiveness perceptions. Using an experimental design, these authors failed to find significant sex differences. In a similar manner, Canary, Cunningham, and Cody (1988) hypothesized that the sexes differ in their conflict strategy use and that women would be more likely to use cooperative tactics in conflict goals concerning relational development. But women and men did not differ on most conflict strategies examined, and contrary to expectations, women reported using more competitive conflict behaviors whereas men reported a greater use of denial tactics. Thus, we have found that competence evaluations of conflict strategies and tactics are rather uniform between the sexes (Canary & Spitzberg, 1987; also see study that follows).

Judgments of appropriateness and effectiveness constitute two criteria of competence relevant to most communication contexts and applicable to conflict episodes specifically (Canary & Spitzberg, 1987, 1990; Spitzberg & Cupach, 1984, 1989). Appropriateness concerns maintaining the expectations of the partner, and effectiveness refers to achieving one's goal in the conflict. However, the context of conflict also appears to pit the criteria of appropriateness and effectiveness against each other. Because interpersonal conflict occurs when people communicate about their perceived incompatible goals, it can be quite difficult to satisfy the partner's expectations while achieving one's personal goal that conflicts with the partner's.

Spitzberg, Canary, and Cupach (1994) indicated how a person could be appropriate or effective, or both, in the management of interpersonal conflict. A person who is inappropriate and ineffective both fails to uphold expectations and to obtain valued goals. Such conflict behaviors are *minimizing* in orientation (e.g., to block out your partner's loud tv, you turn up your own stereo). A person who is appropriate but not effective may meet the partner's expectations but also doesn't obtain his or her own goals through interaction. This person is merely *sufficing* (e.g., you simply ignore your partner's loud tv and hope it will soon cease). A person who *maximizes* may achieve desired goals at the expense of the partner's expectations (e.g., you intimidate your partner with a threat so that she turns down the tv). The person who is both appropriate and effective is *optimal* in achieving valued ends and upholding the integrity of the relational rule system (e.g., you explain that the loud tv prevents you from working, and you ask that it be turned down). The perception that conflict meets competence criteria is very important for relational outcomes, as causal process studies have found that competence perceptions filter the effects of conflict behavior on relational properties, such as trust and satisfaction (e.g. Canary & Cupach, 1988; Canary & Spitzberg, 1989).

In terms of using competence as a conceptual frame of reference for the sex stereotype hypothesis, women would be seen as more competent if they enacted tactics consistent with the sex stereotype of women as nurturing, kind, and supportive, such as calmly discussing the issue, offering disclosure, and seeking areas of agreement. Men, according to the sex stereotype, would be seen as more competent to enact strategies that represent a competitive or an avoidant orientation.

Method

Participants were 132 married couples who were recruited in the following manner. Students at California State University, Fullerton and Illinois State University were offered extra credit if they could obtain the consent of a married couple (either relative or friend) to participate in a longitudinal study on interpersonal conflict. The study entailed having each couple complete, independently of the partner,

TABLE 10.1

Means, Standard Deviations, and Alphas for Husbands' and Wives' Conflict Strategies at Time 1 and Time 2

Strategy	Husbands			Wives			t	r
	mean	(SD)	alpha	mean	(SD)	alpha		
Time 1								
Integrative	2.94	(1.17)	.84	3.12	(1.12)	.77	1.37	.19*
Distributive	5.00	(1.33)	.89	4.74	(1.33)	.88	2.03*	.40***
Avoidance	5.45	(1.29)	.89	5.55	(0.72)	.81	0.72	.23**
Time 2								
Integrative	2.87	(1.25)	.87	3.02	(1.23)	.85	2.07	.34***
Distributive	5.22	(1.29)	.90	4.93	(1.44)	.91	2.17*	.40***
Avoidance	5.54	(1.36)	.87	5.66	(1.22)	.87	1.07	.46***

Note. The lower the number, the higher the reported use of conflict strategy.
$*p < .05. **p < .01. ***p < .001.$

measures of conflict and competence described later at three separate points in time over a 10 week period.[1] Over 200 couples began the project. However, due to either attrition or missing data, only 132 couples' reports for Time 1 (T1) and Time 2 (T2) were usable, with fewer than 100 couples completing all three data collections. Because we opted for a powerful test of the hypotheses, we decided to use the T1 and T2 data only.

Three scales were constructed based on previous items designed to measure *integrative*, *distributive*, and *avoidant* conflict strategies (Canary & Spitzberg, 1989, 1990; Canary et al., 1988; Cupach, 1982; Sillars, Coletti, Parry, & Rogers, 1982). An integrative strategy is marked by a cooperative attitude and was operationalized in such tactics as, "I showed concern about his/her feelings and thoughts," "I reasoned with him/her in a give-and-take manner," and "I expressed my trust in him/her." A distributive strategy is competitive in orientation and was reflected in the following example items: "I used threats," "I criticized an aspect of his/her personality," and "I shouted at him/her." Avoidant tactics seek to distract attention from the conflict issue and were measured by such items as, "I avoided him/her," "I tried to postpone the issue as long as possible," and "I changed the topic of conversation."

In all three data collections, the married couples were first asked to agree on a particular conflict episode that had taken place within the previous 2 weeks and to describe the conflict on the questionnaire. They then completed the integrative (9 items), distributive (15 items), and avoidant (11 items) strategy measures. (The response range for all items was 1 = strongly agree to 7 = strongly disagree.) The means and reliability coefficients of the husband and wife conflict measures are reported in Table 10.1.

In addition, measures of competence and communication satisfaction were completed. The conflict strategy items were counterbalanced with the competence

---

[1] Work in progress by Cupach, Canary, and Serpe (1994) features a detailed report of these measures.

and communication satisfaction items to prevent against any order effects. The 11 item competence measure included such statements as "S/he was effective in achieving what s/he wanted," and "His/her communication was appropriate to the situation." The descriptive statistics for the competence measures were as follows: Husbands at T1 $M = 3.18$ ($SD = 1.20$; alpha = .86); Wives at T1 $M = 3.37$ ($SD = 1.29$; alpha = .86); Husbands at T2 $M = 3.01$ ($SD = 1.15$; alpha = .87); and Wives at T2 $M = 3.18$ ($SD = 1.28$; alpha = .88). Communication satisfaction was measured using Hecht's (1978) scale. The descriptive statistics for the communication satisfaction measure were as follows: Husbands at T1 $M = 3.57$ ($SD = 1.22$; alpha = .91); Wives at T1 $M = 3.64$ ($SD = 1.19$; alpha = .89); Husbands at T2 $M = 3.33$ ($SD = 1.18$; alpha = .91); and Wives at T2 $M = 3.41$ ($SD = 1.30$; alpha = .92).

Results

Based on the sex stereotype hypothesis, we would expect women to enact more integrative conflict strategies and men to enact more distributive and avoidant conflict strategies, relative to their spouses. Table 10.1 reports the paired t-tests between spouses for each of the conflict strategies at T1 and T2. As Table 10.1 reveals, women self-reported that they engaged in distributive actions significantly more than their husbands at both T1 and T2, contrary to the sex stereotype hypothesis. In addition, men self-reported they enacted slightly more integrative and avoidant strategies, although none of the mean differences are significant. These findings also run contrary to the sex stereotype hypothesis.

It is possible that husbands and wives differ in terms of their competence and communication satisfaction perceptions, indicating that either men or women are judged more or less favorably as a group. To examine this possibility, paired t-tests were again computed. None of the t-tests were significant at the .05 level. Accordingly, husbands and wives had equivalent perceptions of their spouses' conflict behaviors.

Based on the sex stereotype hypothesis, we would expect that men would perceive their spouses less competent and they would report less communication satisfaction to the extent their spouses used distributive tactics. That is, given that men are expected to be more competitive, and women are not, men's competence and satisfaction ratings should be more dramatically affected by their spouses' distributive actions, reflecting a "contrast effect" (Eagly & Steffen, 1984). On the other hand, women's competence and communication satisfaction scores should be more powerfully tied to the husband's use of integrative tactics, than vice versa. In order to test these possibilities, z-tests were computed. However, due to the substantial interdependence between husbands and wives on the conflict, competence, and communication satisfaction measures, the z-tests were computed using partial correlations, controlling for the influence of the partner's parallel measures. For example, the partial correlation between husbands' integrative tactics and wives' competence perceptions at T1 are computed, controlling for the wives' use of integrative tactics and the husbands' competence perceptions at T1. Table 10.2

TABLE 10.2
Correlations, Partial Correlations, and z-Tests for Correlation Differences

Strategy	Conflict-Competence r's			Conflict-CommSat r's		
	Husband	Wife	z-test	Husband	Wife	z-test
Time 1						
Integrative	.42 (.29)	.40 (.26)	0.64	.36 (.14)	.47 (.22)	1.46
Distributive	−.23 (−.04)	−38 (−.20)	2.68*	−.32 (−.08)	−.45 (−.18)	1.76
Avoidance	−.05 (−.01)	−.35 (−.28)	4.54*	−.15 (−.00)	−.32 (−.11)	1.77
Time 2						
Integrative	.49 (.26)	.43 (.22)	0.58	.44 (.21)	.37 (.11)	1.79
Distributive	−.45 (−.11)	−.43 (−.05)	0.89	−.31 (−.03)	−.36 (−.08)	0.82
Avoidance	−.17 (−.13)	−.19 (−.14)	0.31	−.23 (−.04)	−.20 (−.00)	0.51

Note. z-tests were performed on the partial correlations; CommSat = Communication Satisfaction.

*$p < .05$, two-tailed.

reports the correlations between conflict and the partner's competence and communication satisfaction measures.

As Table 10.2 reveals, at T1 husband distributive and avoidant behaviors were more powerfully linked to the wife's assessments of the husband's competence and to the wife's communication satisfaction than vice versa. However, husbands' competence perceptions were slightly more correlated with the wives' integrative tactics than vice versa, contrary to expectations based on the sex stereotype hypothesis, although the effect was not significant due to the direction of the hypothesis (i.e., the two-tailed effect bordered on significance, with $p < .10$).

Discussion

The findings from this study show that women were more likely than men to engage in distributive conflict tactics. These behaviors reflect a range of competitive actions, such as insulting, threatening, criticizing, and intimidating the partner. Clearly, these data do not conform to the sex stereotype of women being more relationally sensitive, engaging, and cooperative. Indeed, men showed greater cooperation during conflict as seen in men's slightly higher integrative tactics. Moreover, there were no sex differences in perceptions of partner competence or in assessments of one's own communication satisfaction. What may be more important than the frequency differences of these measures, however, is the manner in which the conflict behaviors affect competence and communication satisfaction evaluations.

The sex stereotype hypothesis would lead us to expect that husbands' competence and communication satisfaction evaluations would be more affected by the spouse's use of competitive behavior. Contrary to this expectation, the z-tests for correlation differences showed that wives were more in tune with husband distributive and avoidant behaviors at T1. That is, although wives self-reported greater use of distributive behaviors, they were actually more affected by the husband's use of such competitive and hostile actions, and avoidance tactics, than were the husbands. In still different terms, husbands relied more than wives did on informa-tion other than the spouse's distributive and avoidant behaviors. Indeed, husbands relied more than wives did on the partner's integrative behavior, though this effect was marginal. In any case, these data clearly show that sex stereotypes did not effectively predict how vigilant men would be in instances where women use competitive conflict tactics, or how women would be aware of men's unexpected use of cooperative integrative tactics. Instead, support for the opposite effect was found. In sum, our data indicates that sex stereotypes have little to say about conflict and corresponding episodic perceptions of communication competence.

CONCLUSIONS AND IMPLICATIONS

The Sex Stereotype Hypothesis and Research on Conflict and Anger

Is the sex stereotype hypothesis supported by research on interpersonal conflict and anger? The answer is clearly *no*; women and men do not consistently behave in ways indicated by traditional sex stereotypes. The conflict and anger literatures suggest that studies supporting the stereotypes probably confuse sex-role expecta-tions with actual behavior. Observations of actual behavior show that, if anything, women are more competitive than men and men have a tendency to avoid conflict, and even these effects disappear when the topic, the relationship, or the partner's communication behavior are taken into account. In addition, with the exception of crying, men and women express anger in similar ways, contradicting the stereotype of men being more dominant.

What explains this lack of support for the sex stereotype hypothesis? One explanation is that reliance on stereotypes provides no meaningful understanding of sex differences in behavior. As Ragan (1989) noted, the use of stereotypes actually contaminates the research on men's and women's interaction. In addition, the socialization processes explaining the adoption of stereotypes sometimes are quite vague. The explanation, "women and men are different because of different socialization processes" hardly says anything beyond the circular statement, "peo-ple are different because they are different" (Deaux & Major, 1990). Even if we do learn something about the genesis and adoption of stereotypes, how stereotypes make their way into the conversations of living people remains a mystery.

Indeed, to the extent that people rely on alternate appropriateness cues relevant to the interaction context (e.g., professional roles, relational rules, personal prefer-ences, etc.), stereotypic portrayals of men and women provide little insight regard-ing standards for behavior, and by extension, what behavior we can predict. In addition, we should consider the many exceptions to the rule: Individuals are complex, goal-directed, and strategic, and act to maximize their successes, not stereotypes.

A second explanation for why stereotypes do not predict conflict behavior is that such views of men and women exaggerate the differences, polarizing the two sexes (Putnam, 1982). Such polarized accounts of men and women do little to inform us about the nature of people communicating with one another (Canary & Hause, 1993; Putnam, 1982; Ragan, 1989).

Implications for Power in Relationships Between Men and Women

Power is certainly a focal concept in the analysis of conflict. We agree with the commonly held view that power does not inhere in individuals. Instead, power is a product of the social or personal relationship shared between people (e.g., Hocker & Wilmot, 1991). Since management of conflict entails mutual influence, the exercise of power is natural in interpersonal conflict.

The lack of support for the sex stereotype hypothesis suggests some implications for power in interpersonal relationships between men and women. In particular, when power differences exist in developed intimate relationships, as opposed to casual or formal role-related relationships, we contend that such differences are less likely to reflect sex differences in stereotypic expectations for behavior in the context of the relationship. In other words, the influence of the sex stereotype on behavior likely diminishes in the context of interpersonal relationships as such relationships become more close and intimate. By definition, the development of close relationships involves increasing interdependence (e.g., Kelley et al., 1983). In general, a greater diversity of resources is exchanged among intimate partners and there are a greater number of issues on which power is exerted. Moreover, couples develop a shared symbolic relational culture that contextualizes relational behavior (Wood, 1982). Consequently, idiosyncratic standards and expectations for behavior are negotiated and developed over time, and these displace more general sociocultural influences on behavior. In short, the partner and the relationship become relatively more important influences in relationship behavior than socially driven stereotypes. Differences in power do not necessarily reflect endemic differences in sex.

Additionally, close relationships involve a degree of shared privacy. In public contexts and non-intimate relationships, social expectations based on sex stereotypes exert a relatively stronger and more constraining influence on behavior. The public and social domains locate where we would expect that sex is itself a source of power, and sex differences in behavior may indicate a power differential. But as the relationship between persons becomes more intimate and private, the context for managing conflict shifts from social to (inter)personal.

We hasten to indicate that sometimes the sex stereotypic pattern is clearly manifest in close relationships between men and women when they have incorporated the social script for behavior into their relational script (Fitzpatrick, 1988). But based on our review of the evidence, this does not occur more often than alternative patterns of behavior. Nor does the lack of sex differences in the management of conflict deny the existence of power differentials in close relationships. But sex differences in influence tactics, to the extent they exist, tend not to be mediated by interpersonal dependence or structural power in the relationship (e.g., Howard, Blumstein, & Schwartz, 1986). Among the greater diversity of resources exchanged in more intimate relationships, it may be that communication is simply a commodity to which men and women have equal access. Indeed, communication seems to be a tool that either males or females can utilize in an attempt to address perceived power imbalances in intimate relationships.

REFERENCES

Averill, J. R. (1982). *Anger and aggression: An essay on emotion*. New York: Springer-Verlag.

Baron, R. A. (1977). *Human aggression*. New York: Plenum.

Baumeister, R. F., Stillwell, A., & Wotman, S. R. (1990). Victim and perpetrator accounts of interpersonal conflict: Autobiographical narratives about anger. *Journal of Personality and Social Psychology, 59*, 994–1005.

Bell, D. C., Chafetz, J. S., & Horn, L. H. (1982). Marital conflict resolution: A study of strategies and outcomes. *Journal of Family Issues, 3*, 111–131.

Berryman-Fink, C., & Brunner, C. C. (1987). The effects of sex of source and target on interpersonal conflict management styles. *Southern Speech Communication Journal, 53*, 33–48.

Betancourt, H., & Blair, I. (1992). A cognition (attribution)-emotion model of violence in conflict situations. *Personality and Social Psychology Bulletin, 18*, 343–350.

Burggraf, C. S., & Sillars, A. L. (1987). A critical examination of sex differences in marital communication. *Communication Monographs, 54*, 276–294.

Burrowes, B. D., & Halberstadt, A. G. (1987). Self- and family-expressiveness styles in the experience and expression of anger. *Journal of Nonverbal Behavior, 11*, 254–268.

Buss, D. M. (1989). Conflict between the sexes: Strategic interference and the evocation of anger and upset. *Journal of Personality and Social Psychology, 56*, 735–747.

Campbell, A., & Muncer, S. (1987). Models of anger and aggression in the social talk of women and men. *Journal for the Theory of Social Behaviour, 17*, 489–511.

Canary, D. J., Cunningham, E. M., & Cody, M. J. (1988). Goal types, gender, and locus of control in managing interpersonal conflict. *Communication Research, 15*, 426–446.

Canary, D. J., & Cupach, W. R. (1988). Relational and episodic characteristics associated with conflict tactics. *Journal of Social and Personal Relationships, 5*, 305–325.

Canary, D. J., & Hause, K. S. (1993). Is there any reason to research sex differences in communication? *Communication Quarterly, 41*, 129–144.

Canary, D. J., & Spitzberg, B. H. (1987). Appropriateness and effectiveness perceptions of conflict strategies. *Human Communication Research, 14*, 93–118.

Canary, D. J., & Spitzberg, B. H. (1989). A model of perceived competence of conflict strategies. *Human Communication Research, 15*, 630–649.

Canary, D. J., & Spitzberg, B. H. (1990). Attribution biases and associations between conflict strategies and competence outcomes. *Communication Monographs, 57*, 139–151.

Christensen, A., & Heavey, C. L. (1990). Gender and social structure in the demand/withdrawal pattern of marital conflict. *Journal of Personality and Social Psychology, 59*, 73–81.

Crawford, J., Kippax, S., Onyx, J., Gault, U., & Benton, P. (1992). *Emotion and gender: Constructing meaning from memory*. London: Sage.

Cupach, W. R. (1982, May). *Communication satisfaction and interpersonal solidarity as outcomes of conflict message strategy use*. Paper presented at the International Communication Association Conference, Boston, MA.

Cupach, W. R., Canary, D. J., & Serpe, R. T. (1994). *Relational and episodic influences on the use of conflict strategies: A longitudinal replication and extension*. Unpublished Raw Data.

Deaux, K., & Lewis, L. L. (1984). The structure of gender stereotypes: Interrelationships among components and gender label. *Journal of Personality and Social Psychology, 46*, 991–1004.

Deaux, K., & Major, B. (1990). A social-psychological model of gender. In D. L. Rhode (Ed.), *Theoretical perspectives on sexual difference* (pp. 89–99). New Haven, CT: Yale University Press.

Eagly, A. H., & Steffen, V. (1984). Gender stereotypes stem from the distribution of women and men into social roles. *Journal of Personality and Social Psychology, 46*, 735–754.

Eagly, A. H., & Steffen, V. (1986). Gender and aggressive behavior: A meta-analytic review of the social psychological literature. *Journal of Personality and Social Psychology, 100*, 309–330.

Felson, R. B., & Tedeschi, J. T. (Eds.). (1993). *Aggression and violence: Social interactionist perspectives.* Washington, DC: American Psychological Association.

Fisher, B. A. (1983). Differential effects of sexual composition and interactional context on interaction patterns in dyads. *Human Communication Research, 9*, 225–238.

Fitzpatrick, M. A. (1988). *Between husbands and wives: Communication in marriage.* Newbury Park, CA: Sage.

Fitzpatrick, M. A., & Winke, T. (1979). You always hurt the one you love: Strategies and tactics in interpersonal conflict. *Communication Quarterly, 27*, 3–11.

Frodi, A. (1977). Sex differences in perception of a provocation: A survey. *Perceptual and Motor Skills, 44*, 113–114.

Frodi, A. (1978). Experiential and physiological responses associated with anger and aggression in women and men. *Journal of Research in Personality, 12*, 335–349.

Frodi, A., Macaulay, J., & Thome, P. R. (1977). Are women always less aggressive than men? A review of the experimental literature. *Psychological Bulletin, 84*, 634–660.

Frost, W. D., & Averill, J. R. (1982). Differences between men and women in the everyday experience of anger. In J. R. Averill (Ed.), *Anger and aggression: An essay on emotion* (pp. 281–316). New York: Springer-Verlag.

Gayle-Hackett, B. (1986). *Do females and males differ in the selection of conflict management strategies: A meta-analytic review.* Unpublished manuscript, University of Portland.

Gottman, J. M. (1979). *Marital interaction: Experimental investigations.* New York: Academic Press.

Gottman, J. M. (1990). Finding the laws of personal relationships. In I. E. Sigel & G. H. Brody (Eds.), *Methods of family research: Biographies of research projects I: Normal families* (pp. 249–263). Hillsdale, NJ: Lawrence Erlbaum Associates.

Gottman, J. M., & Carrere, S. (1994). Why can't men and women get along? Developmental roots and marital inequities. In D. J. Canary & L. Stafford (Eds.), *Communication and relational maintenance* (pp. 203–229). San Diego, CA: Academic Press.

Harris, M. B. (1993). How provoking! What makes men and women angry? *Aggressive Behavior, 19*, 199–211.

Healey, J. G., & Bell, R. A. (1990). Assessing alternative responses to conflicts in friendship. In D. D. Cahn (Ed.) *Intimates in conflict: A communication perspective* (pp. 25–48). Hillsdale, NJ: Lawrence Erlbaum Associates.

Hecht, M. L. (1978). The conceptualization and measurement of interpersonal communication satisfaction. *Human Communication Research, 4*, 253–264.

Hocker, J. L., & Wilmot, W. W. (1991). *Interpersonal conflict* (3rd ed.). Dubuque, IA: William C. Brown.

Howard, J. A., Blumstein, P., & Schwartz, P. (1986). Sex, power, and influence tactics in intimate relationships. *Journal of Personality and Social Psychology, 51*, 102–109.

Junger, M. (1987). Women's experiences of sexual harassment. *British Journal of Criminology, 27*, 358–383.

Kelley, H. H., Berscheid, E., Christensen, A., Harvey, J. H., Huston, T. L., Levinger, G., McClintock, E., Peplau, L. A., & Peterson, D. R. (Eds.). (1983). *Close relationships.* New York: W. H. Freeman.

Kelley, H. H., Cunningham, J. D., Grisham, J. A., Lefebvre, L. M., Sink, C. R., & Yablon, G. (1978). Sex differences in comments made during conflict within close heterosexual pairs. *Sex Roles, 4*, 473–492.

Kopper, B. A., & Epperson, D. L. (1991). Women and anger: Sex and sex-role comparisons in the expression of anger. *Psychology of Women Quarterly, 15*, 7–14.

Levy, B. (Ed.).(1991). *Dating violence.* Seattle, WA: Seal Press.

Margolin, G., & Wampold, B. E. (1981). Sequential analysis of conflict and accord in distressed and nondistressed marital partners. *Journal of Consulting and Clinical Psychology, 49,* 554–567.

Marshall, L. (1994). Psychological and physical abuse. In W. R. Cupach & B. H. Spitzberg (Eds.), *The dark side of interpersonal communication* (pp. 281–311). Hillsdale, NJ: Lawrence Erlbaum Associates.

Parrot, A., & Bechhofer, A. (Eds.). (1991). *Acquaintance rape.* New York: Wiley.

Pryor, J. (1987). Sexual harassment proclivities in men. *Sex Roles, 17,* 269–290.

Putnam, L. L. (1982). In search of gender: A critique of communication and sex roles research. *Women's Studies in Communication, 5,* 1–9.

Ragan, S. L. (1989). Communication between the sexes: A consideration of differences in adult communication. In J. F. Nussbaum (Ed.), *Life-span communication: Normative processes* (pp. 179–193). Hillsdale, NJ: Lawrence Erlbaum Associates.

Renwick, P. A. (1977). The effects of sex differences on the perception and management of superior–subordinate conflict: An exploratory study. *Organizational Behavior and Human Performance, 19,* 403–415.

Rohner, R. P. (1976). Sex differences in aggression: Phylogenetic and enculturation perspectives. *Ethos, 4,* 57–72.

Roloff, M. E., & Greenberg, B. S. (1979). Sex differences in choice of modes of conflict resolution in real-life and television. *Communication Quarterly, 27,* 3–12.

Rusbult, C. E. (1987). Responses to dissatisfaction in close relationships: The exit–voice–loyalty–neglect model. In D. Perlman & S. Duck (Eds.), *Intimate relationships: Development, dynamics, and deterioration* (pp. 209–237). Newbury Park, CA: Sage.

Rusbult, C. E. (1993). Understanding responses to dissatisfaction in close relationships. The exit–voice–loyalty–neglect model. In S. Worchel & J. A. Simpson (Eds.), *Conflict between people and groups: Causes, processes, and resolutions* (pp. 30–59). Chicago: Nelson-Hall Publishers.

Rusbult, C. E., Johnson, D. J., & Morrow, G. D. (1986). Impact of couple patterns of problem solving on distress and nondistress in dating relationships. *Journal of Personality and Social Psychology, 50,* 744–753.

Rusbult, C. E., & Zembrodt, I. M. (1983). Responses to dissatisfaction in romantic involvements: A multidimensional scaling analysis. *Journal of Experimental Social Psychology, 19,* 274–293.

Rusbult, C. E., Zembrodt, I. M., & Gunn, L. K. (1982). Exit, voice, loyalty, and neglect: Responses to dissatisfaction in romantic involvements. *Journal of Personality and Social Psychology, 43,* 1230–1242.

Scheff, T. J., & Retzinger, S. M. (1991). *Emotions and violence: Shame and rage in destructive conflicts.* Lexington, MA: Lexington Books.

Sillars, A. L., Coletti, S. F., Parry, D., & Rogers, M. A. (1982). Coding verbal conflicts: Non-verbal and perceptual correlates of the "avoidance–distributive–integrative" distinction. *Human Communication Research, 9,* 83–95.

Smith, K. C., Ulch, S. E., Cameron, J. E., & Cumberland, J. A. (1989). Gender-related effects in the perception of anger expression. *Sex Roles, 20,* 487–499.

Spielberger, C. D., Jacobs, G., Russell, S., & Crane, R. S. (1983). Assessment of anger: The State-Trait Anger Scale. In J. N. Butcher & C. D. Spielberger (Eds.), *Advances in personality assessment* (Vol. 2, pp. 159–187). Hillsdale, NJ: Lawrence Erlbaum Associates.

Spitzberg, B. H., Canary, D. J., & Cupach, W. R. (1994). A competence-based approach to the study of interpersonal conflict. In D. D. Cahn (Ed.), *Conflict in personal relationships* (pp. 183–202). Hillsdale, NJ: Lawrence Erlbaum Associates.

Spitzberg, B. H., & Cupach, W. R. (1984). *Interpersonal communication competence.* Beverly Hills, CA: Sage.

Spitzberg, B. H., & Cupach, W. R. (1989). *Handbook of interpersonal competence research.* New York: Springer-Verlag.

Sternberg, R. J., & Soriano, L. J. (1984). Styles of conflict resolution. *Journal of Personality and Social Psychology, 47,* 115–126.

Stets, J. E., & Henderson, D. A. (1991). Contextual factors surrounding conflict resolution while dating: Results from a national study. *Family Relations, 40,* 29–36.

Stoner, S. B., & Spencer, W. B. (1987). Age and gender differences with the Anger Expression Scale. *Educational and Psychological Measurement, 47,* 487–492.

Straus, M. A., & Sweet, S. (1992). Verbal/symbolic aggression in couples: Incidence rates and relationships to personal characteristics. *Journal of Marriage and the Family, 54,* 346–357.

Tavris, C. (1984). On the wisdom of counting to ten: Personal and social dangers of anger expression. In P. Shaver (Ed.) *Review of personality and social psychology: Emotions, relationships, and health* (pp. 170–191). Beverly Hills, CA: Sage.

Terhune, T. W. (1970). The effects of personality in cooperation and conflict. In P. Swingle (Ed.), *The structure of conflict* (pp. 193–234). New York: Academic Press.

Thomas, S. P. (1989). Gender differences in anger expression: Health implications. *Research in Nursing and Health, 12,* 389–398.

Ting-Toomey, S. (1983). An analysis of verbal communication patterns in high and low marital adjustment groups. *Human Communication Research, 9,* 306–319.

Wood, J. T. (1982). Communication and relational culture: Bases for the study of human relationships. *Communication Quarterly, 30,* 75–83.

Zammutto, M. L., London, M., & Rowland, K. W. (1979). Effects of sex on commitment and conflict resolution. *Journal of Applied Psychology, 64,* 227–231.

Zillmann, D. (1990). The interplay of cognition and excitation in aggravated conflict among intimates. In D. D. Cahn (Ed.), *Intimates in conflict: A communication perspective* (pp. 187–208). Hillsdale, NJ: Lawrence Erlbaum Associates.

Chapter 11

The Dynamics of Power: Money and Sex in Intimate Relationships

Pepper Schwartz
Davis Patterson
Sara Steen
University of Washington

Decisions about money and sex are among the most contentious that couples make. In this article, we discuss how power and gender affect decision-making and communication on these issues in romantic relationships. The two factors that influence the distribution of power most strongly are social norms about how power should be distributed and the personal options and attributes of each individual. Both norms and resources are strongly influenced, in turn, by a traditional system of gender privileges and placement, historically granting most economic and relationship power to men. These norms, however, penetrate some relationships more than others. Decision-making patterns depend, to some extent, on a couple's social class and the distribution of resources within the couple's relationship (the amount of resources each partner has relative to the other).

Defining power, and who has it, is of course a difficult task. We adopt the classic Weberian definition of power: the ability to carry out one's will, even against the will of others. Implied in this definition is also veto power, the power to prevent another from carrying out his or her will. This is a common conceptualization of power in the study of families and romantic relationships (McDonald, 1980) because it can be operationalized as decision-making power and is consistent with normative resource and exchange theories of power.

To illuminate the dynamics of power in intimate relationships, we choose two topics that are intimately connected with power: money and sex. Not only are decisions about money and sex strongly influenced by power, but negotiation and outcomes symbolize gender patterns of dominance and submission. Thus, an analysis of communication about money and sex brings us closer to an understanding of how power is operationalized in intimate relationships.

In all couples, communication and decision-making are affected by exogenous factors. Differences in income, education, and social class lead to differences in ideology that affect sexual and financial practice (Blumstein & Schwartz, 1983; Rubin, 1976; Van Fossen, 1980; Weinberg & Williams, 1980). Resources also affect relationships on a more personal level. Money, employment, physical attractiveness, and other advantages give individuals an upper hand in their relationships that they use to gain greater decision-making power (Blumstein & Schwartz, 1983). The effects of relative resources occur, at least in part, because the privileged partner has more personal options outside the relationship and therefore lower need for and potentially less commitment to the relationship (England & Farkas, 1986; Waller, 1938). A partner who has the ability to function, both financially and emotionally, without the other worries less about making unpopular decisions, whereas a partner who lacks financial, emotional, and sexual options is less able to take interpersonal risks and unabashedly wield power.

In writing this chapter, we have drawn from a broad range of literature. There is, of course, a great deal written about each of the issues we write about: money, power, sex, and communication. However, there appears to be relatively little research done on the intersection of these issues. We therefore draw heavily from Blumstein and Schwartz's study of American couples done in 1983, as it contains both quantitative and qualitative data about how couples manage issues of money and sex and how power both affects and is affected by these issues. We draw also from sociological, psychological, and communications literature to provide some contrast to these data. We consider decisions about money first, followed by sex, and then take account of the interactions between money, sex, and power, particularly in relationship satisfaction. We conclude with some hypotheses on how these processes may change, if at all, as we approach the year 2000.

MONEY

A review of the literature on money, gender, and power reveals surprisingly little research when it comes to intimate relationships. The dearth of literature on this subject seems to echo what scholars characterize as the taboo nature of discussion about money within relationships (Blumstein & Schwartz, 1983; Felton-Collins, 1990; Hertz, 1986; Pahl, 1983; Pahl, 1989; Treas, 1993). Romance and love are supposed, in American society, to be antithetical to material ambitions, and the pragmatics of earning ability or future lifestyle are not supposed to overshadow emotion and evaluation of character during courtship. Still, Millman (1991) argued that money has become a way to measure the value of all things, including love and one's personal worth. No wonder, then, that money is a delicate matter discussed only within families and between committed partners, and only then with considerable difficulty. Money is one of the most common (if not the most common) issues of discussion in married couples, and also, to a lesser extent, in cohabiting and same-sex couples (Blumstein & Schwartz, 1983). This happens not just because financial matters are at the heart of any couple's present and future plans, but because men and women often view money in fundamentally different ways, and it takes a good deal of conversation or argument to work out opposing positions. Additionally, differences in race, class, and ideology and differences in commitment or likelihood of stability affect the meaning of money and how it is used in the relationship. Whether the partners adopt a traditional marital ideology, attempt to create an egalitarian marriage, or reject the institution of marriage entirely, all couples are also affected by the inequality of male–female relationships in both the workplace and the home.

Gender Norms and the Balance of Income and Power

I think one of the lower things in the world is a man lying around the house letting his wife support him. Maybe I'm conservative but that isn't my idea of how to be a man or how to have a marriage. (53-year-old husband; Blumstein & Schwartz, 1983, p. 71)

Men frame a substantial amount of their identity through work, and the money they receive as reward becomes a measure of personal identity and power. Male orientation toward financial independence dovetails with the norms of traditional marriage, which dictate that the husband should be the main breadwinner. Women are trained in a complementary fashion to seek identity primarily through relationships: Though money represents security, it is secondary to the need for emotional connectedness (Blumstein & Schwartz, 1983; Felton-Collins, 1990; Millman, 1991). Thus the economic provider role is central for husbands, and wives tend to take on the economically dependent roles of nurturer and consumer. This division of goals, activities, and responsibilities, reinforced by the superior earning power of men, creates the basis for marital power differences.

In traditional couples, the provider role also grants husbands a complex of rights and privileges that consolidate and perpetuate male dominance over wives. Reviews of the research on family power indicate that norms are usually more powerful than actual resources in predicting who wields more decision-making power (Kingsbury & Scanzoni, 1989; McDonald, 1980). This conclusion is illustrated by the finding that if either husband or wife believes in the male-breadwinner ideology, the husband tends to have more power in major decisions, even if his wife has a higher income than he does (Blumstein & Schwartz, 1991).

Even those wives who believe they should have an equal say in economic decisions are also aware that a husband's self-esteem may depend on his fulfilling the duties of provider. In particular, Rubin (1976) recorded poignant portraits of working class wives who find it difficult to challenge their husbands on money issues because they understand that their husbands' self esteem is at stake. Further-more, few husbands in working- and lower-class families allow an in-depth discussion of an issue that so frequently threatens their sense of adequacy. The ability to squelch discussion of money illustrates husband dominance in working-class homes; he reinforces his power through control of discussion. Bargaining itself constitutes more of an egalitarian tactic (Howard, Blumstein, & Schwartz, 1986). Wives in dual-career couples have more influence partly because they have an ideology, the right to an equal say, that makes negotiation more likely (Kingsbury & Scanzoni, 1989).

The Struggle for Equality

> I blow up at him when he accuses me of not having put much money in....He gets a much higher percentage of my money than I get of his and while I agree with him that we both should pay for food and entertainment and things like that, I would also like him to acknowledge once in a while how hard it is for me to do. (female cohabitor; Blumstein & Schwartz, 1983, p. 88)

Traditional married couples, couples wedded to the male-as-provider ideology, exist at all class levels. But none hold more strongly to the old ideals than those in the working class (Katz & Perez, 1985; Pahl, 1989; Rubin, 1976). There is little racial variation in ideology between working class African Americans and Whites (Hammond & Enoch, 1976). In contrast, middle-class couples are more likely to subscribe to an egalitarian ideology in marriage (Rank, 1982). It has been suggested that the task repetition and subordinate status of working-class occupations inhibit one's sense of personal autonomy and efficacy, whereas middle-class occupations provide a more satisfying outlet for creativity and the exercise of power (Katz & Perez, 1985; Rubin, 1976). Furthermore, middle-class husbands and wives are more likely to be involved in community and other activities outside the home that also provide alternatives for men to exercise their power and women to demonstrate nondomestic competence. Husbands in the middle class may be less committed to hierarchical marital power ideologies than working-class husbands simply because working-class husbands lack other arenas where they can be in control.

Although Rubin (1976) argued that relative to working-class wives, middle-class wives are likely to draw salaries that are a relatively smaller proportion of the family income than that of their husbands, this disadvantage may be counterbal-anced by the more egalitarian ideology among middle- and upper-class couples (Katz & Perez, 1985; Rank, 1982). Furthermore, with the expansion of career opportunities for women, more wives begin their marriages with well-established careers that continue to give them clout and independence (Hertz, 1986).

However, these class conduct differences do not hold up when we look at race and ethnicity. Beckett and Smith (1981) found that African-American wives are more likely to share the breadwinner role at all levels of husband's income. In their comprehensive review of the literature, Taylor, Chatters, Tucker, and Lewis (1990) also found greater egalitarianism in African-American couples. African-American wives have a longer history of providing for their families, due to economic necessity; the fact that African-American husbands do more housework and childcare than White husbands further supports this conclusion. Ybarra's (1982) study of Chicano families reveals greater egalitarianism than expected, given the cultural emphasis on "machismo" or male privilege. But she found the greatest equalizer, independent of a family's degree of acculturation—and reminiscent of other kinds of families—to be a wife's employment.

For both married and cohabiting egalitarian couples, the challenge to traditional gender roles means that a man must give up some of his power and his central, main-provider identity, in exchange for a relationship based on equity and equality. This process requires learning not to feel threatened or resentful of a woman's success because a male's adequacy has, to some extent, been defined in comparison to his wife, as well as other male providers in general (Blumstein & Schwartz, 1983). But male competition over economic ascendancy is not completely based on male–female relationships. In gay couples, partners are particularly prone to competing economically, with the winner assuming more privileges (Blumstein & Schwartz, 1983; Harry & DeVall, 1978; McWhirter & Mattison, 1984). Taking on a co-provider role brings women more egalitarian treatment; however, women's lesser earning power often makes this difficult. Thus women in egalitarian heterosexual relationships must learn to feel comfortable without an economic provider even while confronting the reality that their economic disadvantage usually makes true equality elusive.

Resource Flows and Patterns of Decision-Making

> She used to handle the money. It was a pretty cut-and-dried affair then, and I didn't need to spend my time on it. But now there's more of it, and there are decisions that have to be made about what we need to buy and when we should buy it. So I do it now. (35-year-old husband; Rubin, 1976, p. 108)

Because a couple's ideology simultaneously affects the partners' relationship and work roles, it affects the partners' relative contributions of income, the way the income is managed, and ultimately, the way the money is distributed and spent. A couple's ideology about money and power within the relationship is heavily influenced by the social world they inhabit. Zelizer (1989) noted clear evidence of class differences in money management from as early as 1921, and Pahl (1983) argued that the level and source of income work with ideology to determine how money and power are allocated. For this reason, we consider further how ideology interacts with class and relative resources to determine patterns of allocation and decision-making between partners.

Owners and Managers

> I don't see the bills so I don't worry about them, so it's a cop-out on my part. I let her worry about them. She's got the bookkeeping background, so that's the official

reason....I'm giving her all the responsibility and she enjoys it; apparently, it gives her a sense of power. It's beautiful. (husband; Blumstein & Schwartz, 1983, p. 65)

Although middle- and upper-class couples exhibit greater variability in patterns of economic dispersement and control, financial latitude constrains working-class couples' decisions about how to handle money (Pahl, 1989). Traditional couples in particular neatly illustrate the distinction Pahl (1989) made between control and management of income, similar to the concepts of orchestration and implementation power (Safilios-Rothschild, 1976). Working class husbands typically exercise control or orchestration power: They make the important but infrequent decisions about how large amounts of money are to be spent. In doing so, they usually delegate the management or implementation power to their wives. Within the guidelines set by their husbands, wives are charged with the time-consuming aspects of spending the money on basic necessities such as food and paying the bills.

Rubin (1976) showed how, for these wives, the job of managing the money brings little satisfaction. It does not give them real decision-making power or even the illusion of power; rather, it constitutes a worrisome burden where few spending decisions even have to be made, because there is little or no discretionary income left over once the bills are paid. The power associated with managing discretionary income—what remains after bills—is evident when we look at traditional middle-class couples. Husbands increasingly take over the role of managing the money from their wives because the traditional marital ideology allows him to control the way money is managed and because at this income level there is real power to be gained by doing so (Rubin, 1976). Clearly, then, the agent is not the same as the owner and the agent's power may be illusory in a conflict situation.

Of course, a working-class wife does have decision-making power about internal household affairs; however, this seeming advantage can backfire, because it comes with consuming duties such as the primary responsibility for raising the children. Her control of this domestic area is also circumscribed. She cannot require male assistance, and her husband holds her accountable for household deficits, including the children's misbehavior or poor school performance (Rubin, 1976).

Rubin argued further that beyond relieving a husband from the responsibility, when the wife does manage the income, he is shielded from facing the reality that he really may not provide enough or as much as he would like to believe. Instead, he can blame her in part for their money problems by holding her accountable for how the money gets spent.

Earning Power Through Employment

Some people think the "toys" he buys for himself are a little excessive....My feeling is that he deserves it all. He works for it....I support him on almost everything he buys, even if I think it is outrageous. (middle-class wife; Blumstein & Schwartz, 1983, p. 58)

When I was married [before] I had to explain why and almost ask forgiveness for spending any money. And now that I've got my own financial situation and my own job...if I goof up, that's my problem. I don't have to rationalize or explain. I just do it. (employed wife; Blumstein & Schwartz, 1983, p. 102)

Money causes a shift in the balance of power even under conditions where male dominance is presumed to be legitimate. Although a wife's power is rarely commensurate with her relative contribution to household income, numerous studies show that her decision-making power increases when she works outside the home (Blumstein & Schwartz, 1983; Katz & Perez, 1985; Pahl, 1983; Rubin, 1976). Thus middle-class wives gain a foothold outside the family and use that leverage internally. When a woman is able to exert influence in her work, she is likely to feel more comfortable exerting influence in other areas of her life, such as her marriage (Kandel & Lesser, 1972; Spade, 1989). Middle-class women are also more likely to have careers where they have a real say in decision-making on the job. They are more likely to demand egalitarian treatment and more likely to be taken seriously by their husbands. It seems, therefore, that both men and women understand the cultural construction of power such that traditionally male activities—earning money and working outside the home—constitute one of the greatest sources of power in intimate relationships (Chafetz, 1991).

Egalitarian beliefs support a system of shared financial management and responsibility, where both partners have access but also must contribute, through employment, to a common pool of resources (Blumstein & Schwartz, 1983; Pahl, 1989). Green and Cunningham (1975) found that more liberal wives, who tended to be younger and with higher incomes, played a greater role in purchasing decisions, providing further evidence that upper income groups are more flexible in sharing conjugal power. Furthermore, money management gives a middle- or upper-class wife more power, not less, simply because a surplus of money gives her more discretionary latitude. Like husbands, a wife who earns money feels freer to spend as she sees fit without being accountable to her spouse; an employed wife is also more likely to have a separate savings account to which a husband has no access (Blumstein & Schwartz, 1983; Pahl, 1989). She may also take advantage of the opportunity to "embezzle" funds to gain more independence in spending or lifestyle. Zelizer (1989) documented family embezzlement all the way back to the beginning of the century:"I skim a little off the top!...Oh, I'll tell him the groceries cost more than they did, or something like that. Nothing spectacular, but it gives me a little breathing room" (homemaking wife; Blumstein & Schwartz, 1983, p. 103).

Pooling is less desirable to either husbands or wives who have had to disentangle themselves financially from a past marriage through the process of divorce (Treas, 1991, 1993). But all things being equal, this management style is still more pleasing to husbands than to wives. Even though pooling theoretically gives wives more economic power than control over just her own, less impressive money, it also keeps her from independent action. Moreover, pooled income only gives wives additional decision-making power if both husband and wife have an egalitarian ideology. Rights of ownership tend to be associated with earning money: Husbands usually remain more comfortable than wives about using joint funds for personal spending (Katz & Perez, 1985). Thus although ideology dictates that couples label their money as jointly controlled, in reality both husbands and wives actually spend with the levels of their relative contributions in mind (Pahl, 1989), with the notable exception of when the wife earns more (McCrae, 1987).

The infrequency of higher earning wives leads us to a consideration of the other ways a woman's ability to equalize the balance of power is inhibited. A husband may limit her opportunity to take outside employment because he very practically perceives that she stands to gain independence and power (Rubin, 1976). A woman who subscribes to the traditional breadwinner ideology is also sensitive to the discomfort her employment can cause: She may relinquish her potential for power simply by not using it, camouflage her earnings by giving them over completely to her husband, or pool the two incomes such that her contribution is effectively "lost" (Blumstein & Schwartz, 1983; Burgoyne, 1990, Pahl, 1989). Even nontraditional wives with higher incomes and higher status occupations than their husbands may resort to pooling as a way not to call attention to their superior position.

Gender differences in the allocation of disposable income also inhibit equality. A wife's income is likely to go entirely toward household expenses, replacing the husband's former contribution; he is then free to spend more of his own earnings as personal discretionary funds. Thus he experiences tangible gains, whereas she loses potential discretionary money—and power. This pattern is consistent with research finding that pooling may increase the wife's power because some of the pooled income at her disposal is not earmarked for household expenses (Blumstein & Schwartz, 1991).

Cohabitation: Where Economic Resources Thwart Ideology

Middle and upper-middle class cohabiting couples are the most sensitive about practicing egalitarian ideals. The most liberal among them may explicitly avoid marriage because of its maintenance of traditional male and female roles and obligations—not the least important of which is the male-provider ideology and its impact on the relationship (Blumstein & Schwartz, 1983). Women are particularly wary of male dominance, but cohabiting men are also less comfortable with dependent partners than married men. Cohabitation is especially attractive to divorced men who feel they have been cheated financially by their ex-wives and divorced women who have had to fight hard for their economic independence. These motivations underscore the importance of both ideology and financial considerations in cohabitation, not merely the desire to have an equal say in decision-making.

Without a marriage contract to help ensure the stability of their relationships, cohabitors find it easiest to avoid conflict and the possibility of male domination by keeping their assets separate. Nevertheless, the male penchant to control decisions may still come into play. As with gay male partners who often compete for control when incomes are unequal, conflict is more frequent among cohabiting couples when the woman has greater influence over spending decisions (Blumstein

& Schwartz, 1983). On the other hand, women may find making equal income contributions especially burdensome on their lower incomes, though the relationship demands it; cohabitation therefore seems to be a more difficult balancing act for women to manage than for men.

Thus despite the potential to avoid the inequities built into traditional marriage, cohabitation also illustrates the limits of ideology to bring about complete equality. Cohabiting couples continue to be affected by gender inequalities that are larger than the relationships they create—the very social forces they attempt to escape.

SEX

Individuals enter relationships with expectations about sexuality that often differ dramatically between partners, particularly in heterosexual couples, where partners bring gender norms and expectations that may be unshared or unknown by the opposite sex. Throughout life, men and women are given covert and subtle messages about how to behave sexually, how to think (or not think) about sex, and how to discuss sex. These messages are almost always very different for men and women, a fact that causes conflicting agendas and frequent miscommunication even in the most committed and intimate heterosexual relationships. Same-sex couples are expected to have somewhat more matched expectations, because both partners have undergone similar socialization, but conflict and misunderstandings still occur. Likewise, male and female feminists, more androgynous egalitarian married couples, and cohabitors, all of whom are likely to share more similar expectations of male and female behavior, may have an easier time understanding one another and negotiating sexual interaction; but that doesn't mean that sexual conflict disappears. Without the gender rules that guide traditional married couples, same-sex, cohabiting, and egalitarian couples are forced to innovate and create their own rules, sometimes finding out that they are more attached to male or female sexual boundaries and prerogatives than they thought they were.

Sometimes partners struggle over how sex will be conducted, when and how frequently it will happen, and how monogamous the relationship will be. The more powerful person determines many of these rules—but there are many ways to have power in sexual relationships. Of course relative income is important, but so are physical attractiveness and relative commitment to the relationship. In this section we see how these kinds of personal resources affect sexual decision-making.

Effects of Gender Norms On Sexual Decision-Making

Many couples choose to distribute sexual decision-making power by adhering to the rules and guidelines available to them. Though some couples try to ignore hierarchical male and female sexual guidelines, it is virtually impossible to be completely unaffected by them. Popular stereotypes of male and female sexuality portray males as more active and aggressive and females as more passive and less interested. These stereotypes, although certainly fading in universal application, are still important and undoubtedly subconsciously affect many couples (DeLamater, 1987; Zellman & Goodchilds, 1983). Traditional sex roles confer virtually all sexual leadership to the aggressive male, leaving the female with only veto power, which she is expected to use only on occasion. Current social norms, however, are moving gradually away from this sharp division of power, giving women additional, though not equal, latitude to both initiate and refuse sex. We describe how gender inequality organizes specific sexual behaviors, including decisions such as when, how often, with whom, and in what position a couple has sex.

Initiating and Refusing Sex.   The first sexual decision a couple negotiates is whether or not sex will occur. Usually, one partner initiates sexual activity (either subtly or directly), and the other partner either endorses or rejects the suggestion. Traditionally, the husband in a heterosexual married couple has had the duty and privilege of sexual initiation, and the wife has had the right to refuse his advance (at least some of the time) if she was not interested (DeLamater, 1987). As the status of women has increased in society, they have gained some degree of sexual independence and initiative. However, research suggests that the norm of male initiation still predominates in most heterosexual couples (most dramatically in older and lower class couples) (Blumstein & Schwartz, 1983; Byers & Heinlein, 1989; Rubin, 1976; Weinberg & Williams, 1980). Some of the major gender issues involved in initiation and refusal are expressed by this husband: "I initiate most of the time, the reason being she has a real hang-up about being rejected sexually. If she catches me in a mood when I'm not interested, she's terribly hurt, and so as a result, she doesn't start anything" (Blumstein and Schwartz, 1983, p. 212).

Women continue to say that they are less comfortable with initiating sexual activity than men, and men often state that they find women who initiate too frequently aggressive and unattractive (Blumstein & Schwartz, 1983; Rubin, 1976; Schnarch, 1991). Men see initiation not only as a male prerogative but as a part of masculinity. Therefore, a woman who exhibits more sexual interest than her partner loses credibility as a woman: "It's not that I mind her letting me know when she wants it, but she isn't very subtle about it. I mean, she could let me know in a nice, feminine way. Being feminine and, you know, kind of subtle, that's not her strong point" (husband, in Rubin, 1976, p. 143).

Even in couples who consider themselves to be egalitarian, the wife is not supposed to initiate more than her husband. This type of role reversal goes too far beyond cultural norms for most couples. Table 11.1 displays these differences.

TABLE 11.1
Sexual Initiation: Who Is More Likely to Initiate Sex?

	Self	*Partner*	*Equal*
Husbands	51%	33%	16%
Wives	12%	40%	48%

Note. From Blumstein and Schwartz (1983). Reprinted by permission.

If men feel that initiation is their right, and women feel it is either out of their realm or dangerous, the implications for same-sex couples are significant. Homosexual couples, who lack sex-based roles to guide their behavior, have to solve initiation and refusal patterns according to more individually derived rules (Peplau, 1981). In the past, homosexual couples were more likely to adopt marital sexual norms by assigning one partner the male role and the other the female role (D'Emilio & Freedman, 1988). This role allocation, however, has become increasingly infrequent, and homosexual couples today tend to operate on a model based either on egalitarian norms or one guided by individual preferences (Harry & DeVall, 1978; McWhirter, 1984). However, it is interesting to note that traditions of male and female behavior still exist in many same-sex couples. Initiation still connotes power, hierarchy, and masculinity, which means that, not infrequently, gay males argue over who gets to initiate more. Masculinity is valued—in some cases even venerated—so both partners insist on the right to initiate (Blumstein & Schwartz, 1983). Initiation predominance correlates with overall power in the relationship and so, as in heterosexual relationships, the less powerful partner must rely on refusal as his only reliable source of power (Blumstein & Schwartz, 1983). A partner who refuses to have sex is using veto power to have a say in the determination of the couple's sexual activity.

The same qualities that men are eager to demonstrate are those that women are eager to avoid. In lesbian couples, both women are normatively allowed to say no, which means that instead of competing for the role of initiator, lesbian partners often try to avoid this role, which they view as aggressive and masculine (Rosenzweig & Lebow, 1992). The lower frequency of sexual activity found in lesbian couples is likely a combination of the fact that women identify initiation with an aggressive male attempt to dominate and other female norms that legitimate lower female desire and authorize higher standards for the emotional conditions that justify and encourage sex (Bell & Weinberg 1978; Clunis, 1988; Peplau, 1981). Thus, the dominant gender norms that legitimate greater male power have a strong influence on even those couples who work to avoid them.

Sexual Frequency. The decision about how often a couple has sex becomes a serious power struggle when partners disagree about how much sex is sufficient (Crain, 1980). Men are stereotyped as being sexually voracious, whereas their female partners are portrayed as less sexually needy. When conflict arises, and one partner wants to have sex once a week and the other wants to have sex more often, both gender and overall power determine what sexual frequency will be established. Clearly, sexual frequency is strongly related to initiation and refusal patterns, but if one partner initiates most frequently and the other refuses equally frequently, who determines the overall rate of sexual activity?

Control over the frequency of sex may go to the partner who desires sex less (Schnarch, 1991). Because he or she wants sex less often, the couple may have sex every time he or she suggests it, although rarely having sex at the more avid partner's suggestion. Thus, lower desire often translates into greater control. Because women are encouraged to be less sexually active than men, control over frequency is one way that women gain the legitimate right to exert control. In some marriages, it may be the only sphere where the wife can accrue real power—and some women use this chit for additional yardage. In a recent focus group organized for a television documentary on male and female roles, the third author heard an unemployed man in his thirties talk about the explicit trades his wife wanted in exchange for sexual access. Because he made no money, he felt he had to barter for sex: "If I carry the groceries, if I am nice, if I do the shopping—when I do the shopping, I *earn* the right to have sex with my wife." (italics added)

Of course, only women with some power have the opportunity to barter in this fashion. A truly powerless wife does not get to refuse (Blumstein & Schwartz, 1983). In completely hierarchical marriages, the husband determines the sexual parameters of his wife's behavior. "I don't use excuses like headaches and things like that. If my husband wants me, I'm his wife, and I do what he wants. It's my responsibility to give it to him when he needs it" (wife, in Rubin, 1976, p. 148).

Some researchers have argued that sexuality in gay male and lesbian couples is an archetype of classic male and female sexuality, and that same-sex couples serve as examples of how men and women would act sexually if they were not constrained by the other gender. Gay males have sex much more often during the early stages of their relationships than any other type of couple, whereas lesbians have genital sex much more infrequently, preferring to have sex under high quality, emotional conditions and substituting cuddling and other kinds of affectional behavior for genital sexuality (Bell & Weinberg, 1978; Blumstein & Schwartz, 1983). Table 11.2 displays a comparison of sexual frequency reported by male and female couples, gay men, and lesbians.

This would appear to suggest that men are more interested in frequent sex than women, whereas women desire less sexual activity and more relational and affectional connection. However compelling this argument may be, it is also true that many homosexuals live in a gay culture with unique sexual norms. Because it is virtually impossible to extricate culture from behavior to determine the "true" sexuality of men and women, the comparison of homosexual to heterosexual couples stops short of being a completely reliable method of teasing apart sexual roles and "natural" sexual proclivities of men and women.

Sexual Positions.   Power is also gained and demonstrated through decisions regarding what types of sex acts (oral, anal, and vaginal) are initiated, allowed, or

TABLE 11.2
Sexual Frequency During the First 2 Years of a Relationship

	Once a Month or Less	Once a Month–Once a Week	1–3 Times/Week	Three Times/Week or More
Married	6%	11%	38%	45%
Gay men	3%	3%	27%	67%
Lesbians	5%	19%	43%	33%

Note. From Blumstein and Schwartz (1983). Reprinted by permission.

vetoed by each partner. The most traditional position for heterosexual activity in our culture is vaginal sex in the "missionary" position (Masters & Johnson, 1966; Victor, 1980). This position gives the man the freedom to determine the pace and movement of the intercourse; the woman has comparatively little flexibility. Blumstein and Schwartz (1983) found that the more equal the power balance in a couple, the less likely they were to have the missionary position be their most frequent sexual position. Women who had more power in their relationships were more able to engage in the decision-making process and were more likely to vary sexual positions, including fewer male dominant positions such as the woman on top or side to side.

Although vaginal sex is part of the sexual repertoire of virtually all heterosexual couples, oral sex occurs less universally (80% of married men in Billy, Tanfer, Grady, & Klepinger's 1993 study reported having received oral sex, and 79% reported having performed oral sex). Oral sex, as much as (if not more than) other sexual positions, has symbolic impact. To some individuals, it is simply erotic behavior that allows one individual to arouse the other, and is viewed as a sexy and generous act. To others, it relegates participants to roles of dominance and submission. Under this conception, most or all of the pleasure involved in the act is experienced by the person on whom the act is performed, with the performer sometimes experiencing physical discomfort or emotional distress. Oral sex can also be seen as perverse, unclean, or humiliating. Thus, if only one partner performs oral sex on the other, it connotes a privilege; reciprocity proclaims equal status as well as equal pleasure. However, there are gender traditions that make it less likely to be reciprocal, even under more or less egalitarian conditions. More women than men are taught that passion is dangerous, that sex may be dishonorable, and that oral sex is disreputable. Such women agree to cunnilingus or fellatio only because they feel they must, and more agree to the former than the latter, because this requires only passive consent (Blumstein & Schwartz, 1983; Hunt, 1974; Kinsey, 1948, 1953). Indeed, a study of prostitutes (Stein, 1974) found that they reported fellatio as their most frequently performed behavior, often because the man said that his wife was unwilling to engage in the act. Lever (1993), in her recent study of Los Angeles street prostitutes and call girls, found that men often paid prostitutes to allow them to perform cunnilingus, indicating that some men eroticize this behavior and do not necessarily impute dominance to the receiver of oral sex (or, if they do, they may find female dominance erotic). Refused by their wives, they nonetheless find the act erotic and seek an opportunity, albeit a paid relationship, to perform oral sex.

Gay and lesbian couples also have issues about oral sex. In gay male couples, the man who performs oral sex most often may end up feeling submissive and "female" if oral sex is not reciprocated (Blumstein & Schwartz, 1983). Some gay male couples resolve this conflict by taking care to share positions equally or by having oral sex at the same time (Harry & DeVall, 1978). Lesbians almost always have oral sex as a main element of their sexual program (Blumstein & Schwartz, 1983). For many it is particularly satisfying because it does not require intromission—and therefore is furthest away from mimicking male–female sex. However, lesbians, like other women, may have ambivalent feelings about oral sex and so there are quite a few couples in which one or both partners refuse to do it. If this is a role playing household there may be no problems—the "butch" takes on the same responsibilities as a male vis à vis sexual orchestration. But if this is a younger, unroled couple, one partner's neglect of sex or sexual reciprocity is likely to become a major relationship problem.

Anal sex is another behavior that has symbolic importance over and above its relationship to physical pleasure. Few heterosexual couples engage in anal sex regularly (Blumstein & Schwartz, 1983), although, according to a *Playboy* sex survey (Petersen, Kretchmer, Nellis, Lever, & Hertz, 1983), half of the men and women surveyed had tried anal sex at least once (with men generally being the most interested). It is notable that only half of this liberal readership had even attempted it; its taboo status may continue because it is associated with homosexuality (and now AIDS) in many people's minds.

Research on gay males shows that sexual preferences about anal sex commonly have little to do with the power structure of the couple (Blumstein & Schwartz, 1983). Nonetheless, if the man on top conveys dominance, the man underneath (the insertee) may feel feminized because he is being entered and is in a female position (Blumstein & Schwartz, 1983). The man on top is more in control because he controls thrust and physical position; this, however, may be mitigated if the man on the bottom is aggressive about giving feedback on how to please him. Nonetheless, if the same partner is always placed on the bottom, it may become conceptualized as control or ascription of less masculine status. "I interpret anal intercourse as being a feminine piece. That doesn't happen between us very much because I don't like it. He doesn't like it either. I've tried, but I have a problem with it because of pain, and I don't like the way he acts when he is on top.... We try not to divide up our sexuality as male–female" (gay male; Blumstein & Schwartz, 1983, p. 242).

Although two-thirds of male couples in one study (Blumstein & Schwartz, 1983) were able to enjoy anal sex (one-third switched positions, while one-third always were a "top" or a "bottom"), approximately one-third avoided it or engaged in it infrequently because of the identity conflicts and power issues it engendered.

Sex Outside the Relationship.   The terms typically used for sex outside of marriage, such as infidelity, cheating, and adultery, are all morally weighted. They demonstrate the general cultural opprobrium for circumventing cultural and religious proscriptions of monogamy. This condemnation, however, is unequal *for* men and women and *by* men and women. Women are both the victims of moral judgments and more likely to be the guardians of the moral status (Glass & Wright, 1992). Blumstein and Schwartz (1983) found that married men felt that monogamy was less important than did married women (75% of husbands said it was important, whereas 84% of wives did) and were also more likely to be nonmonogamous (26% of husbands and 21% of wives had been nonmonogamous during their relationship). In a more recent study, Sprecher and Schwartz (1993) had similar results, finding that women place greater value on "fidelity" and "monogamy" than do men.

Having an affair is a powerful nonnormative act. The ability to have an affair is, to some extent, based on what consequences an individual could or would be willing to absorb. Having an affair is always a high-stakes maneuver because it almost always puts the primary relationship at risk. An affair may be a low risk to a spouse who has an overcommitted partner; it may be a high risk, but high payoff for a partner who hopes to equalize power by asserting sexual independence. The faithful spouse, if he or she finds out about the affair, is left feeling hurt, betrayed, unwanted, or furious, but in any case has lost control, and thus power (Scarf, 1987). Women are generally disadvantaged in this power play because they are usually economically dependent; whatever their emotional exposure, their financial vulnerability discourages nonmonogamy (Blumstein & Schwartz, 1983). If a faithful female spouse disconnects herself from the relationship, she may be out on the street. She is, if she complains, also much more at risk for physical violence, whereas her husband, claiming the rights of male sexual nature—or exercising sheer power—can more usually absorb her anger without physical punishment and may even be able to legitimize his behavior (Lawson, 1988).

Regardless of whether individuals lose or gain power during affairs, the affair is also a manifest communication to the partner that latent messages and feelings have been present. A spouse may be unhappy or bored in his or her relationship, but unable to talk about it. Having an affair, and, often, leaving deliberate clues around for the partner to find, constitutes extremely powerful and effective nonverbal communication (Scarf, 1987). This oblique approach is, of course, not recommended by marriage therapists, but affairs often act as catalysts for events (often separations) that have been long in the making, but have been too difficult to handle directly. The affair forces a crisis and although the crisis may end the relationship, it may also necessitate the long avoided deeper communications and confrontations that could solve relationship problems (Lawson, 1988).

Effects of Resources on Sexual Decision-Making

Although sexuality influences power, it seems the causal order more often goes the other way. The allocation of power within relationships is strongly influenced by factors unrelated to sexuality. For example, a couple's social class has a strong influence on a couple's sexual ideology (Van Fossen, 1977). Lower income, lesser educated couples rely heavily on traditional sexual norms, whereas couples with greater incomes and education feel freer to stray from conventional guidelines and innovate in their sexual behavior (Blumstein & Schwartz, 1983; Rubin, 1976; Van Fossen, 1977). Within couples, the amount of various kinds of resources each partner has relative to the other also affects the distribution of power. Income and physical attractiveness translate into sexual decision-making power in most couples (Blumstein & Schwartz, 1983), because the possession of resources provides an individual with options outside the relationship and because some resources, such as great physical beauty or extreme wealth are hard to replicate if the partner should leave. The partner who is perceived as having better options has more power to make decisions, more power to lead, and more power, in general, to shape the couple's sex life.

Effects of Social Class.   Lower-class couples hold more traditional values about sexuality than middle- or upper-class couples (Kinsey, 1948,53; Van Fossen, 1977; Weinberg & Williams, 1980). Kinsey (1948,53) found that lower-class couples tend to limit their sexual activity to traditional positions, often avoiding activities such as oral sex. Lillian Rubin (1976) quotes a working class wife as "putting up with oral sex": "Even though I hate it [oral sex], if he needs it, then I feel I ought to do it. After all, I'm his wife" (wife; Rubin, 1976, p.139). Whereas a husband said "No, Alice isn't that kind of girl [to have oral sex]. Jesus, you shouldn't ask questions like that. She wasn't brought up to go for all that fancy stuff. You know, all those different ways and that oral stuff. But that's okay with me. There's plenty of women out there to do that kind of stuff with. You can meet them in any bar any time you want to. You don't have to marry that kind" (husband; Rubin, 1976, p.141).

Traditional values about appropriate roles in sex make it less likely for women to be on top, less likely for women to perform or accept oral sex, and generally less likely to have more varied sexual behavior (Blumstein & Schwartz, 1983). More than in other groups, the sex life of lower-class couples is defined by male decision-making (Van Fossen, 1977; Weinberg & Williams, 1980).

Relative Resources Within the Relationship.   Income, prestige, and general external ratification are very important in determining a couple's sex life. If a partner does well, or is perceived to do well, outside the relationship, that partner gains leverage within the relationship, particularly if his or her partner is deemed *unlikely* to prosper outside the relationship. The major issue here revolves around dependence (or lack thereof) on a relationship. If a person has attractive outside options and is aware of this, he or she is less dependent on the current relationship. Thus, what we discuss in this section might appropriately be termed the balance of dependency.

Dependence is, of course, not an accident of traditional marriage. At an extreme end of the world-wide continuum, women are put into sexual and social isolation (purdah), veiled, and deprived of independent income. Sexual control is seen as part of the appropriate subordination of women—even to the point in much of sub-Saharan Africa of requiring genital mutilation (removal of the clitoris and labia) as a part of the ordinary woman's fate. In our own country, we have few such extreme violations of women's physical and sexual freedom; but economic dependency does serve to modify what married women will risk in their relationships. High earning single women or cohabiting women who have less economic dependence might be expected to be more sexually free, and they are (Blumstein & Schwartz, 1983). Again, however, they must be cautious not to go too far beyond the boundaries created by cultural norms, or their relationships are likely to suffer (Apt & Hurlbert, 1992).

A woman who is particularly dependent on her husband's income because she does not have a job or has many children is likely to feel that she has to go along with all of her husband's decisions about sex (even if he decides to have an extramarital affair) because she would have difficulty functioning if he left her. But she may have other chits to play to gain some independence and power. Physical attractiveness, for example, is a potential asset. Beauty, however, is a less manifest quality than wealth, and for it to be a powerful resource, an individual must recognize his or her beauty, realize its worth on the open market, and parlay this knowledge into relationship clout. Thus, although the possession of such a resource contributes to the *actual* likelihood of an individual prospering outside a relationship, what is more important is the *perception* of both partners in terms of the likelihood of that potential being acted upon (Blumstein & Schwartz, 1983). Thus, a wife may be highly attractive, but if neither she nor her husband feels that she has options outside the relationship, her physical attractiveness does not gain her any power within the relationship.

Perhaps the most subtle, but most powerful, form of dependency is love. The ability to love is a resource, but the ability *not to love very much* may be a more potent resource in an ongoing relationship. According to Willard Waller's (1938) principle of less interest, the partner who loves the other less has greater power because the partner who loves more would also be hurt more if the relationship broke up and is therefore forced to work harder to maintain the relationship. Thus, the more emotionally dependent partner is also the less powerful partner. Safilios-Rothschild (1976), in a study of Greek couples, demonstrated that the partner who loves less is able to manipulate affection and sex to obtain relationship power. This critical (and hard to measure) aspect of the balance of power in a couple's relationship has to be factored in when evaluating the impact of other, more tangible resources.

MONEY, SEX, AND POWER IN INTERACTION

A woman's employment and the degree of her success affect more than the couple's economic life. The dynamics of money and sex show how women who upset the traditional balance of power in one area of a relationship experience ramifications in other areas. If men correlate superior earning power with self-esteem and masculinity (and most do) they may lose sexual desire for women who earn more than they do (Blumstein & Schwartz, 1983; Millman, 1991). Traditional men often find a powerful woman less sexy because they eroticize their own power, not a partner's. They may try and retake the senior position. As basic exchange theory proposes, a person who feels that the relationship is unbalanced can withdraw benefits, try to exact costs, or leave. In terms of sexual game-playing, this opens up the possibility of infrequent male initiation, sexual violence, having an affair, or breaking up. Nonsexual ploys of all sorts can also be exacted. Women who earn more than their husbands either put up with less (because they can) and try to create a sexuality of equals, or cave in to traditional expectations and try to protect male feelings of superiority.

The Impact on Satisfaction

Given the impact of cultural values and male marketplace advantages, is it possible to conceptualize relationships where money and sex do not operate, at least to some extent, in the traditional gendered ways? For example, are lesbians and gay men or egalitarian heterosexual couples able to avoid traditional gender roles and therefore power inequities over money and sex? Or are the issues of money and sex so closely connected to a person's gender identity that they can neither be extricated from the constraints of gender nor from their symbolic identification with power? Examining which arrangements seem to create the most satisfaction for different types of couples provides some answers.

Money and Satisfaction

Keeping resources and power in balance promotes straightforward negotiation, allows role innovation, and, the literature indicates, reduces conflict and increases both sexual and relationship satisfaction (Aida & Falbo, 1991; Lind & Tyler, 1988; Pahl, 1989; Sprecher & Schwartz, 1993). Equality in spending decisions correlates with relationship stability among cohabitors and lesbians (Blumstein & Schwartz, 1983). But even equality has complicated consequences.

When wives have the economic resources to leave a marriage, they are more likely to do so: Equality or financial independence not only makes breaking up easier, but keeping incomes separate can mean a real or imagined lack of trust in each other or in the continuity of the relationship that actually undermines the stability of the partnership (Treas, 1991). Thus an increase in women's power can be destabilizing to a relationship. More powerful women can afford higher expectations, and they may be less committed to marriage at any cost. And even though a woman may enjoy a rise in relationship power, her changing status may threaten her own satisfaction. If she desires to have an ambitious partner, and research indicates women do, she may find her partner lacking if her own success makes him seem less of a success by comparison. Both husbands and male cohabitors who are less ambitious tend to have more short-lived relationships (Blumstein & Schwartz, 1983).

Of course, the greater source of instability and dissatisfaction in these circumstances may arguably derive from the male partner's discomfort: Cohabiting men have more conflicts with higher earning women, and husbands whose wives are more ambitious are likely to have less stable relationships (Blumstein & Schwartz, 1983). Just how sensitive men are about maintaining at least financial equality if not superiority is illustrated by the fact that, like heterosexual women, a gay man also tends to disguise his greater success relative to his partner (Blumstein & Schwartz, 1983). So it is more than just a man's provider status that is at stake, for many heterosexual men increasingly welcome the economic contributions of their partners, and the provider role is largely irrelevant to gay couples. It seems that income is so integrated in a man's deeper sense of worth that a man's partner must demonstrate sensitivity to preserve relationship satisfaction.

Women seem more ready than men to relinquish power in the interest of their partner's satisfaction. They especially tend to give up power and autonomy as an expression of their sense of commitment; harmony in the relationship may be more important to women than power in the long run. Consequently, a woman's empathy and nurturing skills can actually sabotage her own needs for autonomy and power in her relationships.

Lesbians believe that the power money exerts on relationships has undermined heterosexual relationships and they are generally committed to preventing it from dominating their lives or determining their satisfaction (Blumstein & Schwartz, 1983). Their experience of inequality as women in a male-dominated world makes fairness and autonomy important to them. This actually causes a catch-22 in some lesbian relationships, because although lesbians do not want money to affect their relationship, they are especially susceptible to the effects of money, as even small imbalances create feelings of dominance and subordination. Either leads to dissatisfaction with the relationship. This may help explain why lesbian couples have been found to have a slightly higher breakup rate than other types of couples (Blumstein & Schwartz, 1983). Thus, even when gender differences do not stack the deck in favor of one partner, the goal of true equality has its own costs and satisfaction is not inevitable.

Sex and Satisfaction

Sex and relationship satisfaction have consistently shown a positive correlation. Mutual and shared initiation correlate with satisfaction in both hetero- and homosexual couples (Blumstein & Schwartz, 1983). Role reversal, however, does not. Therefore, if "liberated" or cohabiting women become assertive in their sexual desires, relationship satisfaction is likely to decrease (Apt & Hurlbert, 1992; Blumstein & Schwartz, 1983).

Nonmonogamy is also correlated with lower relationship satisfaction. Either as an equalizer of power, or as a show of power, it rarely serves in the interests of either the stability or satisfaction of the relationship. When women, either heterosexual or lesbian, are nonmonogamous, it is likely that they are dissatisfied with their relationships or have already made a new emotional commitment. For this reason, nonmonogamous wives and lesbians at any stage of their relationships are more likely to leave their partners than are monogamous wives and lesbians (Blumstein & Schwartz, 1983). Thus, as with monetary success, women more than men are limited in their use of sexual power and freedom by their emotional commitment to a relationship.

CONCLUSION

The long-term social and labor-force trends that have undermined traditional marital ideologies are likely to continue. With the increasing necessity for both partners to work and less of a glass ceiling to limit women's career aspirations, dual-career couples should become more common, both in marriage and as part of a general increase in cohabiting couples. These trends imply two opposing effects: (a) as women increase their options outside the relationship, there is every reason to expect continued instability and unpredictability of lifetime marriage, and (b) as men and women live more similar lives with more similar economic and sexual rules and values, relationship satisfaction will be enhanced.

Nevertheless, power hierarchies are still unlikely to disappear, even net of gender differences. Changing gendered behavior is a difficult challenge. Even though husbands seem more ready than ever to yield some of their decision-making power, and wives seem to want more equality, past ideology, expectations, and socialization resist radical change. Women and men must relearn or unlearn habits while dealing with the ambivalent or confused reactions of society. They often revert to traditionally gendered solutions to problems even when the ground rules and circumstances have changed. Because the expectations of traditional gender roles and identities are fulfilled and reinforced symbolically through the powerful rituals of sex, changing preferences around sexual frequency, initiation, and repertoire may be especially difficult. Likewise, although a man's work still brings home the bigger paycheck and the provider role still exists, it will be hard for men and women to mitigate the power and functions of money in relationships. This state of affairs discourages either husband or wife from giving the wife's employment as much respect as it needs to change the internal organization of the relationship and household. These conflicts over work have serious consequences: Married couples who disagree about the value and place of the wife's employment during the early years of their relationship are more likely to divorce (Blumstein & Schwartz, 1983).

Men also continue to believe that they have a right to their traditional relationship privileges, if not for traditional reasons then as compensation for their greater economic contributions. Even cohabiting men who are more egalitarian often want equal financial partners who will still provide the other relationship benefits that men have come to expect from women, that is, that they be nurturing and sexually available. Thus the transition toward equality is a mixed picture. There is certainly more of a search for equity and equality than ever before, and increasing economic and sexual parity between men and women will make that ever more likely. But social forces such as sluggish opportunities for economic mobility and modest cultural acceptance of egalitarian heterosexual relationships makes change slow, perhaps no longer at a glacial pace—but less quickly than might be predicted given the rapid entry of women into the work force. Equality remains elusive for heterosexual couples.

REFERENCES

Aida, Y., & Falbo, T. (1991). Relationships between marital satisfaction, resources, and power strategies. *Sex Roles, 24*, 43–56.

Apt, C., & Hurlbert, D. F. (1992). The female sensation seeker and marital sexuality. *Journal of Sex and Marital Therapy, 18*(4), 315–323.

Beckett, J. O., & Smith, A. D. (1981). Work and family roles: Egalitarian marriage in black and white families. *Social Service Review, 55*, 314–326.

Bell, A. P., & Weinberg, M. S. (1978). *Homosexualities: A study of diversity among men and women.* New York: Simon and Schuster.

Billy, J. O., Tanfer, K., Grady, W. R., & Klepinger, D. H. (1993). The sexual behavior of men in the United States. *Family Planning Perspectives, 25*(2), 52–60.

Blumstein, P., & Schwartz, P. (1983). *American couples.* New York: William Morrow.

Blumstein, P., & Schwartz, P. (1991). Money and ideology: Their impact on power and the division of household labor. In R. L. Blumberg (Ed.), *Gender, family, and economy: The triple overlap* (pp. 261–288). Newbury Park, CA: Sage.

Burgoyne, C. B. (1990). Money in marriage: How patterns of allocation both reflect and conceal power. *Sociological Review, 38*(4), 634–665.

Byers, E. S., & Heinlein, L. (1989). Predicting initiations and refusals of sexual activities in married and cohabiting heterosexual couples. *Journal of Sex Research, 26*(2), 210–231.

Chafetz, J. S. (1991). The gender division of labor and the reproduction of female disadvantage: Toward an integrated theory. In R. L. Blumberg (Ed.), *Gender, family, and economy: The triple overlap* (pp. 74–94). Newbury Park, CA: Sage.

Clunis, D. M., & Green, G. D. (1988). *Lesbian couples.* Seattle, WA: Seal Press.

Crain, S. (1980). A model of roles and attributions in sexual interactions. *Dissertation Abstracts International, 41*, 684B.

DeLamater, J. (1987). Gender differences in sexual scenarios. In K. Kelley (Ed.), *Females, males, and sexuality* (pp. 127–140). Albany: SUNY Press.

D'Emilio, J., & Freedman, E. B. (1988). *Intimate matters: A history of sexuality in America.* New York: Harper and Row.

England, P., & Farkas, G. (1986). *Households, employment, and gender: A social, economic, and demographic view.* New York: Aldine de Gruyter.

Felton-Collins, V. (1990). *Couples and money.* New York: Bantam Books.

Glass, S. P., & Wright, T. L. (1992). Justifications for extramarital relationships: The association between attitudes, behaviors, and gender. *Journal of Sex Research, 29*(3), 361–387.

Green, R. T., & Cunningham, I. C. (1975). Feminine role perception and family purchasing decisions. *Journal of Marketing Research, 13*, 325–332.

Hammond, J., & Enoch, J. R. (1976). Conjugal power relations among black working class families. *Journal of Black Studies, 7* 107–127.

Harry, J., & DeVall, W. B. (1978). *The social organization of gay males.* New York: Praeger.

Hertz, R. (1986). *More equal than others: Women and men in dual-career marriages.* Los Angeles: University of California Press.

Howard, J. A., Blumstein, P., & Schwartz, P. (1986). Sex, power, and influence tactics in intimate relationships. *Journal of Personality and Social Psychology, 51*, 102–109.

Hunt, M. (1974). *Sexual behavior in the 1970's.* New York: Dell Publishing Co., Inc.

Kandel, D. G., & Lesser, G. S. (1972). Marital decision-making in American and Danish urban families: A research note. *Journal of Marriage and the Family, 34*, 134–138.

Katz, R., & Perez, Y. (1985). Is resource theory equally applicable to wives and husbands? *Journal of Comparative Family Studies, 16*(1), 1–10.

Kingsbury, N. M., & Scanzoni, J. (1989). Process power and decision outcomes among dual-career couples. *Journal of Comparative Family Studies, 20*, 231–246.

Kinsey, A., Pomeroy, W. B., & Martin, C. E. (1948). *Sexual behavior in the human male.* Philadelphia: W.B. Saunders Company.

Kinsey, A., Pomeroy, W. B., Martin, C. E., & Gebhard, P. H. (1953). *Sexual behavior in the human female.* Philadelphia: W.B. Saunders Company.

Lawson, A. (1988). *Adultery: An analysis of love and betrayal.* New York: Basic Books, Inc.

Lever, J. (1993, July). *Prostitutes and the production of intimacy*. Paper presented at the International Academy of Sexual Research, Asilomar, CA.

Lind, E. A., & Tyler, T. (1988). *The social psychology of procedural justice*. New York: Plenum.

Masters, W. H., & Johnson, V. E. (1966). *Human sexual response*. Boston: Little, Brown.

McCrae, S. (1987). The allocation of money in cross-class families. *Sociological Review, 35*, 97–122.

McDonald, C. W. (1980). Family power: The assessment of a decade of theory and research, 1970–1979. *Journal of Marriage and the Family, 42*, 841–854.

McWhirter, D. P., & Mattison, A. M. (1984). *The male couple: How relationships develop*. Englewood Cliffs, NJ: Prentice-Hall, Inc.

Millman, M. (1991). *Warm hearts and cold cash*. New York: The Free Press.

Pahl, J. (1983). The allocation of money and the structuring of inequality within marriage. *Sociological Review, 31*(2), 237–262.

Pahl, J. (1989). *Money and marriage*. New York: St. Martin's Press.

Peplau, L. A. (1981). What homosexuals want in relationships. *Psychology Today, 15*(3), 28–37.

Petersen, J. R., Kretchmer, A., Nellis, B., Lever, J., & Hertz, R. (1983, January). The *Playboy* readers sex survey: Part one. *Playboy*, pp. 108–150.

Rank, M. R. (1982). Determinants of conjugal influence in wives' employment decision-making. *Journal of Marriage and the Family, 44*, 591–604.

Rosenzweig, J. M., & Lebow, W. C. (1992). Femme on the streets, butch in the streets?: Lesbian sex roles, dyadic adjustment, and sexual satisfaction. *Journal of Homosexuality, 23*(3), 1–20.

Rubin, L. B. (1976). *Worlds of pain*. New York: Basic Books, Inc.

Safilios-Rothschild, C. (1976). A macro and micro–examination of family power and love. *Journal of Marriage and the Family, 38*, 355–362.

Scarf, M. (1987). *Intimate partners: Patterns in love and marriage*. New York: Random House.

Schnarch, D. M. (1991). *Constructing the sexual crucible*. New York: W.W. Norton & Company.

Spade, J. Z. (1989). Bringing home the bacon: A sex-integrated approach to the impact of work on the family. In B. Risman & P. Schwartz (Eds.), *Gender in intimate relationships* (pp. 184–192). Belmont, CA: Wadsworth Publishing Company.

Sprecher, S., & Schwartz, P. (1993). Are "her" and "his" similar contributions valued equally? Manuscript submitted for publication.

Stein, M. (1974). *Friends, lovers, slaves*. New York: Berkeley Medallion Books.

Taylor, R. J., Chatters, L. M., Tucker, M. B., & Lewis, E. (1990). Developments in research on black families: A decade review. *Journal of Marriage and the Family, 52*, 993–1014.

Treas, J. (1991). The common pot or separate purses? A transaction cost interpretation. In R. L. Blumberg (Ed.), *Gender, family, and economy: The triple overlap* (pp. 211–224). Newbury Park, CA: Sage.

Treas, J. (1993). Transaction costs and the economic organization of marriage. *American Sociological Review, 58*, 723–734.

Van Fossen, B. E. (1977). Sexual stratification and sex–role socialization. *Journal of Marriage and the Family, 39*(3), 563–574.

Victor, J. S. (1980). *Human sexuality: A social-psychological approach*. Englewood Cliffs, NJ: Prentice-Hall, Inc.

Waller, W. (1938). *The family: A dramatic interpretation*. New York: Dryden.

Weinberg, M. S., & Williams, C. J. (1980). Sexual embourgeoisment? Social class and sexual activity: 1938–1970. *American Sociological Review, 45*(1), 33–48.

Ybarra, L. (1982). When wives work: The impact on the Chicano family. *Journal of Marriage and the Family, 44*, 169–178.

Zelizer, V. (1989). The social meaning of money: Special monies. *American Journal of Sociology, 95*, 342–377.

Zellman, G. L., & Goodchilds, J. D. (1983). Becoming sexual in adolescence. In E. R. Allgeier & N. B. McCormick (Eds.), *Changing boundaries: Gender roles and sexual behavior* (pp. 49–63). Palo Alto, CA: Mayfield Publishing Co.

Part IV

Women and Men in Society

Chapter 12

Television Promotion of Gender Equality in Societies

Everett M. Rogers
University of New Mexico

Thomas M. Hirata
University of Southern California

Ankila S. Chandran
University of Southern California

Jeffery D. Robinson
University of California, Los Angeles

Prosocial television programming is gaining popularity as an effective means of promoting increased gender equality in societies such as the United States and India. Television is an ideal medium for mass dissemination of pro-social messages because (a) television is widely available[1]; (b) television conveys more complex audio and visual information than radio, and requires minimal prior knowledge or education, compared to radio or print; and (c) television is able to sustain viewer interest and deliver information over extended periods of time.

India and the United States are presented here as examples of different societies in which various television strategies have been employed to promote increased gender equality. First, an overview of the research perspectives on media and

---

[1]Almost universally in developed, highly industrialized societies, while many less developed societies are rapidly expanding the reach of their broadcasting systems as television sets become increasingly accessible and affordable.

gender equality are presented. Second, the next section describes an analytical framework for the study of media campaigns. Third, two studies are presented to illustrate previous efforts in the promotion of gender equality. Fourth, the media systems in India and the United States are compared and contrasted. Fifth, several lessons learned from previous media campaigns are discussed.

Increased gender equality is an essential goal in both developed and less developed countries. Large-scale, organized feminism has been diffused from Europe and North America to other parts of the world, so that increased gender equality is now accepted as a prosocial value by many societies. However, structural inequalities persist in most industrialized societies, and less developed countries have more isolated, rural populations that are less exposed to gender equality campaigns. Changing individuals' value structures and societal belief systems is no easy task. Sex discrimination has been entrenched in the values of many societies for thousands of years. However, belief systems can be altered so as to raise consciousness about gender equality through prosocial communication messages.

India and the United States differ in the role played by television in society (Table 12.1). United States television programming is intended to attract large audiences to a commercially sponsored system with relatively little direct governmental control over the content or goals of the television programs. India, like many other less industrialized countries, originally introduced television for development purposes. In India, television broadcasting systems are government owned and operated and there is only one national channel. The government emphasizes prosocial goals and has veto power over any commercially produced television series. The promotion of gender equality is thus effected quite differently in India and in the United States.

TABLE 12.1
Characteristics and Roles of U.S. and Indian Television Systems

	United States	*India*
1. Ownership	Private	Government
2. Goals of television system	Attract large audiences for commercial sponsors	Originally for development; increasingly to attract commercial sponsors
3. Number of channels	4 Networks 3–10 Local	1 National Channel 1–2 Local (only in 5 large cities)
4. Television audience	>98% of all households	50% of population; coverage highest in urban centers
5. Cable television	20–100 channels 70% of all households	3–10 channels 10% of TV-owning households
6. Uses of entertainment-education	Hollywood lobbyists encourage educational themes in television programs	Government encourages prosocial serials dealing with family planning and gender equality
7. Implementation of entertainment-education	Hollywood lobbyists incorporate messages into existing programs	Specific programs created to convey educational messages

HISTORICAL OVERVIEW OF GENDER EQUALITY PROMOTION

Popular media texts have provided the basis for feminist criticisms of the myriad ways in which such texts perpetuate patriarchy in their representation of women and repeatedly oppress women along the lines of race, class, gender and sexual orientation (Faludi, 1991; Mulvey, 1975; Wolf, 1990). Such criticisms in the 1970s initially focused on stereotypical images and portrayals of women (Steenland, 1989; United States Commission on Civil Rights, 1977) and later included the debate over pornography and women's subordination. Attention was also drawn by scholars to discrimination against women in conversational contexts and in television programming (Rakow, 1986) and subsequently it was acknowledged that locating decision-making power (i.e., as producers, directors, and writers) with women and minorities is the principal remedy to such portrayals (Steenland, 1989; Wilson & Gutiérrez, 1985). In the 1980s and 1990s, emphasis increasingly centered on questions concerning interpretation and reception. Researchers realized that the role of the audience must be evaluated in terms of different ethnic, racial, national, and cultural variables. In this period, feminist theorists introduced the concept of oppositional readings of patriarchal texts by interpretive communities of feminist critics and ordinary readers (Ang, 1985; Radway 1984). Radway's (1984) seminal study of female readers of gothic romance novels proposed that ordinary readers used romance novels in ways that helped them escape patriarchal oppression in their daily lives. This trend in feminist scholarship assumes that although the commodification of popular culture provides users pleasure, it also contains within it a subversive potential that can be used to construct an oppositional politics (Ganguly, 1992).

Feminist perspectives on communication and development in First and Third World contexts has also recently sought to correct the habitual use of a predominantly White and European normative referent to evaluate women's situations around the world, and urges more self-reflectivity on the part of scholars in their use of a certain epistemological standpoint (Johnson-Odim, 1991; Mohanty, 1991a, 1991b). So-called post-colonial critiques of representation have also sought to expose the parallels and discontinuities between colonized peoples and women in patriarchy, such as the objectification of the oriental woman/other in Western popular culture (Ganguly, 1992; Said, 1979). Cultural imperialism perspectives (e.g., Salinas & Paldán, 1979; Salwen, 1991) argue that media promotion of social change is illusory, because powerful corporate interests will not allow their positions to be undermined by social transformation. The export of cultural forms, especially television programming, promotes dependence on Western technologies, reinforces the national and international dominance of capital interests, and encourages consumerism and market economics (Lee, 1980). Some cultural imperialism theorists are skeptical of efforts by Western agents to use television for prosocial aims, and of First World goals for Third World development. These theorists argue that corporate intervention in prosocial efforts co-opts middle-class interests and further marginalizes the large lower classes of Third World states (Salinas & Paldán, 1979).

ANALYSIS AND INTERPRETATION OF
TELEVISION PROGRAMS

There are three distinct elements of television programming that are essential to television promotion of any prosocial value: (a) intentions of programs creators, (b) execution of the program (or product) itself, and (c) interpretation of the program (or textual readings). These elements of the television process can be viewed as roughly analogous to the source–channel–message–receiver metaphor (Shannon & Weaver, 1949). A different tradition more recently proposed an encoding/decoding model (Hall, 1980) in which program creators translate (encode) ideas and messages into a cultural code (the program) that is transmitted to, and interpreted (decoded) by, viewers. Creators and viewers each have particular frameworks of knowledge that influence their encoding and decoding of messages. Some components of these frameworks of knowledge include culture, language, experience, and education.

Intent is expressed in the goals of the producers and creators and what they decide to put into the program. In many cases, producers seek only to create entertaining programs, and have few intentions beyond that. In other cases, producers, writers, and directors may deliberately treat topical issues such as discrimination, abortion, or family conflicts. It is entirely possible that writers, producers, directors, and others may have a conflict over the purpose or intent of a program, and have varying degrees of control over the product.

The *execution* is represented by the actual program that is produced and aired. Camera angles, editing, costumes, props, actors' performances, and dialogue are some of the elements that comprise the program. Thus, the program, or the text, is *what is produced*, or the product of the television production process, that will, to a greater or lesser extent, resemble what the creators *intended*.

The *text* is a concept that media theorists have more recently borrowed from literary theory and semeiotics. Fiske (1987) viewed a text as distinct from a program itself, in that a program is an artifact, whereas a text is read by a person. Fiske (1987) distinguished between television programs—the symbolic audio–visual artifacts of the production process—and texts, which are created when programs are interpreted, or read, by audience members. Texts are the products of their readers, such that a television program becomes a text at the moment of reading, that is, when its interaction with one of its many audiences activates some of the meanings/pleasures that it is capable of provoking (Fiske 1987).

The producers' goals or intentions do not necessarily determine the effects on television audiences. The case of "All in the Family," a situation comedy intended to reduce prejudice, is well known. Vidmar and Rokeach (1974) found that highly prejudiced viewers of the prosocial program interpreted the Archie Bunker character's bigoted actions as favorable, justified, and representative of their own views.

The *interpretation* by viewers varies according to who is reading the text. All texts are *polysemous* (Fiske, 1987; Livingstone, 1990) such that a particular program has numerous possible meanings, or *textual readings*. The readers' frameworks of knowledge influence the reading, or readings, that a reader will ascribe to the text. Selective influence theories of mass media effects (cf. DeFleur & Ball-Rokeach, 1989) show that viewers differ in their (a) attention to programs, (b) perception of messages, (c) recall of content, and (d) action in response to texts. Reception theory (cf. Livingstone, 1990) argues that viewers of television actively construct meanings from television texts based in part on their own knowledge, experiences, cultures, and their perceptions of social reality. Viewers differ in their levels of involvement with the text and also in their levels of acceptance or rejection of the various meanings they interpret or decode from the text. Meanings are constructed in social environments, particularly when television viewing is a group activity.

Each of these elements of television programming requires a different analytical approach in order to examine its relationship to the creation, dissemination, and reception of meaning. Message creation necessarily focuses on the writers, producers, and directors of a program, and on the decisions and intentions with which they approach the program production. Critical perspectives often address these analytical elements, but some critical theories are limited because they ascribe—rather than examine—motivations of creators and can underestimate the capacities of different audiences to construct meanings that may not conform to the intentions of the producers of the text.

Analysis of texts themselves (the execution) is even less objective and centers around the program, its aesthetic elements, symbols, actions, and particular meanings that could be ascribed to these elements. Traditional content analysis methods treat specific central messages of programs, and thus ignore the multiplicity of ways in which people interpret the texts, as well as many complexities in the texts themselves (Hall, 1980). Traditional content analysis overlooks oppositional and other less predictable readings of the text.

Analysis of text reception (interpretation) can be conducted through the use of interviews, surveys, or focus groups, particularly those that record viewers' responses and interpretations to viewing of programs. Focus groups are particularly useful in providing an environment in which viewers can socially negotiate meanings in the text (Liebes & Katz, 1989).

SUCCESS OF THE STRATEGIES TO PROMOTE GENDER EQUALITY

Two case studies are presented demonstrating how gender equality can be promoted through television. The first study, conducted in the United States, focuses on television program content. The United States study analyzes how women and men are portrayed on family-oriented situation comedies, and approaches the question of the television promotion of gender equality from a message perspective. The second study is a field survey conducted in India that focuses on audience perceptions of program content. The India study analyzes the extent to which audiences identify with the portrayal of women and men on prosocial Indian soap operas. The study approaches the question of television portrayal of gender equality from an audience effects perspective.

The United States Study

With 21.6 million weekly viewers in 1990, "Roseanne" edged out the popular family-oriented situation comedy "Cosby" with 21.5 million viewers (Monush, 1991). Americans today are quite interested in families in general, because an average of 15.6 millions viewers weekly watch shows such as "Cosby," "Family Matters," "Full House," "Growing Pains," "Major Dad," "Married with Children," "Roseanne," "The Simpsons," "Who's the Boss," and, "The Wonder Years" (Monush, 1991). Theories of mass media effects (Bandura, 1971, 1986; Gerbner, Gross, Morgan & Signorielli, 1980, 1986) suggest that extensive television viewing can affect viewers' beliefs concerning normative, appropriate, and expected behaviors for males and females (Beuf, 1974; Frueh & McGhee, 1975; McGhee & Frueh, 1980; Ross, Anderson, & Wisocki, 1982). With the continued popularity and abundance of prime-time families, television has the capacity to promote the status of women in society, at least by portraying males and females as equal in power, status, and decision-making capabilities.

This study of United States television focused on the presentation of social influence, or power, in the television family. A content analysis of power distribution among males and females in 60 half-hour episodes of family shows was conducted in order to explore five issues: (a) Are females portrayed as pursuing influence goals differently from males? (b) What power tactics are used by males and females in order to achieve various persuasion goals? (c) Are males or females portrayed as more persistent in attempting to influence others? (d) Are males or females more effective in influencing others? (e) Are "traditionally masculine" tactics more effective, as compared to "traditionally feminine" tactics?

The Gender-Based Credibility Gap.   Traditionally, American television has not portrayed women as either credible or powerful in previous decades (perhaps reflecting, as well as shaping beliefs about social life in the 1950s to 1980s). Johnson (1976, 1978) argued that the use of influence tactics in everyday life can be strongly affected by sex-role stereotypes—women, she argued, traditionally have less access to concrete resources (limiting their use of reward and coercive bases of power) and have less access to resources that facilitate building an impression of competence. According to Johnson, females can be expected to use more indirect, personal, and helpless modes of influence, such as the use of personal rewards and appeals to love and affection, whereas males can be expected to use coercion, expert information and legitimate modes of influence. These stereotypical expectations have continued to persist. Females are expected to employ tactics associated with exchange, evasiveness, indirectness, approval seeking, insufficiency, identification, and helplessness, whereas males are expected to employ tactics associated with coercion, confidence, command, and competence (Burgoon, Dillard, & Doran, 1983; Gruber & White, 1986). Television portrayals of social influence tactics have tended to embody the stereotypical view of males as dominant and females as passive. Reflecting on three seasons of television in the late 1970s, Greenberg, Richards, and Henderson (1980) found that in both authority and peer relationships, males gave and received more orders, and received more compliance for those orders, than did females.

Research indicates that the differential use of both amount and type of social influence strategies among individuals is due to perceived differences in social power and tactic efficacy between individuals, and not because of innate individual differences such as gender, sexual orientation, and so on (Falbo, 1982; Falbo & Peplau, 1980; Gruber & White, 1986). Falbo and Peplau (1980, p. 627), for instance, argued that "because men expect compliance to their influence attempts, they use bilateral and direct strategies. Conversely, because women anticipate noncompliance, they are more likely than men to report the use of unilateral strategies." Gruber and White (1986) noted that females used feminine-typed tactics as often as males, and males used masculine-typed tactics as often as females. These authors also reported that males used more power strategies overall, reflecting, "a tendency to feel freer to resort to more influence attempts and to use any effective strategy, masculine or feminine to get their way" (Gruber & White, 1986, p. 17). Enactment of stereotypic power strategies like these by male and female television characters may reinforce differential conceptions of power, encouraging viewers to believe that males and females deserve naturally distinct and unequal statuses within families.

Television portrayals of social influence strategies used by men and women reinforce stereotypical views of dominant males and passive females. A survey of three television seasons looked at order-giving in authority (superior to subordinate)(Greenberg, Richards, & Henderson, 1980). This study found that males gave and received more orders of both types and received more compliance to these orders than did females. Comstock and Strzyzewski (1990) found that females were involved more often, and for longer periods of time, in patterns of family conflict (integrative, distributive, and avoidance). Marital conflicts initiated by wives were portrayed as antisocial, whereas husband-initiated conflicts were portrayed as prosocial.

Few studies have examined effectiveness or persistence (i.e., use of multiple tactics). Credible, competent persuaders should be effective on their first attempt. However, individuals are also portrayed as credible and competent when they are able to resist persuasion attempts effectively. Individuals may be perceived to be weaker or as less credible when (a) they are less effective persuaders requiring more persuasion attempts; (b) they must use multiple persuasion tactics; or (c) they are the targets of multiple persuasion attempts (i.e., targets are not taken seriously when they say "no").

Gender and Goals.   Females are portrayed as having different influence goals than men. Females pursue goals associated with promoting communal and relational goals that maintain egalitarian relationships and that monitor the rights, roles, and obligations of relational partners. In contrast, males pursue more self-interest goals such as competing with others for resources in achieving personal goals (cf. Cody, Canary, & Smith, 1994; Smith, Cody, LoVette, & Canary, 1990). Cody et al. found that females were (a) more supportive and concerned about others; (b) more likely to engage in volunteer work and pursue goals considered *altruistic*, relative to males; and (c) more *dependent* on others than males. Females are more likely to ask for assistance and to ask permission from people in authority (Cody et al., 1994; Smith et al., 1990). A considerable amount of research on "social participation" indicates that females are engaged more often in "status neutralizing" activities, whereas males are engaged more often in "status assertive" activities (Canary, Cody, & Marston, 1986; Cody et al., 1994; Reis, Wheeler, Spiegel, Kernis, Nezlek, & Perri, 1982; Smith et al., 1990). That is, females generally pursue goals that are associated more with the promotion and maintenance of egalitarian relationships where the rights, roles, and obligations of relational partners are monitored, whereas males pursue goals that are associated more with self-interest, such as competing with others for resources and achieving personal goals. Clearly, television portrayals can either reinforce such sex biases, or show their breakdown: Females could be portrayed as equally involved as males in self-interest goals and in their dependence on others, whereas males could be portrayed as equally involved as females in communal goals, and in pursuing altruistic goals.

Method.   The United States study content-analyzed 60 half-hour episodes of the 10 most popular prime-time, family-oriented situation comedies, recorded from July 1, 1990 to November 15, 1990: "The Cosby Show," "Family Matters," "Full House," "Growing Pains," "Major Dad," "Married with Children," "Roseanne," "The Simpson's," "Who's the Boss," and, "The Wonder Years." The study began with a pool of 200 half-hour episodes, out of which 6 were randomly selected from each program, resulting in 60 half-hour episodes. A total of 815 compliance-gaining interactions were analyzed, in which persuader's age (1–20 (child)/over 20 (adult)) and gender (male/female), target's age and gender, and persuader's goal, tactic, and effectiveness (goal explicitly achieved/goal not achieved) were coded. Individual goals and tactics were adapted from Rule, Bisanz, and Kohn (1985) and Cody et al. (1994).

Results and Discussion.   Studies of this type normally focus only on characteristics of persuaders. This study contains information about *both* persuader and target in each compliance-gaining instance. The data indicate that differences in influence behavior were not portrayed as a function of persuader characteristics. Instead, differences in goals, tactics, persistence, and effectiveness were observed almost exclusively as a result of *target* features. In other words, males and females generally did not produce gender-typical messages; rather, persuasive messages were designed differently for appealing to male versus female listeners, regardless of the persuader's gender. In addition, several observed patterns, both overall and age-group specific, suggest general textual messages about normative social influence behavior.

RQ₁: Are females portrayed as pursuing influence goals differently than males?

Table 12.2 shows the relative proportions in which males and females pursued and encountered various goals as persuaders and targets, respectively. Adult male and female persuaders differed in their pursuit of goals. *Dependent goals* were more likely to be shown as pursued by men than by women, whereas *general self-interest goals* were more likely to be favored by women than by men; these patterns may suggest a new trend of portraying males to lose power in relation to females as they transit from children to adulthood. Gender differences were not found for pursuit of *mutual benefit* or *altruistic goals*. Differences by *target* gender were significant both for younger and adult targets. *Dependent goals* were more likely to be directed toward younger female targets than toward adult *females*.

RQ₂: What power tactics are used by males and females in order to achieve various persuasion goals?

Tactic choice did not vary by the persuader's gender during the first, second, or third attempt. *Target gender* did affect persuaders' tactic choice. During first tactic attempts, persuaders were more likely to use *direct tactics* with male targets than with female targets. During second attempts, persuaders were more likely to use *negative tactics* with male targets than with female targets. In sum, male targets showed a greater tendency than female targets to elicit directness and negativity from persuaders in initial attempts.

RQ₃: Are males or females portrayed as more persistent in attempting to influence others?

Male and female persuaders used the same persistence patterns in the aggregate (Fig. 12.1). However, persistence patterns did vary according to the gender of the *target*. Adult males were more likely to receive only one or two attempts. However, females were more likely to receive three or more attempts.

RQ 4: Are males or females more effective in influencing others?

Overall, persuader effectiveness was the same for males and females (Table 12.3). However, gender of the *target* was significantly different for the first and second tactic attempts. Persuaders were more effective with male targets during the first and second tactic attempts. Only at the third tactic attempt were female

TABLE 12.2
Relative Proportions of Goals Pursued by Male and Female Persuaders and Goals Encountered by Male and Female Targets

	Persuaders						Targets					
	Young			Adult			Young			Adult		
	Male	Female	χ^2	Male	Female	χ^2	Male	Female	χ^2	Male	Female	χ^2
Altruistic	30.8	32.6	.26	30.0	31.8	13.0**	40.5	32.7	9.68*	29.8	24.3	9.23*
Self-interest	27.5	25.9	.26	23.1	34.1	7.51*	31.3	23.7	9.68*	28.0	25.7	9.23*
Mutual benefit	14.2	15.6	.26	26.4	22.4	13.0**	16.6	20.5	9.68*	18.8	30.4	8.37**
Dependent	27.5	25.9	.26	20.5	11.7	6.79*	11.6	23.1	9.68*	23.4	19.6	9.23*

*$p \leq .05$. **$p \leq .005$.

TABLE 12.3
Target Compliance (Persuader Effectiveness) for Male and Female Targets

	First Attempt $(x^2 = 4.07)*$	Second Attempt $(x^2 = 6.36)*$	Third Attempt $(x^2 = 1.51)$
Male Targets	53.0	52.7	50.0
Female Targets	45.7	39.8	56.8

*$p \leq .05$.

targets more likely to comply than male targets, though this difference was not statistically significant.

RQ 5: Are persuaders more effective if using "traditionally masculine" tactics as compared to "traditionally feminine" tactics?

Table 12.4 illustrates the effectiveness by persuader gender and tactic gender type. Targets were more likely to comply when "traditionally masculine" tactics were employed than when "traditionally feminine" tactics were used. Additionally, persuader gender differences surfaced at the third attempt, showing males to be more effective than females regardless of the type of tactic employed. Males were significantly more effective than females, when "traditionally feminine" tactics were employed. Notably, females using "traditionally feminine" tactics were the least effective type of persuader.

From the research questions, some important synthetic trends can be found in the portrayal of the sexes on television. The results from research questions three

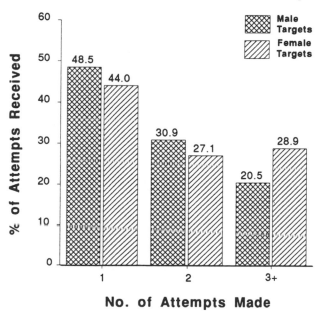

FIG. 12.1. Persistence by target gender.

TABLE 12.4

Target Compliance (Persuader Effectiveness) by Persuader Gender and Tactic Gender-Type

| | First Attempt | | | Second Attempt | | | Third Attempt | | |
| | Tactics | | | Tactics | | | Tactics | | |
	Male	Female	χ^2	Male	Female	χ^2	Male	Female	χ^2
Overall compliance	52.4	34.1	14.03**	24.2	22.6	3.36	50.4	36.0	10.21**
Compliance with male persuaders	52.6	34.8	6.72*	50.9	37.7		56.0	48.4	4.11*
Compliance with female persuaders	52.3	33.3	5.86*	46.5	43.8		43.3	15.8	4.11

*$p \leq .05$. **$p \leq .005$.

and four suggest that persuaders are more persistent with women, and that women were more acquiescent than men when persuaders persisted. Women, then, seemed to require a bit more convincing—or that the female "no" is not as readily believed as the male "no."

Compared to female targets, male targets were shown to receive more direct tactics (requests without explanations being offered), and more negative tactics (such as criticism, threat, deception, and emotionally oriented appeals) from persuaders. When considered in light of the greater tendency of male targets to comply and the greater likelihood that females will be targets of multiple attempts, this pattern suggests that dramatic, confrontational messages were effective alternatives to logic and reasoning for males, whereas females required more elaborate, rational, and carefully considered explanations before they complied. If so, this trend marks a reversal of traditional stereotypical images of women as more emotional than men, at least in their responses to social influence attempts. Finally, the results showing that *females* pursued more *general self-interest* goals, and *males* pursued more *dependent* goals, also reflects a reversal of traditional roles—with younger females as the targets of the dependent goals. Fathers, adults, and other males are portrayed as giving assistance to, and acquiring permission from, their daughters and other young females.

The India Study

The purpose of the India study was to illuminate how the effects of a prosocial soap opera can be understood on the basis of viewers' identification with positive and negative role models in an Indian television series, "Hum Raahi" (Fellow Travellers). "Hum Raahi" was conceived as an application of the entertainment-education strategy. *Entertainment-education* is a communication strategy that seeks to facilitate social change through the mass media by conveying specifically created educational messages that are embedded in popular entertainment forms (such as music, drama, literature, etc.). The appeal of entertainment is used as a vehicle for informative and persuasive messages about alternative ways for viewers to conduct their lives (Rogers, Aikat, Chang, Poppe, & Sopory, 1989; Singhal, 1990). Communicating prosocial messages through entertainment is a development strategy used successfully in many Third World countries.

The basic framework for the entertainment-education strategy was created in Mexico by Miguel Sabido (Sabido, Villaseñor, Dulanto, & Galiendo-Birrueta, 1982), who provided an integrated multitheoretical framework for the creation of entertainment-education programs, whether radio or television soap operas, popular music, or comic books. Sabido's theory for entertainment-education is based on the use of positive and negative role models, and the reward and punishment of these role models in a media drama (see Table 12.5). Positive role models are rewarded for their behavior, whereas negative role models are punished. In addition, there are change-over characters—negative role models who change their ways, and ultimately are rewarded for their transformation (Nariman, 1993). In this

TABLE 12.5
Elements of Miguel Sabido's Entertainment-Education Strategy Applied to the Indian Soap Opera "Hum Raahi"

I. Positive and negative role-models and change-over characters

Positive (Rewarded)	Negative (Punished)	Change-over (Transformed from negative to positive)
1. *Prema* holds out for a career as a school teacher and the chance to choose her own husband. She is rewarded by being allowed to marry Dr. Kumar.	*Angoori* is forced into an early marriage and is punished by death in childbirth.	*Sumitrap* is a negative role model as she has had little education and is a dependent widow. She becomes a positive role model when she learns to be independent and sets up her own cooperative.
2. *Dr. Kumar* supports Prema in her feminist enterprise. He is rewarded by a happy marriage to her.	*Bhairav Prasad* favors his son over his daughters. The son loses money entrusted to him by the mafioso. Bhairav is punished by having to desert his family in order to recover the fortune.	*Shiv Prasad* is a negative role model because he does not educate his own daughter. He becomes a positive role model when he is moved by his daughter's dependent state to support his niece's desire for a college education.

II. *Epilogue*: A 30-second statement reinforcing the moral and educational content of each episode. The epilogue also provides information about services related to the message. In "Hum Raahi," the epilogues were delivered by Tanuja, a popular and respected older Indian film actress as a credible source. Epilogues emphasized the educational message, and the epilogue concept is consistent with traditional Indian folk theater.

regard, Sabido's theory borrows directly from Albert Bandura's (1971, 1977, 1986) social learning theory. Individuals learn from role models with whom they identify.

The basis of the effects that entertainment-education soap operas have on audiences centers around (a) social learning theory, (b) reception theory, and (c) parasocial interaction. Reception theory concerns the processes by which receivers of communication messages construct meanings about the information provided by the media (Livingstone, 1990). Viewers interpret a multiplicity of meanings from television texts, as Livingstone (1990) found in her study of the British soap opera "Coronation Street," and Ang (1985), Katz and Liebes (1986), and Liebes and Katz (1989) found in investigating viewers of "Dallas." The subjective selectivity of individual viewers leads each media consumer to interpret an identical media message in a different way. Conceiving of an active audience individual leads to different approaches to investigating media effects. For instance, if the meanings attached by television viewers to a media message are varied, then one would expect the individual effects of such a message to be varied (Condit, 1989). An entertainment-education television soap opera provides an ideal test bed in which to study the interaction between the media and active viewers who identify in expected, or in unexpected, ways with positive and negative role models. Studies of prosocial media campaigns have applied social learning theory to smoking cessation (McAlister, Ramirez, Galavotti, & Gallion, 1989) and cardiovascular disease campaigns (Flora, Maccoby, & Farquhar, 1989).

Entertainment-education also has its effects through viewers forming parasocial bonds (Horton & Wohl, 1956; Liebes & Katz, 1989) with television characters. Adoption of the educational value in "Hum Raahi" (that is, a shift in values toward increased gender equality) is encouraged through role modelling and the rewards/punishments of the role models. However, viewers must make a connection between the intended value changes, the reward system demonstrated in the media messages, and their own life situations. Involvement—attention to, and participation in, the media—may not be powerful enough to result in a shift in such individual-level value priorities. Brown and Cody (1991) found that viewer involvement was not correlated with prosocial beliefs regarding women's equality in India among viewers of another prosocial Indian soap opera, "Hum Log," that was broadcast in 1984–1985. Viewers with similar high levels of involvement may interpret the program (text) in very different ways.

Identification with role models may be a more fruitful concept than involvement in explaining the effects of entertainment-education. We define *identification* as the degree to which an individual places himself or herself in another person's role. Identification is an emergent property of the viewer's involvement and negotiated reading of a soap opera text, such that viewers perceive characters to be similar to themselves, to be similar to people they know in their daily lives, and to be likeable rather than not likeable (Livingstone, 1990). Moreover, the relationships that viewers perceive among characters is important in determining the meanings that viewers interpret in the soap opera narrative (Livingstone, 1992). Individual identification influences the extent to which a viewer is receptive to prosocial messages embedded in a television text.

We believe that identification is a particularly important factor in causing value change effects of entertainment-education soap operas. Soap operas resemble life in their continuous nature, without resolution, as opposed to an episodic genre where plots are completed in each individual broadcast (Newcomb, 1974). Viewers find soap operas lifelike in their treatment of ordinary people. Soap opera viewers display a high level of emotional investment in characters and in situations depicted in the program (Pingree, 1981). If this emotional investment is with positive role models, then viewers may perceive change to be possible in their own lives. Identification is important for complex social innovations like increased gender equality, as compared to smoking cessation or healthier lifestyles. Adoption of gender equality affects relationships based on socially constructed rules and patterns of interaction. Social interaction behaviors are more difficult to change than individually based health issues.

Methods: Data-Gathering Procedures in India. Because at least a minimum level of identification with a television character is essential for viewers to model their value change, we examined the intensity and nature of Indian viewers'

TABLE 12.6
Respondents in Ten Focus Group Interviews about "Hum Raahi" in India.

Focus Group	Site	Income Level	Gender	# of Ss
1	Bangalore	High	Mixed	11
2	Bangalore	High	Mixed	8
3	Bangalore	Low	Female	19
4	Delhi	Middle	Male	8
5	Delhi	Middle	Female	7
6	Delhi	High	Female	9
7	Delhi	Low	Female	10
8	Delhi	Low	Male	8
9	Delhi	Students	Female	13
10	Delhi	High	Male	6
TOTAL				99

identification with the characters in "Hum Raahi." Focus groups and open-ended questionnaires administered to the participants in 10 focus groups were utilized in order to obtain a textured examination of identification (cf. Morgan, 1988). In July and August, 1992, 10 focus groups of 10 individuals each were conducted in Bangalore and New Delhi. Participants were recruited via interpersonal networks and with the assistance of a marketing research group. Focus groups were composed of high-, middle-, and low-income groups. Both single-sex and mixed-sex groups were interviewed. The interviews were conducted in the local language, in English, or a combination, as appropriate. Video and audio tapes were used to record the focus group sessions. Interviews were translated and transcribed for thematic and content analysis. The number of participants, and a breakdown by site, income level, and gender-composition (in the focus groups) is presented in Table 12.6.

Focus group participants viewed two key episodes of "Hum Raahi." The first segment showed Bhairav Prasad favoring Raju, his wastrel son, over his bright, intelligent daughters. Meanwhile, Prema, a social worker and teacher, is shown in her classroom lecturing to her students, who are all female (Table 12.7). She asks them why they have chosen marriage as their ultimate goal in life and why even a career woman is expected to come home at day's end and serve her husband, fulfilling the traditional expectations of an Indian wife. The second television segment focused on Angoori, a 14 year-old girl who dreams of studying in a university and becoming a government minister. However, she is forced into an early marriage, becomes pregnant, and is dangerously ill. She dies in childbirth, despite the efforts of Prema and Dr. Kumar. Thus, Angoori is a symbol of vital Indian womanhood that has been snuffed out by oppressive forces. This episode, broadcast by Doordarshan in July, 1992, received record viewer ratings of up to 90 in North Indian metropolitan areas.

In most of our 10 focus group interviews, this second segment was followed by a 1-minute epilogue, which entertainment-education soap operas use to reinforce their educational message. Singhal and Rogers (1989) found that epilogues used in "Hum Log" were effective, and that viewers often took the advice offered in them. Tanuja, a respected middle-aged film actress, told viewers that many Indian women die in childbirth because they are married too early and become pregnant before they are biologically ready to have a child. Tanuja also told viewers that

TABLE 12.7
Main Character Descriptions of Positive, Negative, and Neutral Role Models
in "Hum Raahi"

Characters	Role Description
I. Positive	
1. Prema	An independent, educated woman, a teacher and champion of women's rights. The sister-in-law of Bhairav Prasad.
2. Dr. Dilip Kumar	An educated writer, he believes in women's self-empowerment and supports Prema.
3. Suman	Very articulate and bright younger daughter of Bhairav Prasad, who stands up for her rights in the family.
II. Negative	
1. Devaki	A beautiful, rich, and conniving village gossip. She is clever and manipulative and seeks to gain power by interfering in other people's lives. Devaki arranges unhappy marriages for Kusum and Angoori.
2. Bhairav Prasad	The cruel, greedy and heartless father who favors his son Raju, mistreats his wife Manorama, and does not encourage his daughters (Kusum and Suman) to study. Refuses to look after his widowed sister Sumitra when she has nowhere to go and resents the success of his younger brother Subhash and is contemptuous of his father, Shiv Prasad (Dadaji). Bhairav is also heavily influenced by Devaki.
3. Angoori	An intelligent, bright, servant girl, who is the first in her family to receive a formal education, and who is determined to be a government minister, but is forced into an early marriage, and dies in childbirth.
4. Haitram	Malevolent mafioso; elder brother in law of Sumitra.
5. Manorama	Long-suffering wife of Bhairav Prasad.
6. Raju	Selfish, wastrel son and brother of Kusum and Suman. He and his father are more concerned with his stage career than with his sisters.
III. Change-Over	
1. Shiv Prasad	The father of Bhairav Prasad, Devi Prasad and Sumitra, and grandfather to Kusum, Suman, and Raju.
2. Sumitra	The sister of Bhairav Prasad. Sumitra is widowed early in the serial, and is subjected to abuse by her in-laws and her brother. Sumitra successfully sues her in-laws, and establishes a textile cooperative with her lawsuit award.
3. Kusum	The eldest daughter of Bhairav Prasad and a submissive sister. She is talented and intelligent, but her father refuses to let her attend college. Kusum is attracted to Dr. Kumar's nephew, but Bhairav forces Kusum to marry a cruel, divorced wastrel instead.

TABLE 12.8
Respondents' Perceptions of Character Portrayals as Positive, Negative, and Neutral Role Models in "Hum Raahi"

Characters	Intended Perceptions	Viewers' Perceptions
I. Positive		
1. Prema	Positive	Positive
2. Dr. Dilip Kumar	Positive	Positive
3. Suman	Positive	Positive
II. Negative		
1. Devaki	Negative	Negative
2. Bhairav Prasad	Negative	Negative
3. Angoori	Positive	Positive
4. Haitram	Negative	Negative
5. Manorama	Negative	Negative
6. Raju	Negative	Negative
III. Change-over		
1. Shiv Prasad	Change over	Mixed
2. Sumitra	Change over	Mixed
3. Kusum	Change over	Mixed

Note. The designation of characters in "Hum Raahi" shown here was described by scriptwriter Joshi (1992).

information about age at marriage and family planning could be obtained free at family planning clinics.

Viewers' Responses to Hum Raahi.   From our analysis of the focus group data, we found that the viewers of "Hum Raahi" perceived the text in varied ways. Overall, the intended positive and negative role models were "correctly" perceived as such by viewers (Table 12.8). However, our respondents varied widely in regards to their identification with various characters. Perceptions of the change-over characters were the most varied, because these roles changed from negative to positive over time. Specifically, the main target audience of "Hum Raahi"—low income people in India—identified more with the characters and situations and found them more realistic than did people of higher socioeconomic status. More sophisticated upper-income respondents were generally more skeptical of the representativeness of the characters and situations depicted in the serial, as Liebes and Katz (1989) found for Israeli viewers of "Dallas." In addition, low SES viewers in South India agreed with their North Indian counterparts that the situations and characters depicted in "Hum Raahi" were real and ones with which they could identify. However, upper SES viewers in South India felt that the situations and characters were not real and moreover representative of the "backward" North, rather than the South.

The educational content of the entertaining soap opera was taken more seriously as a prescription for action by women rather than by men, and by viewers of lower socioeconomic status than viewers of higher economic status. For instance, a low SES women in Delhi said: "*Rukmini:* [interrupts] Yes, we understand from them [soap operas] that one should not marry at a young age, it leads to complications, problems for the parents. Now, people in the household watch knowledgeful [educational] programs with a lot of attention and interest, and finish up their housework in order to watch. They say that this will come on TV—or that will come on TV, they now get a little knowledge from it." Male respondents, regardless of socioeconomic status, felt that women could not expect a complete equalization of gender relations, especially when women subjugated women as in the case of Devaki, the town gossip. Women, regardless of socioeconomic status, felt they were victims of a social system that subjugated them, and they felt that "Hum Raahi" validated their feelings of injustice.

Viewers expressed a strong desire not to repeat the mistakes of the characters in the serial in their own lives. Gauri, a woman in a low-income focus group interview in Bangalore, said that the character of Angoori resonated with her experiences, and that she learned from the character's suffering: "After watching Angoori suffer and die, I cannot now allow my daughter to get married at a young age, even though my relatives are considering marrying her off." Women and men, across socioeconomic lines, felt that "Hum Raahi" taught them valuable lessons in promoting gender equality for the greater good of society, although women, rather than men, felt these lessons to be more empowering and useful.

The entertainment-education strategy does not preclude oppositional readings of the text. Our respondents were not necessarily influenced by the intended reward/punishment system. For example, an older male focus group respondent in Delhi was asked why Angoori had died. The man responded that she had died of malnutrition. When asked if her early marriage could have caused her death, he said that was not possible, as he had married his own daughters off when they were 14 and 15. On the whole, however, "Hum Raahi" facilitated high viewer involvement with the prosocial text, and, at a minimum, raised consciousness about the problems of gender inequality.

The process of individual identification with television characters in the entertainment-education strategy has important implications for developing communication in the Third World, particularly where didactic campaigns appear to be ineffective, and where exposure to the mass media is widespread.

In conclusion, the viewers of "Hum Raahi" across levels of income, sex, age, and geographical location (North vs. South) identified "Hum Raahi" as an educational television serial that was also very entertaining. Although the target audience of lower SES viewers found it more realistic than did upper SES viewers, identification with the positive and negative role models was not limited to the former. The scriptwriter, Manohar Shyam Joshi, felt that the success of "Hum Raahi's" appeal could be traced to the fact that he sought to "make the [sic] tradition the basis of modernity" (personal interview, Joshi, 1992) and effect change in a context with which everyone could identify, that is, forced marriage, educational restrictions, and so on. In addition, despite the fact that Indian television viewers primarily identified with the positive role models, audience identification was not restricted to these positive role models. Viewers identified with negative role models like Devaki because they embodied power and material success. Scriptwriter Joshi (1992) partly blamed this unexpected identification on the casting and acting of the role models. Joshi was disappointed with the acting of the performers who portrayed positive role models. In contrast, Himani Shivpuri, the actress who portrayed Devaki, turned in a charismatic performance in her role. Thus, intended messages can backfire for production reasons (message effects) as well as for oppositional readings (audience effects).

CONCLUSIONS FROM OUR STUDIES

The similarities in the promotion of gender-equality in the United States and India revolve around the following three observations:

One, family-oriented situation comedies in the United States and soap operas in India both seek to effect changes in behavior by *tailoring their content* to the needs of their audiences. Indian programming is government controlled and is more oriented toward prosocial goals. Prosocial content in United States programming is secondary to profit goals.

Two, both studies explore the effects that male and female role models have on television audiences. The United States study explores changes in television program content. In contrast, the Indian study focuses more on the relationship between audience members and the program content. The two studies point to converging modes of enacting social change.

Three, counter stereotypes are promoted in both the United States situation comedies and the Indian prosocial soap opera. The United States study showed that some female characters responded in ways traditionally characteristic of men. These females required more rational, logical, and careful explanations before they complied than did men; males, on the other hand, were portrayed generally in very helpful ways—considerably different than the image of the father too busy at work to participate in his daughter's baseball games and ballet practices. The Indian soap opera portrayed strong-willed female characters who resisted traditional practices. These role models insisted on further education, a career, and a chance to choose whom to marry.

EAST–WEST COMPARISON: UNITED STATES AND INDIA

Despite some commonalities between types of shows and the goals of both types of programs, the fact that Indian and United States broadcasting systems are markedly different necessitates different approaches to applications of prosocial television strategies. A comparison and contrast of these two societies can provide insights that can guide the design of campaigns in a variety of industrialized and developing countries. First we will discuss four principal differences between these systems: (a) government versus private broadcast ownership; (b) active versus passive role in social change; (c) use of situation comedies versus melodramatic serials; and (d) an industrialized social environment versus a rural environment.

India (and many other less developed countries) has a government-owned broadcasting system, compared to the commercial, privately owned United States system. The United States television system is unique—whereas other developed countries have commercial and cable television, the United States industry is unparalleled in its quantity of output, universal accessibility, and variety of viewer options. United States broadcast stations are privately owned and operated for commercial profit. India and other less developed countries have government-owned and operated systems with a few channels, or only one channel. As public outlets, stations operate as a service for the improvement of society. More importantly, most countries have few television channels, or only one channel, which increases the centrality of those channels programming to individual and social life.

United States media assume a passive (noncontroversial) role in change, whereas media in India (and other countries) assume a more active role. United States media reflect changes in society subtly by showing interpersonal-level deviations from behavioral norms, but avoiding overt deviation from norms on relations between males and females. Commercial sponsors prefer noncontroversial vehicles for their advertisements and avoid programs that may upset or discomfort their viewers. Treatment of controversial topics can bear grave consequences for actors, producers, production companies, networks, and commercial sponsors. Beale (1992) described one of the most celebrated cases: The two-part episode of "Maude" dealing with abortion in 1972. Maude was one of the most popular television shows at the time, and CBS officials approved the abortion script. CBS received 7,000 letters of protest after the first airing, and 17,000 following a repeat broadcast the following August. Nevertheless, "Maude" finished the season as the fourth most popular program. More recently, organized protests, letter campaigns, and sponsor boycotts have proven to be effective punitive measures against programmers who air controversial subject matter, for example the portrayal of a gay male couple on "Thirty Something." Following a boycott organized by Christian fundamentalist groups, the characters' relationship received no further treatment in the show, and their sexual orientation was downplayed in the plot lines.

As the United States study showed, social change is mirrored in United States sitcoms—changes in characters and situations more often follow, rather than lead, changes in society. More recently, prominent actors and producers have applied their influence in order to raise controversial prosocial issues in television programs, including teenage birth control, race relations, and homosexuality. These efforts are sporadic, and withdrawal of sponsorship is a constant threat. Commercial sponsorship also supports a vast array of media alternatives in the United States, which enables viewers to avoid targeted campaigns. Creators are thus discouraged from appearing pedantic.

Social change is portrayed differently in situation comedies than in melodramatic serials. Television, like other cultural products, is a reflection of the social environment. Program creators often try to make their shows relevant to their audiences. Especially for entertainment programs, the extent of program relevance, and the form of this relevance, is constrained in part by the program genre. The situation comedy (sitcom) genre demands (a) that a conflict arise in the plot, and (b) that the conflict be resolved so that harmony will be restored (Newcomb, 1974). Plot conflicts frequently revolve around relations between family members. The genre demands that plot conflicts *must* be resolved in the span of a single episode, usually of 30 or 60 minutes in length. In these compressed narratives, situations may seem to be contrived, or their solutions presented in an oversimplified way. Humorous treatment of situations in sitcoms may also undermine the importance and seriousness of prosocial issues, as was shown for "All in the Family".

In contrast, the melodrama focuses on a continuous disharmony in life (Newcomb, 1974). The melodramatic world is constantly disrupted by the problems of everyday life. Melodramatic serials run for a specified period of several weeks, or months, whereas soap operas run continuously without conclusion (Cantor & Pingree, 1983). The serial format allows for careful plot development over several episodes spanning weeks or even months. Melodramatic narratives are also contrived, so normally serious topics can become unbelievably grave tragedies.

The overall social environment (an industrialized, urban economy and society versus a rural, agrarian economy) influences the impact of gender-equality promotion. Developed populations are more cosmopolite and have greater access to information from various sources. The United States and other industrialized societies are characterized by high literacy rates, urbanized metropolitan areas, and fairly even distribution of wealth. Developed societies typically have diverse media options, ranging from newspapers, magazines, and books, to radio, broadcast and cable television, and audio and video recordings. Substantial majorities of the population have access to most of these media. High incomes and extensive transportation systems allow many people to travel in, and out of, the country. Populations in less developed countries are less educated and have limited access to information. Less developed countries are characterized by agrarian economies and predominantly rural populations. Literacy is low, often less than 50% and much of the population earns subsistence wages. Broadcast systems are limited to a few or one station, and access to radio or television receivers is restricted by the high cost of ownership.

India–United States similarities in television promotion of gender equality are in terms of program content. Despite marked differences in production, ownership and operation of television stations, several key elements in the production of prosocial television are apparent: (a) use of popular media; (b) popularity of family situations; (c) use of familiar and indigenous knowledge; and (d) use of deliberate educational strategies.

Popular media (sitcoms, soaps/serials) are used in gender-equality promotion. Many of the most popular television genres have been employed in prosocial campaigns in the United States and in developing countries. The soap opera, or serialized melodrama, remains popular worldwide, whether imported or indigenously produced in a country. The soap opera is particularly effective in reaching female viewers. The serialized soap opera was always designed to attract United States women viewers, beginning with newspaper comic strips such as "Mary Worth" and "Rex Morgan, M.D.," and radio serials of the 1930s (Allen, 1983), and even to novels of the 18th century (Cantor & Pingree, 1983). Several soap operas, such as "The Guilding Light," originated on radio, and were successfully translated into daytime television programs. Comic books, radio programs, and television all have been employed in entertainment-education campaigns in the United States and in developing countries.

Family situations are popular and successful vehicles for promotion of gender-equality. The serialized drama began with female concerns centered around home and family (Allen, 1983). Soap operas frequently revolve around the activities of one or several families, and on the relationships between the family members (Cantor & Pingree, 1983). Although families have always been featured in United States situation comedies, the family-oriented situation comedy emerged in the 1970s (Newcomb, 1974). The family-oriented, or domestic, situation comedy involves more elements of a family relationship in the plot, particularly concerning personal and emotional issues. Real-life domestic conflicts like those between bigoted Archie Bunker and his liberal son-in-law Mike became the central situations as opposed to the earlier mechanistic, simplistic framework for one-liners and sight gags of earlier sitcoms (Feuer, 1987).

Familiar (indigenous) situations, knowledge, and expertise are used in creation and interpretation of programs. Creators use broad themes and traditions, which are compatible with popular myths (Lozano, 1992) and traditions (Joshi, 1992). Family situations are familiar to most audiences, and encompass conflicts that are common to many traditions and mythologies. The use of such myths in television narratives provides a sense of the familiar, and predisposes the audience to enjoy the story and accept its moral in the manner of traditional story-telling. For instance, Liebes and Katz (Katz & Liebes, 1986; Liebes & Katz, 1989) studied the worldwide popularity of the United States soap opera "Dallas," and found that although non-American viewers saw "Dallas" as a depiction of American society, they saw elements of their own lives in the serial, and used their experiences to explain events in the soap opera. Many viewers interpreted "Dallas" to be a family saga, and related plot developments to Biblical themes and stories. In India's "Hum Raahi," the scriptwriter, Manohar Shyam Joshi, used names that had an association with myths of female power and so emphasized the themes of gender equality and female empowerment.

Family situations are familiar to most audiences, and encompass conflicts that are common to many traditions and mythologies. Many such myths can be alluded to in order to make the concepts and themes more accessible and universal among the audience. However, creators must be careful when using myths and stories that may contain themes or allusions that may run counter to the central value of the intended campaign.

Deliberate educational strategies are employed in Indian and United States television. Planned, coordinated efforts to use media for prosocial purposes are increasing in popularity as their effectiveness is demonstrated. In the United States, educational programs designed to be entertaining range from the engaging but traditional "Mister Rogers' Neighborhood," to the entertaining, yet perceptibly didactic "Sesame Street," to the game-show "Where in the World is Carmen Sandiego?" More popular are the entertaining programs whose content is altered to accommodate or include prosocial concerns. The producers of "Dallas" reduced alcohol consumption in response to pressure from Hollywood lobbyists and an episode of "M*A*S*H" examined the effects of excessive alcohol consumption (Shefner & Rogers, 1992). "Beverly Hills, 90210," a United States program popular among teen and preteen audiences, treated safer sex and birth control, gambling, and the importance of completing school. The Hollywood lobbyist approach and the entertainment-education strategy derive in part from the realization that creative personnel are the most influential agents in television production process. These strategies involve raising awareness and sensitivity among the creators, so that prosocial themes and situations become integral parts of the television programs themselves. Although the efforts of Hollywood lobbyists demonstrate that profit and prosocial themes can be compatible, the primary emphasis of commercial television producers and networks is profit.

The entertainment-education strategy differs from commercial television efforts in that the educational themes are fundamental to the story lines and plot developments. Entertainment-education programs have been produced in India ("Hum Log" and "Hum Raahi"), Pakistan ("Aahat"), Turkey ("Berdel"), Mexico ("Acompáñame, Sangre Joven"), and Jamaica ("Naseberry Street"), among others. Programmers perceive indigenously produced entertainment-education programs to be popular and constructive alternatives to rebroadcast of existing United States and European programs.

DISCUSSION

Ethical dilemmas center around (a) the ethics of deciding what is prosocial; (b) providing fair treatment of the social and cultural groups depicted; (c) responsibility for unintended effects, both prosocial and antisocial; and (d) the ethics of promoting a particular version of development (Brown & Singhal, 1990; Singhal, Rogers, & Brown, 1992). Other ethical issues concern manipulating people's behavior against their will, or without their knowledge. However, to the extent that people are aware that such soap operas are largely didactic, they are not duped. Most respondents in the India study were aware of the educational nature of the program, and viewers actively agreed with the educational messages. Thought-control fears resemble the discarded hypodermic needle model of media effects; television is one among many influential social institutions including religion, the state, the family, social groupings, and so on. Prosocial television is presented in this social context and provides an alternate discourse, not a societal mandate. Theories such as uses and gratifications (Katz, Blumler, & Guerevitch, 1974) and media system dependency (Ball-Rokeach, 1985; Ball-Rokeach & DeFleur, 1976; Ball-Rokeach, Rokeach, & Grube, 1984) acknowledge the importance of the media in the formation of beliefs and opinions whereas acknowledging the limited role of the media in such changes. Use of counterstereotypic characters occurs particularly in situation comedies (e.g., "Mary Tyler Moore," "Who's the Boss?," "Murphy Brown," and "Designing Women"). Such characters can serve as positive role models that represent ongoing social change, and have their own unintended effects, when counterstereotypical characters function as positive role-models. At minimum, counterstereotypical characters can serve as sites of resistance against sexist social structures, as Radway (1984) found for United States readers of gothic romance novels.

The technologies must be adapted to the situations and needs of the social contexts in which they are used, preferably by persons from those societies. Empirical study and theories—both mainstream and critical—clearly indicate that indigenous cultures, traditions, and values need to be integrated with (rather than eradicated by) the promotion of gender equality. Third World countries can use television as an integral part of their development program, rather than a symbol of development success. In all situations, crafting prosocial entertainment that speaks in the viewer's voice will assist the viewer in understanding the implications of the prosocial themes.

In conclusion, prosocial television campaigns are effective if they are viewed as a means, rather than an end. Media campaigns should be programs to promote and effect change. Organizers of campaigns on commercially-sponsored broadcasting systems should forge alliances with supportive sponsors. The producers of "Hum Log" and "Hum Raahi" were fortunate to have the sponsorship of a major industrialist who agreed with their goals. Supportive sponsors can facilitate television production so that the prosocial themes can be treated in the most effective way possible. However, television cannot substitute for social workers and educators who are capable of providing individualized attention to persons or collectives. Contact with viewers helps to maintain feedback so that campaigns can be made more effective, and traditions and cultures can be respected.

ACKNOWLEDGEMENT

This study was supported by a Zumberg Faculty Innovation Fund grant awarded to Dr. Michael J. Cody and Dr. Everett M. Rogers at the University of Southern California. A preliminary report of the project was presented in 1992 (Robinson, Pfefferman, & Cody, 1992). The 1992 data gathering in India was supported by the Annenberg School for Communication at the University of Southern California. A preliminary report of the project was presented in 1993 (Chandran, Hirata, & Rogers, 1993).

REFERENCES

Allen, R. C. (1983). *The Guiding Light*: Soap opera as economic product and cultural document. In J. C. O'Connor (Ed.), *American History/American Television: Interpreting the Video Past* (pp. 306–327). New York: Ungar.

Ang, I. (1985). *Watching Dallas*. New York: Methuen.

Ball-Rokeach, S. J. (1985). The origins of individual media system dependency: A sociological framework. *Communication Research, 12*, 485–510.

Ball-Rokeach, S. J., & DeFleur, M. L. (1974). A dependency model of mass media effects. *Communication Research, 3*, 3–21.

Ball-Rokeach, S. J., , Rokeach, M., & Grube, J. (1984). *The great American values test: Influencing behavior and belief through television*. New York: Free Press.

Bandura, A. (1971). *Social learning theory*. New York: General Learning Press.

Bandura, A. (1977). *Social learning theory*. Englewood Cliffs, NJ: Prentice Hall.

Bandura, A. (1986). *Social foundations of thought and action: A social cognitive theory*. Englewood Cliffs, NJ: Prentice Hall.

Beale, L. (1992, November 10). An abortion that shook prime time. *Los Angeles Times*, p. F1.

Beuf, A. (1974). Doctor, lawyer, household drudge. *Journal of Communication, 24*, 142–145.

Brown, W. J., & Cody, M., (1991). Effects of a pro-social television soap opera in promoting women's status. *Human Communication Research, 18*, 114–142.

Brown, W. J., & Singhal, A. (1990). Ethical dilemmas of pro-social television, *Communication Quarterly, 38*, 1–13.

Burgoon, M. J., Dillard, J. P., & Doran, N. E. (1983). Friendly or unfriendly persuasion: The effects of violations of expectations by males and females. *Human Communication Research, 10*, 283–294.

Canary, D. J., Cody, M. J., & Marston, P. (1986). Goal types, compliance-gaining and locus of control. *Journal of Language and Social Psychology, 5*, 249–269.

Cantor, M. G., & Pingree, S. (1983). *Soap operas*. Beverly Hills, CA: Sage.

Chandran, A. S., Hirata, T. M., & Rogers, E. M. (1993, May). *Using entertainment for development: Viewer identification with a pro-social Indian soap opera*. Paper presented to the Intercultural and Development Communication Division, International Communication Association, Washington, D.C.

Cody, M. J., Canary, D. J., & Smith, S. (1994). Compliance-gaining goals. In J. Wiemann & J. Daly (Eds.), *Communicating strategically* (pp. 33–90). Hillsdale, NJ: Lawrence Erlbaum Associates.

Comstock, J., & Strzyzewski, K. (1990). Interpersonal interaction on television: Family conflict and jealousy on primetime. *Journal of Broadcasting and Electronic Media, 34*(3), 263–282.

Condit, C. M. (1989). The rhetorical limits of polysemy. *Critical Studies in Mass Communication, 6*, 103–122.

DeFleur, M. L., & Ball-Rokeach, S. J. (1989). *Theories of mass communication* (5th ed.). New York: Longman.

Falbo, T. (1982). PAQ styles and power strategies used in intimate relationships. *Psychology and Women Quarterly, 6*, 399–405.

Falbo, T., & Peplau, L. A. (1980). Power strategies in intimate relationships. *Journal of Personality and Social Psychology, 38*(4), 618–628.

Faludi, S. (1991). *Backlash: The undeclared war against American women*. New York: Anchor Books.

Feuer, J. (1987). The MTM style. In H. Newcomb (Ed.), *Television: The critical view* (4th ed., pp. 52–84). New York: Oxford University Press.

Fiske, J. (1987). *Television culture*. New York: Routledge.

Flora, J. A., Maccoby, N., & Farquhar, J. W. (1989). Communication campaigns to prevent cardiovascular disease: The Stanford community studies. In R. E. Rice & C. K. Atkin (Eds.), *Public communication campaigns* (2nd ed., pp. 233–252). Newbury Park, CA: Sage.

Frueh, T., & McGhee, P. E. (1975). Traditional sex role development and amount of time spent watching television. *Developmental Psychology, 11*, 109.

Ganguly, K. (1992). Accounting for others: Feminism and representation. In L. F. Rakow (Ed.), *Women making meaning: New feminist directions in communication* (pp. 60–79). New York: Routledge.

Gerbner, G., Gross, L., Morgan, M., & Signorielli, N. (1980). The "mainstreaming" of America: Violence profile No. 11. *Journal of Communication, 30*(3), 10–29.

Gerbner, G., Gross, L., Morgan, M., & Signorielli, N. (1986). Living with television: The dynamics of the cultivation process. In J. Bryant & D. Zillmann (Eds.), *Perspectives on media effects* (pp. 17–40). Hillsdale, NJ: Lawrence Erlbaum Associates.

Greenberg, B. S., Richards, M., & Henderson, L. (1980). Trends in sex-role portrayals on television. In B. S. Greenberg (Ed.), *Life on television: Content analyses of U.S. TV drama* (pp. 65–87). Norwood, NJ: Ablex.

Gruber, K. J., & White, J. W. (1986). Gender differences in the perceptions of self's and others' use of power strategies. *Sex Roles, 15*, 109–118.

Hall, S. (1980). Encoding/decoding. In S. Hall, D. Hobson, A. Lowe, & P. Willis (Eds.), *Culture, media, language* (pp. 128–39). London: Hutchinson.

Horton, D., & Wohl, R. R. (1956). Mass communication and para-social interaction: Observations on intimacy at a distance. *Psychiatry, 19*, 215–229.

Johnson, P. B. (1976). Women and power: Toward a theory of effectiveness. *Journal of Social Issues, 32*, 99–110.

Johnson, P. B. (1978). Women and interpersonal power. In D. N. Ruble & G. L. Zellman (Eds.), *Women and sex roles* (pp. 301–320). New York: W.W. Norton.

Johnson-Odim, C. (1991). Common themes, different contexts: Third World women and feminism. In C. T. Mohanty, A. Russo, & L. Torres (Eds.), *Third world women and the politics of feminism* (pp. 314–327). Bloomington, IN: Indiana University Press.

Joshi, M. S. (1992, July 31). Personal interview.

Katz, E., Blumler, J., & Guerevitch, M. (1974). Uses of mass communication by the individual. In W. P. Davidson & F. Yu (Eds.), *Mass communication research: Major issues and future directions* (pp. 11–35). New York: Praeger.

Katz, E., & Liebes, T. (1986). Decoding *Dallas*: Notes from a cross-cultural study. In G. Gumpert & R. Cathcart (Eds.), *Inter media: Interpersonal communication in a media world*, (3rd ed., pp. 97–109). New York: Oxford University Press.

Lee, C. C. (1980). *Media imperialism reconsidered: The homogenizing of television culture.* Beverly Hills, CA: Sage.

Liebes, T., & Katz, E. (1989). *The export of meaning: Cross-cultural readings of Dallas.* New York: Oxford University Press.

Livingstone, S. (1990). *Making sense of television: The sociology of audience interpretation.* New York: Pergamon Press.

Livingstone, S. (1992). The resourceful reader: Interpreting television characters and narratives. In S. R. Deetz (Ed.), *Communication yearbook 15* (pp. 58–90). Newbury Park, CA: Sage.

Lozano, E. (1992). The force of myth on popular narratives: The case of melodramatic serials. *Communication Theory, 2*, 207–220.

McAlister, A., Ramirez, A. G., Galavotti, C., & Gallion, K. J. (1989). Antismoking campaigns: Progress in the application of social learning theory. In R. E. Rice & C. K. Atkin (Eds.), *Public communication campaigns* (2nd ed., pp. 291–307). Newbury Park, CA: Sage.

McGhee, P. E., & Frueh, T. (1980). Television viewing and the learning of sex role stereotypes. *Sex Roles, 6*, 179–188.

Mohanty, C. T. (1991a). Introduction/cartographies of struggle: Third World women and the politics of feminism. In C. T. Mohanty, A. Russo, & L. Torres (Eds.), *Third world women and the politics of feminism* (pp. 1–47). Bloomington, IN: Indiana University Press.

Mohanty, C. T. (1991b). Under Western eyes: Feminist scholarship and colonial discourses. In C. T. Mohanty, A. Russo, & L. Torres, *Third world women and the politics of feminism* (pp. 51–80). Bloomington, IN: Indiana University Press.

Monush, B. (1991). *International television and video almanac* (36th Ed.). New York: Quibly Publishing.

Morgan, D. L. (1988). *Focus groups as qualitative research*. Beverly Hills, CA: Sage.

Mulvey, L. (1975). Visual pleasure and narrative cinema. *Screen, 16*, 6–18.

Nariman, H. N. (1993), *Soap operas for social change: Toward a methodology for entertainment education television*. Westport, CT: Praeger.

Newcomb, H. (1974). *TV: The most popular art*. New York: Anchor Books.

Radway, J. (1984). *Reading the romance: Women, patriarchy, and popular literature*. Chapel Hill, NC: University of North Carolina Press.

Rakow, L. F. (1986). Rethinking gender research in communication. *Journal of Communication. 36*, 11–26.

Reis, H. T., Wheeler, L., Spiegel, N., Kernis, M. H., Nezlek, J., & Perri, M. (1982). Physical attractiveness in social interaction II: Why does appearance affect social experience? *Journal of Personality and Social Psychology, 43*, 979–996.

Robinson, J. D., Pfefferman, R. J., & Cody, M. J. (1992, October). *Who's the Boss?: Sex differences in influence attempts on prime-time, family-oriented, situation comedies*. Paper presented in the Interpersonal Division of the Speech Communication Association, Chicago, IL.

Rogers, E. M., Aikat, S., Chang, S., Poppe, P., & Sopory, P. (Eds.). (1989). *Proceedings from the Conference on Entertainment-Education for Social Change* (pp. 1–37). Los Angeles: Annenberg School for Communication, University of Southern California.

Ross, L. D., Anderson, R. & Wisocki, P. A., (1982). Television viewing and adult sex role attitudes. *Sex Roles, 8*, 589–592.

Rule, B. G., Bisanz, G. L., & Kohn, M. (1985). Anatomy of a persuasion schema: Targets, goals and strategies. *Journal of Personality and Social Psychology, 48*, 1127–1140.

Sabido, M., Villaseñor, M., Dulanto., G, & Galiendo-Birrueta, C. (Eds.). (1982). *Handbook for reinforcing social values through day-time TV serials*. Mexico City: Communication Research Department, Televisa Institute for Communication Research.

Said, E. W. (1979). *Orientalism*. New York: Vintage Books.

Salwen, M. B. (1991). Cultural imperialism: A media effects approach. *Critical Studies in Mass Communication, 8*, 29–38.

Shannon, C. E., & Weaver, W. (1949). *A mathematical theory of communication*. Urbana-Champaign, IL: University of Illinois Press.

Shefner, C. L., & Rogers, E. M. (1992, May). *Hollywood lobbyists: How social causes get in network television*. Paper presented at the International Communication Association, Miami.

Singhal, A., (1990). *Entertainment-education communication strategies for development*. Unpublished doctoral dissertation, Annenberg School for Communication, University of Southern California, Los Angeles.

Singhal, A, & Rogers, E. M. (1989). Prosocial television for development in India. In R. E. Rice & C. Atkin (Eds.), *Public communication campaigns* (2nd ed., pp. 331–350). Newbury Park, CA: Sage.

Singhal, A., Rogers, E. M., & Brown, W. J. (1992, August). *Entertainment telenovelas for development: Lessons learned about creation and implementation*. Paper presented at the International Association for Mass Communication Research, Sao Paulo, Brazil.

Smith, S. W., Cody, M. J., LoVette, S., & Canary, D. J. (1990). Self-monitoring, gender, and compliance-gaining goals. In M. J. Cody & M. L. McLaughlin (Eds.), *The psychology of tactical communication* (pp. 91–135). Clevedon, England: Multilingual Matters Ltd.

Steenland, S. (1989). *Unequal picture: Black, Hispanic, Asian and Native American characters on television*. Washington, DC: National Commission on Working Women of Wider Opportunities for Women.

U.S. Commission on Civil Rights (1987, August) *Window dressing on the set: Women and minorities and television*. Washington, DC: U.S. Government Printing Office.

Vidmar, P., & Rokeach, M. (1974). Archie Bunker's bigotry: A study in selective perception and exposure. *Journal of Communication, 24*, 36–47.

Wilson, C. C., & Gutiérrez, F. (1985). *Minorities and media: Diversity and the end of mass communication*. Newbury Park, CA: Sage.

Wolf, N. (1990). *The beauty myth: How images of beauty are used against women*. London: Vintage.

Chapter 13

Men and Women in the Market Place

Michael J. Cody[1]
University of Southern California

John Seiter
Utah State University

Yvette Montagne-Miller
California State University, San Diego

Contributions to this volume detail discrepancies in power and credibility between men and women in a number of important areas. One area that has witnessed little change over the decades deals with the assignment of tasks involving shopping and related "domestic" or "family" chores. The task of shopping for the vast majority of goods, such as food, clothing, and gifts (Christmas, birthday, anniversary, etc.) is assigned to women. Further, it appears that it may take quite some time to change expectations concerning who, and how, basic daily tasks are assigned to, and completed by, males and females.

Our analysis of how people shop for clothing reveals that (even in the 1990s) males approach the activity as a "task" or "chore" to be completed as quickly as possible, giving less thought to their purchases than do women. When compared to women, men are less likely to shop for clothing, spend more money in less time, and are more compliant when influenced by salesclerks. Oddly, these results contradict the "traditional" view of women as more easily influenced than men. Indeed, our central thesis is that neither sex is generally, or universally, more easily influenced than the other, once we take into consideration individuals' *goals, plans* that are developed for achieving those goals, available *resources*, and *beliefs* regarding men, women, and the world in general. To illustrate, we will first overview the literature and history of research on gender differences in persuasion.

---

[1]Inquiries regarding additional information on this chapter should be directed to Michael J. Cody.

Second, we will report the results of an observational study completed in major retail stores in California.

GENDER AND PERSUASION

Historically, persuasion research on gender differences perfectly illustrates the "Woman as Other than Male" approach to social science; that is, how men are persuaded, and resist being persuaded, has been considered the *standard* against which female "influenceability" is compared and contrasted. Decades of research, in fact, have been devoted to the study of how women are more easily influenced than men. When the general hypothesis of "women as easily influenced" could no longer be maintained, scholars sought to identify *types* of women who presumably were easy to influence (i.e., "traditional sex-typed," women who adopted "traditional roles," etc.). Pointedly, there exists no comparable body of literature concerning *males* who might be more easily influenced, or a comparable typology of male receivers—despite the fact that such a typology is not particularly difficult to imagine, given that substantial numbers of males are sensation seekers, sports enthusiasts, chronically lonely, and so forth. The traditional bias has been to assess female-related influenceability. A brief chronology of events is in order.

In the 1950s an attempt was made to identify receivers who were more susceptible to influence than others. Championed in the 1940s and 1950s, the attempt was to identify a *personality*-based type of receiver who was more easily influenced than others (Hovland & Janis, 1959; Janis & Field, 1956; Janis & Rife, 1959; also see McGuire, 1969). However, while some work did identify and confirm that some people are more generally influenced than others, the differences between "high" and "low" persuadable receivers were often weak. Research subsequently switched direction from work on a general persuasibility index and focused attention on a number of individual difference variables also considered as important determinants of influenceability; such as self-esteem, intelligence, and gender (Cohen, 1959; Hovland & Janis, 1959; McGuire, 1969).

Indeed, a standard social psychology textbook in the 1940s had already concluded (Bird, 1940, p. 274; cited in Scheidel, 1963, p. 357): "Many researchers covering several topical areas and involving different kinds of tests and apparatus have shown girls and women to be more suggestible than boys and women to be more suggestible than boys and men." Exceptions are strikingly few. By the late 1960s and early 1970s, persuasion scholars continued to be confident that women were more easily influenced than men. For example, one popular volume used as a supplemental text in persuasion courses in the 1970s concluded that "one of the most consistent and reliable findings in the field" is that females are more easily influenced than males (Karlins & Abelson, 1970, p. 89). Scheidel's (1963) often-cited work is still considered exemplary research of this era; reacting to messages concerning political and governmental policies, women receivers were found, compared to males (a) to be more easily influenced; (b) to transfer attitude change from one topic to a range of topics [showing greater overall influence]; and, (c) to retain less information from the persuasive messages.

However, Eagly (1978) thoroughly reviewed research on gender and persuasion, and rejected the general conclusion that females are more easily influenced; she found little evidence in support of greater susceptibility in either *persuasion* studies, or in *conformity* studies *not* involving *group* pressure. When female influenceability was observed, Eagly argued that the results could partially be "explained by researcher's tendency to choose experimental materials somewhat biased against the interests and expertise of women" (p. 86). For example, Chaiken (1979), in a classic study on beauty and compliance, argued that women signed petitions restricting the serving of (red) meat on campus not because they were more easily influenced than men, but because they eat less meat, were less committed to a meat diet, and reflected greater health-consciousness (than men).

Eagly's (1978) review also made it clear that the "consistent and reliable" finding of female influenceability was invalid: although 32% of the studies published before 1970 found women to be more easily influenced than males, only 8% of the post-1970 studies reached such a conclusion. Other meta-analyses conducted in the 1980s further questioned the generality of, and the strength of, the gender-influenceability relationship. Becker (1986, p. 195) concluded that the correlation between gender and influenceability to be a lowly .05 to .08. Later, Eagly (1983, p. 976) estimated the correlation between gender and influenceability to be between .08 and .13 based on a sample 148 conformity and persuasion studies.

Because it is impossible to claim a *general* effect for gender, scholars sought to study gender differences as possibly attributable to the *topics* employed, to the *sex* of participants involved in persuasion research (sex of experimenter, sex of speaker, and sex of receiver), to the *status* of men and women in society, and to the expectations or stereotypes people hold concerning male/female differences in credibility and persuasibility. In the latter approaches, Eagly (1983) can be credited with demonstrating that people generally *expect* men to be more persuasive and women to be more easily influenced largely because of the fact that men typically hold positions of formal status, and higher status individuals are considered persuasive and/or worthy of deference and respect. Some progress in gender equality would follow after women increased in visible levels of status, and stereotypes and expectations of gender bias change: "the role analysis predicts that sex differences will lessen as women become more frequent occupants of higher status roles" (Eagly, 1983, p. 979).

However, the male-formal status/greater female influenceability relationship does not account for *all* of the gender differences in persuasion and conformity research. Much of the research reviewed through the decades is flawed by the fact that the majority of scholars were male (79% of the authors were men), and that male scholars reported stronger gender effects than did female authors; *the* correlation between the sex of the authors and the effect size of reported sex difference was .41 (Eagly, 1983). Presumably, stripping away assumed greater male status and power reduces the extent to which females will display greater compliance. However, Eagly (1983) did state that there may be a "true" (but small) gender effect in the direction of stereotypical differences in "studies of small-group interaction carried out in laboratories and other settings (e.g., juries) where interaction is initiated in the absence of preexisting role hierarchies and formal status inequalities between the sexes" (p. 977).

Over the years, it was proposed that the *topic* of persuasion probably contributes greatly to whether or not males or females are influenced. Three years after Eagly's (1978) first review, Eagly and Carli (1981) examined the question of topic bias critically, believing that increased male knowledge and expertise in certain topics may have placed men in a better position to counterargue and resist persuasion. However, Eagly and Carli concluded that male-oriented topics were *not* substantially or significantly overrepresented in the persuasion and conformity research. We also would like to point out that such an hypothesized effect would still not account for differences involving juries, in which both males and females are presumably equal in expertise concerning legal matters (copyright infringement, proof of guilt beyond reasonable doubt, etc.), yet there is a small effect for females to be more compliant in juries (according to Eagly, 1983).

However, it is possible that the topic that is selected interacts with both the speaker's sex and the receiver's sex to affect influenceability. The *cross-sex influence* effect hypothesis was offered as a way of explaining and accounting for some of the research findings over the decades. Through the 1950s, 1960s, and 1970s most research employed males as speakers. Thus, male receivers heard a same-sexed speaker, whereas female receivers heard an opposite-sexed speaker. Obviously, any number of confounding variables can stem from such a situation. For example, at least some of the male college students in these studies were reared to be competitive, and could have counterargued the male speaker as part of this competitive nature (i.e., men compete with other men). On the other hand, females (at least young ones) may have been reared to comply with speaker's requests, especially speakers who are presumably older, mature "male researchers," who possess relatively higher levels of "expertise," or status.

Nonetheless, a "cross-sex effect" may be obtained when (a) the persuasive messages are presented by communicators who are physically present (as opposed to contexts when speeches are presented through remote channels of communication, such as written, audio-taped recordings, etc.); and, (b) the procedure involves a context in which receivers believe that their opinions will (or may) become known to the communicators; that is, receivers are aware (or can infer) that their agreeing or disagreeing with the speaker will be made known to the speaker (cf. Ward, Seccombe, Bendel, & Carter, 1985). Under these conditions, Ward et al. found that females did show a greater amount of "agreeing responses" to male speakers (topics studied dealt with how federal money should be spent in Reagan's "New Federalism" budget proposals). However, most of the male speaker/female receiver agreeing responses were transitory—the changed opinions did *not* persist over time. Rather, there was greater *persistence* in changed opinions over a 2 month period when female receivers heard the speech by a female speaker, not a male speaker; that is, male speakers prompted only temporary "yeah saying" responses that should not be viewed as real long-term persuasive outcomes.

However, the other half of the "cross-sex effect" is sometimes not fully supported: Males are only occasionally influenced significantly by female speakers.
In the Ward et al. study, female speakers significantly influenced male receivers on
only one topic: how to combat poverty effectively. Such an observation highlights
the importance of studying the sexes of both speakers and receivers, along with
expectations and beliefs concerning who is likely to be a credible speaker on
various topics (i.e., poverty, domestic matters/violence, safety of nuclear power,
etc.).

The attempt to keep the myth of female influenceability alive continues. First,
research has speculated that if not *all* women are easily influenced, then perhaps
some are, and the resistant women might be characterized as more male, or at least
showing more masculine characteristics. A number of studies demonstrate that
traditionally sex-typed females (females who score high on femininity and low on
masculinity) are more easily influenced than either traditionally sex-typed males
(low femininity scores, high masculinity scores), who resist influence the most, or
individuals who are "androgynous" (i.e., males or females possessing characteristics of both masculinity and femininity)(cf. Bem, 1975; Montgomery & Burgoon,
1980). Thus, the argument goes, only the *really* feminine and "traditional" female
is easily influenced and gullible.

Although Montgomery and Burgoon (1980) found that scores on masculinity
and femininity were much stronger and significant predictors of persuasibility than
physiological sex, before the decade was over marketing scholars such as Schmitt,
Leclerc, and Dube-Rioux (1988) questioned the predictive utility of gender schema
theory, arguing that physiological sex was predictive of persuasibility when one
took into account exposure to advertisements and reactions to gender-related
products (e.g., perfumes and perfume containers). That is, females (regardless of
sex-role orientations) are generally likely to read different magazines than males,
and are therefore more likely to recall different advertisements and show more
liking for and interest in perfumes and perfume containers than men. Note that other
marketing projects (Qualls, 1987) do in fact demonstrate that sex-role orientations
predict a number of important features, such as dominance in decision-making in
marital contexts. In regard to reactions to specific messages, however, Schmitt et
al. found that men and women (based on biological sex, not androgyny) have quite
different reactions and thoughts regarding perfumes and other merchandise.

Advertising and marketing experts continue to focus on identifying *some* group
of women ("career women," "housewives," and so on) who might be relatively
easy to influence (Barak & Stern, 1986; Barry, Gilly, & Doran, 1985; Bellante, &
Foster, 1984; Jackson, McDaniel, & Rao, 1985). For instance, substantial interests
have been placed on the "Career Woman" versus the "Homemaker," each being
influenced by messages that appeal to the woman's particular interests. On one
hand, both the "Career Woman" and the "Housewife" value variety in meals and
low prices. However, whereas the "Housewife" is concerned more about serving
nutritious meals and about receiving praise for cooking, the "Career Woman" rates

food shopping as less enjoyable (than the "Housewife") and is more likely to value ease of preparation and ease of cleaning when considering purchases.[2]

More recently, Leigh, Rethans, and Whitney (1987) emphasized the importance by which women perceive or identify themselves as being a traditional, or modern woman. Acceptance of traditional roles ("If being a housewife is a full-time job, a woman should be able to find time to cook," etc.) results in a profound difference in orientations toward, and reactions to, advertisements (compared to when ads feature "modern" roles). Commercials that show women purchasing gold jewelry, buying their own stocks and bonds, receiving and using their own *American Express* cards, and so on, attempt to appeal to the working, modern woman, whereas ads that show women making good choices for family members appeal to traditionals. Based on our experiences teaching persuasion, we have found that one set of advertisements that polarize these two types of receivers are the Robitussin's "Dr. Mom" advertisements, which portray all family members (except the mother) as helpless in fighting cold symptoms; and when the mother is sick, the household environment is shown as deteriorating. We have found that the "Dr. Mom" advertisements are offensive to a number of career women because they "force" women into the roles of nurturer and carer; as if all males are incompetent at taking care of themselves.

Finally, persuasion experts have begun to study aging receivers, those who have retired or who are over 70 years of age (Burnett, 1991; Day, Davis, Dove, & French, 1988; Davis & French, 1989; Greco, 1988; Lazer, 1985; Lumpkin & Festervand, 1988; Rubin & Rubin, 1982; Ursic, Ursic, & Ursic, 1986). The most recent of these attempts at studying 70+-year-old receivers almost exclusively involves examining women (Davis & French, 1989; Day et al., 1988), because the sample of males diminishes quickly in the 70 to 80+ age group.

Although the elderly *poor* may be under-represented in these studies, this research does succeed in providing a clearly consistent pattern of difference between the middle class elderly and the affluent elderly women. Presumably, this latter category included women who were affluent because they were career women, and/or because of inherited wealth. These projects indicate that affluent receivers are more suspicious and less trusting of advertisements and are less dependent on the advertisements as sources of information concerning purchases. It is the middle-class elderly receiver who perceives that advertisements provide information to them, whereas the affluent receiver believes that all advertisements are fundamentally biased or untrustworthy.

The more affluent elderly indicated agreement with the statement that advertising is insulting to their intelligence, that women are portrayed in negative light, and

---

[2]Despite the plethora of research on woman and food shopping, it is virtually impossible to find a comprehensive assessment of how men shop for food. (Although we have read in marketing newsletters that men [presumably those who value the view of themselves as "good providers"] like to shop and do a good deal of the grocery shopping. However, their use of coupons, their competence at shopping, maintaining budgets, etc., are clearly understudied, highlighting just how profound a bias there is in the literature.)

that advertisements should not be used as primary sources of information in decision-making. The affluent read more materials (books, magazines) and have a wider range of resources than do the middle-class elderly (Bettinghaus & Cody, 1994). Thus, the women who have the financial resources enabling them to purchase advertised products are actually the group who are *most resistant* to being influenced by persuasion to buy the products—at least in regards to mediated advertisements (television, radio).

WOMEN, MEN, AND SHOPPING

By now the reader should be convinced that there does *not* exist any sort of general trend for women to be more easily influenced than males. However, the "woman as easily persuadable" claim can also be assailed from the position of the male shopper: Men often claim they do not feel competent at shopping, defer to women's opinions, and, generally, shun shopping. Part of this orientation also includes devaluing shopping as a relatively unimportant task (but we will return to this issue later).

There are relatively few published articles on actual retail behaviors (excluding news reports concerning the increased use of catalogue sales, especially by career-oriented women), but two recent publications show consistent views of how men and women shop. Fischer and Arnold (1990) reviewed existing literature and conducted a field study regarding gift-buying behavior. Although it might be true that men who hold egalitarian attitudes are more inclined to help and become involved in gift buying and Christmas shopping (than the traditional male), the general conclusion is that Christmas shopping is still "woman's work." The existing literature not only suggests that women *do* more of the Christmas shopping and the gift buying, but they are also more likely (than men) to *plan* what to buy, to buy *appropriate* gifts, and to spend *more time* shopping—especially given that men traditionally view shopping (for gifts, clothing, etc.) as a low-status activity (cf. Fischer & Arnold, 1990). Further, Fischer and Arnold found that women gave more gifts to others (12.5 on the average, versus 8.0 by men), started shopping earlier in the year (October, while men waited until November), and spent more time involved with buying an appropriate gift (2.4 hours per gift, to a man's 2.1 hours). Men, however, spent more money for a gift ($91.25 per gift, compared to $62.13 by women). Despite the expenses, however, 16% of the gifts purchased by men were returned or exchanged, compared to 10% of the women's gifts.

A second study by Peters (1989) concluded that teenagers spend a good deal of income on clothing (19% to 23% of a teenager's budget) and that parents are equally likely to financially assist both male and female teenagers. Teenage females are more likely to plan purchases and read about fashions than teenage males, who tune into radio, tv ads, or are influenced by store displays. Peters' own project indicated that females were more likely to have shopped sometime in the last month (compared to males), and that teenage boys are more likely to shop with their mothers, or to have their mothers engage in the shopping for them. Females were more likely to shop with friends. Fathers *rarely* shop with either child.

The Importance of Goals, Plans, Resources, and Beliefs

It should be clear that there is *no* simple model that links "gender" or "sex" to influenceability. Rather, gender may be linked to influenceability only through a set of conditions involving the person's motives, beliefs about a credible persuader, plans, and resources. Indeed, we have adapted Miller and Read's (1991, 1987; Read & Miller, 1989) interpersonalism model of personality when characterizing male and female interests, plans, and behaviors in interpersonal communication in general (Canary & Cody, 1994). The Miller–Read model specifies that any individual difference (male versus female, high versus low self-monitoring, lonely versus non-lonely, etc.) is best viewed as stemming from one or more of four components: Goals, plans, resources and beliefs.

We introduce the interpersonalism model here for the obvious reasons that (a) the interpersonalism model is a parsimonious way to characterize a number of differences between men and women in interpersonal relationships (cf. Canary & Cody, 1994) and, (b) the model provides an explanation for the ways in which men and women differ in orientations to the marketplace, and to persuasion. We will first overview our conclusions concerning goals, plans, resources, and beliefs regarding women and men in general, prior to commenting on the specific task of shopping.

Goals.   A substantial amount of work by communication scholars and psychologists in the last 10 years has focused on goals and goal achievement (such as Bisanz & Rule, 1989, 1990; Cody, Canary, & Smith, 1993; Rule & Bisanz, 1987; Rule, Bisanz, & Kohn, 1985). Scholars have in fact documented a number of differences between women and men in the goals that are pursued (Cody, Canary, & Smith, 1994; Smith, Cody, LoVette, & Canary, 1990), and noted that women are typically more expressive, affiliative, cooperative, status neutralizing, and communally oriented (also see Booth, 1972; Wheeler & Nezlek, 1977).

Cody et al. (1994) studied the social participation of men and women (the term "social participation" is used to denote the quality and quantity of activities that individuals actively construct for themselves), and found that women more frequently pursued goals of *sharing activities* with others, *gaining assistance* from others, *giving advice* to others, engaging in *volunteer work*, proposing *relational changes* (planned relational escalations, devising tests of relational trust, and devising ways to initiate relationships), and *protecting rights* and *enforcing obligations* with others.

Most of these differences can be explained in terms of the fact that women pursue more communal goals in which they engage in more status-neutralizing activities, whereas men pursue more competitive, individualistic goals in which they engage in more status-assertive activities. Communal goals are reflected by the fact that women give more advice to each other, share more activities with one another, are more preoccupied with the quality of their interpersonal relationships, and are more concerned with ensuring that people (friends, roommates, brothers, and sisters) adhere to rights and obligations (i.e., others should reciprocate favors, fulfill obligations in cleaning, paying bills, etc.; women act in ways to help others treat one another fairly).

There are, of course, some negative aspects concerning goal orientations of women. Women (in surveys conducted up until 1990) are more *dependent* on assistance from others for a number of tasks, and are forced into roles of *seeking permission* from people in authority. Indeed, when we were preparing the Cody et al. (1994) chapter we found that many women were quite ambivalent, even angry, over their parents' inconsistent, or blatantly unfair, set of rules established for boys and girls. For example, many parents give sons greater license and freedom, but restrict and "protect" daughters. Another negative aspect stems from the fact that young males (high school through college) still appear to possess greater credibility in influencing others in position of authority at work than do young females (who claimed greater success at influencing police officers, security guards, etc.), suggesting another way society has changed little in regards to gender equality over the decades (Cody et al., 1994).

Nonetheless, women, as noted above, are more likely than men to perform the tasks of retail shopping. Further, we also expected that males and females would pursue different sub-goals when shopping. Clearly, some shoppers can be classified as "focused shoppers," because they believe they have a good idea of what they are seeking (i.e., a particular shirt, a certain type of outfit, etc.). Other shoppers can be classified as "gift-buyers," because they are purchasing an object for another, or for some holiday. A third set of shoppers can be classified as "recreational" because they are browsing, or at least claim to the clerks that they are "just looking," so that they can leisurely look at the merchandise without a clerk's presence, and without any explicit (or implicit) pressure applied. We expected that men and women would both participate in "focused shopping," whereas women would engage in more "recreational shopping" and "gift-buying" than men.

Plans.   Plans deal with the sequences of communicative actions a person will employ to attain a goal. Women pursue relational and communal goals (as listed above) by asking friends to do things with them (to shop, eat, spend time together visiting, etc.), whereas males typically have to have some focal activity when they get together with other males (watch a game, work on some task). We are, frankly, amazed that in this society it is permissible for a woman to ask a friend over to chat because she is bored and needs companionship, but the same request from a male to another male is judged as nonnormative. Instead, men need to watch a game, play poker, and so on. (Recall President Bush being criticized by the media in the late 1980s for being a "wimp," because he used "feminine" terms such as a "splash" of coffee, and he would have a "chat" with someone.) Nonetheless, plans for pursuing the general relational and communal goals include showing interest in others, disclosing appropriately, being open to others, treating others as equal, and avoiding bragging (Canary & Cody, 1994; McLaughlin, Louden, Cashion, Al-tendorf, Baaske, & Smith, 1985; Miller, Cooke, Tsang, & Morgan, 1992).

In regards to retail shopping, women are obviously expected to spend more time planning and thinking about purchases than men. Women are more likely to develop *plans* for buying effectively, appropriately, and within a budget; males make *plans* to buy something adequately as soon as possible. Also, because men are more task-oriented shoppers (i.e., they want to get in, find what they need, purchase it and get out), helpful selling tactics (i.e., tactics that facilitate the goal of quick shopping) on the part of the salesclerk should be more effective on them than on women. On the other hand, women, who have more interpersonal goals, should prefer "friendliness" as a selling tactic.

Resources.   The implementation of any plan requires that the individual possess certain resources that make it possible to pursue the goal. These resources include the personal, situational, and relational talents, abilities, knowledge, status, money, or connections that a communicator may have at his/her disposal in order to implement a plan in order to achieve a goal. In general interpersonal communi-cation, women communicate most emotions accurately, smile more, use higher levels of eye contact, adopt a more direct position to other speakers, display increased levels of involvement, and are more expressive than men, who use more space, are louder, are more likely to interrupt others, make more speech errors, and employ more "filled pauses" (Burgoon, Buller, & Woodall, 1989; Deutsch, 1990; Hall, 1984, 1985; Henley, 1977; Knapp & Hall, 1992; c.f. Hyde & Linn, 1986; Mayo & Henley, 1981). Women and men also have a different orientation toward self-disclosure; women are more concerned with making sure that the person they disclose to is discreet, trustworthy, sincere, liked, respected, good at listening, warm, and open. Women engage in "remedial work" that has a greater chance of successfully avoiding conflict and resolving disputes (c.f. Canary & Cody, 1994). For example, they employ more detailed and more elaborate apologies when communicating accounts (Gonzales, Pederson, Manning, & Wetter, 1990; Roth-man & Gandossy, 1982).

With regard to retail shopping, we expect women and men to allocate resources differently. Specifically, we suspect that women will be motivated to expend *time* as a resource in studying merchandise in order to buy effectively (price-wise) and appropriately. Men, on the other hand, will be "focused" shoppers, and will expend *money* as a resource in order to buy a desired object quickly.

We also suspect that the resources men and women allocate may also make them susceptible to different sales tactics. Once again, if men want to shop quickly, then the salesclerk who helps them make decisions and helps them to quickly fulfill their assignment and exit the store will also be effective in increasing sales. Thus, the use of helping tactics and expertise claims may help men make their decisions, purchase the objects, and leave.

On the other hand, women (whom we presume to be spending more time shopping and who are likely to want to shop leisurely) are likely to be influenced by *low* amounts of pressure (i.e., they would be resistant to being led and to expertise claims by clerks), and may value *friendliness* on the part of the clerks. Indeed, the *Los Angeles Times* newspaper for September 15, 1993, indicated that the largest retail stores in California have decided that it is cost-effective to train workers to be friendly, and to have them stay physically close to check-out areas where they can be found easily, rather than wander isles, attending clients, and employing various tactics. Further, Hornik (1992) found that females may be positively affected by a friendly touch in a restaurant setting (although there were a number of interaction effects dealing with sex of toucher, initiator, and level of physical attraction). Thus, we expected that woman would be positively influenced by a friendly environment, whereas males would be positively influenced by salesclerks who facilitate their goals.

Beliefs. Beliefs about the world and about interpersonal relationships will affect whether men or women will devote resources to a plan in the interest of achieving a goal. Beliefs regarding what is a male or female behavior continues to play an important role in whether men or women will fully commit the resources to fulfilling the goal, among other things. For example, we believe that men believe that *female* clerks are likely to be better sources of information than men, because they perceive that women possess greater knowledge about fashion and merchandise than do men. Peters (1989) found that men rarely shopped with their children, and teenage boys learned to defer to mothers and other women. Thus, we expect that men would be compliant or more easily influenced by women salesclerks.

In sum, women (mothers, teenage daughters) shop more often than do men, plan their shopping purchases, are more likely to be informed (based on print media), are more likely to purchase appropriate merchandise, and are more likely to spend a longer period of time shopping than men. Also, we expect that shoppers would have different motives (subgoals) for shopping; women are more likely (than men) to be recreational shoppers or gift-buyers. Further, men and women are expected to allocate different resources when involved with the task: Men are likely to spend more money to complete the "task" or "chore" as quickly as possible, whereas women spend more time shopping. Beliefs are also likely to play an important role in the persuasion process (also noted above), with men more likely to defer to the opinion of women regarding merchandize to be purchased.

Observations of Shoppers

We completed a project in which several hundred buyer–seller interactions were observed in major department stores. After training coders in the identification of Cialdini's (1993) compliance principles (see Table 13.1), pairs of students spent hours on Thursday evenings, Friday evenings, Saturdays, and Sundays observing and coding the interactions between shoppers and clerks, and coding types of sales tactics used as well as whether the shopper *agreed* with the salesclerk or *rejected* the recommendations, assistance, or advice of the clerk. Only commission-based stores were sampled, and the pairs of coders were asked to first record a communication exchange in one area of the store (i.e., women's clothing), and to move to

TABLE 13.1
Tactics Used in Selling Clothes

Tactics	Examples
Liking/Ingratiation	
Praise	I have seen the kind of clothes you buy and you look great in the more sophisticated fashions like this one.
Opinion conformity	Oh, yes! I agree. The blue one does look better.
Rendering favors	Let me call the other store and see if one can be sent over this afternoon.
Friendliness	Hi, how are you? Has the sun come out yet?
Similarity	I have a St. John's knit similar to that in a light blue. Don't you just love it?
Source Competence	
Expertise	Oh, you're in luck. We just received a shipment of some wonderful casual dresses made out of a very light linen. The weave of our new line is more open than last year's line to let more air pass through and keep you cooler.
Honesty/trust	The only problem is that they have to be dry cleaned and treated very gently if you want the quality to last.
Helping/Reciprocity	
Helpfulness	May I help you? May I carry those up to the front for you? Shall I start you a [dressing] room?
Leading helpfulness	Did you see our sales display on the Ralph Lauren sweaters? 25% off is a great buy.
Inducements	
Commitment	Would you like a belt with this?
Contrast	A suit? May I show you these...$1,000 is too high? Let's look at...
Social proof	Everybody is buying these this year. We sell out of them as soon as they come in.
Scarcity	This is the last one in blue in your size.

another (men's clothing, women's shoes, etc.), so that different types of shoppers, and clerks, were included. Despite the fact that different areas of the store were sampled, the majority of observed shoppers were female ($n = 322$), and relatively few were male ($n = 94$).[3]

Coding Compliance Principles

Anchoring and Contrast Effects.   Is $80 a lot of money to pay for a belt? Is $75 too much to spend for a tie? In comparison to a $500 new suit, do such expenses

---

[3]For details concerning methods, coder training, and reliability, contact the senior author, Michael J. Cody.

seem large or small? There can be no denying that many things in life are *relative*. Happiness, the evaluation of what is "expensive," what is a "gruesome crime," what is "beautiful," what is "generous," and many other judgments are influenced by comparisons and contrasts to other events.

Contrast effects are important in compliance settings in several ways. Most typically, sales clerks can affect the sales process by showing customers the most expensive items first, so that other items do not seem quite as expensive. When shoppers become "anchored" at the expensive, and high-quality, end of the line of products (a $900 St. John knit dress, $300 imported shoes, $240 slacks, etc.), the price of a $400 dress, $120 shoes, and so on, appear to be a "good" deal. Showing the customer the most expensive item first, before showing more "reasonably" priced items, is referred to by Cialdini (1993) as the "contrast" tactic in Table 13.1.

Reciprocity.   The reciprocity principle is used to gain compliance from others in several ways. First, and most obviously, reciprocity is used to gain compliance from others simply due to the fact that one can create a feeling of obligation on the part of others by doing them favors, or giving them objects, or services. Amway corporation, for example, relies on reciprocity when members of Amway leave the BUG (a collection of samples of shampoo, detergents, polishes, etc.) with potential customers so that the customers can try any product they want to try "without obligation to buy." However, there is some *felt* obligation to buy something: The sales representative left a wide array of nice products for the customer to use at his/her pleasure, and the LEAST a customer could do is buy something. Other companies will offer free samples of food items in the stores in order to activate the reciprocity principle. For our purposes here, however, it should be obvious that when salesclerks offer frequent aid and assistance (especially for a certain length of time) shoppers may experience some obligation to compensate or reciprocate the favors.

As shown in Table 13.1, two types of helpfulness can be distinguished. General helpfulness refers to offers by the clerk to assist the customer with needs such as finding a dressing room, checking sizes, and so forth. Leading helpfulness occurs when a clerk "pilots" a customer from one place to the next, demonstrating merchandise, sales, and so forth.

Commitment.   The commitment principle simply means this: The more a person is *committed* to a group, organization or cause, the more likely the person will comply with requests to aid or assist the group, organization, or cause. Research on the commitment principle has focused on two procedures: the *foot-in-the-door* tactic (once a person agrees, or is committed to a decision, the person is likely to agree to a second, larger request), and the *low ball* procedure (a person agrees to a request, or commits to a decision, and later learns that there are unexpected costs involved with such a commitment; see Cialdini, 1993, for additional details and examples; also see Bettinghaus & Cody, 1994).

The use of a general commitment principle in sales encounters rests on the notion that once a customer selects the first object to buy (kakhi pants, a blue blazer, etc.), that the individual is "committed" to a particular look, color scheme, or type of fashion, and the individual will be influenced by the claim that a particular belt, shirt, or pair of shoes will complement the object to which she or he has committed. In a sense, the "commitment" tactic is used to help the customer "accessorize" a wardrobe so that certain items fit together to provide a fashionable look.

Liking.   The *liking principle* is simply this: We are more likely to comply to requests of likeable, good-looking people than people who are unlikable and not good-looking. As indicated in Table 13.1, there are a number of ingratiation tactics that also promote liking, these being *similarity, opinion conformity, general friendliness, rendering favors,* and *praising* shoppers.

Social Proof.   Sometimes, people just don't know how to behave. They do not know what the appropriate action should be, or what etiquette requires. When people do not know what to do, or when they do not have guidelines, prior experience, evidence, or research proof, they use others' behavior to learn what is appropriate. This type of influence is known as social proof. *Social proof* is used when people do not have access to evidence, statistics, facts, logic, insight, or some other form of *logical proof.* Clearly, this form of influence is used in sales encounters when the salesclerk explicitly or implicitly informs others that "this fashion is what is currently popular," "this is what everybody is buying this year," "this is the hottest Fall color," and so on. The claim is that what is popular is good, and people should wear, listen to, vote for, or buy what is popular.

Authority.   The *authority principle* is a frequently employed tactic and examples are quite common. One way to tap into the authority principle is through the use of expertise. Because shoppers are observed in specialty shops that feature imported shoes, "designer" clothes, and so on, an "expert" can tell shoppers information about how the products are made, materials that were used, the history of a company or family that makes the Scottish knits, and so forth. Customers often buy products based on the information supplied by experts.

A second way that the authority principle can operate is through the establishment of trust. That is, shoppers who trust a salesclerk are more likely to believe the clerk when the clerk tells them about the qualities of a product.

Scarcity.   The scarcity principle is simply this: objects appear to be more valuable when the opportunity to obtain or own them is limited or restricted in some way. There are several ways in which our daily behavior is shaped by the scarcity principle: *the desirability of scarce objects, planned scarcity,* and, *restricted freedom.* The first two are easy to describe and most relevant to shopping. First, people are willing to spend more money on "one of a kind" objects that they will own, and that no one else will own. Rare baseball cards, first edition books, coins or stamps printed with errors, and so forth, are items collectors will spend a considerable amount of money to purchase. Given that scarce objects will fetch higher prices, it shouldn't be surprising to see that marketers actually *plan* shortages of certain desirable products so that shoppers will pay more of hard-to-find objects. Finally, there are times when the scarcity principle is activated when a person's freedom to behave in a particular way is restricted, such as when a sale ends at midnight, and they will not be able to buy the object if they wait.

Results: Gender, Goals, Tactics, and Reactions

Preview of Results. Pairs of coders worked collaboratively to listen to buyer–seller interactions of "randomly" selected shoppers; first, the pair would appear at a designated section of the store (e.g., "women's clothing") and select the shopper who entered the store at a particular time (e.g., 6 pm). The pair of coders then followed the shopper, and re-constructed the sequence of tactics employed, along with the shoppers' reactions (accepting or rejecting of the salesclerks' tactics), the sex of shopper and salesclerk, and the duration of the encounter. During the observations, coders were allowed to take notes, discretely; but no electronic eavesdropping was permitted for legal reasons. After the shopper completed the task (either buying merchandize, or declining a purchase and leaving the store), the pair of coders left the immediate area to write out a transcript of the interaction, and recorded the sales price (if a purchase had been made). Some tactics were used more than once. Several of the tactics (*helping/reciprocity, liking/ingratiation,* and *source competence*) were sometimes used two or three times during an exchange, whereas others (*scarcity, contrast*) were rarely used a second time during an exchange.

Table 13.2 presents the correlations between the frequency by which tactics were used with the frequency by which shoppers accepted or rejected the various tactics, along with the purchased amount. As Table 13.2 suggests, the importance of accepting the advice or tactics of the salesclerk is clear: Acceptances of the salesclerks' messages clearly followed from the use of Praise and other Liking/Ingratiation tactics ($r = .73$) and from Helping/Reciprocity tactics ($r = .73$), and corresponded with higher sales ($r = .51$). Rejecting the salesclerk's tactics, however, did not have a *negative* effect on sales, only a small positive effect ($r = .19$).

TABLE 13.2
Correlations Between Tactics and Reactions

Tactics	Accept	Reject	Amount
Liking/ingratiation	.73**	.58**	.36**
Source competence	.57**	.54**	.30**
Helping/reciprocity	.73**	.37**	.34**
Commitment	.41**	.23**	.36**
Contrast	.15**	.02	.09*
Social proof	.36**	.26**	.20**
Scarcity	.23**	.15**	.13**
Purchased Amount	.51**	.19**	

*p significant beyond .05. **p significant beyond .01.

TABLE 13.3
Effectiveness of Sales Tactics on Male and Female Shoppers

	Male Shoppers			Female Shoppers		
		Not			Not	
Tactics	% Used	Used	Used	% Used	Used	Used
Liking/ingratiation	54%	63.85	127.32*	40%	45.95	107.39*
Praise	40%	58.56	156.84*	34%	44.71	122.34*
Opinion conformity	23%	85.14	141.32	12%	65.23	109.70*
Render favors	36%	81.82	127.35	24%	58.70	107.83*
Friendliness	51%	72.67	122.83	45%	57.82	86.35*
Similarity	19%	93.77	117.34	12%	65.24	110.77*
Source competence	62%	68.62	116.70	43%	45.82	103.16*
Helping/reciprocity	90%	64.09	132.49*	94%	45.67	91.82*
Commitment	28%	74.05	161.67*	22%	51.98	138.32*
Contrast	10%	96.64	113.89	9%	66.47	115.71*
Social proof	29%	81.80	139.21	27%	56.02	110.53*
Scarcity	16%	90.55	139.04	15%	64.51	105.55*

*Indicates that the tactic was significantly, reliably, related to increased sales.

Generally speaking, most sales tactics were significantly related to sales, but the use of tactics pertaining to *contrast* effects ($r = .09$), *scarcity* ($r = .13$), and *social proof* ($r = .20$) were somewhat less effective than other tactics (see Table 13.2).

Table 13.3 presents the general results pertaining to gender differences, use of compliance tactics, and purchase amount. For both male and female shoppers, we compared the purchased amount when the tactic was *used* at least once on the (male or female) shopper, compared to when the tactic was *not used* on the (male or female) shopper. A series of *t*-tests (among other statistics) was used to test whether men (or women) purchased more when the tactic was used, or when the tactic was not used on them. Generally speaking, tactics involving some type of *source competence, liking/ingratiation*, and *helping/reciprocity* were substantially more often used than tactics involving *commitment* and *social proof*, whereas *scarcity* and *contrast* tactics were less frequently employed. Tables 13.4, 13.5, and 13.6 present results for each *type* of shopper (recreational, focused, and giftbuyer).

We now turn attention toward assessing the issue of gender differences in regards to goals, resources (dollars), resources/beliefs (time commitment), beliefs (deference to salesclerks), sales tactics, and frequency of influence attempts.

Goals.   Our observations revealed that males and females differed substantially in motives for shopping. More women than men were observed shopping; women represented 77.4% of all shoppers. Of the 106 "recreational shoppers," 82% were female, and 18% were male, a clear difference ($z = 5.54$). Of the 257 "focused" shoppers, 77% were female, 23% were male, a clear difference ($z = 7.61$). However, there was little difference in the frequency by which women (62%) and men (38%) were gift buyers ($z = 1.69$).

Resources: Dollars. Men spent more money ($M = 107.31$) than women ($M = 78.34$ $t(414) = 1.96$, $p = .051$), and spent more money per minute ($M = 4.51$) than did women ($M = 3.31$ $t(414) = 2.00$, $p = .046$).

Resources/Beliefs: Time Commitment. There was a significant Shopper Sex by Salesclerk Sex interaction for the length of time spent shopping ($F(1/415)$

TABLE 13.4
Effectiveness of Sales Tactics Used on Recreational Shoppers ($N = 105$)

Tactics	% Used	Purchase Amount Not Used	Purchase Amount Used	t-value	p
Liking					
Praise	20%	9.21	109.42	7.76	.001
Opinion conformity	10%	18.14	132.53	6.20	.001
Render favors	13%	19.06	101.96	4.69	.001
Friendliness	52%	16.68	42.37	1.99	.050
Similarity	8%	22.92	106.43	3.77	.001
Source competence					
Expertise	19%	19.95	73.34	3.33	.001
Honesty/trust	5%	26.73	96.27	2.30	.024
Helping/reciprocity					
Helpfulness	95%	4.40	31.28	.87	.387
Leading help	32%	6.92	78.91	5.90	.001
Commitment	10%	19.04	124.75	5.59	.001
Contrast	5%	26.78	95.29	2.29	.026
Social proof	15%	17.60	99.81	4.98	.001
Scarcity	12%	19.71	103.69	4.59	.001

TABLE 13.5
Effectiveness of Sales Tactics Used on Focused Shoppers ($N = 256$)

Tactics	%Used	Purchase Amount Not Used	Purchase Amount Used	t-value	p
Liking					
Praise	42%	62.46	141.89	4.91	.001
Opinion conformity	16%	92.26	114.86	1.00	.317
Render favors	32%	84.18	121.46	2.09	.037
Friendliness	43%	73.76	125.45	3.12	.002
Similarity	13%	89.65	137.24	1.95	.053
Source competence					
Expertise	50%	76.35	115.90	2.39	.018
Honesty/trust	16%	87.77	140.25	2.30	.022
Helping/reciprocity					
Helpfulness	96%	89.82	96.25	.16	.876
Leading help	30%	75.03	143.76	3.89	.001
Commitment	26%	73.38	161.00	4.79	.001
Contrast	9%	92.12	133.17	1.44	.152
Social proof	31%	84.43	121.83	2.08	.038
Scarcity	16%	90.69	122.87	1.43	.154

TABLE 13.6
Effectiveness of Sales Tactics Used on Gift-Buyers (*N* = 54)

Tactics	% Used	Purchase Amount Not Used	Purchase Amount Used	t-value	p
Liking					
Praise	29%	75.47	91.75	.77	.443
Opinion conformity	17%	67.98	135.01	2.65	.011
Render favors	35%	74.96	87.92	.61	.546
Friendliness	56%	76.46	81.82	.27	.791
Similarity	27%	87.13	57.73	1.30	.199
Source competence					
Expertise	46%	69.07	91.79	1.13	.263
Honesty/trust	23%	70.70	108.97	1.62	.111
Helping/reciprocity					
Helpfulness	94%	75.43	79.69	.11	.912
Leading help	42%	68.62	94.51	1.28	.206
Commitment	35%	68.10	101.26	1.59	.118
Contrast	13%	79.97	75.36	.15	.878
Social proof	36%	60.38	113.33	2.68	.010
Scarcity	17%	78.57	83.22	.16	.863

= 5.57, p = .019). Female shoppers spent the same length of time shopping when attended by either female salesclerks (M = 23.99 minutes) or male salesclerks (M = 22.16 minutes). However, male shoppers spent more time shopping when attended by female salesclerks (M = 30.51 minutes) than by male salesclerks (M = 17.13 minutes).

Beliefs: Deference to Salesclerks. For frequency of "rejecting" reactions to the salesclerk, there was no effect for Shopper Sex (p = .323) or Salesperson Sex (p = .801). Both male (M = .93) and female (M = .93) shoppers used rejection infrequently. For frequency of "accepting" reactions to the salesclerk, there was a significant effect for Shopper Sex ($F(1/415)$ = 4.881, p = .028), but not for Salesclerk Sex (p = .415), or for the interaction (p = .604). Males were more accepting of sales tactics (M = 6.30) than females (M = 4.93). As noted above, Table 13.2 illustrated the importance of employing tactics with which shoppers voiced acceptance. The fact that male shoppers accepted the salesclerks' tactics significantly more often than female shoppers supports the notion that males were more compliant (and possibly more dependent on others' opinions and advice), and that males were motivated to hurry thought the processes; by accepting advice quickly, they could spend more money in less time and leave the "task" of shopping behind them.

Sales Tactics. Table 13.3 presents the results concerning how often these tactics were used on male and female shoppers, how much money shoppers spent, and whether we can conclude that the use of a tactic was statistically, or reliably, related to improving the sales. Males received many *source competence* tactics from sales clerks (62% of clerks used these tactics on males, 43% on females) and males received more overall *liking/ingratiation* tactics (54%) than did females (40%). Few overall differences were obtained for *helping/reciprocity* tactics (50% males, 54% females), *commitment* tactics (28% males, 22% females), *contrast* effects (10% males, 9% females), *social proof* (29% males, 27% females), and *scarcity* (16% males, 15% females).

As indicated in Table 13.3, men spent more money when they were helped (*helping/reciprocity*, $132.49, versus not helped, $64.09), when they were praised ($156.84 versus $58.56 when not praised), and when the *commitment* tactic was used on them (i.e., men agreed to buy some accessory, such as a belt, etc.)($161.67 versus $74.05). We further wish to point out that female shoppers never reached the male shoppers' expenses. Praised males spent $156.84 compared to $122.34 for praised females, helped males far outspent helped females ($132.49 to $91.82), and men spent more when the *commitment* tactic was used on them ($161.67), compared to females ($138.32).

As indicated in Table 13.3, women spent a good deal of money when the salesclerks used *commitment* ($138.32), *praise* ($122.34), *contrast* ($115.71), and *social proof* ($110.53). It can be inferred that females desired to buy what was popular (i.e., *social proof*), what made them look good, what was a good buy (relative to the more expensive objects used in the anchoring and contrast effect), and they were motivated to accessorize.

It can also be noted in Table 13.3 that females appear to be influenced by *every* tactic; they spent more money when any of the particular tactics were used on them than when the tactics were not used on them. However, this does not mean that females are indiscriminantly influenced by *any* sales tactic. Recall that the vast majority of "recreational shoppers" were female (82%). An assessment of the sales interactions with just the recreational shoppers indicate that when these shoppers announced that they were "just browsing," they spent very little money if they were, in fact, left alone. However, the use of *any* tactic employed on recreational shoppers was related to increased sales. The data on this issue is presented in Table 13.4. A careful examination of Table 13.4 indicates that recreational shoppers were particularly influenced by four of the *liking/ ingratiation* tactics (spending over $100 when all but the general "friendliness" tactic was used on them), and they were strongly influenced by *commitment* (spending $124.75 when accessorizing), and *scarcity* ($103.69). There were no significant differences in the influence of recreational shoppers (for either Shopper sex or Salesclerk sex). Recreational shoppers spent less money ($30.01) than either Focused shoppers ($95.48)($t(360)$ = 4.83, p = .001), or Gift-buyers ($80.89)($t(156) = 4.23, p = .001$).

Because recreational shoppers differ from others in regards to motives and goals (being that they claim only to be browsing, and are [presumably] more uncertain of purchasing preferences), the selling task is considerably different than when the clerk confronts the more focused and gift-buying shopper. Some comment is in order, then, concerning the *sequential* requests involved in "piloting" a shopper from being noncommittal browser to being a spender. It is difficult to show the *sequential* use of effective tactics statistically; our assessment of an effective salesclerk's strategy is: First, win over the shopper's trust by using similarity, opinion conformity, rendering favors, or praise. Second, use the commitment principle to help the shopper assemble an ensemble. Third, suggest or indicate that the store is running out of the desired object(s) and/or the objects will no longer be on sale after the weekend (or whatever). Why this is a good sequence rests in the fact that recreational shoppers do in fact want to be left alone, in part because the shopper does not want to be pressured or manipulated by a salesclerk. Therefore, the salesclerk should groom an image of a friendly individual, who is not likely to manipulate or pressure the shopper; the worse choice is to apply pressure on the recreational customer too early.

Focused shoppers, who were typically women, were most strongly influenced when "leading helpfulness" ($143.76, versus $75.03), when *committed* (or when accessorizing)($161.00, versus $73.38), when praised or when other tactics of *liking/ingratiation* were employed; also effective were expertise, and *social proof* tactics (see Table 13.5); ineffective tactics included general Helping, *scarcity*, the use of a *contrast* effect, or via conformity of opinion. Why are the above tactics effective? Presumably, focused shoppers already have a good idea what they want. So a tactic such as leading helpfulness, which directly facilitates the attainment of their goal, is more effective than general helpfulness. For similar reasons, *scarcity* should not be as effective. If a shopper found exactly what was being sought, it does not matter if it is the last one of its kind–he or she has decided to purchase it anyway. Similarly, leading a focused shopper to merchandise that is too expensive (*contrast*) will not facilitate his/her goals and is therefore not effective. On the other hand, once a clerk had found what a focused shopper is interested in, *expertise, social proof, liking/ingratiation*, and *commitment* tactics help convince the shopper to buy.

Finally, gift-buyers were significantly influenced by two tactics: Being told what was popular (*social proof*), coupled with agreeing with the opinion voiced by the shopper (presumably, telling gift-buyers what is popular among the targeted group (i.e., high school graduates, etc.), was persuasive. Second, salesclerks clenched the sale of the recommended merchandize by agreeing with the opinion voiced by the shopper ("Yes, I agree, the red one looks the best.").

Frequency of Influence Attempts. Males received more *total number of tactics* ($M = 17.66$) than did females ($M = 16.98$)($t(414) = .013$). However, males ($M = 7.94$) were not recipients of more different strategies than females ($M = 7.22$)($t(414) = 1.07, p = .29$). This indicates that males received repeated uses of several tactics (i.e., praise, expertise, help), more so than did female shoppers.

Summary and Implications

First, a summary of our results indicates:

1. More women shopped at clothing stores than did men, and more women were "recreational shoppers" and "focused" shoppers. Both women and men were motivated to shop for gifts.

2. Men spent more money than women, and spent more money per minute than women; men also spent a significantly longer time shopping when aided by a female salesclerk, relative to a male salesclerk.

3. Men were more verbally compliant (accepting more tactics) than women, and the acceptance of sales tactics were significantly related to increased sales.

4. Men received more frequent, repeated tactics than did females.

5. Generally speaking, shoppers tended to be influenced by tactics that facilitated achieving their goals. Males spent more money when they were helped, praised, and when the *commitment* approached was used. Gift-buyers were influenced by appeals to popularity (*social proof*) and by conforming opinions. Female shoppers, who typically were "recreational" and "focused" shoppers, were also significantly influenced by the sales tactics—but different tactics were effective for different types of shoppers.

We argued, based on the Miller and Read (1989) *interpersonalism model*, that influenceability is not so much related to one's biological sex as to one's *goals, plans, resources*, and *beliefs*. The all too stereotypical male shopper demonstrated that his goal was to shop as quickly as possible, traded one resource (money) for another resource (time), and apparently believed and trusted the salesclerks recommendations (by agreeing with the recommendations), and also showed a preference for interacting with female salesclerks. Female shoppers, however, were also influenced by a number of sales tactics, but effective tactics differed based on their goal (as a recreational shopper, focused shopper or gift-buyer), but females were not as compliant, spent the same length of time in the store whether a male clerk (22 minutes) or a female clerk (23 minutes) helped them, and spent less money than did men.

What does our essay, review of literature, and set of observations say about gender equality, and about the relationships between men and women? First, our observations revealed that males and females differed substantially in their *goals* for shopping. Most recreational and focused shoppers were females and there was little difference in the frequency by which women and men were gift-buyers. Our expectations were only partially supported, then, because we anticipated that women would be both recreational shoppers and gift-buyers; and we thought there would be little difference between men and women in regards to frequency of "recreational shopping." Besides the obvious fact that fewer men were observed, we have to concede that we did not distinguish (when the data were collected) between buying a gift for someone else, or buying a "self-gift." We had thought that women would engage in more gift-buying *for others,* compared to men, and this trend may still be true. Further, note that because men are still socialized to devalue retail shopping, they may have lied–claiming that some fashionable object was for someone else when it was in fact for themselves.

Whatever the case, it can be argued that such goal differences, in addition to differences in the use of *resources*, may be related to influenceability and the effectiveness of particular sales tactics. For example, men spent more money when they were helped, praised, and when the commitment tactic was used on them. Why were these particular tactics useful on the men? Clearly, if the typical male simply wants to buy several objects as quickly and as efficiently as possible (and get out of the store), an effective approach is simply to *help* him find the desired object, praise his selection when he picks a particular shirt, sweater, or whatever, and then recommend an accessory that complements his choice.

Our observations also suggest that individuals' *beliefs* play an important role in determining the effectiveness of a salesclerk or a particular tactic. For instance, male (clothing) shoppers do in fact spend more time and money when clerks are female, rather than male—either because they *believed* female clerks are more knowledgeable concerning fashions and clothing, and they deferred to them because of this expertise, and/or because men are susceptible to the praise statements and other statements of ingratiation used on them.

What, then, does our chapter say about the relationships between men and women? Clearly, the two most significant statements we can make about relationships are (a) that shopping should not be, and in the future will not remain, solely in the domain of "women's work;" and (b) that shopping should be recognized as a necessary, valuable task that should not be devalued. Changes in expectations for who is responsible for shopping, however, will not be implemented easily. Indeed, despite the fact that the media may portray men shopping, cleaning, and vacuuming (e.g., Tony Danza in "Who's the Boss?" and the "Tanners in Full House"), expectations concerning who and how basic daily tasks are assigned to and completed by men and women have not been significantly altered (also see Rogers, Hirata, Chandran & Robinson, this volume). We've already noted, for instance, that fathers rarely shop with their children, and teenage boys rely on their mothers to shop. Why should such a bias continue? Ironically, women have learned (over the decades) to purchase their own automobiles, computers, and so on, whereas many males have not learned to engage in *basic* and *necessary* activities such as buying clothes, or buying gifts (that will be not returned or exchanged). However, as the number of working women continues to increase, and economic and/or other conditions produce families with more than one "bread-winner," changes are inevitable. As such conditions induce more men into the marketplace, we may not only witness dramatic shifts in individuals' goals, plans, and resources for shopping, but also in individuals' beliefs about the importance of sharing shopping duties. If so, there will be fewer gender differences, and a movement toward greater gender equality.

REFERENCES

Barak, B., & Stern, B. (1986). Women's age in advertising: An examination of two consumer age profiles. *Journal of Advertising Research, 25,* 38–47.

Barry, T. E., Gilly, M. C., & Doran, L. E. (1985). Advertising to women with different career orientations. *Journal of Advertising Research, 24,* 26–35.

Becker, B. J. (1986). Influence again: An examination of reviews and studies of gender differences in social influence. In J. S. Hyde & M. C. Linn (Eds.), *The psychology of gender: Advances through meta-analysis* (pp. 178–209). Baltimore: Johns Hopkins University Press.

Bellante, D., & Foster, A. C. (1984). Working wives and expenditure on services. *Journal of Consumer Research, 11*, 700–707.

Bem, S. L. (1975). Sex role adaptability: One consequence of psychological androgyny, *Journal of Personality and Social Psychology, 31*, 634–643.

Bettinghaus, E. P., & Cody, M. J. (1994). *Persuasive Communication* (5th ed.). Ft. Worth, TX: Holt, Rinehart & Winston.

Bird, C. (1940). *Social psychology.* New York: Appleton-Century-Crofts.

Bisanz, G. L., & Rule, B. G. (1989). Gender and persuasion schema: A search for cognitive invariants. *Personality and Social Psychology Bulletin, 15*, 4–18.

Bisanz, G. L., & Rule, B. G. (1990). Childrens' and adults' comprehension of narratives about persuasion. In M. J. Cody & M. L. McLaughlin (Eds.), *Psychology of tactical communication* (pp. 48–69). Clevedon, England: Multilingual Matters.

Booth, A. (1972). Sex and social participation. *American Sociological Review, 37*, 183–192.

Burgoon, J. K., Buller, D. B., & Woodall, W. G. (1989). *Nonverbal communication: The unspoken dialogue.* New York: Harper & Row.

Burnett, J. J. (1991). Examining the media habits of the affluent elderly. *Journal of Advertising Research, 30*, 33–41.

Canary, D. J., & Cody, M. J. (1994). *Interpersonal communication: A goals-based approach.* New York: St. Martin's Press.

Chaiken, S. (1979). Communicator physical attractiveness and persuasion. *Journal of Personality and Social Psychology, 37*, 1387–1397.

Cialdini, R. B. (1993). *Influence: Science and practice* (3rd ed.). New York: Harper Collins.

Cody, M. J., Canary, D. J., & Smith, S. W. (1994). Compliance-gaining goals: An inductive analysis of actors' goal types, strategies, and successes. In J. Daly & J. Wiemann (Eds.), *Strategic communication* (pp. 33–90). Hillsdale, NJ: Lawrence Erlbaum Associates.

Cohen, A. R. (1959). Some implications of self-esteem for social influence. In C. I. Hovland & I. L. Janis (Eds.), *Personality and persuasibility* (pp. 102–120). New Haven: Yale University Press.

Davis, B., & French, W. (1989). Exploring advertising usage segments among the aged. *Journal of Advertising Research, 29*, 22–29.

Day, E., Davis, B., Dove, R., & French, W. (1988). Reaching the senior citizen market(s). *Journal of Advertising Research, 27*, 23–30.

Deutsch, J. F. (1990). Status, sex, and smiling: The effect of role on smiling in men and women. *Personality and Social Psychology Bulletin, 16*, 531–540.

Eagly, A. H. (1978). Sex differences in influenceability. *Psychological Bulletin, 85*, 86–116.

Eagly, A. H. (1983). Gender and social influence: A social psychological analysis. *American Psychologist, 38*, 971–981.

Eagly, A. H., & Carli, L. L. (1981). Sex of researchers and sex-typed communications as determinants of sex differences in influenceability: A meta-analysis of social influence studies. *Psychological Bulletin, 90*, 1–20.

Fischer, E., & Arnold, S. J. (1990). More than a labor of love: Gender roles and Christmas gift shopping. *Journal of Consumer Research, 17*, 333–345.

Gonzales, M. H., Pederson, J. H., Manning, D. J., & Wetter, D. W. (1990). Pardon my gaffe: Effects of sex, status, and consequence severity on accounts. *Journal of Personality and Social Psychology, 58*, 610–621.

Greco, A. J. (1988). The elderly as communicators: Perceptions of advertising practitioners. *Journal of Advertising Research, 28*, 39–46.

Hall, J. A. (1984). *Nonverbal sex differences: Communication accuracy and expressive style.* Baltimore, MD: The Johns Hopkins University Press.

Hall, J. A. (1985). Male and female nonverbal behavior. In A. Siegman & S. Feldstein (Eds.), *Nonverbal behavior in interpersonal relations* (pp. 195–225). Hillsdale, NJ: Lawrence Erlbaum Associates.

Henley, N. M. (1977). *Body politics: Power, sex, and nonverbal communication.* New York: Prentice-Hall.

Hornik, J. (1992). Tactile stimulation and consumer response. *Journal of Consumer Research, 19*, 449–458.

Hovland, C. I., & Janis, I. L. (1959). Summary and implications for future research. In C. I. Hovland & I. L. Janis (Eds.), *Personality and persuasibility* (pp. 225–254). New Haven, CT: Yale University Press.

Hyde, J. S., & Linn, M. C. (Eds.). (1986) *The psychology of gender: Advances through meta-analysis.* Baltimore: Johns Hopkins University Press.

Jackson, R. W., McDaniel, S. W., & Rao, C. P. (1985). Food shopping and preparation: Psychographic differences of working wives and housewives. *Journal of Communication Research, 12*, 110–113.

Janis, I. L., & Field, P. B. (1953). Sex differences and personality factors related to persuasivility. In I. L. Janis, C. I. Hovland, P. B. Field, H. Linton, E. Graham, A. R. Cohen, D. Rife, R. P. Abelson, G. S. Lesser, & B. T. King (Eds.). *Personality and persuasability* (pp. 55–69). New Haven CT: Yale University Press.

Janis, I. L., & Rife, D. (1959). Persuasibility and emotional disorder. In C. I. Hovland & I. L. Janis (Eds.), *Personality and Persuasibility* (pp. 121–137), New Haven, CT: Yale University Press.

Karlins, M, & Abelson, H. I. (1970). *Persuasion: How opinions and attitudes are changed* (2nd ed.). New York: Springer-Verlag.

Knapp, M. L., & Hall, J. A. (1992). *Nonverbal communication and human interaction* (3rd edition). New York: Holt, Rinehart & Winston.

Lazer, W. (1985). Inside the mature market. *American Demographics, 7*, 23–25, 48–49.

Leigh, T. W., Rethans, A. J., & Whitney, T. R. (1987). Role portrayals of women in advertising: Cognitive responses and advertising effectiveness. *Journal of Advertising Research, 26*, 54–62.

Lumpkin, J. R., & Festervand, T. A. (1988). Purchase information sources of the elderly. *Journal of Advertising Research, 27*, 31–41.

Mayo, C., & Henley, N. M. (Eds.). (1981). *Gender and nonverbal behavior.* New York: Springer-Verlag.

McGuire, W. J. (1969). The nature of attitudes and attitude change. In G. Lindzey & E. Aronson (Eds.), *The handbook of social psychology* (2nd ed., Vol. 3, pp. 1130–1187). Reading, MA: Addison-Wesley.

McLaughlin, M. L., Louden, A. D., Casion, J. L., Altendorf, D. M., Baaske, K. T., & Smith, S. W. (1985). Conversational planning and self-serving utterances: The manipulation of topical and functional structures in dyadic interaction. *Journal of Language and Social Psychology, 4*, 233–251.

Miller, L. C., Cooke, L. L., Tsang, J., & Morgan, F. (1992). Should I brag? Nature and impact of positive and boastful disclosures for women and men. *Human Communication Research, 18*, 364– 399.

Miller, L. C., & Read, S. J. (1987). Why am I telling you this? Self-disclosure in a goal-based model of personality. In V. J. Derlega & J. H. Berg (Ed.), *Self-disclosure: Theory, research and therapy* (pp. 35–58). New York: Plenum.

Miller, L. C., & Read, S. J. (1991). Inter-personalism: Understanding persons in relationships. *Advances in personal relationships, 2*, 233–267.

Montgomery, C. L., & Burgoon, M. (1980). The effects of androgyny and message expectations on resistance to persuasive communication. *Communication Monographs, 47*, 56–67.

Peters, J. F. (1989). Youth clothes-shopping behavior: An analysis by gender. *Adolescence, 24*, 575–580.

Qualls, W. J. (1987). Household decision behavior: The impact of husbands' and wives' sex role orientation. *Journal of Consumer Research, 14*, 264–279.

Read, S. J., & Miller, L. C. (1989). Inter-personalism: Toward a goal-based theory of persons in relationships. In L.A. Pervin (Ed.), *Goal concepts in personality and social psychology* (pp. 413–472). Hillsdale, NJ: Lawrence Erlbaum Associates.

Retailers change ploys to improve sales. (1993, September 15). *Los Angeles Times*, pp. D1, D4.

Rothman, M. L., & Gandossy, R. P. (1982). Sad tales: The accounts of white-collar defendants and the decision to sanction. *Pacific Sociological Review, 25*, 449–473.

Rubin, A. M., & Rubin, R. B. (1982). Older Persons' TV viewing patterns and motivations. *Communication Research, 9*, 287–313.

Rule, B. G., Bisanz, G. L., & Kohn, M. (1985). Anatomy of a persuasion schema: Targets, goals, and strategies. *Journal of Personality and Social Psychology, 48,* 1127–1140.

Rule, B. G. & Bisanz, G. L. (1987). Goals and strategies of persuasion: A cognitive schema for understanding social events. In M. Zanna, P. Herman, & J. Olsen (Eds.), *Social influence: The fifth Ontario symposium on personality and social psychology* (pp. 185–206). Hillsdale, NJ: Lawrence Erlbaum Associates.

Scheidel, T. M. (1963). Sex and persuasibility. *Speech Monographs, 30,* 353–358.

Schmitt, B. H., Leclerc, F., & Dube-Rioux, L. (1988). Sex typing and consumer behavior: A test of gender schema theory. *Journal of Consumer Research, 15,* 122–128.

Smith, S. W., Cody, M. J., LoVette, S., & Canary, D. J. (1990). Self-monitoring, gender, and compliance-gaining goals. In M. J. Cody & M. L. McLaughlin (Eds.), *The psychology of tactical communication* (pp. 91–135). Clevedon, England: Multilingual Matters.

Ursic, A. C., Ursic, J. L., & Ursic, V. L. (1986). A longitudinal study of the use of the elderly in magazine advertising. *Journal of Advertising Research, 13,* 131–133.

Ward, D. A., Seccombe, K., Bendel, R., & Carter, L. F. (1985). Cross-sex context as a factor in persuasibility sex differences. *Social Psychology Quarterly, 48,* 269–276.

Wheeler, L., & Nezlek, J. (1977). Sex differences in social participation. *Journal of Personality and Social Psychology, 35,* 742–754.

Chapter 14

Gender and Power

Judy C. Pearson
Ohio University

Leda Cooks
University of Massachusetts

difference: 1. an instance of differing in nature form or quality; a characteristic that distinguishes one from the other or from the average. 2. distinction or discrimination in preference.

— Webster's New Collegiate Dictionary (1981)

differánce: a structuring principle that suggests that definition rests not on the entity itself but on its positive and negative references to other texts. Meaning is changed over time and ultimately the attribution of meaning is put off, postponed, deferred, forever.

— Derrida (1972, 1981, pp. 39–40)

The relationship between gender and communication has been of interest to researchers since the beginning of this century (Jespersen, 1922; Parsons, 1913; Stopes, 1908). Within the past two decades, the research has increased at a geometric rate. Perhaps of greater importance, issues of *how* gender and communication should be studied have arisen. The significance of this shift lies, in part, in the fact that the relative power between and among women and men is affected by how gender is conceptualized. This essay will explore the development of inquiry on gender and communication. Attention will be paid to the implications of studying gender from particular perspectives.

This chapter reflects first on the history of gender research and then reflects on its reflection. We begin with a discussion of *Gender as Difference* by the first author. Followed by a description of *Gender as Differánce* developed by the second author, which also distinguishes between gender as difference and gender as differánce, and between gender research and feminist research. We then consider power in gender research and discuss radical feminism, arguments for and against ontological difference, and the location and understanding of oppression. This section is followed by our criticisms of the traditional, quantitative research that is used to study gender and human relationships. We then conclude with some thoughts on re-visioning gender as scholars in an academic community.

GENDER AS DIFFERENCE

Perhaps it is essential, at the beginning, to discuss the term *gender*. Until the 1970s, *sex* was the term of choice among researchers investigating women and men. The first textbook in speech communication, for example, was entitled *Sex Differences in Human Communication* (Eakins & Eakins, 1978). Not surprisingly, early studies treated *sex* as a demographic variable that had no more theoretical grounding than age, race, or socioeconomic class.

During the 1970s a number of forces came together to encourage researchers to refine the word *sex*. Biologists viewed *biological sex* as their province and continued to seek answers to biological questions. Researchers in the social sciences and humanities replaced the term *sex* with *gender* in order to clarify the linguistic, social, moral, and mental aspects of individuals.

A team of psychologists and an individual psychologist presented similar reconceptualizations of gender almost simultaneously in 1974. Spence, Helmreich, and Stapp (Spence & Helmreich, 1978; Spence, Helmreich, & Stapp, 1974a, 1974b) chronicled their findings in a book entitled *Masculinity and Femininity: Their Psychological Dimensions, Correlates, and Antecedents* and operationalized them in an instrument known as the Personal Attributes Questionnaire. For her part, Bem (1974; 1975a; 1975b) developed the Bem Sex Role Inventory and contributed to both the scholarly and the popular literature.

At that time, I was completing my doctoral studies at Indiana University. My dissertation considered the influence of teachers' and students' biological sex and the teacher's predisposition toward sexism on speech evaluation in high school classes (Pearson, 1975b). I learned that male and female students were graded differently—particularly by sexist teachers. I had also published an article in *Today's Speech* (now Communication Quarterly) that dealt with Abigail Adams' conceptions of women's rights within some of her personal correspondence (Pearson, 1975b).

I had an opportunity to meet and talk with Sandra Bem just after I had completed my Ph.D. We talked about our common interest in sex roles and sexism. I was intrigued to learn that we were both motivated to investigate this area for personal reasons. Bem felt that she had been "miscategorized" by earlier instruments in which she could only be masculine or feminine rather than masculine and feminine. I was nurtured by a masculine mother and a feminine father and thus grew up cross-sexed and with the belief that most women were as closely in touch with their masculine selves as I was.

The work of Bem and the Texas psychologists called into question older conceptions of masculinity and femininity as the end points on a single scale and replaced them with two bipolar scales. Individuals were thus not simply categorized as masculine *or* feminine but as having unrelated greater and lesser endorsements of masculine traits and of feminine traits. An individual could be both high in masculinity and high in femininity (androgynous), high in masculinity and low in femininity (masculine), low in masculinity and high in femininity (feminine), or low in masculinity and low in femininity (undifferentiated).

This difference in conceptualization might appear to be simplistic or even irrelevant. However, the perspective dramatically altered the way men and women were categorized. Neither men nor women were limited in their self-conceptions based on their biological sex. Women could be masculine and men could view themselves as more feminine. Ideally, both could be flexible and adopt masculine and feminine characteristics when appropriate. Scholars might have long known that masculinity and being a man and femininity and being a woman are not identical constructs.

One's masculinity or femininity became known as a *sex role*, a *gender role*, or simply as *gender* that could vary independently from one's *biological sex*. When the term *sex* is used, it refers generally to one's biological or physical self; the word *gender* points to psychological, social, and interactive characteristics (see, for example, Bernard, 1971, 1975; Lipman-Blumen & Tickamyer, 1975; Pearson, 1975b; Stroller, 1968). Social scientists soon learned that although gender and sex could diverge, they tended to covary. Women are more likely to be feminine than are men, and men are more likely to be masculine than are women.

The close affiliation between biological sex and psychological gender has been explained in a variety of ways. MacCorquodale (1989) summarized the dialogue:

> The relative weight given by a belief system to social versus biological factors results in an ideology that maximizes or minimizes sex differences. Within both feminist and traditional systems of belief, there is a division between those who believe the influences of biology are indirect and mediated by society (social constructionists) and those who believe that direct effects of biology endow each gender with certain essential characteristics (biological essentialism). (Sayers, 1982, p. 95)

The nature versus nurture question has been debated extensively; it is continually revitalized by new research findings.

More recently, an even more provocative problem has surfaced. When does gender become known and stable? Research in the United States has been relatively unequivocal. Money (1972) argued that gender identity is formed during a child's first 3 years. Sex roles continue to develop between the ages of 3 and 5 (Seegmiller, 1980). Gender constancy, or the tendency to view oneself dependably as a male or female, is achieved between the ages of 5 and 7 (Tibbits, 1975).

Evidence from other cultures suggests that gender roles might be far more fluid. Imperato-McGuinley and her colleagues (1979) examined sexually incongruous children from rural Santo Domingo villages. These children displayed an acquired inadequacy known as DHT-deficiency, and they had ambiguous genitalia. Eighteen people with this condition were raised as females. At puberty, these "females" developed a penis and scrotum and their voices became lower. The familiarity of the phenomenon encouraged the development of a word that literally translates as "penis at twelve." Sixteen of the 18 children raised as females were successful in adopting a male gender role and in marrying and fathering children. Two experienced sex role confusion.

The researchers drew two conclusions. First, they observed that when biological evidence and socialization are in contradiction, biology seems more basic. Second, they concluded that gender identification might evolve throughout childhood and not be fixed at the early ages postulated by research completed in the United States. The study both supports biological determinism and the fluidity of one's sex role.

Traditional research on sex differences treats sex as just another variable, "as a property of individuals and their behaviors rather than also of social structures and conceptual systems" (Harding, 1986, pp. 33–34). Gender researchers "have focused on the idea of gender identity in terms of psychological sex, that is, the degree to which a person identifies with characteristics associated with masculinity or femininity" (Jenkins & Kramarae, 1981, p. 14). Indeed, most of my own work and the work of many people in communication adopted either a biological or psychological notion of gender in the 1980s (see, for example, Pearson, 1980a, 1980b, 1981a, 1981b, 1984; Pearson, Miller, & Senter, 1983; Pearson & Trent, 1986; Serafini & Pearson, 1984; Shea & Pearson, 1986). When we did this, we tended to ignore the sociological contribution and the "fact that both masculinity and femininity are man-made creations" (p. 14). Jenkins and Kramarae (1981) added, "If gender is considered primarily a psychological rather than sociological phenomenon, then individuals are thought free to choose to change their behavior to best suit themselves" (p. 14).

Feminist researchers have criticized traditional scientific approaches and have worked to shift the paradigms, to change the ways we think about the process of learning and discovery. Indeed, feminists have argued for a "new world view." Broadly speaking, feminist research has recognized that traditional scientific research is a patriarchal enterprise, that information pertaining to women has been viewed through an "ideological" lens, and that male experience has been the panorama from which others—both male and female—have been judged. Feminists discourage researchers from seeking additional answers to old questions, but encourage investigators to pursue new questions about women's experiences from their own positioning. Feminist scholars such as Rich (1986) and French (1985) defined feminism and sexuality as a multiplicity of diverse experiences, models, and cultures.

GENDER AS DIFFERÁNCE

A title more in line with the purposes of this section of our chapter might be gender *as* power or the power *in defining* gender, rather than gender and power. To use the conjunction "and" separates power from the label we give it. To speak of gender is simultaneously to speak of power; indeed, the development of "gender" as a particular area of scholarship has emerged out of a need to validate women's experiences as equivalent to those of men. What constitutes gendered knowledge? Concerns about gender, the way it is expressed, the ways it is socially constructed or created, are concerns raised by those who are *other than men*. Yet, studying gender and researching the ways that men and women experience the world differently routinely inscribes women as literally *not Man*. The power in defining and categorizing gender, then, is the power of defining difference, of epistemological understandings of self and other, of subject and object, and of autonomy and constraint. These are precisely the politics of empowerment that have concerned (male) scholars for centuries. In defining gender, however, we need to ask whose word we are representing and whether we are empowering women through changing the language of oppression or merely redefining a "lack of" what is male.

I begin my section by first noting that I make a distinction between feminist research and gender research. I believe that the focus of gender research (in the tradition of Gilligan, 1982, Kramarae, 1981; Thorne, Kramarae, & Henley, 1983) has been specifically on differences between men and women as the means by which women can become empowered to change their lives. I differentiate gender and feminist scholarship in that I believe the former to be a focus on the means by which (White, middle-class) women are created as *Other*, whereas feminist scholarship has focused on the consequences of gendered experiences and the ways women can resist or re-evaluate those consequences. Much of what has been called feminist research I have lumped into the label "gender" research in and on communication. Also, although much of this scholarship has been conducted in departments other than communication (e.g., linguistics, sociology, and psychology), each has examined the "different" ways that women and men communicate. Foss (1988) included both feminist scholarship and gender research in her definition of "women's communication scholarship." She defined the scope of this research as all research done by women, regardless of topic or content, to scholarship "'about women or gender,' whether done by women or men," to "feminist scholarship, which brings to the research the self-consciously political values of the women's movement and challenges traditional notions of research" (p. 1). While I am critical of the representation of traditional research on women and gender *as* feminist scholarship, I do not always assume that gender research has been interpreted as feminist scholarship. However, given the differentiation that both Foss (1988) and I make, little of the research called "women's communication scholarship" can be defined as feminist scholarship.

Although most feminists and gender scholars agree that women need to re-vision (as Rich named it) themselves in history, literature, philosophy, art, and science, appeals to difference have primarily been based on essentialist arguments. Gender researchers who have advocated the "nurture" approach to understanding gender as a social construction have based their arguments on notions of a different essence of maleness and femaleness. In its implicit essentialization of sexuality, gender research has made "difference" the ontology from which its "nature versus nurture" epistemological arguments emerge. In effect, such arguments about being and knowing naturalize "difference," while critically examining and challenging only the epistemological assumptions that categorically define and explain the "nature" of men and women.

Whether the philosophy and politics of explaining difference have changed over the centuries or not, the sociopolitical climate in the United States has shifted toward increasing awareness of cognitive and emotional differences between men and women. Television shows have replaced the physical separation of men and women (women in the home, men on the streets and at work) with narratives/discussions about psychological and linguistic differences represented in popular studies on gender and communication (e.g., Gilligan, 1982; Kramarae, 1981; Tannen, 1990). Popular television talk shows and sitcoms (such as "Mad About You," "Love and War," "Seinfeld") focus on the misunderstandings/misinterpretations that arise when males and females attempt to communicate. News columns and magazine articles devoted to understanding male/female communication dominate space in these media as well. Yet, the increasing awareness of differences in popular culture, along with the recent focus on empowering women through emphasizing the social construction of language and identity has led to a double bind for many women who have fought to be recognized as both different and equal. An important questions to ask is, "How are the very ways difference is studied disempowering to women?"

Although not proposing to answer this question, this chapter is an added voice to this discussion. Although many studies have examined feminism, femininity, and power (e.g., Bartky, 1990, Gordan, 1991; Weedon, 1992), few have examined the place of power in gender research in communication. Rarely have either feminist or gender studies turned their focus inward in an attempt to understand the ways women are constructing power in their very articulation of empowerment. For instance, although much of the work in feminist and gender scholarship has advocated conversation among multiple standpoints, multiple authored works are usually presented as harmonious in point of view. This perpetuates the notion that knowledge (and therefore, power) is contained within the form; therefore, a research paper contains more "intelligence" than a conversation, and a lecture more than a discussion.

POWER IN GENDER RESEARCH

Parker (1989) observed that power emerges as a central concern to any focus on identity/self-consciousness. Within gender research, power and identity have always been bound in one another. For women to "find" themselves, to value their identity as women, meant that they had power and control over their lives. The goal of gender research was to show the differences in the ways men and women communicate, thereby allowing women to value their experiences as different in comparison to male experience. Therefore, gender research in communication has concerned itself with power as one half of a complementarity. As with the heterosexist construction of men and women, powerful and powerless behavior exist in opposition, as a struggle between contesting (complementary) forces over stable territory. Therefore, as Lakoff (1975) suggested, women often use "power-less" terms, or as Tannen (1990) wrote, women use the language of relationship whereas men converse in the language of status and hierarchy.

The bipolarization of power terms allows a focus on difference without consideration of the various ways men and women are positioned within the discourse itself. For instance, the consideration (long present in the work of many feminist scholars of color) that language does not position one as exclusively male or female but in terms of race, sexuality, age, and class as well displays language itself as the site of multiple constructions of identity. Thus, language and power do not exist in isolation, nor is the territory over which the "gender wars" are fought ever immutable. Such constructions of race, class, and gender as fixed and stable belie a politics of location that constitute fe/male subjectivities within gender research. hooks (1990) observed that this "politics of location' necessarily calls those of us who would participate in the formation of counter-hegemonic cultural practice to identify the spaces where we can begin the process of re-vision. . . for many of us, that movement requires pushing against oppressive boundaries set by race, sex and class" (p. 143).

For hooks, this movement begins as a gesture of defiance—as movement *against* oppression—but is transformed through the "ever shifting realms of power relations" (p. 145). In this manner, movement *against* becomes movement *toward* the creation of new spaces and openings for awareness. Such an awareness is informed by intersecting moments of race, gender, and class that are intimately bound in relation to others.

In this sense, power is not the proprietary struggle between oppressor and oppressed over the territory of rights but, rather, exists as both freedom and domination within discursive relations. Thus, one answer to the primary question posed above is that knowledge of gender is knowledge of difference not just as oppression, but as both lack and excess. Yet, notions of power/identity are constructed in flux: defined in situations, as time and place, in the space of organizations/institutions, within boundaries and categories.

Gender Research and the Paradox of Difference

Gender is usually defined as difference or as equality. This section examines the struggle over definitions of identity, power, and difference that have characterized the women's movement in this country since the 1970s. As our earlier discussion indicated, biological and psychological distinctions between male and female affirmed women's differences from men while legitimating their status as other to men. The dichotomization of difference through categories of gender presented the women's movement with several (new?) epistemological problematics. Dichotomies are useful in that they offer a means for clearly distinguishing good from bad, often serving to empower emancipatory movements (such as the women's movement). However, dissatisfaction with "separate but equal" models of gender such as those proposed by Chodorow (1978), Gilligan (1982), and Kramarae (1981) emerged over the dichotomization of male/female as a totalizing system of difference. This led to debate (among White feminists) about difference versus equality with men. Should women attempt to prove themselves as men's equals by defining equality and identity according to male standards, or should women attempt to validate their differences through preserving what is uniquely female?

The treatment, according to MacKinnon (1984) of sex as distinction and of equality as equivalence, has placed women in the bind of routinely defined (represented) according to male standards (although the referent is seldom recognized). MacKinnon (1984) noted:

> Virtually every quality that distinguishes men from women is already affirmatively compensated in this society. Men's physiology defines most sports, their needs define auto and health insurance coverage, their socially designed biographies define workplace expectations and successful career patterns, their perspectives and concerns define quality in scholarship, their experiences and obsessions define merit, their objectivication of life defines art, their military service defines citizenship, their presence defines family, their inability to get along with each other—their wars and rulerships—defines history, their image defines god and their genitals define sex. (p. 84)

MacKinnon's argument is that difference and equality both exist to perpetuate domination of males over females.

Frye (1990) concurred with this view in a provocative essay entitled *Lesbian "Sex"*. She focused on the representation of sex—both as a way of being (noun) and as a specific act (verb) between two consenting adults—in a series of studies on American couples published by Blumstein and Schwartz (1983, cited in Frye, 1990). Frye took a critical look at the way "sex" is defined and measured in these and other reputable studies that have looked at duration and frequency of lesbian "sex" in relation to other (gay and heterosexual) couples. Frye's questioning of what has traditionally defined hetero sex and the importance attached to some acts over others raises important issues regarding *whose* sex and sexuality are being defined. Frye (1990) wrote:

> When I put myself to the task of theorizing about sex and sexuality, it was as though I *had* no experiences, as though there was no ground on which and from which to generate theory. But (if I understand the terminology rightly) I have in fact been what they call "sexually active" for close to a quarter of a century. . . heterosexually, lesbianly, and autoerotically. Surely I have experience. But I seem not to have the *experiential knowledge* of the sort I need. (pp. 309–310)

Although Mackinnon's discourse is critical of the "advancements" in the legal system made under the guise of special benefits and equal protection under the law and Frye's concern is with the power of language, their work may serve as commentary on the moves to understand gender and communication. The advances made in understanding women's communication as relational, indicating their connectedness to others, perpetuate epistemological assumptions about women as nurturers. That women relate through sharing, understanding, and work for inclusion bespeaks their historical *exclusion* from male society. To acknowledge "generic" male terms in our language is not enough if women are to escape the traps that language itself creates. Yet, creating terms unique or specific to female experience or valuing women's ways of communicating as different raises again the question *different from what?* To define against a standard suggests that the standard has already been established.

Radical Feminism: Uniting Against Patriarchy

The rise of radical feminism in the late 1970s and early 1980s can be seen as a call for unity and the need for a coherent movement where all women could unite against all forms of oppression. However, although many radical feminists claim that patriarchy is the universal experience of oppression, they also assume that the language of patriarchy itself hinders any attempt at unity among women.

The radical feminist argument about language, identity and difference suggests an essential being (perhaps not woman or female as Wittig, 1990, suggested) that exists apart from (male) society's definition of sex and sexuality. MacKinnon (1984) perhaps best illustrated the radical view of "difference," stating that, "Division may be rational or irrational. Dominance either seems or is justified. Difference *is*" (p. 82).

As a logical extension of the radical argument, separatist feminists have attempted to avoid patriarchy altogether, articulating the need for women to create a society totally apart from men, and have considered men a burden to society and a threat to civilization in general (Echols, 1991). Yet, as Jehlen (1990) noted, the universal characterization of any experience leads to the denial of other forms and ways of knowing—of the complex ways in which we experience the world.

Arguments for/against Ontological Difference

Radical and separatist feminists have suggested a unified understanding of "difference" as a unified essential Other-than-man. Yet, questions of difference and equality, while immanent concerns of white feminists, do not account for differences among women themselves. Still, some White feminists are attempting to silence the voices of those (lesbians and women of color) who are different within the feminist movement itself. Indeed, many radical feminists feel that the category of gender difference articulates the ultimate (essential) distinction between peoples and should, therefore, speak to the experiences of all women who call themselves "feminists." Indeed, many women who criticized the assumption that gender is the ultimate trope of difference and spoke instead of many overlapping and intersecting moments of race, sexuality, and gender were alienated and isolated from the (White, middle-class) women's movement. Higgenbotham has observed (cited in Gordon, 1991), the debate among White feminists about difference verses equality was pre-dated by the debate among African Americans about separation verses assimilation.

To the extent that Third World women and women of color have not been represented in the experiences of White, middle-class American women, they did not (and do not) consider themselves to be part of the feminist movement. The debate over the "hierarchy" of oppression left many women of color wondering how their experiences should or could ever be represented in feminist discourse. As hooks (1984) argued, the oppression experienced by a White housewife [reflecting on Friedan's *The Feminine Mystique*] can never and should never be equated with the experience of a poor, lesbian African American. Yet, hooks herself did not advocate further separation of women according to their differences but, rather, the awareness among all women that such a hierarchy of oppression should create.

On the Edge of Difference; Locating and Understanding Oppression

Third World women scholars, who often choose not to identify themselves as feminists, have long recognized the imperialism of Western "progressive" movements (such as feminism) in the name of a benevolent multiculturalism and ethnic pluralism (see, for example, Loomba, 1991; Mani, 1992). The problematic issue here, as is the case in many of the feminists of the United States, is *who* can empower the oppressed and under what circumstances participation should occur. For many women scholars in the Third World, the question is not "how do we want to be defined?" but "who has the right to define us?" Identity is problematic only insofar as others (First World nations) identify the oppressed as needing transformation. Mani (1992) criticized the elitism that allows First World feminists to view other cultural practices as oppressive. Spivak (1991), too, argued that the difference that makes a difference is that of learning and knowing about other women: "if you do it in such a way that we can really talk to you. . . but if you just talk about doing it in a superficial way so that people can say that you are also interested in the third world then you will get nothing. It's not *easier* to do than other kinds of work." (p. 228)

Only those who speak from the margins, as hooks (1990) noted, can reflect consciousness of the boundaries and constraints placed on those defined as different within the dominant system of meaning. Culture is recognized as such by those who stand outside the center. The boundaries of symbolic meaning, both visible and invisible, are what make all people realize that they are somehow at the fringes, on the radical edge between reason and cultural insanity. For those who recognize themselves and their experiences reflected in culture, choices and opportunities present themselves as natural and predetermined. Lack of recognition of the mobility and constraints placed on all those who are different has been cited more than once as the reason gender research has not provoked much of a response by women outside the White, middle-class mainstream.

ON RESEARCHING GENDER

Criticism of Traditional, Quantitative, Scientific Research

Science is not value free (Bowles & Duelli-Klein, 1983; DuBois, 1985; Fox Keller, 1985; Rosser, 1988). It is fabricated by scientists who are constructed within a society. As a social enterprise, science embodies the values and attitudes of the culture. Science is sexist if the society that produces it is sexist. Not surprisingly, social science has generally reinforced dominant social values and conceptions. (Some exceptions, though, include research that shows that stereotypical ideas about women and men are sometimes not demonstrated in behavioral studies). Although feminist critiques are varied, four major criticisms of traditional research can be identified (e.g., Bowles & Duelli-Klein, 1983; DuBois, 1985).

First, such inquiry sustains sexist and androcentric values. The "male-as-central" perspective in scientific research has rendered women invisible. Although social science examines women, it generally can not see them. Issues that are important to women are left unexplored. Gynocentric values are rarely espoused. In general, men serve as the archetype for all humans. Johnson (1984) observed that women continue to be viewed as the "other" and noted that they are further alienated because of "male language that is foreign to their experience" (p. 77). Bate (1984) added, "Difference as a concept in our research is problematic . . . it is extremely hard to talk about differences without implying inequalities. If women's language is different from men's . . .then one of the two sex-linked languages is superior and the other should be changed" (p. 101).

Second, research is not available to those who need it. A great deal of research makes no tangible difference to women, individuals of color, and those who are poor or otherwise disenfranchised. In addition, research findings are rarely accessible to anyone except a handful of academicians. The language that is adopted is specialized jargon rather than the language of average people. "Pure" research is in abundance; applied information is demeaned.

Third, exploitive and elitist relationships mark traditional scholarship. The research process, itself, suggests a hierarchical nature. The language of science implies a power relationship. Individuals are viewed as "subjects" (which incorporates a metaphor of royalty). Worse, people are dehumanized as they are referred to impersonally as the "objects" of study. Participants may also be deceived or manipulated in the name of science.

Fourth, the political nature of research is not acknowledged. Instead, research is viewed as "objective," and results are readily accepted without question because they embody such qualities as impartiality, neutrality, and lack of prejudice or bias Such studies thus gain persuasive appeal (Bowles & Duelli-Klein, 1983). Bate (1994) added, "Training in laboratory research methods promotes the belief that category differences are central and that individual differences within categories are error. None of us would argue in daily life that stereotypes are better than knowing individual people, but experimental research often promotes the continuation of stereotypes" (p. 101). Johnson (1984) concurred:

> What any of us knows about the reputed linkages and reciprocities of gender and social relationships is a function of very diverse ways of knowing. This, of course, is true of any domain of knowledge. But in the field of gender and communication, the diversity in ways of knowing carries special implications because the subject matter is political-ideological... Furthermore, any particular knowledge gains or fails to gain legitimacy according to the degree to which it meets a person's criteria for what type of knowledge is important. (p. 78)

Emerging Themes in Feminist Constructions of Method

Four central themes emerge in feminist constructions of a method. These include (a) valuing women and their experiences, (b) studying gender as a social construction, (c) recognizing the role of self-reflexivity and intersubjectivity in the research process, and (d) doing research that has value for women.

Valuing Women and Their Experiences.   A decade ago, Wood and Phillips (1984) summarized the Pennsylvania State University Conference on Gender and Communication Research: "Conferees recommended research on women in women's environments and—separately—of men in men's environments" (p. 63). In the last 10 years, feminists have echoed the importance of examining women's cultures. Creating theory grounded in the actual experiences and language of women is one goal of a feminist research methodology. Feminists believe that research should embrace women's values, experiences, and ideas in their own right rather than to examine women through men's frames of reference. Women's experiences, in and of themselves, should be examined.

This research would go beyond traditional inquiries that include hypothesis testing and the isolation of variables. Feminists view such approaches as lacking holistic understanding (DuBois, 1985). Consequently, feminist methods are often phenomenological. Such research respects women's experiences and views them in their entirety within their unique circumstances. It allows for a transaction between the observer and the observed (Harding, 1987).

Studying Gender as a Social Construction.   Feminist researchers reject the notion that gender is a natural, biological phenomenon. Feminists view gender as a socially learned construction. As such, gender is central to experience and to research. Some writers believe that gender is the most fundamental issue to culture (see, for example, Foss & Foss, 1989).

As a cardinal characteristic, gender permeates all social practices, myths, and ideologies. Research thus cannot simply dispense with gender as a biological variable or a psychological construct. Instead, gender becomes a central categorizing classification (Thorne, Kramarae, & Henley, 1983). Gender is a ubiquitous social creation of human experience that is culturally constructed. Gender is basic to all human socialization and knowledge.

Recognizing the Role of Self-Reflexivity and Intersubjectivity in the Research Process. Self-reflexivity and intersubjectivity are sometimes used equivalently, but they are different concepts. Self-reflexivity in research requires that the researcher acknowledge the hierarchy implicit in gathering *data* from a subject and retrieving it for the purposes of scientific knowledge. When a feminist researcher recognizes her own location in the research process, she also retrieves the aspects of *relationship* important to feminist research. Positioning the researcher in research makes the differing interests, biases, and concerns of feminists visible. The historical contributions of race, class, and social status in which the researched and the researcher are situated must be acknowledged. When the researcher examines herself in the process, as Harding (1987) observed, the research is no longer an invisible, anonymous, disembodied voice of authority.

Intersubjectivity is the complementary exchange of information between the investigator and the investigated (Spitzack & Carter, 1989). The researcher shares her experiences and the goal of her research with the researched individuals. The researched people become collaborators in the project; they are co-researchers. Frequently, they become acquaintances or friends of the researcher. Nearly 5 years ago, the first author conducted research for *Lasting Love: What Keeps Couples Together* (Pearson, 1992). Today, she continues to receive letters, cards, and phone calls from those individuals who served as co-researchers. In her current project, *Marriage after Mourning* (Pearson, 1995) the first author has become acquainted with couples across the country who have lost children but have remained in satisfying marriages. These couples have become part of a network of individuals who are helping her to understand the marital process.

Intersubjectivity allows the investigator to continually relate her experiences with her current perceptions and to communicate those experiences and perceptions with those being investigated. Building on this notion, Lather (1991) suggested that sequential interviewing (taking interpretations of interviews back to the participants) is necessary for women to make research a community interest and value. In this manner, intersubjectivity is only experienced within the process of coming to knowledge of the other. Although this process is never fully complete, the sharing of research creates new spaces for questions and conflicting ideas of what occurred.

Doing Research that has Value for Women. Research should have value for women in two senses. First, it should deal with the practical situations that characterize the ordinary lives of women. Research should consider the pragmatic and the applied rather than the exotic and the theoretical. It should have the potential to contribute assistance in the form of insights and information to women. Similarly, research should go beyond academic boundaries and professional forums to share information.

Second, research should have value as it frees people from those conditions that are oppressive to them (Bowles & Duelli-Klein, 1983). Feminist research must be instrumental in improving women's lives. Some researchers believe that the *means* (interviewing women and valuing their stories and lives) may be more important than the product of the research itself. Feminists such as Steinem (1991) noted that the goal lies in providing women with both a heightened understanding *and* the tools to act on behalf of themselves to improve their social and economic conditions. Research that deals with topics like battering, incest, abuse, and so on, often exemplify this goal of feminist research.

What Kind of Research Should We Do?   Johnson (1984) observed that "one can 'know' about gender and social relationships from several very different positions and that these varying positions affect not only what is studied but how the phenomena selected for study are interpreted" (p. 78). She labeled these positions as *actor, social scientist, cultural anthropologist,* and *feminist.*

Johnson (1984) explained that when the actor is the knower then "the conscious knowledge of everyday life" is made "legitimate." She referenced Lakoff's research as an example of using data based on introspection and intuition.

When the social scientist is the knower, a very different picture emerges. Johnson (1984) noted, "The social science knower mistrusts the bias and limited experiences of any actor." These knowers have explanation and prediction as their goal and they use observation and measurement to achieve them. Social science generally relies on comparisons and thus often compares males and females.

When the knower is a cultural anthropologist, she values naturalistic inquiry and ethnography. Johnson (1984) added, "Methods for naturalistic analysis of the influences of gender in interaction vary from qualitative to quantitative, but in all cases, the researcher's knowledge must be acquired by understanding the natural, undisturbed properties of human behavior *in situ*" (p. 79).

The fourth possible way of "knowing" is that of feminism. Feminist knowers assume the patriarchal, oppressive nature of society on women's experience and consciousness. Johnson (1984) wrote, "Knowledge within this frame is an interesting fusion of archaeological pursuits and naturalistic inquiry: archaeological in its attempt to uncover and free the suppressed cultural forms of women and naturalistic in its attempts to be free of preconceptions about the meanings of interactional patterns" (p. 79).

Three of Johnson's ways of knowing seem to hold promise. The fourth, the social scientist as knower, also has some potential, particularly if it is used in conjunction with other ways of knowing, in a triangulated design. We are uncomfortable suggesting only one kind of research or one kind of knowing. Oral histories, simulations, hermeneutics, ethnography, triangulation, and other approaches have all been recommended by feminist writers (see, e.g., Anderson & Jack, 1991; Bowles & Duelli-Klein, 1983; Fee, 1981; Harding, 1986, 1987; Hawkensworth, 1989; Langellier & Hall, 1989; Spitzack & Carter, 1989). Harding (1987) may have the final word as she noted that the strongest feminist research studies are not notable because of the methods they employ. The best studies use women's lives and perceptions as their inception. They consider race, class, and ethnicity; they fashion methods that are compatible with the research problem; and they incorporate researcher partiality in their findings.

Some feminist scholars have shifted from an emphasis on the need for valuing women's experience to criticizing the ways women have identified themselves through male experience of the world (see, e.g., Borland, 1991; Hale, 1991; Kauffman, 1992). Indeed, this is the primary basis for the differences between liberal and radical/socialist/postmodernist feminism. Whereas liberal feminists have uncritically valorized women's experiences of the world, other feminists have recognized the danger for women in identifying with or against male experience. hooks (1990, 1991, 1992) argued for the need for women to create a space apart from, rather than in opposition to, male knowledge of the world. Comley (1990) noted that "to identify against oneself is to devalue one's experience and to place oneself—if one is a woman—on the margins of privileged experience" (p. 179).

Similarly, de Lauretis defined experience as "the general sense of a process by which, for all social beings subjectivity is constructed. . . not by external ideas, values or material causes, but by one's personal subjective engagement in the practices, discourses and institutions that lend significance (value, meaning, and affect, to the world)" (p. 159).

Yet, both subjectivity and objectivity, the knowledge of people and things, is intimately connected to power. Whether the experience is viewed as ascertaining a shared knowledge of things or socially constructing views of the world, the assumption remains that humans are capable of generating knowledge of some reality.

CONCLUSION

What Are the Possibilities for Re-visioning Gender as Scholars in an Academic Community?

Scholars are beginning to reevaluate their constructions of intercultural and interpersonal relationships. We need to move beyond the superficialities of sex distinctions and look more deeply at what lies at the center of our knowledge of ourselves and others. Scholars need to move away from the theories of the past and toward the more complex and detailed articulations of the discursive *locations* at which power is articulated and reality constructed.

Although several feminist scholars have disparaged Foucault's uncritical acceptance of gendered knowledge (e.g. Bartky, 1988; O'Brien, 1982), his theories of power, identity and the body have strongly influenced poststructural feminism (see, e.g., Gore, 1993; McNay, 1992; Weedon, 1991). Foss (1984) applied Foucault's notion of the discursive formation to research in gender and communication: "This formation (gender research) is governed by certain rules about what is able to be talked about—and thus known—in our research and kinds of discourse that must be produced in order to 'count' as research. An examination of the discursive practices that govern our research reveals some very clear rules about what is considered be a "true" statement or to be of significance in research" (p. 73).

Foucault raised some interesting possibilities for gender research because he positioned experience within the discursive formations that constitute identity, although, as O'Brien (1982) observed, he failed to contemplate *how* men and women's experiences are positioned differently. Perhaps somewhere between either understanding oppression as a common enemy or focusing only on the fragmented and indeterminate "moments" of gendered meaning, gender research can look towards a more complete and complex understanding of the *situated* female self.

Certainly, there are many other rules that govern our research and that tell us what knowledge is valid and what is not. But what is interesting about these rules is their conformity to what has been labeled the "male perspective" or the "male system." Psychologist Anne Wilson Schaef (1981) discussed how a "White Male System" operates in our culture, surrounding and permeating our lives: "We all live in it. We have been educationally, politically, economically, philosophically, and theologically trained in it, and our emotional, psychological, physical, and spiritual survival have depended on our knowing and supporting the system" (p. 5). Although this currently is the dominant system in our culture, Schaef argued alternative systems or perspectives exist, including Black, Chicano, Native American, and female systems of knowing.

Still, gender is critical to the feminist perspective. Gender is not just a variable. It is relevant to all aspects of culture. Gender challenges the traditional research paradigm that stresses objectivity and tries to determine precise laws that describe, explain, and predict stable, linear, and causal relationships among observables (Foss & Foss, 1989).

Past research on gender did not adopt a feminist perspective. Just as women (and other minorities) have been silenced, the feminist perspective, itself, has often been muted in past research efforts (Foss & Foss, 1989; Spitzack & Carter, 1989). It is more consistent to study gender using a feminist perspective. Pearce and Freeman (1984) noted, "The crucial issue in gender research, as we see it, is that of becoming and remaining 'sufficiently radical'" (p. 65).

REFERENCES

Anderson, K., & Jack, D. (1991). Learning to listen: Interview techniques and analyses. In S. B. Gluck & D. Patai (Eds.), *Women's words: The feminist practice of oral history*. New York: Routledge.

Bartky, S. L. (1988). Foucault, femininity and patriarchal power. In I. Diamond & L. Quinby (Eds.), *Feminism and Foucault: Reflections on resistance* (pp. 61–86). Boston: Northeastern University Press.

Bartky, S. L. (1990). *Femininity and domination: Studies in the phenomenology of oppression*. New York: Routledge.

Bate, B. (1984, Fall). Submerged concepts in gender/communication research. *Women's Studies in Communication*, 7(2), 101–104.

Bem, S. (1974). The measurement of psychological androgyny. *Journal of Consulting and Clinical Psychology*, 42, 155–162.

Bem, S. (1975a). Androgyny vs. the tight little lives of fluffy women and chesty men. *Psychology Today*, 9, 58–59.

Bem, S. (1975b). Sex-role adaptability: One consequence of psychological androgyny. *Journal of Personality and Social Psychology, 31*, 634–643.

Bernard, J. (1971). *Women and the public interest: An essay on policy and protest.* Chicago: Aldine Pub. Co.

Bernard, J. (1975). *Women, wives, mothers: Values and options.* Chicago: Aldine Pub. Co.

Borland, K. (1991). "That's not what I said": Interpretive conflict in oral narrative research. In S. B. Gluck & D. Patai (Eds), *Women's words* (pp. 63–74). New York: Routledge.

Bowles, G., & Duelli-Klein, R. (Ed.). (1983). *Theories of women's studies.* Boston: Routledge & Kegan Paul.

Chodorow, N. (1978). Family structure and feminine personality.

Collins, P. H. (1991). *Black feminist thought.* New York: Routledge.

Comley, N. R. (1990). Reading and writing genders. In B. Hendricksen & T. Morgan (Eds.), *Reorientations* (pp.179–192). Urbana, IL: University of Illinois Press.

de Lauretis, T. (Ed.). (1986). *Feminist studies/critical studies.* Bloomington, IN: University of Indiana Press.

Derrida, J. (1972). *Marges.* Paris: Editions de Minut.

Derrida, J. (1981). *Positions.* Chicago: University of Chicago Press.

DuBois, E. C. (1985). *Feminist scholarship: Challenge, discovery, and impact.* Urbana: University of Illinois Press.

Eakins, B. W., & Eakins, R. G. (1978). *Sex differences in human communication.* Boston: Houghton Mifflin Company.

Echols, A. (1989). *Daring to be bad.* Minnesota: University of Minnesota Press.

Fee, E. (1981). Is feminism a threat to objectivity? *International Women's Journal of Women's Studies, 4*, 378–392.

Foss, K. A. (1988). Feminist scholarship in speech communication: Contributions and obstacles. *Women's Studies in Communication, 11*(1), 1–9.

Foss, K. A., & Foss, S. (1989). Incorporating the feminist perspective in communication scholarship: A research commentary. In K. Carter & C. Spitzak (Ed.), *Doing research on women's communication: Perspectives on theory and method* (pp. 65–90). Norwood, NJ: Ablex.

Foss, S. K. (1984, Fall). A female perspective on the research process. *Women's Studies in Communication, 7* (2), 73–76.

Fox Keller, E. (1985). *Reflections on gender and science.* New Haven, CT: Yale University Press.

French, M. (1985). *Beyond power: On women, men, and morals.* New York: Summit Books.

Frye, M. (1990). Lesbian "sex." In J. Allen (Ed.), *Lesbian philosophies and cultures* (pp. 305–316). Albany, NY: State University of New York Press.

Gilligan, C. (1982). *In a different voice.* Cambridge, MA: Harvard University Press.

Gordon, L. (1991, Spring). On "difference." *Genders, 10*, 91–111.

Gore, J. (1993). *The struggle for pedagogies.* London: Routledge.

Hale, S. (1991). Feminist method, process and self criticism: Interviewing Sudanese women. In S. Gluck & D. Patai (Eds.), *Women's words: The feminist practice of oral history* (pp. 121–136). New York: Routledge.

Harding, S. (1986). *The science question in feminism.* Ithaca: Cornell University Press.

Harding, S. (Ed.).(1987). *Feminism and methodology: Social science issues.* Bloomington: Indiana University.

Hawkensworth, M. E. (1989). Knowers, knowing, known: Feminist theory and claims of truth. In M. R. Malson, J. F. O'Barr, S. Westphal-Whil, & M. Wyer (Eds.), *Feminist theory and practice* (pp. 327–350). Chicago: University of Chicago Press.

hooks, b. (1984). *Feminist theory: From margin to center.* Boston, MA: South End Press.

hooks, b. (1990). *Yearning: Race, gender and cultural politics.* Boston: South End Press.

hooks, b. (1991). *Breaking bread.* Boston, MA: South End Press.

hooks, b. (1992). Representing whiteness in the Black imagination. In L. Grossberg, C. Nelson & P. Triechler (Eds.), *Cultural studies* (pp. 338–346). New York: Routledge.

Imperato-McGuinley, J., Peterson, R., Gautier, T., & Sturla, E. (1979). Androgens and the evolution of male-gender identity among male pseudohermaphrodite with a 5-alpha-reductase deficiency. *New England Journal of Medicine, 300,* 1236–1237.

Jehlen, M. (1990). Gender. In F. Lentricchia & T. McLaughlin (Eds.), *Critical terms for literary study* (pp. 263–273). Chicago: University of Chicago Press.

Jenkins, M. M., & Kramarae, C. (1981). A thief in the house. In D. Spender (Ed.), *Men's studies modified: The impact of feminism in the academic disciplines* (pp. 11–22). New York: Pergamon Press.

Jespersen, O. (1922). *Language: Its nature, development and origin.* London: Allen & Unwin.

Johnson, F. (1984, Fall). Positions for knowing about gender differences in social relationships. *Women's Studies in Communication, 7*(2), 77–82.

Kauffman, B. (1992). Feminist facts: Interview strategies and political subjects in ethnography. *Communication Theory, 2*(3), 187–206.

Kramarae, C. (1981). *Women and men speaking.* Rowley, MA: Newbury House Publishers.

Lakoff, R. (1975). *Language and woman's place.* New York: Harper & Row.

Langellier, K. M., & Hall, D. L. (1989). Interviewing women: A phenomenological approach to feminist communication. In K. Carter & C. Spitzak (Ed.), *Doing research on women's communication: Perspectives on theory and method* (pp. 193–220). Norwood, NJ: Ablex.

Lather, P. (1991). *Getting smart: Feminist research and pedagogy with/in the postmodern.* New York: Routledge.

Lipman-Blumen, J., & Tickamyer, A. R. (1975). Sex roles in transition: A ten-year perspective. *Annual Review of Sociology, 1,* 297–338.

Loomba, A. (1991). Overworlding the Third World. *Oxford Literary Review, 13,* 164–192.

MacCorquodale, P. (1989). Gender and sexual behavior. In K. McKinney & S. Sprecher (Eds.), *Human sexuality: The societal and interpersonal context* (pp. 91–112). Norwood, NJ: Ablex.

MacKinnon, C. (1984). Difference and dominance: On sex discrimination. In K. Bartlett & R. Kennedy (Eds.), *Feminist legal theory* (pp. 81–94). Boulder, CO: Westview Press.

Mani, L. (1992). Cultural theory, colonial texts: Reading eyewitness accounts of widow burning. In L. Grossberg, C. Nelson, & P. Treichler (Eds.), *Cultural studies* (pp. 392–404). New York: Routledge.

McNay, L. (1992). *Foucault and feminism.* Boston: Northeastern University Press.

Money, J. (1972). *Man & woman, boy & girl: The differentiation and dimorphism of gender identity from conception to maturity.* Baltimore: Johns Hopkins University Press.

O'Brien, P. (1982). *The promise of punishment: Prisons in nineteenth century France.* Princeton: Princeton University Press.

Parker, I. (1989). Discourse and power. In J. Shotter & K. Gergen, (Eds.), *Texts of identity* (pp. 56–69). London: Sage Publications.

Parsons, E. C. (1913). *The old-fashioned woman: Primitive fancies about the sex.* New York: G. P. Putnam's Sons.

Pearce, W. B., & Freeman, S. (1984, Fall). On being sufficiently radical in gender research: Some lessons from critical theory, Kang, Milan, and MacIntyre. *Women's Studies in Communication, 7* (2), 65–68.

Pearson, J. C. (1975a). Conflicting demands in correspondence: Abigail Adams on women's rights. *Today's Speech, 23,* 29–33.

Pearson, J. C. (1975b). *The effects of sex and sexism on the criticism of classroom speeches.* Unpublished doctoral dissertation, Indiana University, Bloomington, IN.

Pearson, J. C. (1980a). A factor analytic study of the items in three selected sex-role instruments. *Psychological Reports, 47,* 111–118.

Pearson, J. C. (1980b). The influence of the level of instruction and the sex of the teacher on the criticism of classroom speeches. *Iowa Journal of Speech Communication, 12,* 28–34.

Pearson, J. C. (1981a). The effects of setting and gender on self-disclosure. *Group and Organizational Studies: The International Journal for Group Facilitators, 6,* 334–340.

Pearson, J. C. (1981b). Sex differences in speech criticism: An annotated bibliography. *Women's Studies in Communication, 4,* 47–54.

Pearson, J. C. (1984). What's the square root of 69?: Sex differences in sexual humor. *Ohio Speech Journal, 22,* 27–47.

Pearson, J. C. (1992). *Lasting love: What keeps couples together.* Dubuque, IA: Brown & Benchmark.

Pearson, J. C. (1995). *Marriage after mourning: The secrets of surviving couples.* Dubuque, IA: Kendall Hunt.

Pearson, J. C., Miller, G. R., & Senter, M. M. (1983). Sexism and sexual humor: A research note. *Central States Speech Journal, 34,* 257–259.

Pearson, J. C., & Trent, J. S. (1986). Successful women in speech communication: A national survey of strategies and skills, contributions and conflicts. *Association for Communication Administration Bulletin, 49,* 92–94.

Rosser, S. V. (1988). *Feminism within the science and health care professions: Overcoming resistance.* New York: Pergamon Press.

Sayers, J. (1982). *Biological politics.* London: Tavistock.

Schaef, A. W. (1981). *Woman's reality: An emerging female system in the white male society.* Minneapolis: Winston Press.

Seegmiller, B. R. (1980). Sex-typed behavior pre-schoolers: Sex, age, and social class effects. *Journal of Psychology, 104,* 31–33.

Serafini, D. M., & Pearson, J. C. (1984). Leadership behavior and sex role socialization: Two sides of the same coin. *Southern Speech Communication Journal, 49,* 396–405.

Shea, B. C., & Pearson, J. C. (1986). The effects of relationship type, partner intent, and gender on the selection of relationship maintenance strategies. *Communication Monographs, 53,* 352–364.

Spence, J. T., & Helmreich, R. L. (1978). *Masculinity and femininity: Their psychological dimensions, correlates, and antecedents.* Austin, TX: University of Texas Press.

Spence, J. T., Helmreich, R. L., & Stapp, J. (1974a). The personal attributes questionnaire: A measure of sex-role stereotypes and masculinity–femininity. *JSAS Catalog of Selected Documents in Psychology, 4,* 127.

Spence, J. T., Helmreich, R. L., & Stapp, J. (1974b). Ratings of self and peers on sex-role attributes and their relation to self-esteem and conceptions of masculinity and femininity. *Journal of Personality and Social Psychology, 32,* 29–39.

Spitzack, C., & Carter, K. (1989). Research in women's communication: The politics of theory and method. In K. Carter & C. Spitzak (Ed.), *Doing research on women's communication: Perspectives on theory and method* (pp. 11–37). Norwood, NJ: Ablex.

Spivak, G. C. (1991). Neocolonialism and the secret agent of knowledge: An interview with Robert Young. *Oxford Literary Review, 13,* 220–251.

Steinem, G. (1991). *Revolution from within: A book of self-esteem.* Boston: Little, Brown and Co.

Stopes, C. C. (1908). *The sphere of "man": In relation to that of "woman" in the constitution.* London: T. Fisher Unwin.

Stroller, R. J. (1968). *Sex and gender, on the development of masculinity and femininity.* New York: Science House.

Tannen, D. (1990). *You just don't understand: Women and men in conversation.* New York: William Morrow and Co.

Thorne, B., Kramarae, C., & Henley, N. (Eds.). (1983). *Language, gender and society.* Rowley, MA: Newbury House Publishers.

Tibbits, S. (1975). Sex role stereotyping in the lower grades: Part of a solution. *Journal of Vocational behavior, 6,* 255–261.

Weedon, C. (1991). Post structuralist feminist practice. In D. Morton & M. Zavarzadeh (Eds.), *Texts for Change: Theory/Pedagogy/Politics* (pp. 47–63). Urbana: University of Illinois Press.

Webster's New Collegiate Dictionary (1981). Springfield, MA: G. & C. Merriam Co.

Wittig, M. (1990). *The straight mind and other essays.* Boston: Beacon Press.

Wood, J. T., & Phillips, G. M. (1984, Fall). Report on the 1984 conference on gender and communication research. *Women's Studies in Communication, 7*(2), 61–64.

Author Index

Subject Index

DATE DUE